JOHN SEMLEY

Hater

On the Virtues of
Utter Disagreeability

VIKING

VIKING

an imprint of Penguin Canada, a division of Penguin Random House Canada Limited

Canada • USA • UK • Ireland • Australia • New Zealand • India • South Africa • China

First published 2018

www.penguinrandomhouse.ca

LIBRARY AND ARCHIVES CANADA CATALOGUING IN PUBLICATION

Semley, John, author
    Hater : on the virtues of utter disagreeability / John Semley.

Issued in print and electronic formats.
ISBN 978-0-7352-3616-5 (hardcover).—ISBN 978-0-7352-3617-2 (electronic)

    1. Popular culture. 2. Art appreciation—Popular works. 3. Criticism—Popular works. 4. Criticism (Philosophy)—Popular works. 5. Critical theory—Popular works. 6. Critical thinking—Popular works. 7. Aesthetics—Popular works. 8. Acquiescence (Psychology)—Popular works. 9. Aversion—Popular works. I. Title.

NX640.S46 2018   700.1   C2018-902387-2

                                                 C2018-902388-0

Cover and interior design by Andrew Roberts

Printed and bound in the United States of America

10 9 8 7 6 5 4 3 2 1

Penguin
Random House
VIKING CANADA

To all opposed.

CONTENTS

- *The Contrarian Impulse* -

The stupidest fight I've ever started erupted in late August 2017 when, while distractedly switching between Twitter and a PDF of Sammy Davis Jr.'s autobiography, *Yes I Can*, and listening to heavy metal music on YouTube, a random thought occurred to me, and so I tweeted:

"why?" > "smalltown boy"

The songs are both singles from British synthpop trio Bronski Beat's 1984 debut record, *The Age of Consent*. Neither song, it's fair to say, is especially well known to a general audience. Nor were they smash hits (though "Smalltown Boy" got to #1 on the charts in a few Benelux countries). They're relatively minor songs by a relatively minor group, and the idea of suggesting that one is better than the other (especially the one that's *least* well known of the two)—more than thirty years after their original release—had all the marks of a hollow provocation.

As they say, I know whereof I speak. I've been in some totally pointless, idiotic fights—fights that ran the gamut from self-defeating to smugly self-affirming.

I once tried to stir up an argument by asking, halfway honestly, who would win in a full-out, drag-down fight between the anthropomorphic bad-boy baseball from the VHS cover of the 1989 baseball comedy *Major League* and the anthropomorphic good-ole-boy football from the VHS cover of the 1991 football comedy *Necessary Roughness*.

In Grade 7 debate club, I fiercely led a rebuttal against the ludicrous resolution that Barq's Famous Olde Tyme Root Beer possessed, per its ad campaign, "bite." I once vexed someone, largely for my own amusement, by mounting the argument that "musically, everyone agrees that Iron Maiden is the best band, music-wise, in sheer terms of the music." I have defended the Lou Reed/Metallica team-up album *Lulu*, which everyone hates, in part just because everyone hates it. Because if I don't, who else will? (Also, I sincerely stand by *Lulu*'s howling opener "Brandenburg Gate" as being a very interesting hard rock song, if not necessarily a conventionally "good" one.)

Those were good fights, in their own way. But of all the dormant beehives to kick around for sport, this would-be contretemps about the songs "Why?" and "Smalltown Boy" was no doubt the *stupidest*. It's pretty much a joke at the expense of the idea of even having an opinion about anything at all. But it proved to be the most revealing. Because somehow, it worked. Someone took the bait. A few people, even.

One Twitter follower immediately told me to "stay in my lane." Another chimed in to say that *both* songs are timeless classics, a sentiment that carried with it the assumption that pitting one against the other was a futile exercise. Yet another interjected to mention The Communards, another British synthpop duo carried by the piercing falsetto of Bronski Beat singer Jimmy Somerville.

Granted, the back-and-forth was never elevated to the level

of a true argument. Nobody discussed how the experience of being a young gay man in the early 1980s is framed differently in each song: the fantasy of escapism and retreat from oppression and familial rejection of "Smalltown Boy" weighing against the more upright, defiant tone of "Why?" with its imperative call for an explanation of oppression and hate ("Can you tell me whyyyyyy-auuuuurrrrghhhhh?!").

But more to the point, this exercise cut to the heart of a deeper instinct. Starting a fight on social media about two singles nobody really remembers by a band nobody really cares about? This is the essence of the contrarian impulse.

And it is at the heart of what it means to be a hater.

In 2009, the word *hater* found its way into the *Oxford English Dictionary*, which is pretty much *the* dictionary you want to be in if you're an aspiring Legitimate Word. Here's how the English-language gatekeepers at the *OED* define it:

> **hater *n.*** a person who greatly dislikes a specified person or thing: *a man hater* | *he's not a hater of modern music.*
> **informal** a negative or critical person: *she found it difficult to cope with the haters.*

The Oxford folks, as is often the case, were merely playing catch-up, well after the word had already gained purchase in the everyday parlance. A top-rated entry on the website Urban Dictionary dates back to 2005 and defines *hater* on a slightly different axis, more attuned with the *OED*'s informal definition (itself formalized by virtue of inclusion in the *Oxford English*

Dictionary). Here's their definition, all typos and grammatical eccentricities *sic*:

> **hater**
> A person that simply cannot be happy for another person's success. So rather than be happy they make a point of exposing a flaw in that person.
>
> Hating, the result of being a hater, is not exactly jealousy. The hater doesnt [*sic*] really want to be the person he or she hates, rather the hater wants to knock somelse [*sic*, again] down a notch.
> **Susan:** You know, Kevin from accounting is doing very well. He just bought a house in a very nice part of town.
> **Jane (hater):** If he is doing so well why does he drive that '89 Taurus?

This book, *Hater*, is preoccupied with these latter, informal, somewhat clumsier definitions. It's not about hating as a matter of preference, as one might hate (per the *OED*'s example) modern music or (per my own) corn on the cob.*

And—I feel like maybe I should **bold**, *italicize*, ***ALL CAPS*** and **<u>UNDERLINE</u>** this bit, lest anyone miss the point, though I bet some are bound to deliberately miss it anyway—it is most certainly not concerned with the kind of hatred that is truly repellant, as in an aversion to a person or group of people that

---

* I don't hate it per se; I just don't like the idea of chewing on a cob of fresh seasonal corn, slathered in butter and salt, like some kind of grotesque man-beaver.

emerges from some perceived (and often entirely preconceived) difference in identity, gender, ability, sexuality, race, religion, color, creed, ethnicity, etc., etc.—I'm sure you get the idea. This is not about justifying that kind of prejudice. Like, *at all.*

This book concerns hating as a cultural practice, and being a hater as an expression of cultural identity. It's about being the person who stands up, who is willing to make every modest protuberance in the pop cultural landscape a hill to die on, who kicks the stupidest conceivable beehives. Because for a while now (since at least 2005, if we're to take the online Urban Dictionary as a relevant reference point), hating has entrenched itself in the cultural firmament. The "hater" has become a cultural archetype: contemptuous of seemingly everything, dismissive of everything else, wholly unimpressed, eyes caught in an exaggerated roll, lip half-snarled, locked in a perpetual sneer. Hating has likewise become a common attitude in contemporary Western culture. And, when done right, I think it's a defensible one.

This book sets out from what I'll admit is a somewhat smugly contrarian premise: that hating is good.

If we're constantly leaned on by the gentle pressure to nod and smile and agree upon the ever-expanding constellations of cultural consumption and appreciation, then disagreeability, scowling, and shaking one's head feels urgent, and even necessary. Our culture seems largely defined by either an overstated performance of enthusiasm or a painfully convoluted different *kind* of enthusiasm. Take so-called think pieces, like "Why *Game of Thrones* Is About Single Payer Healthcare" or literally whatever. That's a lot of effort going into intellectualizing something because it's popular. But where is the conversation on whether it is even any *good?* In this environment, being smug, annoying, and contrarian strikes me as having an inherent virtue.

The content and character of that virtue may not be immediately apparent. It certainly won't make you a hit, especially online. I can't estimate the number of articles and opinions I've purveyed as a writer and critic that are met with their own smug dismissals, usually phrased along the lines of "You must be fun at parties." But to cop the parlance of the endless parade of competitive reality TV shows we're all expected to keep abreast of, I didn't come here to make friends. And, more to the point, if picking at assumptions and the taken-for-granteds of culture, of the way we all relate to everyday life—if only by stirring the pot, and staging arguments about Bronski Beat singles for no real reason—is deemed un-fun by people at parties . . . well, then you're probably going to the wrong parties.

This book aims to make the case for haterism as both a symptom of and potential cure for the current cultural climate. After all, in order to repair the rot and decay worming through our culture, the same rot/decay must be (a) addressed, with righteous vehemence, and then (b) rejected, with an even more honest anger. This book also aims to reclaim the hater mantle from the wing-nut pretenders of contemporary contrarianism, those who use dissent not to challenge or clarify reality, but to further obfuscate it.

We need to take hating back. Why? Because criticism is vital for shaping, and sharpening, that shared cultural world we all waft through. When done well, it opens a dialogue, facilitating a give-and-take. And even when it is done reflexively, it serves a meaningful symbolic function, as it dares to howl "NO!" in the wan faces of grinning agreeability. Even in its most performative, utterly insincere iterations, hating offers an alternative, piercing the fog of consensus and lighting the path of a new way forward.

Life, after all, is a struggle against not just the rushing tide of inevitability but also the seductive whirl of conformity. We're like . . . what did Fitzgerald say? Boats against the dang current? If we can't preserve the necessary muscle memory to keep beating on, then we risk drowning in the deluge of damnable sameness.

So, raise a tall glass of triple-proof Haterade.* Here's to keeping our heads above water. And to acquiring the critical muscles necessary to jam a pointy finger into the soft solar plexus of the flabby culture industry and undermine its assumptions, its fundamental laziness, demanding, in shrieky, self-consciously annoying faux falsetto, "Tell me whyyyyyy-auuuuurrrrghhhhh?!"

---

* A fictional beverage designed to replenish a hater's ability to hate. The idea dates back to Gucci Mane's 2010 song of the same name.

— 1 ►—

You're Doing It Wrong

— DISCUSSED HEREIN —

"Love trumps Hate" | *Thirteenth-century Latin* | *Taylor Hackford's*
The Devil's Advocate | *Diogenes vs. Alexander* | *Rotten fruit
and other highly chuckable foodstuffs* | *The fate of one John Richie of
Long Island* | *Thumbs as a critical metric* | Black Panther |
The Algorithm | Bigger Cages, Longer Chains |
Technological determinism | *Donald Trump*

— Friends of the Devil —

Consequently love must needs precede hatred; and nothing is hated, save through being contrary to a suitable thing which is loved. And hence it is that every hatred is caused by love.

—THOMAS AQUINAS

We have forgotten how to hate.

This may seem like a counterintuitive—or even gallingly stupid—assertion in a world rocked by partisan political infighting, by global-scale ideological conflict, and by a renewed activity in formalized hate groups. Indeed, in 2018 the Alabama-based Southern Poverty Law Center reported that the number of hate groups in the United States has swelled by twenty percent since 2014. On the face of things, the problem would not seem to be too little hate, but far too much of it. Hate is a boom industry.

So let me clarify. We have forgotten how to hate *well*. We have forgotten how to hate rigorously, and virtuously. The modern co-opting of resistance and disagreeability by far-right interests has shamed hate. Popular, and utterly vacuous, slogans like "Love trumps Hate" have exacerbated the problem, by twisting love and hate in a binary of diametrically opposed ideals. Their relationship, as the history of hating illustrates, is far more complex than all that.

Hatred and love are entwined, like two knotty earbud strands tangled in your jeans pocket.

If, like me, you're a little tripped up by the syntax of that Aquinas quote up there, don't despair. The *Summa Theologica* was written in Latin in the thirteenth century, and not translated or released until the late fifteenth century, when the Fathers of the English Dominican Province delivered their English translation to the Benziger Brothers Printers.

Way back then, even reading itself was a rarefied activity undertaken by clearly demarcated classes of scholars and clerics and other distinguished wise-type gatekeepers. As far as your average person: he/she/they were deeply illiterate, and impoverished, and generally too preoccupied with the mucky, grueling work of serfdom to care much about reading, or about the screechy scraping together of two dissonant-seeming words.

Still, Aquinas's general thrust remains intact: Hatred isn't just the formless, frothing resentment toward something. (Though, yes, it certainly can be, and often *is*, that.) Hatred can work as a corrective, a way of clarifying and refining a more profound love for a thing—like pruning the tatty, dead leaves from an otherwise beautiful flower.

I am aware that this defense may sound horribly contrarian. Like: "Well *actually*, hating isn't about hating! It's about . . . I don't know . . . uh . . . love!" But then, that's precisely what this book is: a defense of the contrarian attitude and its usefulness. Hating is a form of righteous dissent that can often be used to clarify ideas and positions. Which brings us right back to Saint Thomas Aquinas.

I invoke Aquinas above not (merely) for the sake of being rangy and eclectic. Nor am I especially interested in grounding this discussion of hating, dissent, and contrarian thought in speciously theological grounds.* I am, however, interested in bringing the conversation around to Christianity in order to offer a brief historical sketch of haterism, beginning with the function of the so-called devil's advocates.

I'm sure we've all heard the phrase before. Perhaps it has been employed by some tertiary acquaintance in a fedora trying to bogusly undermine a conversation about political correctness. Or maybe you've heard it bandied about in reference to director Taylor Hackford's 1997 absurdly Miltonian legal thriller *The Devil's Advocate*.** But the term has its origins in the Counter-Reformation Roman Catholic Church.

While references in extant Vatican literature date back as far as Pope Leo X (1513–1521), the position was formally enshrined by Sixtus V (née Felice Peretti di Montalto) during his relatively short stint as pope, circa 1585–1590. The actual technical term for this role was *Promoter Fidei* (Promoter of the Faith), but it was colloquially known as *Advocatus Diaboli*, or Devil's Advocate. It's not really an official posting within the organizational structure of the Catholic Church anymore; the job was drastically revised under the rule of Pope John Paul II in the late 1970s. Still, the Church may, from time to time, summon people

---

* Though, to be fair, when one squirms through twelve years of state-funded Catholic-school education, one feels a certain pinch to cash in on it (figuratively, but also literally) whenever an opportunity presents itself. And if it's not clear, this mysterious "one" happens to be me.

** In which a peak-Keanu Keanu Reeves plays a Florida lawyer summoned to a fancy New York City legal firm overseen by a peak-Pacino Al Pacino, who is, in fact (spoiler alert), the Devil Himself.

to support the role. Christopher Hitchens, who I'll talk more about later, was actually retained in 2002 to sportingly speak against the canonization of Mother Teresa of Calcutta. It would, admittedly, be a very fun gig, suited as it is to the skill set of any hardened hater.

The explicit task of the Promoter Fidei was to call into question the legitimacy of would-be Catholic saints during the process of beatification—which is the step directly preceding canonization. They played the role of the pro skeptic: undermining the legitimacy of supposed miracles, and generally calling into question just how saintly the proposed saint was.

They'd attempt to poke holes in the would-be saint's character, cast a chary eye on the legitimacy of their miracles (proceeding, of course, from the belief that there can be wholly legitimate, nonfraudulent miracles), and generally play the part of the Church's Official Skeptic. They'd square off against the *Advocatus Dei* (that's "God's Advocate," as you have likely guessed), who was arguing in favor of canonization, of miracles, and of the unimpeachable saintliness of the person in question.

The Devil's Advocate would mount a case against the prospective saint. And not necessarily because they detested the person, or even thought them unworthy of sainthood. (Though Hitchens, for what it's worth, was genuinely unimpressed with Mother Teresa, calling her an "ally of the status quo" who essentially exploited the wretched and suffering she professed to help, all to the end of expanding the profile of the Roman Catholic Church.) Generally speaking, the aim was to perfect the case for sainthood, to ensure that the given individual was free from damning blemishes. It's sort of like when a politician's public relations team scours the would-be candidate's closets for skeletons—something that most public relations teams could probably do a much better job of.

In all this, the Devil's Advocate is not a doubter but a Promoter of the Faith. Even the twin titles speak to the dialectic interplay between hatred and love, antagonism and advocacy. While ultimately contrarian, political, and even more than a bit disagreeable, they are so by design. At the end of the day, the Devil's Advocate is a force of good.

This force precedes the orthodoxy of the hoary old Catholic Church, believe it or not.

It says a lot about another spiritual friend o' the devil, Diogenes of Sinope, that he wasn't really big on writing things down. When your whole "thing" is being a wanton social pariah and self-styled degenerate who sleeps in a ceramic pot[*] with a dog and spits, both figuratively and literally, in the faces of the powerful and well-to-do—going home and sitting at a desk to record your thoughts and ideas doesn't really track. It would be like the coolest guy in high school going home after dating cheerleaders, racing convertibles, smoking cigarettes, and swirlying[**] nerds to work on a public blog called "How To

---

[*]   Basically, the Before Common Era equivalent of living in a dumpster.

[**]   If you don't know what a swirly is, chances are you've never swirlied, or had a swirly performed on you. In which case, I offer you heartfelt salutations on a charmed life.

Be Cool As Hell." A truly cool guy would never do that.* And Diogenes of Sinope was, truly, the coolest guy.

What we know of Diogenes—his life, his words, his deeds, whom he spat upon and why—we know from secondary sources concerning the history of philosophy, and of the ancient Greek world more generally. In his extensive biography of earlier Greek philosophers, Diogenes Laërtius (no relation) writes that Diogenes of Sinope was born in 412 BCE and died in 323 BCE. The son of a banker, Diogenes's early life was beset by scandal when either he or his father (or he *and* his father, depending on your source) debased the local currency by smashing it with a large chisel, thus rendering it useless. As a result of his fiscal blasphemy, Diogenes was stripped of his citizenship and all his possessions and cast out of the Ionian colony of his birth—his fate cast to the winds.

For Diogenes No-Longer-of-Sinope, exile and impoverishment were gifts. Later in his life, one person approached to ask how he felt about being banished from his homeland. Did it ever bother him? "Nay," came Diogenes's response. "It was through that, you miserable fellow, that I came to be a philosopher." When asked where he came from, Diogenes would call himself a "citizen of the world"—thus essentially minting the word *cosmopolitan*.

Likewise, he would commonly invert the terms of his exile, to make it seem that it was not *he*, Diogenes, who suffered a punishment, but rather the poor people of Sinope, who had been sentenced to "home-staying." Here we have a very basic, very useful rhetorical inversion that would become a standby of

---

* That said, Diogenes is reported in some primary sources as having written something like ten books, in addition to a whole bunch of letters.

the hater's arsenal. Where one might reasonably claim that, factually, Diogenes was sentenced to exile from his birthplace of Sinope and, qualitatively, that the consequence of that exile was bad, the bedraggled philosopher responded that, actually, (a) exile rules, and (b) I wasn't even exiled at all, but rather I sentenced my exiles to "home-staying." When the ancient world gave Diogenes lemons, he made lemonade—then chucked the lemonade in his doubters' eyes.

He preached a life of virtue and honesty, and of peeling away the bogus veneer of civility, and civilization itself. What's more: he actually *lived* this life. He wasn't like these hoity-toity Marxist professors you read about these days who preach class-consciousness and labor solidarity over cheeky cocktails at the Faculty Club. He embodied his philosophy. He spat in the faces of the rich. He became a historical avatar of asceticism, contrarianism, cynicism, haterism, and the virtues of doglike living.

Inarguably, the coolest thing Diogenes ever did was this: he told Alexander the Great, essentially the most powerful person in the ancient world and one of the most powerful people *ever*, to go jump in a lake. Given the Macedonian king's tendency toward the nasty business of massacring his enemies, selling captured foes into slavery, and razing ancient Western Asian capitals to cinders during bouts of drunken idiocy (he is called "Alexander the Conqueror" in many Persian histories, with good reason), merely talking back to Alexander seems bold, impudent, even a bit stupid. But the real kicker? Alexander didn't even seem to care. As a matter of fact, he loved it.

As Plutarch describes it in his *The Life of Alexander the Great*, the Macedonian leader arrived to meet the slovenly philosopher, who was dwelling in a suburb called the Cranium.* Having heard a great deal about Diogenes, Alexander was keen to meet him and, when he did, asked if he could gift him with anything. Diogenes responded: "I would have you stand from between me and the sun." Alexander was reportedly so gobsmacked by the request, and by Diogenes's sheer ballsiness, that he told his followers (who were hitherto laughing at and mocking the homeless roustabout), that were he not Alexander, he would be Diogenes.

Different translations of the account, from Cicero and others, offer slight variations on Diogenes's request. But the thrust is always more or less the same: "Stand out of the sunlight," buzz off, go away. By the standards of the fourth century BCE, this is an absolutely savage burn. It's as if you were living today in a shitty bachelor apartment with no water and Elon Musk knocked on your door and said, "Hey, I'll give you anything in the world you desire, including unlimited access to my infinite wealth and fleet of rockets," and you told him you wanted a week on Mars with his mom. Beyond being funny, and a burn ward–worthy insult, it suggests a level of integrity that's pretty much unfathomable, if not a little insane.

It's not just the crassness and pithiness of the comment but also Alexander's response (usually summed up as "If not Alexander, I would be Diogenes") that rings out across history. If you can't be the most powerful, respected, well-appointed person in the world, one before whom entire civilizations bend their knee, then it's just as good to be the most venal rapscallion on planet Earth, beholden to naught but oneself.

---

*   What an amazing detail, eh? A philosopher living in a big jar in a part of town called the "Cranium"?!

As the Advocatus Dei has the Advocatus Diaboli, so Alexander has Diogenes. If there were a patron saint of haterism, it would be Diogenes. And considering his nasty habit of sending bodily fluids flying in the faces of his enemies, you'd be hard-pressed to find anyone who could successfully call into question his hater bona fides. It wasn't just a matter of his being consummately uncouth, or venomously witty, either. In his pure detest—of money, of the material world, of the divine rights of fancy-lad Macedonian kings—Diogenes served as a model for the social and political underclass. He afflicted the powerful. So much so that the most powerful, perversely, held him in high estimation. Alexander the Great could conquer Egypt, Syria, Phoenicia, Anatolia, Persia, and the bulk of the known ancient world. But Diogenes served as his greatest foil. He was unconquerable. An existential threat.

There are similar institutional examples of contrarian thought, such as the *Dissoi Logoi*, a Greek form of rhetoric in which students are charged with making points from an opposing view. Not unlike the Catholic Church's Devil's Advocate.

The aim of the Dissoi Logoi is firmly entrenched in more formalized rules of debate. As mentioned earlier, there was a time in elementary school debate club I argued against the ludicrous proposition "Barq's Has Bite," a reference to a then-popular root beer, which, unlike some other big-name root beer brands, contained caffeine. The proposition seemed daffy, not least of all because I was a total Barq's Boy at the time.

I think my team ended up arguing that Barq's doesn't have "bite" because the caffeine it does contain is insufficient to register anything like a biting assault on the nervous system. Of course, Barq's and its reported, much-ballyhooed "bite" were incidental to the exercise itself. The point was to mount a case defending something you don't necessarily believe in yourself.

The problem with debate club, of course, is that a central idea is never refined or synthesized. One side merely wins while the other loses. It is either true that Barq's has bite or it isn't. Here we come across a problem central to hating: at what point does the passionate condemnation of something-or-other constitute (or appear to constitute) a mere exercise? When does contrarianism become *just* a game? When does vociferous, sustained disagreement curdle into trolling? It's a question addressed in Part 3 of this volume. For now, it's worth keeping in mind, even if it's somewhere near the back: What is the distinction between a sincere and a purely sporting attack on (or defense of) a thing? And moreover, does this distinction *matter*?

There is certainly a lively school of thought that holds fast to the idea that criticism—all criticism, and the fiercer the better— is of inherent value. I'm not yet sure if I'd consider myself an alumnus of this school, but I've certainly audited a few classes, maybe even a whole course load. Perhaps the clearest, pithiest articulation of this I've ever heard comes from German philosopher and political theorist Karl Marx.* Who else?

---

* If you are one of those people for whom the very name "Karl Marx" constitutes some kind of red (no pun) flag then, well, I'm sorry. Despite wholly reductive and moronic contemporary claims to his personal responsibility for Soviet and other genocides, it's not like he personally cut the ribbons on the gulags. Whatever you make of the tenets of communism itself, many of Marx's ideas as a philosopher, historian, and political theorist are wholly valuable.

In an 1843 letter to his friend Arnold Ruge, in which he decried "the old university of philosophy," "the anarchy of the mind," and the "reign of stupidity," Marx summed up the animating spirit of his emerging critical philosophy:

> If constructing the future and settling everything for all times are not our affair, it is all the more clear what we have to accomplish at present: I am referring to *ruthless criticism** of all that exists, ruthless both in the sense of not being afraid of the results it arrives at and in the sense of being just a little afraid of conflict with the powers that be.

Granted, Marx was talking about the criticism of philosophy, of political economy, of whole states and social structures. But that one bit rings clarion-clear, like a rallying cry: "ruthless criticism of all that exists." It's so damn good that every time I read it I want to pinch my fingers to my thumb and blow one of those satisfied chef's kisses. *The ruthless criticism of all that exists.* It's perfect.

Let's begin.

---

* The italics here belong to Marx's original letter. I'm not *entirely* sure how one italicized a letter in 1843, but nevertheless.

— *Metacriticism and the Rotten Fruit of Consensus* —

Consider the rotten tomato. First, think of the plump red fruit of the *Solanum lycopersicum*, all meaty and juicy and glistening in the mind's eye. Instead of slicing it to toss in a salad or serve alongside some bulbous buffalo mozzarella, imagine it putrefying past its prime. Now that red has deepened to murky near-brown. But where the ugly, squishy rotten tomato has been drained of its palatability as a foodstuff, it has blossomed in its putrescence into something even greater: an instrument of protest. Tomatoes weren't the first protest food. That would probably be turnips, which were chucked at Roman governor of Africa Vespasian during a tour through the pre-Carthaginian North African colony of Adrametum circa 63 CE.

In a similarly revolutionary act, the sunshine-joke band Smash Mouth was pelted with free bread gifted to attendees at the 2015 Taste of Fort Collins food festival. Here bread—that foodstuff so metaphorically crucial to the French Revolution, that food so symbolic of accessibility to food itself—was wielded as an ad hoc weapon against a lame '90s alt-rock band best known for contributing songs to the *Shrek, Rat Race*, and *Mystery Men* sound tracks. Smartphone videos of lobbed loaves told the whole story: The people had spoken. Smash Mouth sucks.

Yet bread, in its flinty stiffness, is a relative outlier in the history of disapproving food-hurling. For millennia, eggs were big—to such a point that having egg on one's face has become a euphemism referring to embarrassment at one's own actions. Throw a stone and you're liable to end up in jail. Whipping some eggs or turnips or rotten tomatoes, on the other hand, is a way of displaying similar contempt, without the genuine threat of injuring the object of scorn.

And what's a shiner or a bruise on the forehead, anyway? Being covered in stinky egg yolks or rancid tomato splatter seems even more dehumanizing. When you're physically injured by someone, the moral burden tends to shift to the perpetrator of that injury. When you're dressed in chicken ovum, fruit innards, or cream pie filling, you tend to just look like a bit of a goof.

Unlike eggs or turnips, however, the capturing of past-prime tomatoes has a more specific history. The weaponization of over-ripe tomatoes is a fairly modern invention.

An 1883 review in *The New York Times* gives an account of a performance in which a John Richie of Long Island, "who aspires to be an actor and lecturer" was "demoralized by tomatoes." Curiously, while the review mentions that "a bushel or two" of rotten tomatoes had been distributed among the audience, the chain of events is unclear. Richie was pelted with tomatoes for fumbling during a somersault. But he fumbled *because* he was being hit with tomatoes. Likewise, when he attempted to regain the audience's faith with an acrobatic trapeze number, things got even worse: "A large tomato thrown from the gallery struck him square between the eyes, and he fell to the stage floor just as several bad eggs dropped upon his head. Then the tomatoes flew thick and fast, and Richie fled to the stage door. The door was locked, and he ran the gauntlet for the ticket office through a perfect shower of tomatoes."

As described by the *Times*'s savvy theater/acrobatics critic, it almost sounds as if the tomato barrage was the main event. The article is also unclear as to whether Richie's performance was met with disapproving fruit because it stunk, or if it stunk because of fruit that registered a kind of preemptive disapproval. "Why would they come just to boo us?" wonders an incredulous Lisa Simpson, dreaming of an audience turning on her subpar supergroup of rock music also-rans. Poor John Richie of Long Island offers as persuasive a case as any. It's fun to boo things, to lose oneself in the collective ecstasy of rowdy, passionate protest—even of something as innocuous as a public gymnastics display.

The people had spoken. Tomatoes are fun to throw.

In 1998, a Bay Area web designer named Senh Duong launched the website Rotten Tomatoes. The idea sprang from a desire so pure that anyone who has ever been seriously interested in art or culture can recognize it: He wanted to know about Jackie Chan movies. Specifically, Duong wanted to know what people had to say about Jackie Chan movies.

For years, whenever a Jackie Chan film was released, Duong would crawl the internet looking for reviews and commentary, driven by the fan's urge to see what other people were saying about one of his favorite action stars. The relative pre-1998 obscurity of Chan (at least in the United States) made this tricky. In 1998, Jackie Chan, then an acclaimed actor/director/comedian/stuntman/martial artist in his native Hong Kong, was poised for a major Hollywood breakthrough with the buddy-cop action-comedy *Rush Hour*. So the prospect of something like a comprehensive online Jackie Chan resource likely appealed to the wider culture, and not just Duong himself.

Duong was clever enough to realize that such a resource would not only extend beyond his own fandom but also beyond

Jackie Chan's stardom. His website would aggregate reviews about movies, allowing like-minded film buffs to easily peruse the relevant news and views. Long story short: Rotten Tomatoes went from a Jackie Chan fan's after-work side project to a major source for movie news and commentary. With plugs from Roger Ebert, profiles in *Rolling Stone*, and mentions from other prominent tastemakers, it grew from a modest, Usenet-promoted resource, collecting 100 unique daily users to a top-scoring website drawing something like 26 million global visitors every month. As of this writing, in early 2018, it's pretty safe to say that Rotten Tomatoes is where you go to find opinions about movies. Alternatively, you go to Wikipedia, which invariably leads you to Rotten Tomatoes, via some prominent and very deliberate links.

Now, sure, aggregating news and opinions was nothing new. Documents ranging from a parish bulletin to a major daily newspaper to a subreddit thread are all aggregations of news, commentary, opinion, advertising—basically any relevant piece of "content" targeted toward a specific group. Where Rotten Tomatoes became truly revolutionary (for better or worse) was in its distillation of aggregation. Staff members began combing the relevant reviews of given films, gleaning their general attitude, and, in turn, assigning scores to movies. Any review that scored three out of five on your classic Five Star rating scale was "Fresh." Anything south of that was "Rotten." Then the aggregation of these assessments resulted in one of two ratings. Any movie with a fresh rating over 75% was Certified Fresh. Anything south of that? Forget about it.

In a low-key ironic twist, a website christened after the historical process of hucking tainted fruit at the lousy became a registrar of quality. In an inversion of title, the culture began looking to a website called "Rotten Tomatoes" for assurances of Freshness. This new criterion for freshness reeks. To paraphrase English deathrockers Alien Sex Fiend's 1986 single "I Walk the Line": this tomato's rotten, rotten to the core.

Sometime in 2017, I remember seeing a commercial for the superhero blockbuster *Spider-Man: Homecoming*, which was either the 7th or 308th Spider-Man movie made in my lifetime.[*]

In this ad, the lithesome wall-crawler scales the side of a New York City skyscraper, which is digitally embossed with the film's aggregated critical rating, calculated by the website Rotten Tomatoes. When I was a kid, movies were pushed, in part, by pull-quotes of critical enthusiasm, even if it was just Peter Travers from *Rolling Stone* comparing one or another thrill-a-minute spectacle to a "roller coaster ride." At the very least, you could count on a movie being endorsed by an agreeably upturned thumb.

The basic algebra was always, "Well, so-and-so likes this movie, and I like movies so-and-so likes, so maybe I'll like this movie too." Even if you didn't particularly agree with so-and-so, or even recognize so-and-so's name, at least there *was* a so-and-so. That is, there was a basic modicum of communication, however implicit, with another person—or even just

---

[*]   At the risk of tipping my hand, age-wise, I grew up in a faraway time when the prospect of a big-screen Spider-Man movie carried with it the promise of genuine excitement and spectacle, and wasn't just a way of marking eighteen months of time passing.

another person's thumb. Now the prospective blockbuster film-goer is met only with steely percentages, as if taste and opinion and discernment have been conflated with scientific consensus. Now the thinking goes, "Ninety-seven percent of people who saw this movie and registered their opinion to some arbitrary website think this movie is good, so statistically, if you don't think it's good, you're an anomaly, and also probably weird." Now the algebra is literally just algebra.

So what is the problem with this, one might reasonably wonder. Surely a weighted score based on a broad sampling of reviews from established, and at least semi-professionalized, film critics is a fair way of determining a given film's quality. Right?

As is often the case with questions having obvious-seeming answers, the response is both yes and no. Firstly, some might reasonably respond that judging the artistic merit of something based on percentage score and the presence of some conspicuously branded juicy vine fruit constitutes an affront to criticism itself.* Instead of thoughtful argumentation or engaged conversation, instead of thinking and, in turn, encouraging readers to think, criticism in the age of Big Data has mutated into a consumer scorecard. And while consumer scorecards are all well and good, if you want to know whether to buy an LCD or LED TV, or are curious about which model of SUV won't roll over and kill your whole family, the point of what we call art is that it

---

* This may appear to be a counterargument lodged on behalf of some film-snob straw man. Fair enough. But as someone who has made these arguments—and, indeed, is making them right now—I feel well positioned to credibly account for the stuffing of this particular straw man.

stands outside of (if not in opposition to) such crassly consumerist concerns. That you can, as of this writing, buy tickets to major North American chain cinemas via the Rotten Tomatoes website further entwines the often-entwined bedfellows of art and commerce. Any daylight between consensus and commerce has been effectively blotted out.

Plenty of film critics took issue with this flattening as far back as Siskel and Ebert's *At The Movies*, in which the generally game, intelligent hosts reduced their own arguments to Thumbs-Up/Thumbs-Down verdicts. It's not like there was some clear rubric shared with the audience or anything. Instead, two boring-looking guys from the American Midwest became arbiters of taste, of quality, of the culture as a whole. Just think about the way in which the show's trademark (and trademarked) phrase "two thumbs-up" has become a common idiom for the expression of hearty approval. Their power was almost total, like the fickle emperors of Rome who also determined fates with their thumbs. As the ancient Roman satirist Juvenal put it in his lacerating long-form poem "Against the City of Rome," this thumbs-up/thumbs-down* display constituted its own public spectacle: "Now they give shows of their own. Thumbs up! Thumbs down! And the killers Spare or slay, and then go back

---

* The American anthropologist Carleton S. Coon, in his book *The Story of Man*, noted that Barbary macaques can be seen in the wild performing similar hand gestures. Coon suggests that this is a way of boasting about even having opposable thumbs. While I don't find this argument especially persuasive, I *do* find it very funny. Think of it: The thumbs-up emerged as a way of bragging about being able to make a thumbs-up. Take *that*, bears!

to concessions for private privies." As in the case of poor John Richie of Long Island (or even a syndicated TV show dedicated to movie reviews), the evaluation of a thing becomes, if not the thing itself, then an independent event adjacent to the thing.

A fundamental difference between Roger Ebert and Gene Siskel (or Richard Roeper, or whomever should find themselves hosting any given version of *At The Movies*) and the Tomatometer is that theirs was a system of their own design. If they wanted to streamline their arguments into a binary system of hand gestures then, well, that was their business. Rotten Tomatoes universalizes the practice, and the problem. Tellingly, the site's founder was as inspired by the Siskel and Ebert thumb metric as he was by Jackie Chan. "When I was picking a domain name for Rotten Tomatoes, I was gonna call it 'Thumbs Up' as a tribute," Senh Duong said in 2008, in an internal oral history published on the occasion of the site's tenth anniversary, "but luckily (for copyright reasons), all variations of the show's trademarked rating system were taken." The name may be different, but the problem—from an aesthetic, intellectual, and critical standpoint—persists. In a turn that may qualify as ironic, a website that originally began operations as a portal to film criticism has come to diminish (if not wholly obviate) the vital importance of that same criticism. Moreover, the Tomatometer tends to work in service of the culture industry we all pretend to despise, encouraging not criticism but brain-dead enthusiasm.

I burrow into these grandiose issues of criticism's function, and the vitality of the so-called Aesthetic Dimension, a little later (talk about suspense). The larger, and more insidious, issue is that Rotten Tomatoes and similar knockoff websites such as Metacritic don't *even* account for a given movie's quality in a meaningful way.

All they account for is consensus. The Tomatometer score assigns Fresh ratings to any film about which critics have been, by and large, positive. But this positivity exists on a sliding scale. A Fresh rating can refer to an enraptured, five-star, two-thumbs-*waaaaay*-up, go-out-and-see-it-now rave as well as a three-out-of-five-stars review, which ranks a movie just slightly better than so-so.

One can conceive of a scenario in which a north-of-middling film that barely scrapes by the formula's 60% Fresh cut-off* in every single review is resultantly certified 100% Fresh. Sure, nobody loved it. But nobody really hated it either. Forget the ambitious, potentially divisive works that aspire to artfulness. The ultimate must-see movie becomes the one that barely surpasses total critical ambivalence, a work so wholly middlebrow and stabilized in its just-okayness that it could be used to level a shelf. Audiences rave: "It was fiiiiiiiine," while wiggling their open hands back-and-forth. Two atrophied, barely extended thumbs-up.

Consensus criticism—or aggregated "metacriticism"—doesn't stand as a mark of quality. It stands as a mark of sufficient quality. It can't tell you if a film is good, only if it's good *enough*.

The ascendancy of consensus-as-criticism has bred even more curious consequences. Some people take a Tomatometer rating

---

* In aid of conceiving of such a movie, here are some films that scored precisely 60% on the Tomatometer, ranging from underrated sci-fi epics to middlebrow legal thrillers to direct-to-video sequels (and back again to underrated sci-fi epics): *Starship Troopers, Arlington Road, Throw Mama from the Train, A Civil Action, Stuck on You,* and *Starship Troopers 3: Marauder.*

as holy writ. These people tend to be predisposed to like a film because they have a vested interest in the filmmaker, the star(s), or, most typically, the franchise. With only slight disparagement, I'll call these people "fans."* Fan, from *fanatic*, means (per *Merriam-Webster*) "a person who is extremely enthusiastic about and devoted to some interest or activity" or, even more on point, "a person exhibiting excessive enthusiasm and *intense uncritical devotion*" (emphasis my own). As the recent history of Rotten Tomatoes has shown, there are few fan cultures whose devotion is as intense and blindly uncritical as superhero blockbuster fans.

Explaining why people feel so fanatically about superhero movies (or similarly souped-up blockbuster franchises, such as *Star Wars*) could fill reams of pop-psychology textbooks. Maybe kids who were raised on comic books, once a nerdy and pseudo-subcultural medium, feel a sense of ownership now that these characters and scenarios have come to dominate mass culture. Maybe the character of the superhero, generally a brooding or alienated social misfit vested with incredible power, encourages a chip-on-the-shoulder attitude among fans who regard themselves as similarly alienated, if conventionally powerless. Maybe there's some secret arrangement whereby

---

* Lest I be accused of positioning myself as above-it-all, I too have my own fannish devotions, things I'll defend to the point of hysterical apologetics. I fork over money to podcasts I don't even really listen to, out of some sense of obligation or guilt for the hours of pleasure and insight they've afforded me. And I'll probably always buy a ticket to a James Bond movie, or listen to a new Iron Maiden album. And likewise, I'll twist myself out of shape trying to defend even their minimal merits, even when I know, deep in my heart of hearts, that they might just actually be bad.

every longtime Spider-Man reader is entitled to a portion of the profits of a new Spider-Man movie? I don't know. What I do know is that the culture of consensus around superhero movies specifically has had a documented, net-negative effect on not just critical thinking but also pop culture as a whole.

There are likely no fans more fanatical or maniacally uncritical than Batman fans. In the summer of 2012, many moviegoers eagerly awaited *The Dark Knight Rises*, the third and final film in director Christopher Nolan's rebooted Batman trilogy. These films invested the cinematic franchise with a newfound seriousness, trading in Jack Nicholson's giddy, scenery-chewing supervillain the Joker for Heath Ledger's morose, anarchic take on the character, and swapping armies of penguins strapped with rocket launchers for ponderous dialogues about the nature of good, evil, and civic responsibility. This ain't your grandmother's Batman, etc.[*]

The anticipation around *The Dark Knight Rises* had reached such a spiked pitch that die-hard Bat-fans began hectoring critics who dared to give the film negative reviews, thereby "ruining" the film's score. It got so bad that Rotten Tomatoes suspended its system of anonymous user comments. "The job of policing the comments became more than my staff could handle for that

---

[*] Any claims that the new generation(s) of Warner Bros./DC Comics movies aspire to a certain seriousness, maturity, and oft-cited "grittiness" were severely undercut by the boy of about eight years old I saw at a matinee screening of 2017's *Justice League* who came barreling into the sticky-floored cinema shouting, "*Weeeeeeeeeeeeee* Batman! Superman! *Weeeeeee!*" Beyond being more amusing than anything in *Justice League*, I keep this young man in mind whenever I'm trying to remember the real target audience of such entertainments.

film, so we stopped the comments altogether," Matt Atchity, the website's editor-in-chief, said at the time. "It just got to be too much hate based on reactions to reviews of movies that people hadn't even seen."

A similar kerfuffle erupted in early 2018, on the cusp of Marvel Studios' *Black Panther* movie. The hype around *Black Panther* was comparable to that surrounding *The Dark Knight Rises*, albeit for different reasons. As the first major Marvel Studios superhero blockbuster featuring a black superhero—but not, as was commonly misreported, the first black superhero movie[*]—the stakes surrounding *Black Panther* were high. And so were the expectations. The film was emerging into a culture in which issues of diversity and representation in Hollywood (both on-screen and behind the cameras) were front of mind, accelerated by cultural movements/hashtags such as #OscarsSoWhite, #BlackLivesMatter, and #TimesUp.

More than just another Marvel Studios project, *Black Panther* carried on its lithe, robotically besuited shoulders the hopes of whole cultures, races, and ethnic groups. Members of the global African diaspora rallied around the character, and around his fictional African kingdom of Wakanda—a technologically advanced, Afro-futurist monarchical civilization imagined as the modern end point of a national history free of European conquest, colonization, the slave trade, and other all-too-real historical horrors. Advance ticket sales were better than brisk, setting and surpassing the record for most ticket presales for a superhero movie, surpassing DC's joyless *Batman v Superman:*

---

[*]   Lest we forget *Blade*, *The Meteor Man*, *Blankman*, and *Spawn*.

*Dawn of Justice.** Groups organized public screenings for disadvantaged urban youth. Even the heart of the hardened cynic must surely swell, however slightly, at such news.

Black Panther wasn't just about another hero prancing across car rooftops in a fancy super-suit and felling bad guys. It was (to borrow the tagline of the first Obama campaign) about all-caps HOPE. Marginalized groups with so little faith to vest in systems like Hollywood or Marvel Studios vested *Black Panther* with their faith. It was too full of hope to fail.

As happened with *The Dark Knight Rises*, this hype fueled a toxic fervor. The first less-than-sterling review of *Black Panther* reached the Tomatometer courtesy of *Irish Independent* critic Ed Power. (This is another weird result of Rotten Tomatoes: it draws attention to otherwise below-the-radar scribes writing, for example, for Irish daily newspapers.) And people weren't having it. Power's review had punctured the film's coveted 100% Rotten Tomatoes score, kicking off a predictable tempest-in-a-teapot Twitter storm. Power was accused of trolling—the practice of being nasty for the purpose of goading, or merely for the sake of nastiness itself (more on this later)—or of merely trying to differentiate himself from the wash of positive early reviews. There was also the matter of what, precisely, Power didn't like about the movie. As he wrote of the character:

---

* DC fans apparently conspired to sink *Black Panther*'s "audience score" out of sheer fanboy animosity for all Marvel products. This is a cultural melee so inane and minor that I'm frankly a little embarrassed to even admit knowing about it.

What he doesn't get to do much of is jump around beating-up bad guys. That's a shame. Marvel has finally given us an African superhero. The hope surely was that he would be allowed to do superheroic things.

The criticism of Power's criticism was commonly reduced to: This guy is mad that Black Panther doesn't beat up enough bad guys. As one irate Panther-holic tweeted, "So there's a critic that gave #BlackPanther a bad review for not beating up enough bad guys. I say they add a scene where everyone beats up the critic." At the risk of sounding confused (or coy), and with due respect to *Black Panther*'s status as a cultural object signifying well beyond its ostensible narrative and aesthetic boundaries, isn't this sort of what superheroes do? Beat up bad guys? Isn't it reasonable enough that someone buying a ticket to a Marvel Studios mega-blockbuster be treated to the basic element of the genre, in the same way one buying a ticket to a classic American western may well expect to see a gunfight and a jug of whiskey labeled with three *X*s and an impromptu acoustic musical number?

The electrifying energy and amplified aspirations attributed to *Black Panther* established a kind of preconsensus. And this time it was less about the character, the property, or the franchise itself. It was about the hyped-up hopes that the film might singlehandedly reshape the way black talent (and black faces) are prefigured in American pop culture. Yet, in another case of Rotten Tomatoes's formula feeling arbitrary, and a bit confused, this critic had filed a largely positive review, grading the film a three out of a possible five stars. It's not even that Ed Power didn't like *Black Panther*, but that he didn't like it enough. And in this particular case, "enough" meant unqualifiedly, without reservation, with the frenzy, excessive enthusiasm, and intense uncritical devotion of the fan. Critical dissent is drubbed even when it's not actually that dissenting.

The consensus groupthink and blind faith in the Tomatometer bred a nasty mob mentality. And while mobs can be fine, say, in those cases when they're mustered in the defense of the defensible, here they were marshaled to rally for the product of a major corporation. Working critics often serve as a check and balance against the grinding machinations of the Hollywood culture industry. Think back to those earliest examples of fruit, turnips, or eggs being turned upon parading Roman imperial bureaucrats. A dissenting review of something that looms as auspiciously in the cultural firmament as a new Batman or Marvel movie[*] is not only an evaluation of its qualities (or lack thereof) but also a register of complaint against a whole culture otherwise happy to overlook those qualities (or, again, lack thereof).

Acolytes subservient to the cult of the Tomatometer wield their own weaponized rotten fruit against those who perform the public service of wielding rotten fruit of their own. It's like those splattery scenes from La Tomatina of Buñol, the annual Valencian festival during which people purchase tickets for the privilege of hurling tomatoes at one another, just for kicks. Yes, tomatoes are fun to throw—for

---

[*] Oh man, how I wish that new Batman and Marvel movies didn't loom quite so auspiciously in the cultural firmament. But, well, here we are.

protest, for constructive criticism, for the exhilarating thrill of a splat. But they're now being thrown en masse, in all directions, in chaos that actually enforces consensus over criticism. Once again, we find ourselves facing another substitution. Judgment, and especially the breathless rush to judgment, has supplanted evaluation, thoughtfulness, discernment, taste—the very *stuff* of criticism itself.

To wield a rotten tomato comes with a certain power. To paraphrase the guiding ethos of one of those countless Spider-Man movies: With great power comes great responsibility. Or at least, you know, *some* responsibility.

Upworthiness and the Dangers of Being so Damn Agreeable

Like pretty much everyone on planet Earth, I was surprised by the events of Tuesday, November 8, 2016. The night Donald Trump was elected the forty-fifth president of the United States of America.

I remember it with a nightmarish clarity. I was at my apartment. I had intended to host an ironic election party themed after Infowars, the ad hoc media empire of wing-nut conspiracy theorist Alex Jones. I put some M&M's candies in a tin bowl labeled "nutraceuticals," a reference to the dietary supplements hawked on the Infowars website. I prepared a pitcher of wretched limeade margaritas labeled "Goblin Vomit," inspired by one of Jones's more deranged rants about then–presidential hopeful Donald Trump "charging into a goblin's nest." I ordered a pizza and labeled it "John Podesta's

Spirit Cooking Pizza," a reference to . . . well, if you don't know, you're probably better off.*

It was meant to be all snark and fun as a few friends and I waited for Hillary Clinton to be named the next president of the United States. Of course, that did not happen. Adding insult to injury, barely forty-eight hours later, I found out that Leonard Cohen had died. I didn't sleep for four days.

Something else I had in common with pretty much everyone on planet Earth—including, I wager, Donald Trump and everyone inside his campaign—was needing to know *why*. In the immediate aftermath of the 2016 election, people were groping for answers. Answers to pressing questions like, "How did this happen?" and "How *could* this happen?" and "Is this surely the worst of all conceivable worlds, including a world where the only song ever recorded was Aerosmith's 'Pink,' and so you had to hear it every time you turned on a radio?" But before such weighty issues could be interrogated, the reactionary instinct was to assign blame.

Blame for Trump fell at the feet of many: white nationalists, Russian internet trolls, Bernie Sanders voters, Jill Stein voters, the Electoral College, the media, James Comey, "brocialist" podcasters, Lena Dunham's asinine pro-Clinton rap video, an ideologically confused GOP, a Democratic Party wholly out of touch with the American middle class who ran a

---

* But if you *are* curious, just plop the words "John Podesta spirit cooking" into your web browser. Then cancel any plans, silence your phone, and get ready to lose yourself in the warrens and blind alleys of one of American politics' more hairy conspiracy theories in recent memory.

wildly uninspiring candidate, etc. But one among this expansive rogues' gallery of culprits seemed particularly reproachable: The Algorithm.

"I doubt I would be here if it weren't for social media, to be honest with you," Donald Trump told *Fox News* in October 2017. He was referring to his own prolific, and highly erratic, Twitter account, which often seems to be the singular motor of the modern news cycle. But the statement rang true, however incidentally, in a broader context. For many speculators and commentators, it was The Algorithm—the bubble—that made a Trump presidency not just conceivable but also attainable.

To paraphrase Marx in *The Poverty of Philosophy*: as the hand mill produced the feudal lord and the steam mill the industrial capitalist, The Algorithm gave us Donald Trump. Or so some argued in the wake of Trump's election. Where Marx held that the character of a given society was determined by its economic model, so it was similarly posited that technology—not economic technology like a loom or printing press, but the cultural technology of everyday life—was in part responsible for radically destabilizing the institutions and operations of American democracy. As *The Guardian* newspaper noted, using their own distinctly Marxian verbiage, "The 2016 election took place under the spectre of a bubble."

The bubble in question was really two bubbles, which more or less overlapped, like a Venn diagram in full eclipse. The first was the social media bubble, constituted by Facebook, Twitter, YouTube, Instagram, Reddit, and other products of so-called Web 2.0 that prioritize user-generated content of stories, news, polls, etc., produced by major media companies. The second bubble was one of existing bias. More than merely lapping over one another, these two bubbles were mutually reinforcing. Imagine the monster from that movie *The Blob*, which mindlessly absorbs anything it touches. Now imagine a blob that devours *other* blobs. This was the noxious, blobby bubble that loomed over the Trump election.

Writing about social news media algorithms is like trying to catch a greased pig. They're mercurial and ever-changing, with developers constantly fiddling with them. But to take Facebook circa 2016 as an example, the main problem with social media is that it tends to support existing biases. Facebook's "newsfeed" landing page is programmed to serve a given user, privileging content that a given user's friends may be sharing or liking, and pushing types of content that a user typically interacts with to the top of their feed. Share a lot of posts about food? You're likely to see a lot of those *Tasty* videos where recipes are prepared on electric hot plates, shot from dead-on overhead angles. Are you the kind of person who shares memes about "Crooked Hillary"? Well, you're bound to see a lot more of that stuff. These feeds are intelligent, adapting in real time. Engagement is king.

In a way, this all makes intuitive sense. If I log in to *my* Facebook page, or Twitter profile, why would I want to see stuff I don't care about? If social media is truly "social," then it follows that we'd be interested in defining the perimeters of our social circles. You're not likely to invite some guy you can't stand to a housewarming party. So why follow Facebook pages or Instagram accounts that don't jive with your interests and predilections? What's wrong with this kind of personalization?

In his 1995 book *Being Digital*, MIT Media Lab founder Nicholas Negroponte spoke of the "post-information age." Where the information age relied on data, statistics, and the numerical proliferation of consumer habits in order to "narrow-cast" media and information to consumers, the post-information age sees digitized iterations of the *actual* consumers themselves. Negroponte compares the information age to "Have It Your Way," that old burger slogan that suggests personalization but, in fact, only offers customization within a radically delimited range of possibilities.* Negroponte juxtaposes this with the post-information age and the rise of what he terms "the Digital Me." As he writes, "Everything is made to order, and information is extremely personalized . . . True personalization is now upon us. It's not just a matter of selecting relish over mustard." More recently, and employing even more phantasmic, fanciful language, American political philosopher Jodi Dean described the '90s-era internet as constituting a "fantasy of abundance."

We now live in a kind of inverted version of this extreme personalization; fantasy revealed as nightmare. Users—that is, real people, voters, the atomic units of a functioning democracy—who tend to follow conservative news-and-views sources are bound to find themselves unknowingly stuck in a bubble structured by that ideological leaning. Likewise, liberals who follow pages dedicated to Colin Kaepernick and Democracy Now! are likely to have their worldview confirmed. When *The Guardian* developed a quick experiment to test the theory (by having

---

* I am reminded of a favorite line from my favorite book, Theodor Adorno and Max Horkheimer's *Dialectic of Enlightenment*: "The diner must be satisfied with reading the menu."

liberals and conservatives switch feeds and report on the different media served up via algorithm), the results were as dispiriting as they were unsurprising. As one test subject put it, reading across the political aisle, "It's like reading a book by a fool." Both sides accused the other of being stuck in a bubble, failing to recognize that this attitude is necessarily informed by their being stuck in a bubble of their own. At the risk of sounding hopelessly cheesy, the problem with the endlessly customizable "Digital Me" is that it forgets the "Digital You," to say nothing of the "Digital Us."

This may seem relatively harmless when it comes to matters of taste or cultural engagement, but becomes more complicated when the same social news landscape is mapped over the terrain of politics and democracy. And it is even further complicated, and rendered deeply sinister, by revelations that some of the memes and social news users engaged with were (a) totally made-up, (b) deliberately calculated by foreign state actors* to skew election results, and (c) both. A new phraseology emerged following the Trump election, which seemed to take its cues from Negroponte's post-information terminology: "fake news" (or "post-facts") was immediately weaponized on both sides of the political aisle.

---

*   I am hesitant to buy into the popular "Russian troll" conspiracy whole hog. While it increasingly seems to be the case that social media trolls operating outside of the United States set up social media pages to sway opinion, the desperate belief that Russia "fixed" the election, even if it's undeniably true, feels like scapegoating. Such an explanation is entirely too convenient, and deliberately ignores the more root-and-branch ideological and institutional rot endemic in American politics.

When political critics and commentators talk about polarization, this is precisely what they mean. We have become so polarized that we fail to recognize the conditions of our own polarization. We take our position as being some natural, untampered-with state of affairs and any other position as being a chimerical construction. And absurdly, we tend to take our positions as verifiably true even if they're subject to patent absurdities, like a harebrained belief that a Democratic operative is involved in a Satanic child sex ring operating out of a D.C.-area pizzeria, or that Donald Trump is a mere puppet whose strings are being pulled by a stone-faced Russian kleptocrat. As the prolific French sociologist Gustave Le Bon noted way back in 1895, "the philosophic absurdity that often marks general beliefs has never been an obstacle to their triumph."

Another likely unintended, and absurd, consequence of the previously unfathomable Donald Trump presidency is that it has imbued antiauthoritarian punk rock records with a renewed urgency and relevancy. Thinking of how The Algorithm structures an individual's reality, I'm reminded of a 2002 EP by Swedish socialist garage rockers The (International) Noise Conspiracy: *Bigger Cages, Longer Chains*. Our cages are so roomy, our chains so lengthy, that we don't even feel caged or chained. The uptick in sales of the book *1984* following Donald Trump's election speaks to the tendency to view our present condition as Orwellian. But it is more like the dystopia of Aldous Huxley's *Brave New World*: our ideological bondage has become so cozy and accommodating that we fail to notice it at all.

———

The Algorithm reproduces existing political biases, tastes, and distastes. Yet it also reproduces existing attitudes, ways of orienting oneself toward the world. In the previous section, we looked at the ways in which consensus hamstrings critical thinking. Similarly, I'd argue that the operating principle of The Algorithm is agreeability. The purpose of The Algorithm, after all, is to serve content that we agree with. This runs the gamut from click-baiting listicles that appeal to large swaths of the public ("15 Reasons Why Pizza Is Actually Really F*cking Good For You") to image macros and memes that reinforce a political bias (a photo of Canadian prime minister Justin Trudeau superimposed on a picture of Yoda from the *Star Wars* movies, overlaid with blocky text reading "THE FAIL IS STRONG IN THIS ONE").

Every retweet, every like, every share, every upvote consolidates a sameness of opinion. This has been shown to be true within differing spheres of opinion and belief (e.g., liberals will share stuff that other liberals tend to agree with). We share stuff that reflects our existing prejudices, or even our aspiring prejudices. Anecdotally, a friend who wrote for a comedy website once told me that they operated under an editorial instruction to "write stuff that people look good sharing." That is, stories that, by virtue of being shared, would reflect well on the sharer's character, projecting an image of them as some sort of Good Person. The result was a kind of totally frictionless satire— "Area Woman Fed Up With Man's Crap"—that primarily functioned to reflect well on the person who shared it, as opposed to being actually wry, sardonic, insightful, or, you know, funny. This tendency also calls to mind a 1995 episode of the ABC sitcom *Roseanne*, in which the Connor clan is tapped to become a

"Nielsen Family," and so must diarize their TV-viewing habits. Insistent on proving that their family is not "white trash," the titular matriarch instructs her family to watch brainy, educational programming that will reflect well on their viewing habits, and on the Connors as people. Here taste (in comedy writing, in TV programming) becomes less about what one might like, and more about how what one likes (or pretends to like) shapes perception. We share content that is—to borrow the name of a popular website that manufactures such content—"Upworthy." We want to control our presentation-of-self through social media.

To return to Marx's technologically determinist quote from earlier, about the hand mill producing the conditions of feudalism, it is the very nature of retweet/upvote/like to reproduce bias. That is, the nature of these technological functions is the driving of consensus. As the Korean-German writer Byung-Chul Han has written, digital technologies, from the black boxes of our smartphones to the algorithms of appeasement that fill them, "prolong *the same*." Digital technology and digital space, he writes, "undermines our ability to encounter and work with negativity." Likes (or upvotes, or retweets) generate similarly likeable material. Consequently, our prejudices are so fully reinforced that even the suggestion of undermining feels inconceivable, like being told that the law of gravity isn't so hard and fast after all. Another participant in *The Guardian*'s 2016 feed-switching experiment told reporters, "I never see positive stuff about Hillary Clinton. I didn't know that existed."

The burrowing into these self-reproducing digital seedbeds of consensus creates a fundamental disjoint in our encounter with the Other. It's no longer just a matter of disagreeing with (or reserving white-hot contempt for) those with whom we disagree, but a matter of not even being aware of them. This is what's lost when we lose our ability to encounter negativity. Negativity, after all, isn't just conceived as a critical judgment or censure that rankles. It is the emergence of something previously unknowable in our sense of self and of the world we inhabit. One imagines a modern Red voter meeting a modern Blue voter as a conquering conquistador might have greeted a member of an Indigenous population: not as a peer or contemporary, but as an anomaly, something whose existence had hitherto been *unthinkable*.

The Algorithm functions to drive toward accord and preclude divisiveness and contrarian chirping. It has created a new, dangerous standard of agreeability. We respond to content that appeals to our biases. We like and click and share in search of consensus. And not only with some perceived bloc to which we might belong. We desire consensus with ourselves—an internal accord.

While aspiring to such internalized entente may make life more pleasing by sanding off the flinty edges of disagreeability, it is a death sentence for a species that tends to thrive and evolve through the process of conflict and interrogation—both internal and external. Since "holistic" ascended as a grating buzzword co-opted by the stilted New Speak of corporate communications, there's been a trend toward a cultural standard of wholeness, or completeness.

Compounding the problem, holism—i.e., the viewing of all things as constituent parts of some grand architecture of completeness—is often used in the equally grating argot of New Age health and wellness as synonymous with "natural." American author Barbara Ehrenreich has phrased the detente between a belief in naturalized holism and a belief in contradiction as a war between the very ideas of conflict and harmony themselves.

Beware of anyone claiming that any one way of living, or of thinking, is somehow natural and thus unmoored from the mitigating tendrils of ideology. Such claims tend to be, historically, the *most* sneakily ideological, because they hide their arbitrariness behind the veil of nature and specious claims of how things *should* be.

It's precisely for this reason that I'm hesitant to ascribe any one particular essence to the whole of human existence. Still, it strikes me that it is *more* natural to struggle through hypocrisy, to feel ill at ease with oneself, to succumb to feelings of fraudulence or impostor syndrome, to feel fully alive in contradiction. This is what Saint Paul was talking about when he pronounced, cryptically, "I do not understand what I do. For what I want to do I do not do, but what I hate I do." Or, if all the Catholic theology stuff is wearing on you, reader, then look to the writing of one of the great disbelievers, Albert Camus. For Camus, revolution and art "live in the same contradiction." Likewise, the rebel, the revolutionary, the freethinker is one who embraces the contradictions of life instead of attempting to suppress or resolve them.

Holism is itself a relatively new concept. (And, as Ehrenreich unpacks, one that is inexplicably bound up with the reproduction of capitalism and the subtle enforcement of ideology.) Contradiction's history runs longer, and the concept of contradiction offers a more stable bedrock for situating oneself in the world. Common sentiments regarding the essential roughness of life reappear in various traditions of wisdom, from Buddhism's First Truth (life is suffering) to scowling German philosopher

Arthur Schopenhauer, a Diogenes-level historic grouch* who declared that "the life of the individual is a constant struggle . . . he discovers adversaries everywhere, lives in continual conflict and dies with a sword in hand." To live is to live in conflict, and in struggle, both with the world and with oneself.

Moreover, the drive toward consensus and agreeability is ultimately a drive toward simplicity, and a dangerous reduction. For Camus, it was the drive toward the elimination of freedom itself. Such knowledge should breed wariness around the comfort of consensus and internalized self-satisfaction. To disagree with the world, and with oneself, is, after all, to be alive.

The election of Donald Trump offers many harsh lessons. Don't elect Donald Trump as president of the United States would probably sit smack at the top of the list. But right up there is the danger of being so damnably agreeable.

---

* He also, like Diogenes, preferred the company of dogs to men, finding companionship late in life with pet poodles. He once wrote approvingly of a chained dog that tore its master's arm off, in apparent protest at having its life reduced to subservience and bondage.

— 2 —

What We Like and Why We Like It

— DISCUSSED HEREIN —

Paul Valéry's most famous pronouncement | *The KFC Double Down* |
Distinction | *Living sociologically* | *Cultural omnivorousness* |
Hegemons | *The necessity of eating one's veggies* | The Sopranos |
"In Defense of Guy Fieri" | *"Against Interpretation"* | *Think pieces
and hot takes* | *Horniness* | The Aesthetic Dimension

— *The New Tastelessness* —

It's pretty much impossible for a book about hating to not also be, at least in some respect, a book about taste.

"What really matters is what you like, not what you *are* like," insists John Cusack's sad-sack record store schlub in the 2000 film *High Fidelity*. It's a line that has doubtless been repeated by similarly self-styled sullen young men who define their identities through their placement in some expansive matrix of cultural consumption. Employing haterism's fundamental value of negation (and following poet Paul Valéry's proclamation that "what is called taste is made up of a thousand distastes"), we might rework this to "What really matters is what you *don't* like, not what you are like."

The matter of taste, at least judging by the number of books and essays published on the subject in the past decade, seems key to the way we think through our culture. And yet it also, weirdly, simultaneously, seems like we've never cared *less* about it. These days, taste is only interesting to us to the extent that we can destabilize it: salvaging crap movies as cult movies; creating cockamamie frameworks for justifying a later-life interest in Dad's collection of corny soft rock records; eagerly upsetting hierarchies of "high" and "low" by, say, plating fried chicken alongside caviar or plating fried foie gras as if it were a KFC Double Down sandwich.*

---

*   As of this writing, the latter dish can be procured at Montreal's Joe Beef, while the former is served at David Chang's fine-ish dining chain Momofuku. Both restaurants, and their animating personalities,

To some extent, to write about taste is to write about the outmodedness or superfluity of taste. For the serious-minded gourmand/cinephile/music snob/man o' letters/whatever, no genre or flavor profile is too lowbrow. Nothing is verboten. The only thing truly taboo is taste itself.

Well, I wonder, in my pitchiest, most-quavering, David Byrne–iest voice, *how did we get here?*

Another thing that's pretty much impossible: writing about taste without beginning a paragraph with, "In his landmark 1979 study *Distinction: A Social Critique of the Judgment of Taste*, French sociologist Pierre Bourdieu writes . . ." So, let's just get that out of the way.

In his landmark 1979 study *Distinction: A Social Critique of the Judgment of Taste*, French sociologist Pierre Bourdieu writes:

> Taste, the propensity and capacity to appropriate (materially or symbolically) a given class of classified, classifying objects or practices, is the generative formula of life-style, a unitary set of distinctive preferences which express the same expressive intention in the specific logic of each of the symbolic sub-spaces.

Dense academic jargon, maybe. But hey, I chopped the abutting bits where he uses acutely technical sociological patter

---

exhibit a too-eager desire to fold high-end dining into junky fast food. Thinking of these (types of) restaurants, I am reminded of the *Simpsons* joke about going to a restaurant and ordering "your finest food stuffed with your second finest," only to be served lobster stuffed with tacos.

like "synthetic unity" and "body hexis." What Bourdieu's getting at, in a very basic sense, is the manner in which taste serves as an expression of a given subject's position in a class hierarchy. Taste is a product of social conditioning and part of a complex system that determines the very way we view the world. Bourdieu and other sociologists call this system the "habitus."

Distinction is notable for explicitly connecting cultural capital (one's acquired understanding of books, films, artworks, wines, hefty sociology textbooks, etc.) to plain ol' capital (that is, money). It's a fairly commonsensical equation: more money creates more access to things like education and rarefied artworks (the opera, the ballet, and so on), thereby accommodating both access to and a more nuanced understanding of the whole field of culture. In Bourdieu's study of mid-twentieth-century French culture and society, "good taste" was the taste of the dominant culture, for example, those with the greatest stocks of economic and cultural capital. Such good taste trended toward more rarefied art and culture that has a purely aesthetic function, like a Rothko painting or a purely decorative bauble. These are things that can be enjoyed in and of themselves; art (or fashion) for art's (or fashion's) sake.

Contrarily, what Bourdieu terms the working-class aesthetic is oriented toward more instrumental ends, like a useful pair of utility overalls or a film designed to excite and entertain. Bourdieu discusses "manual workers" who dismiss a photograph of some pebbles "as useless, perverse or bourgeois." From the vantage of the working-class habitus, such a banal photo constitutes "a waste of film." For the more culturally savvy consumer, for whom such issues are less pressing, waste matters not. Indeed, the conspicuous consumption and display of such everyday banalities for their own sake may be the essence of the art. Just think of Warhol's soup cans and soapboxes, Duchamp's *Fountain*, and the whole bourgeois artistic notion of the ready-made and objet trouvé. Here the artistic object's everyday-ness is its point, or part of it. It is precisely because Warhol's boxes of soap pads cannot be used for laundry that they become art, as they transcend the rudimentary utility en route to offering something like a "pure" aesthetic experience.

If I am merely skating over the surface of Bourdieu's hefty tome, it is because nowadays *Distinction* is just as likely to be mentioned for being "seminal" and "oft-cited" as it is for being a bit old hat, if not out-and-out irrelevant. Cultural consumption and the formation of taste now transpire not only in the shadow of Bourdieu but also in full self-conscious knowledge of him. Think of the arrival of the oft-maligned, tritely caricatured "hipster," whose sartorial sense indexed geeky Ray-Ban Clubmaster eyeglasses, vented "trucker hats," vintage bowling shirts, and waxed handlebar mustaches à la Rollie Fingers/ Archduke Franz Ferdinand. Such a figure stages a knowing collapse of good taste and bad, high and low signifiers, legitimate and illegitimate taste, suggesting the formation of a new megahabitus that contains all others.

The post-distinction (and post-*Distinction*) taste culture is perhaps best signaled by the ascension of Miller High Life, a crisp, clean-drinking, and relatively cheap lager that advertises itself in a '70s-styled anachronistic label as "The Champagne of Beers." Not only does a "working-class" beer advertise itself with reference to pricey French sparkling wine but also most savvy modern consumers know that the comparison is a bit of a joke, and thus part of the drink's appeal. Likewise, we all know a guy who savors the apparent contrast in liking both extreme heavy metal and fine wine.* Or, more precisely, savors that *there is* no contrast.

People are so acutely, cripplingly conscious of their expression of taste—and how that expression situates them within larger cultural, social, and economic fields—that they've come to adapt in real time. Skewing too highbrow? Better pepper a conversation with quotes from *The Simpsons* or, even better, acutely ironized lines from *Family Guy*. Feeling like a lowbrow pleb? Time to pop on that *L'Année dernière à Marienbad* Blu-ray you've been using as a coaster. And it's not enough to (per the expression) favor champagne taste on a beer budget. These categories of high and low must be exploded altogether. Such a pose is essentially the physical embodiment and social expression of the destabilization of high and low. It is turning oneself into a plate of fried chicken and caviar. Giggity-giggity-goo, *mon chou*!

The reason for this is "meta" in a way that sufficiently befits our age. Bourdieu's theories of distinction and the dominance hierarchies of cultural capital have become (in certain quarters)

---

* I was once told a story of a mutual acquaintance who explained that a fun way to blow people's minds was to walk into a dimly lit and pricey wine bar, "wearin' a fuckin' Bathory T-shirt," a reference to a Swedish heavy metal outfit that makes full use of spooky-evil genre clichés (goat heads, skulls, burly Vikings, pale moons) in their album art and iconography. Since then, the phrase "wearin' a fuckin' Bathory T-shirt" has come to connote, in my mind, the self-conscious collapsing of ostensibly diametrically opposed spheres of cultural operation. I invite you, reader, to use it liberally. "You can go to the Metropolitan Opera, wearin' a fuckin' Bathory T-shirt . . . ," "I performed an angioplasty on her, wearin' a fuckin' Bathory T-shirt . . . ," and so on.

so ubiquitous that they have invited response in the calibration of taste, distinction, and the very presentation of self. "We live," as Marco Roth and the editors of the magazine *n+1* write, "in an emerging mainstream moment of the sociology of taste." Exhibiting some knowledge of these sociological theories of taste—be it via dinner party patter or garish sartorial configuration—has itself become a structuring element of taste. As Roth and Co. put it, "This spread of sociological thinking has led to sociological *living*—ways of thinking and seeing that are constructed in order to carry out, yet somehow escape, the relentless demystification sociology requires."

As with many trends discussed in this volume, this shift from thinking through the sociology of taste to living the sociology of taste constitutes not so much a progressive evolution as a cyclical recursion. The anxiety around taste, and the corresponding desire to collapse high into low and, further, to eliminate the high/low distinction altogether has resulted in a geographical flatland of distinction—a desert of taste. More recent theories of taste tend to focus less on Bourdieu's divide between illegitimate and legitimate, working-class and dominant culture, and more on the patterns of cultural consumption along omnivore/univore lines. Where the high-class cultural omnivore devours a range of texts, giddily pecking at even working-class or crass "mass" entertainments, the univore's tastes are (to nip a line from a wildly popular recent trash erotic novel that entrenched itself in the cultural firmament) very singular. Where the univore may just listen to Taylor Swift, the omnivore *redeems* her.

What matters is not even what you like (or what you don't like) but how you can rework and appropriate an endless sprawl of cultural signifiers. In this culture of buffet-style omnivorousness, reactions of love and hate risk becoming wholly irrelevant, sloping ever toward a mushy middle. Expressing unique affection for the highbrow opens one to accusations of snobbery. Likewise, an unself-conscious enjoyment of low culture risks betraying an eagerness to appropriate and elevate the culture industry's assembly-line junk.* Caught in contemporary taste culture's cruel double bind, the only safe refuge is, increasingly, the ever-ballooning middle.

And so Valéry's equation has been effectively inverted. Taste is no longer comprised of whole constellations of distastes. Now, distaste stands as the only thing more gauche than taste. To live in this hemmed-in, brutally self-reflexive, archly sociological way is to deny the charge of personal passions, positive or negative.

And yet, in a world where a corporate mega-CEO such as Jeff Bezos cops the jargon of sociology** to push his company's self-publishing platform, the language of Bourdieu's sociology of taste feels facile. Worse, it has been rendered hostile to culture—an instrument of cultural knowledge weaponized against culture itself. The cultural producers, the wielders of political power, the contemporary hegemons have become so kind as to do the work of thinking through the world for us. They are like the savvy dad who attempts to hedge his son's defiance by blasting hard rock

---

* Alternatively, such enjoyment may just reveal one as being uncultured. It's tricky to know which is worse.

** See Bezos's 2012 shareholder meeting address, in which he castigated "well-meaning gatekeepers" of culture. This despite being, you know, a mega-rich gatekeeper of actual capital.

and punk records, as if to prove that their righteous rebelliousness will only ever narrow toward lameness. Effrontery is made to seem deeply pointless, all well-intentioned cultural rebellions stamped out before they can even catalyze.

High and low have been replaced by an extreme middle, with taste and distaste supplanted by the new tastelessness. And the valuation of cultural omnivores doesn't so much expand the circle of tastemakers as carefully hide and obfuscate the cultural and class positions that were once explicit in the public formation of taste—like a drunk upper-cruster giving himself away when his monocle falls into his pint of $4 High Life.

Deep-Fried Chocolate Broccoli:
— *Premium Cable, Poptimism,* —
and the Extreme Middlebrow

In this brave new millennium of collapsed, destabilized, double-bound tastelessness, don't dare to tell a critic to eat their vegetables. In what parades as a bold, defiant thesis, published in *The New York Times Magazine* in 2011, pop culture writer Dan Kois wrote against engaging with art movies and other conspicuous markers of refined acculturation. For Kois, expressions of taste are variously "aspirational" or a "performative act." "As I get older," Kois writes, "I find I'm suffering from a kind of culture fatigue and have less interest in eating my cultural vegetables, no matter how good they may be for me."

Kois need not worry: he's not alone. Despite the well-meaning protestations of "elitist" and "snob" cultural gatekeepers—whose job is, you know, helping to convey the meaning or value of more difficult art to the public writ large—nobody seems to really care about cultural vegetables these days. Or rather, the valuation for what passes as worthwhile cultural sustenance has changed. Reading so much pop culture writing and criticism (or "criticism") these days, I'm reminded of the *j'accuse* Jerry Seinfeld's character aimed at his junk-foodie postman neighbor: "Newman, you wouldn't eat broccoli if it was deep-fried in chocolate sauce." At the risk of further tapping the figurative taste/literal taste metaphor, deep-fried chocolate broccoli proves an apt metaphor for the new culture of tastelessness.

Has the culture of tastelessness resulted in a new, extreme middlebrowing of culture? Or has a renewed middlebrow encouraged the taboo on taste?

At the risk of sounding cheeky, I maintain that the two trends are irrevocably bound up with one another, with the middlebrow and the taste taboo producing each other in a co-constitutive fashion. To dig into this, it helps to understand the manner in which culture and how we talk about culture has changed over the past two decades. In particular, I want to look at the relationship between a certain kind of cultural production—premium cable television—and a corresponding kind of cultural response—the so-called think piece.

As defined by good old *Merriam-Webster*, *think piece* is "a piece of writing meant to be thought-provoking and speculative that consists chiefly of background material and personal opinion and analysis." The dictionary traces its first known use to 1941, but the most fittingly modern use I can track down is in Buckley Barry Barrett's 2000 index *Churchill: A Concise Bibliography*, in which the author describes the "journalistic, think-piece nature" of an early biography of the British prime minister.

The year 2000 feels like an appropriate, or at the very least instrumentally *useful*, place for locating the emergence of the think piece. A new millennium. The era of Bush II. The adolescence of serious-minded premium cable dramas. The dawn of the Golden Age of TV. Because beyond being the single greatest television show ever produced, and the defining piece of American art of the last quarter-century, *The Sopranos* was epochal. It is the sort of rare cultural artifact whose influence can truly not be overstated. What better proof of this than the fact that even typing the words "*The Sopranos* was epochal" feels so trite and clichéd? Because it is not so much an opinion as a matter of fact: a statement of plainspoken, self-evident truth.

Creator and show-runner David Chase's HBO American epic entered into a culture that had been primed for it. By the late 1990s, the established order of broadcast television was being threatened. The arrival of high-resolution home video (in the form of DVD), the proliferation of channels via cable and satellite subscriptions, and the stuffy sameness of network programming created the perfect conditions for a sea change. At the risk of indulging a bit of Whig historiography—that is, the belief that past events constitute a coherent teleology that advances irrevocably toward the present—it seemed as if all of popular culture was working toward *The Sopranos*.

As Ian Leslie noted in a lengthy 2017 analysis of television's new "Golden Age," subscription cable networks like HBO were beholden directly to the viewer, and not meddling interlocutors like corporations buying ad time. This new landscape also resulted in a new breed of viewer. "Chase's novelistic, multi-layered narrative perfectly answered the needs of TV's new audience," Leslie writes. "They enjoyed grappling with complex, difficult characters, and genre-busting shifts in tone. Crucially, they were also willing to pay for this kind of storytelling." This new philosophy of televisual storytelling was best summed up by David Chase, creator of HBO's other "novelistic" critical hit, *The Wire*. In an interview with BBC2 in 2008, Chase was accused of exhibiting contempt for the "casual viewer." At this he leaned across the table and, in a hushed tone, confirmed the charge, declaring, "Fuck the average viewer."

The advent of the "avid viewer,"* a term coined by *New Statesman* pop culture critic Anna Leszkiewicz, demanded new frameworks for writing about television. Where, pre-2000, a major television show might expect a few kind write-ups in broadsheets and magazines, and (if they were extremely lucky) a *TV Guide* cover, the coverage emerging during TV's Golden Age constituted its own journalistic ecosystem.

Publications such as *Vulture* and *The A.V. Club* began churning out episode-by-episode recaps, which as a rubric for evaluating long-form storytelling feels about as fair as writing

---

*   One may reasonably wish to trace the advent of such slavishly devoted viewership further back, to *The X-Files*, *Twin Peaks*, or even *Star Trek*. While no doubt fervent, the fan bases of such programs constituted a relatively small cult. With *The Sopranos*, such intensity of interest emerged as the de facto way to watch television. While a program like *Twin Peaks* or *Homicide: Life on the Street* may likewise be held up as an early example of game-changing television, both did little to perpetuate a full-blown cultural shift. It's sort of like people trying to claim that Cream or Blue Cheer were the first heavy metal bands, when in fact their heaviness and sonic assaults were mere preludes to the genre-inventing originality of Black Sabbath.

chapter-by-chapter reviews of a novel, or attempting to divine the figure in a carpet that is still on the loom.* Podcasts emerged as another medium for talking about (or listening to other people talk about) television. Eventually, the postmortem gabfest became an event in itself, with AMC (a network whose profile improved drastically during the post-*Sopranos* cable boom) airing "after shows" with names like *Talking Dead* or *Talking Bad* (dedicated to recapping *The Walking Dead* and *Breaking Bad*, respectively).

Desperate to capture readers in the wide-open, revenue-draining wilds of the internet, publications began behaving like the late-'90s cable networks: playing to the tastes and interests of the avid viewers. When people weren't watching *Mad Men* (or *Breaking Bad* or *The Walking Dead* or *Boardwalk Empire* or *Westworld*), they were reading about it, or listening to commentators chat about it. Not only had the viewer been apprehended but also their imagination had been colonized. The once exacting, demanding avid viewers of this new Golden Age weren't just watching *Walking Dead*, or even *Talking Dead*, they were thinking *Walking Dead*.

I'd like to circle back to that dictionary definition of *think piece*, which proves helpful. I'm particularly interested in the idea that

---

* The futility of such a process recalls Pee-wee Herman's funny description, in the 1986 film *Pee-wee's Big Adventure*, of solving a conspiratorial mystery: "It's like you're unraveling a big cable knit sweater that someone keeps knitting and knitting and knitting and knitting and knitting and knitting and knitting!"

the contemporary think piece, as critical substitute, "consists chiefly of background material and personal opinion and analysis." The definition recalls what in university literature or cultural studies classes used to be called "reflection papers." (A quick skim across modern syllabi suggests that some professors are now just straight up calling such papers "think pieces.") The reflection paper was distinguished from the more comprehensive, critically investigative form of the essay.

Where the formal essay is defined, in William Harmon's *A Handbook to Literature*, as possessing "serious purpose, dignity, logical organization, length," the think piece constitutes more of a first-blush reflection. At best, it can relate an author's enthusiasm for a given work through personal anecdote, or persuasively yoke a work and a salient social moment. See, for example, "Black Superheroes Matter: Why a 'Black Panther' Movie Is Revolutionary." Superhero movies, and especially the Marvel Studios superhero movies, emerged post-2008 as the cinematic equivalent of the premium cable drama: devoted to large-scale "world building," governed by a consistent(ly dull) aesthetic sensibility, and shot through with enough critical catnip to keep lights on at the Think Piece Factory. At worst, such think pieces are devoid of any serious consideration, clouded by the prejudice of preference, utterly ignorant to matters of aesthetics, and rushed to market under extreme duress. (To this last point, a snarky, funny *VICE* guide called "How to Write a Think Piece" offers this important criterion: "Don't worry about your work being good. Just get it out there.")

This shift in watching, and receiving, TV and brain-dead blockbuster cinema was accompanied by the trend toward "poptimism" in music criticism. As defined by journalist Jody Rosen, poptimism (or popism) operates on the principle that "Beyoncé is as worthy of serious consideration as Bruce Springsteen, and ascribing shame to pop pleasure is itself a shameful act." Poptimism was pluralist, uncaringly commercial, and—as the portmanteau itself suggests—cheerily optimistic. The think piece was the perfect format for the poptimist turn in music criticism. The Pollyannaish exalting of popular taste, often taking the form of what I've previously described as enlightened philistinism ("Yeah, it's popular and commercial. But *so what*?"), was charily regarded by more perspicacious critics as fundamentally reactionary. As Saul Austerlitz wrote in *The New York Times Magazine* in 2014, in a rare screed against the poptimist reaction:

> Poptimism embraces the familiar as a means of keeping music criticism relevant. Click culture creates a closed system in which popular acts get more coverage, thus becoming more popular, thus getting more coverage. But criticism is supposed to challenge readers on occasion, not only provide seals of approval.

Poptimism provoked a shallow rethinking of the function of criticism itself. Criticism's once serious, dignified function mutated. The impulse quickly spread to other forms of cultural journalism, with film critics ("In Defense of Zack Snyder"), book reviewers ("In Defense of Young Adult Fiction"), and even gourmands ("In Defense of Guy Fieri") seizing on the trend. They sang the praises of zero-calorie entertainments with a wholly unearned air of defiance, using space formerly afforded to criticism to justify their own (poor) tastes. There is also a grating sense that such criticism disingenuously tries to flatter readers by speaking to them on their own terms. As one of my favorite film critics, Kent Jones, wrote in 2001 following a widely circulated broadside against the insularity of criticism (written by, unshockingly, another film critic): "Critics were suddenly coming on like the Red Cross, giving aid to the tender-hearted majority. What's up with all this compassion for the common man?"

Indeed—what's up? It strikes me that much of the poptimist impulse is wholly disingenuous. And this isn't just because questions like "What's the difference between Bruce Springsteen and Beyoncé" feel unfairly loaded. (One writes his own songs; the other is an inspiring and economically powerful black woman whose music is secondary to the text of her stardom and public profile.*) It's because poptimism sometimes feels like an abdication of criticism itself. It's not that writers toeing the poptimist line aren't intelligent or cultured, but that they'd rather use their

---

*   Yes, I'm aware that Beyoncé has writing credits on her records, alongside a dozen-plus collaborators. And the question of sole vs. collaborative authorship in art is an interesting one. That said, it is a question that often remains unasked in favor of a pop star like Beyoncé (or Taylor Swift, or The Weeknd, or Kanye West) as a massive popular artist, without even interrogating the character and content of that artistry. If someone can construct their superstardom as a kind of large-scale performance art, as many have done, then that has value. But it is undoubtedly a *different* value than that of being a singer-songwriter who writes and performs his/her own music. The Boss/Beyoncé question is also loaded along lines of race and gender. Nobody should praise Springsteen over Knowles because the former is a white guy. But framing an artistic comparison in such terms invariably encourages such reduction. Perhaps a more fitting question would be: Why is Beyoncé less worthy of critical admiration than Joni Mitchell? Or than Odetta?

intelligence and acculturation to assuage their class anxiety. I am reminded of Proust's comments on the "vanity of intelligent people," those who "having become more intelligent" are thus entitled to be less so. It's fine that Dan Kois or whoever doesn't want to eat their cultural veggies or grapple with high art. But why should I, or anyone, want to read about them? What purpose does poptimism serve other than the validation of middlebrow, deep-fried chocolate broccoli taste? It's as if the critic's role has slumped from that of guide or interlocutor to mere sponsor, patting the befuddled filmgoer on the back while cooing, "It's cool, buddy. I can't stand that Tarkovsky shit either."

Where what might be snobbishly termed "proper" criticism once stood in antagonism (or, at the very least, ambivalence) to the larger culture industry, the think piece operates in service to it. When AMC's *Mad Men* went off the air in 2015, I joked on Twitter that pink slips served to its writing staff saw *Slate*, *Salon*, *Vulture*, *The A.V. Club*, etc., hand down the same to their writers as the single-track content conveyor belt driving both production and reception ground to a halt. The think piece and the premium cable drama formed a constitutive, codependent bond. How a work relates to the existent history and tradition of its medium (or of culture itself) and, indeed, whether it is good or bad, hardly matters.

In her landmark treatise "Against Interpretation," Susan Sontag warned of a content-driven style of criticism that was inherently reductive. When one distills *A Streetcar Named Desire*'s Stanley Kowalski and Blanche DuBois into archetypes of barbarism and Westernized civility (respectively), Sontag writes, the range and possibility of Tennessee Williams's play is delimited; the text becomes narrowly "intelligible." For Sontag, such intelligibility was only one constituent part of art's sprawling tapestry of possibility. "Against Interpretation" was published in 1966, and Sontag's concerns have proved almost embarrassingly prescient, if not more relevant now than ever. "Interpretation," she wrote, "violates art. It makes art into an article for use, for arrangement into a mental scheme of categories."

The think piece doesn't so much diminish art as render it wholly incidental. The mere existence of a work—and the contemporary proliferation of work after work after work—is enough to justify the think piece. The fundamental problem with so much of contemporary criticism is that the prospective critic is structurally encouraged to not care, to treat the value of one-or-another book/TV episode/movie as wholly irrelevant to the task of writing about it. Sontag wrote that desperate, interpretive searches for meaning constitute "the compliment that mediocrity pays to genius."

The think piece effectively inverts this formulation. Now it is more common to see genius (or perhaps "genius," the work of people who, to nip a phrase from the controversial and cuttingly mean critic Armond White,* "think they think") pay compliments to mediocrity. The clarity of critical judgment alights on every rotten movie, grating pop singer, or paperback book written for awkward adolescents alive in the throes of their protean horniness, and dissolves, ultimately, into a sprawling field of meaninglessness.

Enormously erudite and intelligent expositions about extremely stupid things have degraded both the standard for

---

* Much more on this gentleman in a bit, I assure you.

writing about serious things, and the seriousness of those serious things themselves.

— *The Sleeper Has Awokened* —

In more recent years, this irrelevance has mutated again, into a kind of mis-relevance: a categorical confusion between the work of art itself and the whole social and historical world. The accursed think piece has precipitated the rise of what *Vox* author Jaime Weinman has called "socially conscious criticism," which reveres (or condemns) art based on its ability to embody some woozy consensus of what the world itself should be. Details of character, plot, theme, and even quality itself are subsumed in investigations of "larger" issues of diversity and representation, with films, TV shows, and even YA novels living and dying on the perceived strength of casting calls and plot synopses.

The move toward socially conscious criticism seems like a natural extension of the poptimist impulse. Mainstream Hollywood movies or trashy novels devised by megacorporations are not merely acceptable for enjoyment but may well be, to use the contemporary parlance of the internet, "EVERYTHING," that is: an uplifting, inspiring, and even reproducible model for civilization itself.

The problem with the argument—and the whole culture of "socially conscious criticism"—is not that it privileges politics over aesthetics. It's that it tends to totally ignore aesthetics, and form, and craft. It values art purely on the basis of its perceived political efficacy or usefulness. And in so doing, it does a disservice to both art and politics.

The "new turn" in socially conscious criticism, it should be said, is not at all new. That contemporary critics and practitioners of scorching hot-takery fail to historicize this is not that surprising. The popular term "woke" implies this very kind of blinkered thinking. It's as if, just now, a generation of writers has arisen bed-headed to the very idea of politics itself. In their haste to bring this new awareness to bear on cultural criticism, they neglect to consider the long history of such thinking. It's hard to see clearly when your eyes are still heavily crusted with sleep dirt. Nowhere is this trend toward ahistoricity more evident than in the click-baiting headline style "[Such-And-Such Text] Is More Relevant Now Than Ever!" Really? More relevant now than in the historical and social context in which it was produced, or the historical and social context into which it entered? How could such a thing even be conceivable?

While socially conscious criticism is generally treated (ahistorically) as some new trend, it recalls the hoariest history of literary criticism, in which intensely partisan publications like *Edinburgh Review*, *The London Magazine*, *Blackwood's Magazine*, and the Tory-boasting *Quarterly Review* used literary essays as mere vehicles for smuggling political agendas. Criticism of such eighteenth- and nineteenth-century schools treated a given book review like an ideological Trojan horse—albeit one that is shoddily built, the exterior all but exposed, such that the Trojans crammed inside are plainly, absurdly visible to the naked eye. In a case of history being not so much progressive as cyclical, the contemporary trend of socially conscious criticism constitutes less a major leap in critical thinking than a reversion—all just another bit of history repeating.

More modern critical writing, thinking, and theory was marked by turf wars between formalists and those who wished to interpret works of art in their larger social context. In the early 1970s, literary scholars like Kenneth Burke and Hazard Adams (and later, Franco Moretti) drastically revised the prevailing mode of "New Criticism," which regarded texts as self-contained worlds, by considering the social and historical contexts in which these texts were produced and read. This movement was termed "sociological criticism."

Around the same time, great English-Canadian film critic Robin Wood afforded previously maligned genres (horror movies, specifically) with serious critical attention, dividing them into "progressive" and "reactionary" camps that more or less reflected liberal and conservative political ideologies. Even earlier, Marxist thinkers of the Frankfurt School fled Nazi Germany, landed in Los Angeles, and studied mass culture as an appendage of totalitarianism that (to paraphrase the seminal work by Frankfurt scholars Theodor Adorno and Max Horkheimer, *Dialectic of Enlightenment*) toxified society with its sameness.

What the new socially conscious criticism—which isn't really new so much as it is accelerated, in the same way that the internet and social media accelerate pretty much everything— takes from this genealogy of thought is an underlying belief that all media is inherently political. What such writing so often forgets is the emphasis on aesthetics and form as the very expression of that political potential.

In 1977's *The Aesthetic Dimension*, philosopher and critical theorist Herbert Marcuse synthesizes this long history of theory on the relation between art and politics into a (relatively) clear thesis: that art is valid not in its ability to represent (or shape) the social world, but in its ability to stand outside of it. As he writes in his introduction, "I see the political potential of art in art itself, in the aesthetic form as such." For Marcuse, it wasn't just that aesthetics—form, style, craft, the very way a work of art is made and presents itself—could reflect the political. It was that all these things were political in and of themselves. In rising above (or in Marcuse's word, "transcending") their social and material bases, works of art held potential to radically oppose those very bases, and to reshape the public consciousness.

Some examples may help make sense of this idea. When motion pictures became the rage in the United States in the early part of the twentieth century, there was a genuine moral panic about their professed deleterious impacts on impressionable audiences (read: women, children, the working class). It had little to nothing to do with the contents of a given filmstrip. It was the medium itself, and its tendency to rouse audiences in rowdy urban nickelodeons. Until 1952 in the United States, movies were not afforded the constitutional protections of the First Amendment granted to other arts, precisely because they were seen as too vivid and corrupting.

There are also the legendary stories of audiences running out of the way of a moving train at early movie screenings, or rioting when Igor Stravinsky premiered his ballet *The Rite of Spring* at the Théâtre des Champs-Élysées in Paris in 1913. Musical subgenres from hip-hop (with its repurposing of turntables as themselves musical instruments) to noisy, violently unlistenable black metal (with its aesthetic assault against the very idea of music) have likewise formally reoriented our expectations of the very idea of art. In so doing, they challenge that rigidity and sameness from which the governing political regimes draw their power and tacit authority. After all, it is the delimitation of imagination—artistic and political—that inures us to the status quo and acclimatizes us to accepting it. Great art disturbs this relationship and invites us to consider new forms, to conceive of alternatives to the grinding way things are. It's not merely that art *can* do this. This is what art *is*. Its function is to transcend the constraints of functionality. These are true, radical stakes of art and culture. These are the real politics behind the art.

What is troubling and dispiriting about contemporary socially conscious criticism is that it forgets all of this. Instead of considering forms and alternatives, it narrows the possibilities of thinking and critiquing. If they're not altogether ignored, then aesthetics are at the very least instrumentalized, marshaled in the service of one or another ideology instead of affronting, or even flicking at, the existence of that ideology. We talk about casting, about release strategies, about how Kendrick Lamar's *DAMN.* album was made with beats created on an iPhone 6. We talk about industry and play into the marketing buzz in a way that renders art itself irrelevant.

In a reflection of the results of *The Village Voice*'s annual Pazz & Jop year-end best-of poll, music critic Carl Wilson spoke of "the narrative," that is, "the loose conglomeration of gossip, images, anecdotes, outsize claims, invective, and controversy that these days positions a work as culturally significant, as either speaking to 'the moment' or clangingly missing it." This is increasingly (and verging on exclusively) how critics talk about pop culture, i.e., they talk *around* it, of everything around a record/film/TV episode, but not so much the record/film/ TV episode itself. It's like a weird perversion of the old idea of commodification, in which historical and social processes can be crystallized inside a discrete object, like that bug trapped in amber at the beginning of *Jurassic Park*. The difference is that the commodity (say, Beyoncé's new album) is itself irrelevant. What matters is only "What We Talk About When We Talk About Beyoncé."* Objects of art, culture, and entertainment are understood purely through their relationship to the field from which they emerge, and, in turn, re-enter. The narrative does not so much result in the commodity as the commodity occasions the narrative. Still more despairing, beyond even the hyped-up claims that a given Beyoncé album is "EVERYTHING," is the underlying assumption here: that the objects of culture themselves do not matter one bit.

At the risk of sounding like an old fogey counterreactionary, I want to restate the stakes here. The issue is not only that criticism itself has become a rarefied commodity but also that this vanishing of the critical impulse ends up diminishing the experience of

---

* Beyoncé Knowles is the definitive cultural object of this age, precisely because she is a "pure text"—that is, she seems to exist purely to have meaning projected onto her, instead of generating that meaning. Take her recent (as of this writing) headlining performance at the 2018 Coachella Valley Music and Arts Festival. It was a performance lauded for its costume changes, energy, and incorporation of various modes of African, and African-American, iconography. It was a performance, in the purest way. Beyoncé's art is not her music but her presentation and consistent reinvention of herself. She is a pure text. I once had a professor say of Madonna, "If she did not exist, the field of cultural studies would have to invent her." To a considerable extent, I think the same can be said about Queen Bey.

culture itself. Sontag's call in "Against Interpretation" was to replace hermeneutics with "an erotics of art"—a push toward feeling in lieu of meaning. Sontag was writing more than half a century ago, and her diagnoses of sensory-dulling "culture based on excess, on overproduction" feels downright quaint from today's vantage. Now this sense of meaningless glut extends not only to the system of cultural production but also to the system created to make sense of it.

As is almost always the case, solving the problem proves much thornier than diagnosing it. Better to resign oneself to an enlightened participation in the machinery of cultural production and perception, like that guy in *The Matrix* who gobbles down a juicy steak, perfectly cozy in the knowledge that it's the product of a high-level computer simulation programmed to enslave humanity. A culture that vaunts the popular, gives voice to the amateur, and drives toward the mellow middle of consensus is invariably chary of experts, of snobs, of anyone who can be cut down with a damning accusation of *pretentiousness*.

Yet isn't this precisely why one turns to criticism? Not merely to validate one's own taste, but to be met with a rare insight born from deep knowledge of a subject, to encounter the pleasure of a new text, to rise above one's delimited cultural horizons and assume a love of alien cultures in a way that is, pretty much by definition, pretentious?

The problem facing the prescriptivist wondering "What's to be done?" may not be that Sontag is too old-fashioned, but rather that she is not quite old-fashioned *enough*. We may look back, productively, to older models. Not poptimism or oldfangled rockism (with its daft valuation of Authenticity above all else) or even

Sontagian erotics of art. The real danger held by the rise of the think piece, poptimism, and the subsequent renewal of a self-consciously "socially conscious criticism" is that it not only forgets the contemporary caricature of the culture industry but also shills on its behalf. It's not even that, following Sontag, erotics has replaced bloodless hermeneutics. It's that we're now subject to soft, dopey forms of both.

What the dopey, bloviating culture of think piece–y optimism needs is renewed, radical pessimism: an acknowledgment that the machinations of the culture industry are bad, and that it is the duty of the critic to oppose them. It is a cruel function of late capitalism that it makes all righteous complaint seem clichéd, rendering its critics foolish, like mid-'90s stand-up comedians wondering "what's the deal" with the price of popcorn at the multiplex or the swelling cost of a cup of coffee.

In even identifying such hardened contours of daily life, one runs the risk of sounding like a sneering front man from a 1980s hardcore band.* But I'd argue that it's an unflattering pose worth assuming. In such a climate, the hater can serve a vital function in calling attention to the stupidities and ironies of contemporary discourse. If the critic—or journalist, or aspiring

---

* In a 2017 interview with *Yahoo*, industrial music icon-cum-sound track composer Trent Reznor decried the "vicious cycle" of artists debasing their own creative visions to appease fickle online tastemakers. I felt pangs of acute humiliation, precisely because I wholeheartedly agreed with the guy who made a name sing-screaming lines like "God is dead! And no one cares! If there is a hell! I'll see you there!"

belle-lettrist, or run-of-the-mill writer—encourages hostility toward the products and operations of mass culture, attempting to lay bare its machinations and schemes, then perhaps the so-called average consumer may absorb something of this productive skepticism.

A fundamental myth of our times is that culture *gives us what we want.* This is an obscenity. As anyone who has napped through an episode of AMC's prestige advertising-and-philandery drama *Mad Men* likely knows, the culture only gives us what we want after dictating what it is that we want. Before it can satisfy desire, first it must structure that desire.

If, as a quote commonly attributed to Picasso goes, "art is a lie that tells the truth," then mass culture is a lie that tells a lie. Criticism that does not speak truth to this lie only serves it. Criticism orients itself toward the sharpening of reason and the awakening of passion. It is the painstaking marriage of hermeneutics and erotics. It is not enough to enthuse. It's about the constant interplay of enthusiasm and the ruthless enquiry of that enthusiasm. And sometimes, the best way to be inquisitive is to be plainly, brutally adversarial.

Think of one of TV's most memorable critics, the Jon Lovitz–voiced Jay Sherman from the short-lived prime-time animated sitcom *The Critic.* Just because Sherman almost always decried a given work—using his pitchy catchphrase "It stinks!"— doesn't make him incorrect. The post-taste desire to transcend cliché poses its own problem, namely, that cliché sometimes serves to helpfully condense a certain truth. This is why one may be reasonably tempted to, even now, reengage with something like anti-capitalist critique by (re)watching John Carpenter's consumerist sci-fi satire *They Live* or dropping the needle on a Dead Kennedys record.* Restating premises in contemptuous, bold, even basic terms has a revitalizing usefulness: The culture industry is bad. Art is good. *The Sopranos* is epochal.

Attempting to yoke the meaning of things to the demands of our time is (to use a favorite simile) like trying to catch a greased pig. The instant you think you have your mitts around it, that muddy sucker skedaddles away. The trend toward wokeness presents a similar problem: Those who are wide-eyed today may be revealed as asleep at the switch—in an awful dream where you snap awake only to find yourself still dreaming. What's demanded is not a mere expansion of correct-sounding verbiage, but a more substantive reorientation of consciousness: of what constitutes art, and meaning, and how we respond to it. Instead of turning art into artifacts, of reducing its possibilities to a sprawling supermarket aisle of bulk "takes," the critic aims to account for the unknown and ambiguous, and so expand the horizons of culture, of art, of entertainment, of civilization itself. It's not even so much about explaining the mystery of the text as restoring a belief *in* that mystery—less about finding the figure in the carpet still on the loom than in the faithful, half-mad belief that there is one.

And if this all sounds horribly highfalutin, then let's put it this way: eat your goddamn vegetables. Because you know,

---

* Though, come to think of it, D.K. front man Jello Biafra may have issued one of the earlier woke rallying cries, bellowing on a lengthy collaboration with industrial icon Ministry, "When people are asleep / We must all become alarm clocks."

generally speaking, if you don't eat *some* vegetables, you're probably going to die. Or at least end up unhealthy—a bloated cadaver pouch jammed with junk and refuse, puckering and sundering at the seams like an overstuffed Glad® bag, wallowing in your putrescent crapulence, and howling, "To hell with the world!"

◄─ 3 ─►

The Uses and Abuses of Contrarianism

─ DISCUSSED HEREIN ─

Henrik Ibsen | Armond White | Embarrassing doormen and garbagemen | What we don't talk about when we talk about . . . | Cranks, trolls, and normies | The problem of going from Simon Cowell to Piers Morgan | Pepe the Frog | Citizen journalism | South Park | "Steal My Sunshine" | Neil deGrasse Tyson, Bill Nye, and Jesse Pinkman

— *To Thyself Be Enough* —

In the second act of Henrik Ibsen's *Peer Gynt*, the titular Danish peasant gets drunk with a trio of dairymaids and smashes his head on a rock. The next day, under the spell of a beguiling woman dressed in green and adrift in the wan toxic fog of a brutal hangover, he is lured to a cave to meet the Old Man of the Mountain, the king of all the local trolls.

During a bickering, confrontational back-and-forth, the Old Man poses a serious question to Peer: "What difference is there 'twixt trolls and men?" Peer concludes that troll and man are more alike than it seems, with trolls being slightly more virtuous in their open displays of ferocity, where man tends to hide behind timidity. The Old Man agrees and offers up the troll credo. Where man hews to Polonius's famous maxim in *Hamlet*, "Man, to thyself be true,"* trolls are more defiantly egocentric, following the edict, "Troll, to thyself be enough!"

In more liberal English translations of *Peer Gynt*, the troll's mission statement is rendered even plainer: "Be true to yourself and to hell with the world."**

---

* Properly, "This above all: to thine own self be true" (*Hamlet*, I, iii, 564).

** I would be remiss if I did not mention that Ibsen's play was itself something of a trolling text: prodding notions of Norwegian identity and the idea of what constitutes poetry or theater, blending styles and modes. It was also notoriously difficult to actually stage, with its multiple settings and shifts between the diegetic spaces of reality and a lavish dreamworld.

———

To thyself be enough! To hell with the world!

These words bounce around in my head manically whenever I find myself thinking—as I, perhaps, too often do—of author, critic, and professional provocateur Armond White.

Because if anyone lives the motto of Ibsen's Old Man in the Mountain, it's Armond White: a film critic who has earned a reputation as a shit-disturbing troll for his consistent tendency to cut against consensus opinion, sink perfectly plump 100% Fresh ratings on Rotten Tomatoes, and publicly antagonize peers and filmmakers. In 2014, White made headlines when he was ousted from the prestigious New York Film Critics Circle (NYFCC) by majority vote, after allegedly berating *12 Years a Slave* director Steve McQueen. Among the reported insults hurled by White, which he roundly denies: "You're an embarrassing doorman and garbageman," "Kiss my ass," and, quite simply, "Fuck you."

In a very sharp profile of Armond White (one which White himself described to me as a "hit piece"), writer Stephen Kearse plucks a choice line from White's review of the widely lambasted blockbuster *Suicide Squad*: "These comic-book characters are interesting in ways that abandon the nihilism Christopher Nolan brought to the previous Batman franchise, which merely continued Tarantino's jokey, sadistic film noir." Kearse neatly arrests the bogusness of such seemingly defiant writing: "White nearly bursts a lung blowing on his anti-comic book nerd dog whistle, and for what? To irk a few Nolanites? To rile up some Tarantino nerds? He's gone from writing about movies to writing against viewers."

This is precisely the sort of curdling that marks the change from charming curmudgeon, or even bitterly recalcitrant contrarian, to out-and-out troll. It's as if Armond White's writing and critical preoccupations have warped from the hatred lobbed at him by slobbering Marvel/Pixar fanboys and (perhaps righteously) annoyed members of his own former critics' circle.

But it's not that Armond White reflexively hates everything. He likes plenty of stuff. It's just not the stuff other critics tend to like. Where Michael Bay's *Transformers: Revenge of the Fallen* is what we seasoned, hard-bitten pros of the film criticism game might call "a bad movie," White's ecstatic review employs verbiage like "fantastic," "dreamlike," and "wonderful," with one sentence praising Bay's ability to apprehend, in a film about warring car-robots, "the enormity of life itself." At his very best, Armond White sees (or pretends to see) the things other critics miss in their rush to hasty judgments. Even *if* he's being coy or insincere or a bit stupid (which he, again, denies), White feels he's not just writing about movies, but defiantly writing against the way we write about movies, standing *against* the looming hierarchies of value and bastions of critical consensus, even if it's just for the hell of it. That he is triply marginalized as a black, gay Republican in a field crowded by white liberal voices only adds to his outcast status.

As a longtime reader and sometimes-writer of film criticism, I've long been fascinated, and invigorated, by White. He's the madman-sage who says and does what he wants, like a bitchy contestant on *RuPaul's Drag Race* who stirs up drama just for fun. In 2014, following White's booting from the NYFCC, I rushed to his defense. I praised White's contrarianism and his indelicacy, writing for Toronto's *NOW Magazine* that rudeness is precisely the point, stating "that anyone regards him as a problem is the problem." I was attempting my own, tooth-and-nail, defiantly contrarian defense of a defiant contrarian challenging the boundaries of decency. I was, in hindsight, being generous. But the fact remains: White is a compelling figure precisely for his ability to challenge (or just ignore) boundaries and to rouse aspiringly like-minded defenders. I have little doubt that Armond White would hate (or profess to hate) such borderline-sycophantic pledges of patronage. The very smart, acutely acerbic, and genuinely funny critic Nick Pinkerton once described White's posture as "that of a gate-keeper who would ward off pretenders to the citadel of criticism with a flaming sword."

White's professional conduct has proven so unbecoming that even Roger Ebert, that genial nice-guy face of film criticism, called him a troll. Following White's booting from the NYFCC, *Entertainment Weekly*'s critic Owen Gleiberman wrote, "Armond tosses out provocations like grenades and eats acclaimed films for breakfast." Others have been much worse.

But what, exactly, *is* Armond White doing? Is a knowing contrarian, the hater's hater, chucking grenades and causing drama for his own amusement? Or is he guided by some deeper mission to expand the parameters of critical thought? Or is he, by now, a creature of pure, curdled resentment?

On paper, Armond White shares several concerns already eluci-dated here. He's Old Guard. He studied journalism and criticism in academic contexts, at Michigan's Wayne State University and Columbia University in New York (respectively). That White committed himself to writing with a certain seriousness and severity distinguishes him from many modern fans-cum-content-evaluators. In his 2008 thesis essay "What We Don't Talk About When We Talk About Movies,"* nailed on the door of the *New York Press* website, he writes: "Does the training of movie critics matter if they aren't taught to preserve the idea that movies must affirm our humanity? The public deserves critics who appreciate when an audience wants to be moved, encouraging them to experience catharsis." Armond White, in his own estimation, is such a critic.

To historicize it a bit, the shift from professionalized critics emerging from academic departments to more self-schooled reviewers may mirror something of the shift in filmmaking itself. By the early 1990s, formally educated film school grads such as George Lucas and Martin Scorsese were supplanted by "movie brats" such as Quentin Tarantino and Robert Rodriguez. These new filmmakers learned their craft not from sitting through lectures and seminars, but by gobbling down TV movies and home video releases. In film culture, the 1990s and the ascent of the internet in the late 1990s and early 2000s led to what it sometimes described as a "democratization." Just as anyone with an iPhone can (theoretically) make a movie, anyone with an internet connection and WordPress blog can review one. Yes, *in theory*. But theory, to paraphrase Mark Twain, often fails in the presence of fact.

White calls bullshit on the myth that the internet democratized expertise. He sees it more as the barbarians crashing the

---

* The title of which is a modestly clever inversion of the clichéd think piece headline format: "What We Talk About When We Talk About _____."

gate. The intellectuals and experts have been replaced by fans and other enthusiasts, who seem all too content to bark for the culture industry instead of questioning it. "People who go into criticism these days are not serious journalists," says White.* "They're not serious about film. The real problem is they're not serious about what they're doing. They get into criticism to promote Hollywood: to get screeners,** to get free movies. That in itself is not a bad motivation. But after you see the free movie, what do you do? Do you perform as a critic? Or do you perform as a fan?"

I'm sympathetic to White's claims that the profession of criticism, at least in the second decade of this millennium, encourages shallowness. Publishers scramble to retain the joint interest of the major corporations providing "content" and of the would-be readers who constitute an audience predisposed to pay for that content. (And the blurred line between fandom and "real" criticism is something I looked at earlier with think pieces.) It's the disappearance of that real criticism at the expense of the beaming, blindly enthusiastic, semiprofessionalized fandom that is a particular bugbear for White. His call is loud, seductive, vaguely uplifting—a martial march calling like-minded partisans into the street.

---

* All unattributed quotes here are from an in-person interview with White, conducted in March 2018 at the Red Cat Restaurant in New York City's swanky Chelsea district. For the record, Mr. White ordered fish tacos. I ordered a paté, either in an effort to seem fancy (I don't especially care for paté) or simply in a flustered bit of panic-ordering. We both had Negronis, on Mr. White's recommendation.

** A screener is a cheapo DVD sent out to members of critics' guilds during awards season, so that they may have access to major releases at their leisure.

Like when he says, "It's a reviewer's job, no matter what, to apply critical thinking to their subjects. If they do that, I like to think it will inspire the same in audiences. When critics praise whatever happens in Hollywood, what signal are they sending to their readers? It's that everyone in Hollywood is good, and if you don't like it then you're weird." Again: hard agree.

White is also smart and savvy on certain issues of ideology. As a writer for the conservative, William F. Buckley–founded *National Review*, as well as the LGBT glossy *OUT* (where his author bio declares him "the world's most contrarian film critic"), White wears his politics, if not necessarily as a point of defiant pride, certainly as a matter of fact. "Part of the hostility I receive has to do with the fact that I admit my political perspectives," White says. "It's very arrogant to think you don't have a perspective, and what you think is just right."

And yet, if anyone seems to think that he's staunchly, infallibly right, it's Armond White. There is a gurgling resentment in White's treatises, which profess to speak on behalf of the "public" (whatever that even means) but actually speak most defiantly against White's own contemporaries. And, even worse, his righteous contempt for the culture of consensus and critical dumbing-down has mutated into very thinly veiled disdain for that very same public he pretends to care about.

Which brings us to the thing that may divide the contrarian from the troll: sincerity. As Henry James—about as fine a writer and thinker and combative old soul as there ever was—knew, debate and discussion and contrarianism only function well (or, in his words, prove "fertilizing") when they are undertaken with both frankness and sincerity. As a yardstick for measuring the usefulness of what might appear to be hollow shit-disturbance, it's as good as anything. But where frankness—or one of its crueler cousins, rudeness or incivility—is in no short supply these days, sincerity gets very dicey. It is, as anyone who has ever cranked out an utterly insincere apology knows, a quality that proves very easy to fake. It is also nearly impossible to gauge, unless you're some sort of human lie detector. Ultimately, deciding if someone really *means* what they say can come down to a matter of faith.

More troublingly, the idea of someone being sincere and true and exhibiting utter fealty to themselves loses importance when their self is wholly insincere. "To thyself be enough!" declared Ibsen's Troll King. But that sense of "thyself" can feel so unstable. There's a cheap bit of wisdom (variously attributed to Nazi propagandist Joseph Goebbels and sky-high self-help guru Tony Robbins) dictating that if you tell a lie long enough, it warps into the truth. Based on this, it's possible that insincerity can be taken as sincerity. Maybe a person can only be derided and mocked as a troll for so long before they start believing it, before they confuse their Diogenes-in-defiance with self-martyrdom. The persecutor maintains that they are the persecuted. This is the weird logical loophole through which the troll might scurry, all the while fending off the pitchforks and torches of the mob.

At the end of one of my very favorite movies, James Whale's *Bride of Frankenstein*, Boris Karloff's maladroit monster has been mocked and rejected and chased away with pitchforks and torches so many times that he eventually believes himself to be a monster. And so, he climactically destroys his creator's lab, along with his jerry-rigged, would-be bride (who, too, was immediately repulsed; and fair enough), and the possibility for any such future stitched-up aberrations. Maybe you can only be called a monster, an aberration, a troll so many times before you start believing it.

Here's the thing about Armond White: it's pretty much impossible to prove, but speaking with him, drinking with him, dining with him, I got the sense that he was being wholly disingenuous.

When asked if he was playing the role of the troll, or the proverbial Frankenstein's monster, he denied it: "That's a popular response. But it's not *even* a response. It's a defense against what I'm trying to say."

When asked if he was writing against fans, or other critics, or the culture of filmgoing and cultural appreciation writ large, he was similarly obstinate: "If I thought there was good criticism out there, I wouldn't need to write criticism. That's absolutely true. I wouldn't write criticism if I didn't have anything special to say. There's no point praising another Marvel movie. There's no point in writing another good review of a Paul Thomas Anderson movie. Why become a film critic if you have nothing to add beyond nodding your head? Why do it?!"

When asked if he bears grudges against other critics, he lied to my face: "I would welcome anyone to challenge an idea I write, rather than attacking me. I would never attack a person. Only their ideas. And if you can't defend your ideas, you're in the wrong profession." (For evidence to the contrary, I would encourage you to look up White's quarrel with fellow critic Georgia Brown, which culminated in his calling for the abortion of her fully adult son, the filmmaker Noah Baumbach.)

Armond White can hammer, like a heavy metal drummer, the idea that criticism has slouched into enthusiasm, that professionalism has been supplanted by amateurism, that free-thinking has been replaced by groupthink. He can defend himself. Or at least the idea of himself.

But some things can't be defended. In the weeks after the 2018 school shooting in Florida, White took to his sometimes-used twitter account @3xchair (a reference to his being the three-time chair of the NYFCC before being canned) to snipe at what he called the "Parkland Puppets," survivors of gun violence who mobilized to challenge American gun laws:

> Sick of the Parkland Puppets yet? Why their ubiquitous presence on TV news shows? Who's their publicist? Obviously not just being picked up off the street, no 16-year-old has quick access to network news producers. Clearly, some PR exec is handling these Alt-Left kids.

This sentiment betrays any meaningful adherence to some ethic of criticism. Or even contrarianism. It's not just that comments like this scan as someone desperately trying to get a rise out of people. It's that they betray a malfunction in critical thinking, and a point where open political bias becomes shameless water-carrying for the powers that be. With tweets like that, fissures shoot through the veneer of somber civility. The self-professed freethinker reveals himself as a conspiratorial, tinfoil-hat wingnut.

It is, of course, unfair to hold a movie reviewer to task for their views on gun violence in America. And, as he made clear, as a black man, White has very deep-rooted opinions about the way American media treats white victims of gun violence vs. black victims of that same violence. But the feeling is the same:

that his opinions arise from a spiky resentment, rather than a sober-minded approach to the goings-on, or even a coy and knowingly reactionary "troll" approach.

He explains he is a skeptic, that he sees things that others don't. He lectures stridently about how the media is deceiving us all. And again, I don't *necessarily* disagree.

A final anecdote: When he went on Facebook and voiced his opinions about what he calls the "Parkland Puppets," a long-time friend unceremoniously unfriended him online. "I've known her for years," he says, his voice shot through with equal parts resentment and remorse. "Is that all it took? This is not the right response."

Perhaps he's right. Perhaps in our ever-sprawling market-place of opinion that invariably reduces to suffocating echo chambers of belief, we need more wild, wing-nut, wonderfully contrarian opinions. Maybe Armond White, not despite but *because of* his resentment and trolling of consensus and disdain for good taste, is a vital figure. Maybe he and I, people who agreed on some points and disagreed on others, who represented in my own mind some compelling Venn diagram of accord and dissent, could get on like gangbusters.

"How'd the interview go?" a friend texted me, as I strolled back to my hotel from my lunch with the formerly intimidating, now wholly human Armond White.

"Pretty good!" I thought. Pretty good.

A few hours later, I checked on Armond online. No dice. In the intervening hours, he'd blocked me on Twitter. His words echoed in my head, buzzing with their hypocrisy: "This is not the right response."

Then again those words from Ibsen: "To hell with the world."

I thought I'd been engaged in an open, mutually interrogating conversation with an occasionally like-minded hater. But maybe I'd just been trolled by the Troll King.

— *The Contrarian Deformation* —

Beyond my own borderline perverse interest in the man, *why*, one might reasonably wonder, does Armond White matter?

Well, he matters because the calcifying of his persona signals a broader culture shift from healthy (even if performative) contrarianism to a more malignant form of trolling. To paraphrase a snappy bit of dialogue from Armando Iannucci's British parliamentary satire *The Thick of It*, he has shifted from the kind of person people love to hate to the kind of person people just straight-up hate, completing the turn "from Simon Cowell to Piers Morgan." And lord knows the world doesn't need more Piers Morgans.

In what is often called "our present moment," contrarianism has turned against itself. Where the mantle of hater may once have been worn by the skeptical, the chary, the rigorously contemptuous, it has now fallen to a new, mutated model of the troll. While pugnacity, and plain cattiness, are by no means the invention of the internet, these tendencies were, like much else, accelerated by the social media boom. And so we arrive at the hallmarks of the modern troll:

(a) Immediacy: The idea of frantically sending a poorly thought-out tweet has itself become something of a jokey Twitter meme.

(b) Anonymity: Far from a democratizing effect creating meaningful debate, it supports proliferation of the most vile and common groupthink.

(c) Misguided provocation: The keyed-up desire to provoke is not a means to critical thought but a way to shake off the atrophied empathy of modern life while, in fact, only extending it.

Where "trolling" may have previously connoted the ego-centric, or the reactionary, it now marks an anarchic, highly ironic form of confrontation mobilized purely in the service of (to cop a bit of 4chan slang—more below) rustling people's jimmies. Where the contrarian might aspire to the barbed wit of H.L. Mencken, Karl Kraus, or Dorothy Parker, the trolls are more than content calling people "fags" and "'tards," and egging on people to kill themselves. Instead of being haters, these new trolls plainly *hate*.

It's a Contrarian Deformation that has given rise to improbable cultural icons such as Milo Yiannopoulos, memes like the smirking Pepe the Frog, a revived neofascist and white supremacist politics, and, most notably, U.S. President Donald Trump.

In her book *Kill All Normies*—one of the earliest volumes to enter a now-cluttered publishing microcosm tracking the rise of the so-called alt-right—Angela Nagle traces the historical rise of trolling. It's a far-reaching history, from the Romantic "cult of the moral transgressor as a heroic individual" to Dostoyevsky's Raskolnikov to Norman Mailer's "hipster" (which is not quite the same as the Miller High Life–swilling millennial hipster described earlier) to "contemporary transgressive anti-moral cultures like 4chan that later fused with the alt-right." In the misty sorta-underground of the internet, the troll finds its antecedent in what used to be called the "crank": a conspiratorial sort who used to populate early online forums and Usenet groups, exploring their online soapboxes to prattle on about byzantine conspiracy theories that were previously the domain of late(-late-late)-night talk radio and self-published pamphlets.

If the modern troll has a proverbial cavern under the mountain, it's /b/, a dingy ghetto of the online forum 4chan. Back in 2008, *Gawker* writer Nick Douglas described /b/ as a random-image posting board "where completely anonymous— no login, no username—people try to shock, entertain, and coax free porn from each other." Boards such as 4chan, reddit, Twitter, and even Facebook are somewhat premised on the idea that "anyone" can have a voice. The regime of authority is therefore decentralized—and often with disastrous results. Rhetoric around the internet tends to employ unfaltering, and often wholly unfair, images of cesspools, sewers, and (most prominently) "garbage fires." While such broadsides may wildly generalize the whole of the internet, there's little argument that /b/ *is* the fetid cesspool, the gurgling sewer, the simmering, stinking garbage fire.

Stewed in the gnarly stock of sundry references to suicide and ejaculate and anilingus, the internet trolls bred on /b/ thrive on shock, confrontation, and a desperate sense of troubling standards of morality and good taste. The guiding creed of this subculture is the "lulz"*: the idea of disturbing shit strictly for the fun of it. Irony is used less as a tool of subversion than as a bulwark to hide behind, permitting a disavowal of consequences, or even of any sort of meaning. "Sure I deluged a female video game enthusiast with rape threats and sent Holocaust photos to a Jewish person on Twitter," rations the troll. "But I only did it for the lulz."

Nothing is off-limits for the troll. Rules and social taboos are meant to be broken. Nothing is sacred and everything is profane. They use transgression and memes and cruddy Microsoft Paint doodles of frogs and genitalia to enliven the suffocating ennui of modern life. They joke about rape, about suicide, about genocide; they recycle nasty racist caricature and indulge reprehensible misogyny. They abhor morality, liberal standards of good taste, and sensibilities of so-called "normies."

It's easy enough to look at this, moralize, and decry it as bad. It *is* bad. But it is vital to understand the emergence of the modern trolls—who, among other dickheaded assaults, have helped give hating a bad name. In a formidable switcheroo of cultural politics, the trolls have effectively co-opted tactics of transgression and grotesquerie from the left. In so doing, the cesspool has leaked into the mainstream of contemporary political and social life. On the political front, the online trolls' professed ethic of anarchism is betrayed by their consistent support for, first, the Trump campaign and, now, the Trump administration. Donald Trump was held up as an icon in this community precisely because he affronted "libtard" standards of political

---

*   A 4chan perversion of the more common online acronym "LOL," for "laugh out loud."

correctness. He was crass, sexist, racist, cruel, conceited, contemptuous of democratic institutions and traditions of civil governance, and physically grotesque. He was their Troll King as a commander in chief, a leader of the free world who couldn't give a damn for it.

Will the new troll herds' rabid, hostile disdain for the status quo manifest, post-Trump, as an attack on emerging conservative, far-right attitudes in American life? Doubtful. If anything, the opposite is proving true, as trolls and far-right hate groups claim Trump, and even credit themselves with electing him. As one 4channer posted on the fateful November night in 2016 when Donald Trump was elected president of the United States, "We actually elected a meme as president." It scans as a lament, but there is actual, un-ironic pride there. Instead of being consistently anarchic and ruthlessly critical in their online pranksterism, as they were in pre-Trump's America, the online trolls are now just carrying water for the world's most powerful administration, like dutiful little minions. The emancipatory promise of the internet hasn't been so much supplanted by a reactionary power as fused with it. Like Trump rallies and similar right-populist gatherings, the internet provides the freedom to be reactionary, regressive, racist, intolerant, just plain awful.

We've seen how the democratization of criticism and cultural gatekeeping has hobbled culture. Similarly, the internet's democratization and decentralization of voices helped serve the destabilization of democracy itself. Cheerier techno-optimists had long praised the internet and social media for its ability to give a voice to anyone with an internet connection, which could (hypothetically) amplify voices marginalized by traditional media. Look at the Arab Spring! Citizen journalism! Ain't It

Cool News! But in November 2016, as the ballots were counted, the egalitarian Shangri-la promised by the internet revealed itself as a sulfur-stinking hellworld.

In my own personal, proverbial backyard, the transition from the crank to the troll to the out-and-out terrorist has unfolded with horrifying verity. While I was working on this very chapter, a man drove a van on a sidewalk, targeting and killing pedestrians in North York City Centre, a Toronto business district. The alleged suspect was revealed to be a member of "incel" (involuntary celibate) communities online, where lonely men who believe themselves deprived of sex and female affection indulge all manner of bitter, deeply misogynistic fantasies. As the putrid runoff of the already plentiful trolly "manosphere"—and, in turn, whole ideological systems of patriarchal order and male supremacy—the incel subculture reveals just how brutally and manifestly violent online ideologies can become when their denizens are no longer content to settle for lulz. They indulge this behavior in service of a historically dominant ideology.

It's now a troll's world. We're all of us denizens of the craggy, putrid cave under the mountain.

There is a tendency to want to write off trolls as pathetic, or pitiable.

In conversation with Armond White, he repeatedly compared the upset fans and film buffs who harangue him online to either children or "demented" people. Clichés circulate of pimply twerps living in their mom's basement, or logging on to Twitter using a public library computer (the implicit insult being that such users can't afford their own computer). They are desperate, or misguided, or keen ironists who are reasonably alienated by political and social life.

But what if they're not?

In an episode of the animated sitcom *South Park* (itself an expression of contemporary, "equal opportunity" trolling[*]), elementary school students are bedeviled online by an anonymous abuser known only as "Skankhunt42." The kids at school naturally assume that Skankhunt42 is Eric Cartman, ever the small town's sociopathic antagonizer. In a nifty twist, it's revealed that the mysterious troll is actually Gerald Broflovski, a middle-aged father who simply enjoys ruthlessly mocking middle schoolers and doodling penises on pictures of PTA moms while enjoying a glass of wine late at night. As he puts it, coyly speculating on the motivations of the troublesome troll: "Well, you never know, could be someone who just, kind of thinks it's funny to stir the pot and watch everyone freak out."

Far from being socially alienated or otherwise maladjusted, Gerald is a model of middle-class normalcy, his nightly Twitter trolling sustaining a sprightly spring in his step, as he struts through his neighborhood to the peppy strains of "Steal My Sunshine" by Canadian sibling–pop act Len. Here is a powerful

---

[*]   Indeed, *South Park*'s connection, whether imagined or explicit, to modern fringe far-right movements has merited plenty of digital ink-equivalent. See: Janan Ganesh's "Did *South Park* Accidentally Invent the Alt-Right?" in the *Financial Times*, or Sean O'Neal's "*South Park* Raised a Generation of Trolls" in *The A.V. Club*, in which the author astutely describes the show's ethic of "hostile apathy," which has come to be a standard of contemporary trolling.

image of the modern troll: inconspicuous, chipper, spiritually sustained by their hate-mongering and cyberbullying, appearing to the outside world as just another workaday normie. This is the harsh reality of the modern troll. They are normal to the point of seeming unremarkable, if not wholly banal.

As we saw with "woke" criticism, the normie-troll may itself be less of an epochal shift than an acceleration, or a mutation, of a long-standing style in Western thought: paranoia. Way back in 1964, Pulitzer Prize–winning critic Richard Hofstadter wrote that "American politics has often been an arena for angry minds." As Hofstadter diagnosed it, American thinking has been obsessed with conspiracy, and has employed paranoid rhetoric from the McCarthy-era Communist witch hunts and the John Birch Society back to anti-Catholic agitating ("Jesuits are prowling about all parts of the United States in every possible disguise," read a piece published in a December 1934 issue of the *New York Protestant Vindicator*) and anti-Masonic rabble-rousing against Illuminism that dates back to the Republic's founding.

Throughout history, the paranoid style has relied on special claims of evidence to prove that "the unbelievable is the only thing that can be believed." Such conspiratorial thinking strives, in its own inverse way, toward a holism that stands in stark contrast to the messiness of actual, real life. (As Hofstadter notes, "the paranoid mind is far more coherent than the real world.") The 9/11 Truther movement is perhaps the best modern example of this. In a way, it is easier to believe that the attacks of September 11, 2001, were the work of a well-oiled government cabal than to accept the more troubling notion that a handful of fanatics could abhor America so much that they'd want to hijack airplanes with box cutters and attempt to destroy several of the country's more prominent landmarks. Its special evidence: "Jet fuel can't melt steel beams!"

As I noted earlier when looking at the online bifurcation of political communities into self-justifying and self-reproducing bubbles, such thinking may appear controversial or contrarian. However, in actuality, it is an attempt to conjure a totalizing worldview free from contradiction or competing information—an internal accord. As David Neiwert describes it in his book of the same name, such thinking imagines an "Alt-America," a doppelgänger of the real deal where "facts and the laws of political gravity do not apply." Thus, the skeptical, hater-ish instinct to question government and media narratives only works against itself, hardening a radical, paranoid consensus that is increasingly common in everyday life. Or rather, as Hofstadter's essay advances, has *always* been common in everyday life. After all, "the idea of the paranoid style as a force in politics would have little contemporary relevance or historical value if it were applied only to men with profoundly disturbed minds. It is the use of paranoid modes of expression by more or less normal people that makes the phenomenon significant."

While it might be a stretch to say trolling is the new normal, there's no question that trollish thinking has come to colonize what constitutes normalcy. From Pizzagate to the Russian election tampering to news items about how Justin Trudeau just might be the illegitimate son of Fidel Castro, the media is preoccupied with conspiratorial thinking. In large part, it's a function of mainstream media responding to the bizarro social media echo chambers. People online talk about John Podesta serving semen to schoolchildren, and then that and other distracting canards effectively become news. And not because they constitute legitimately newsworthy items. But, somehow, the very fact that people are talking about them *does* render them newsworthy.

Just think of the exhaustive news coverage of Donald Trump's tweets, which often read as little more than the resentful, half-mad ramblings of a brain-wormy ogre raging against the "haters and losers" while squatting on the toilet. As political scientist Yascha Mounk notes, the mainstream media is forced into a no-win scenario when it comes to covering the president's half-coherent social media blasts. He was able to circumvent the existing relationship between politicians, the media, and the public by using any opportunity to tweet directly to his followers. As Mounk writes, "Once he had done so, established broadcasters faced a stark choice: ignore the main subject of conversation and make yourself irrelevant—or discuss each Tweet at length, thereby amplifying Trump's message even as they ostensibly scrutinized it." In other words: damned if they did, damned if they didn't. Though, naturally, one wonders if we'd be *as* damned if they didn't.

The reinforcement (or, to use buzzy contemporary parlance, "normalization") of such way-out thinking, and the media's hapless promotion of it, is a perversion of haterism. Healthy skepticism rots into a self-reinforcing conspiratorial rationality. Doubt collapses into paranoia. Interrogation becomes inquisition. The vigilance of cross-examining contrarianism hardens into plain, unadorned, unbecoming hate. The free play of thought and intellect freezes as rationality becomes irrational. There is, perhaps, no better illumination of this than the contemporary attitude toward the systematic human enterprise of science.

— *The New Irrationality (or I Fucking Hate Science)* —

In late July 2014, in what may be considered a good (or at least funny) use of social media trolling, a Twitter user named @dogboner posted a photo of a man on a subway train working on his laptop, accompanied by the caption, "Some guy using his laptop on the train like a dumbass nerd lol." The "dumbass nerd" in question was astrophysicist, author, and TV host Neil deGrasse Tyson. Instantly, @dogboner (whose real name is Michael Hale) faced a tweet-storm of abuse and haranguing from social media users for whom Tyson has emerged as a kind of messiah of modern rationalism.

The photo was shared on the popular Facebook page "I Fucking Love Science" (which currently engages some 25 million-plus users), leading to even more angry call-outs. Hale was called "stupid," an "underachieving burnout," and worse. One person encouraged Hale to "fall into an ocean of A.I.D.S." The thing is, Hale *knew* it was Tyson. Few had bothered to consider that the original tweet was nothing but the sort of stupid, ironized joke that savvy Twitter users major in. Legions of self-satisfied rationalists and armchair logicians, who pride themselves on their superior intellect, were totally snookered.

Beyond being (really, really) funny, the incident was revealing. It spoke to the vehemence and belligerence science seems to inspire in popular culture, and in people more generally. It also laid bare the frothing cults of personality surrounding people like Tyson, Bill Nye, Canadian astronaut Col. Chris Hadfield (who live-streamed parts of his 2013 mission to YouTube, including a much-shared acoustic guitar rendition of David Bowie's "Space Oddity"), and other modern pop-star scientists.

It's consistent with a broader cultural trend. Recent films about science and scientists, like *The Imitation Game* and the Stephen Hawking biopic *The Theory of Everything*, have earned critical acclaim and commercial success. CBS recently renewed its uber-popular science dork sitcom *The Big Bang Theory* for what feels like its forty-seventh season. Even fictional characters— from the *Big Bang* boys to Matt Damon's marooned astronaut in *The Martian* vowing to "science the shit" out of problems to Aaron Paul's skeezy Jesse Pinkman in *Breaking Bad* exclaiming, "Yeah science, bitch!"—speak to the cultural ascendency of scientific thinking.

Or something like it.

Neil deGrasse Tyson wrote a book called *Astrophysics for People in a Hurry*. It's dedicated to "all those who are too busy to read fat books yet nonetheless seek a conduit to the cosmos." The dedication functions as a mission statement for the contemporary culture of pop science: take mind-bogglingly complex ideas, strip them down to their nuts and bolts, pad them with colorful allegories and dorky jokes, and make them accessible to the layperson.

As expressed in his books, his documentary TV series *Cosmos: A Spacetime Odyssey*, and his popular Twitter account (boasting some 7.3 million followers), Tyson is a master of streamlining and simplification. *Astrophysics for People in a Hurry* makes a previous pop-physics landmark like Stephen Hawking's 1988 bestseller, *A Brief History of Time*, look like Charles W. Misner, Kip S. Thorne, and John Archibald Wheeler's dense 1973 doorstopper *Gravitation*. Likewise, Tyson's writing is given to colloquialism ("Quarks are quirky beasts," he writes, early on) and unadorned, let-me-break-it-down-for-you anecdotes. In one section, about physical laws being inarguable, Tyson explains density with a story about sending back a mug of hot cocoa that didn't come dolloped with whipped cream, after arguing with the waiter about whether or not the missing cream had sunk to the bottom.

This folksy, brass-tacks approach to science is not without its problems. Indeed, the whole domain of "pop science" and "pop-star scientists" like Tyson is wrought with controversy, both inside and outside the larger scientific community. In his "An Introduction to Science and Technology Studies," philosopher of science Sergio Sismondo describes the widespread popularization and dissemination of science to the general public as "a necessary evil, not to be done by working scientists still engaged in productive research." Coming from a scientist—or a philosopher of science—this is a third-degree savage burn.

Beyond such negative effects on the perception of hard science, popularization and simplification pose a broader cultural problem. With their paraphrased ideas, relatable yarns, and mic-dropping, "Yeah science, bitch!" approach to the field, the pop-star scientists command a genuine authority. And they pass that authority on to their readers and fans, who rush to their defense to attack smirking Twitter jokers and share "I Fucking Love Science" memes. Pop science offers the general public the air of authority and credibility of science without all the . . . you know, science. There's a word for this highly empirical, authoritative worldview: *scientism*. And it's the preeminent embodiment of irrationality dressing itself up in the sheep's clothing of cold, calculated rationality. It is also, I should mention, not even a particularly new or novel idea.

The publication of Thomas S. Kuhn's *The Structure of Scientific Revolutions* in 1962 marked a major turning point in thinking about science. Kuhn challenged the old Enlightenment ideal that pitched scientific discovery as a straight line trending ever upward, with knowledge and discoveries accruing across time.

According to Kuhn's historical research, scientific discovery was marked by stops and starts, dead ends, and plain wrongheaded thinking, occasionally reoriented by major discoveries and revolutions in scientific thought (such as those undertaken by Copernicus, Newton, Einstein, etc.). Such discoveries tend to be regarded as "inevitable" only after the fact. It's sort of like the old adage about history books being written by the victors. The history of science is similarly revisionist, positioning all discoveries as necessary stages in an ongoing process of unfolding. In truth, they may really be the result of revolutionary thinking, anomalistic approaches to scientific thinking, and crises in knowledge as well as the mitigating influences of society and culture. Kuhn called these—minting what is now a pretty much meaningless buzzword—"paradigm shifts."

Kuhn's book undermined the idea that science and the scientific method held a unique relationship to the truth of existence and being. Facts and truths are tinkered with to fit the idea of scientific methodology as a grand process that is slowly unpeeling itself like some coy, gargantuan banana. In reality, facts are slippery, and sometimes malleable to the point of meaninglessness. Just think back to those old kitschy magazine ads with boastful claims like "More doctors smoke Camels than any other cigarette!" for examples of how science, and facts, can be wrested to serve the most malicious agendas.

Earlier critics of scientism, like economist Friedrich Hayek, looked at the way in which so-called soft sciences (i.e., the social or moral sciences) adopted the scientific method in order to acquire the patina of objectivity, as if things like human action, motivation, and consciousness itself could be measured as quantifiably as an apple bonking someone on the head. The modern pop science preached by Tyson and others poses a similar threat: privileging the hard, the quantifiable, the unproblematically knowable at the expense of other disciplines, like the humanities, or philosophy.*

On his career-rebooting Netflix series *Bill Nye Saves the World*, the sixty-one-year-old "science guy" (who, while he has a degree in engineering, is not an actual scientist so much as a sort of science mascot) constantly explains natural phenomena by exclaiming "It's science!"

He does so to canned hurrahing, whoops, and rounds of applause. The studio audience isn't cheering the result of one or another experiment, or even Nye, but science itself. There's something disturbingly antiscientific about all this. The pop-star scientists become modern-day soothsayers. They are something to believe in. As long as we believe in them, we don't have to do the work of science, or even understand it with any nuance. Under such conditions, science—that legendary realm of experimentation and freethinking—becomes nothing more than another

---

* To say literally nothing of the comfort and spiritual ballasting that religion offers to believers. But that's a whole other bag of bad-faith thinking.

form of indoctrination. And why should we be surprised? Guys like Tyson and Nye offer the rarest, and perhaps most desirable, of promises: certainty. They grant the authority and conviction that science is said to provide, wielded like a blindly bright iPhone flashlight to ward off the consuming dimness of uncertainty and unknowability.

There's no doubt that science is important. Everybody—well, almost everybody—wants to see a cure for cancer and more cheap, renewable energy sources. And science is increasingly under threat, be it from lack of government funding, vocal anti-vaccination activists, or plain moronic young-earth creationists and flat-earth truthers. But anti-scientism is not the same as being anti-science, any more than deciding not to wear purple shirts would be a denial of the existence of purple as a color. Interrogating scientism is merely a way of making sure the cultural regime of science can weather the scrutiny of its own methodology. Science has become subsumed in the very kind of mystification it attempts to callously dispel. In lieu of the sort of critical thinking advocated by the sciences, it has become easier (and, improbably, cooler) to simply "fuckin' love" it.

After all, what good is the authority of science, of what inherent value is a dog-eared, half-skimmed copy of "Astrophysics for Dummies," when the smugly scientifically minded frontliners in baggy Bazinga! T-shirts, shoring up the battlements of loving science, can be so dumb as to be duped by a social media snarkster maneuvering under the ludicrous nom de guerre "dog boner"? Of what use is a fetishistic vaunting of the scientific method when people are too thick to even pick up on a joke?

Rhetorical questions, sure. But I'll offer an answer all the same. The @dogboner prank is valid because it suggests a positive contemporary use for trolling. Instead of merely provoking or harassing people, Michael Hale—whether intentionally or by the sheer accident of making a dumb joke—created the perfect storm, subjecting himself to the volleys and rabid insults of others. In so doing, he revealed the blind faith, animosity, and abounding "paranoid style" animating the worldview of ostensibly scientifically minded Enlightenment bros. It was a troll that lured the trolls out of their online caverns, hollows, and begrimed goblins' nests.*

In playing the role of the hater to such self-serious science lovers, he laid bare the stupefying faith that so many people (perhaps ironically) put in science. I mean, @dogboner's stupid-as-hell Twitter joke doesn't even pass the Occam's razor test: the problem-solving principle that the most likely answer to a question is the one carrying the fewest assumptions. How could the rationally minded possibly believe that someone riding a New York City subway *wouldn't* recognize the most popular and public science guy of this generation? Why wouldn't the most reasonable solution be that this guy was joking? Worse than being slavishly devoted to their fuckin' love of science, these total dorks are (even worse) entirely humorless.

When it comes to the ascent of scientism, and of undermining the cultural authority of fab favorites like Neil deGrasse Tyson, that stupid @dogboner tweet offers an almost Socratic lesson. When something, even something as seemingly positive as the scientific method, is taken for granted as sound and solid, the hater pokes and prods the foundations of that solidity, demanding that a culture account for all the things it takes

---

* To borrow a phrase from barking-mad far-right conspiracy monger Alex Jones.

for granted. The aggressive trolling that enabled the Trump phenomenon (and, if the trolls themselves are to be believed, accounted for his election) proved similarly destabilizing, challenging not just pearl-clutching notions of good taste, decorum, and propriety but also the core values of liberal democracy itself—all things that were seemingly taken for granted.

As soon as you squint a bit and view it through the hater's inverted lens, the ascent of the modern troll offers an ass-backwards encouragement. Here we have a bunch of apathetic, empathetically arrested deplorables essentially turning the tide of American politics. If they're not the motive force of Trump's election, at the very least, in their own estimation, they aided in the election of a meme to the highest office in the nation. It's a stock rallying cry among liberals (pre- and post-Trump) that "Love trumps hate"—but the sheer efficacy and prominence of the modern troll proves the opposite. Loath though we may be to admit it, hate often takes the cake.

The auspicious lesson here is that hate can be efficacious. And that hate marshaled against haters, trolls launched against the trolling, can be productive weapons in the long haul. As Richard Hofstadter wrote of the paranoid style in American thought, "Nothing really prevents a sound program or demand from being advocated in the paranoid style. Style has more to do with the way in which ideas are believed than with the truth or falsity of their content." In other words, trolling offers another wackily, crudely inverted, funhouse-mirror image of the hater. As a tactic, trolling has proven highly effective. But it's more a mode of behavior—a style, in Hofstadter's terms—than a program. The question for the hater becomes: What is worth trolling, and why?

Understanding how contrarianism has given rise to trolling, and how haterism has mutated and curdled in "the present moment," is just the first step. The mission now is to find a way to save dynamic contrarianism from vicious trolling, to free healthy skepticism from the muck and mire of paranoia, to disentangle hating from hatred.

We must be contrarian and adversarial while remaining not just frank but also sincere. We must relearn how—and why—to hate.

— 4 —

How to Hate

— DISCUSSED HEREIN —

Misers, churls, and evil hearts | *Martin Crane* | *Haunting tweets* |
The theme music to HBO's Entourage | *Hating with care* |
Anti-fandom | The Sorrows of Young Werther | *Lifestyles of the
rich and famous and very annoying* | *Upside-down hearts* | *Starbucks
coffee cups* | *Ideology* | *Brexit* | *Trump (again)* | *KoЯn* |
the Judgment Night *sound track* | *The comfort of Bad Things* |
Bartleby | *Dissensus* | *Thes inedibility of Rimbaud's poems* |
The vigilance of piss and vinegar

— *Reconsidering the Curmudgeon* —

Curmudgeon is one of those great words that sounds like what it means. It feels satisfyingly self-describing: an obstinate chunk of letters that don't so much roll out of the mouth as make harsh demands of it. *Cur* . . . like a mongrel, Diogenes's dog, Diogenes himself. *Mud* . . . silty and earthy and sort of gross. *Geon* . . . like bludgeon or a truncheon, bullyingly wielded. As a word, *curmudgeon* is utterly curmudgeonly.

In his 1755 *Dictionary of English Language*, all-purpose English intellectual Samuel Johnson describes the "curm'udgeon" as "An avaritious [*sic*] churlish fellow; a miser; a niggard; a churl; a griper." Tracing the word's etymology leads the curious down dead ends and blind alleys. Take the French *coeur méchant*, for "evil heart." Such a definition discredits the curmudgeon as a mere misanthrope: one who abhors the world and all the people in it, who is, to paraphrase Byron, least alone in hermetic solitude. I find myself in accord with American writer Jon Winokur who, in his handy bathroom reader *The Portable Curmudgeon*, rejects such purely misanthropic characterizations. "They're neither warped nor evil at heart," he writes. "They snarl at pretense and bite at hypocrisy out of a healthy sense of outrage. They attack maudlinism because it devalues genuine sentiment. They hurl polemical thunderbolts at middle-class values and pop culture in order to preserve their sanity . . . Offense is their only defense."

Such lavish, heroic descriptions (of what might just be plain meanness) are intoxicating, in a sentimental, self-flattering fashion. Through sniping, backbiting, and a ruthless, often very funny, criticism of damn near everything existing, the curmudgeon is no mere misanthrope. Instead of stooping to society's compromised standards, the curmudgeon provokes the world to rise to meet him. And at least since the time I facilitated my seventh birthday party at a screening of the late-period Jack Lemmon/Walter Matthau vehicle *Grumpy Old Men*, the curmudgeon has occupied a place of pride in my own drooped, desiccated prune of a heart.

A hypothetical list of historical and cultural curmudgeons is long, and runs as far back as old Diogenes, if not as far back as Homer, who, in *The Iliad*, expresses the essence of unadulterated misanthropy, writing: "Nothing is more miserable than man, / Of all that breathes and moves upon the earth." There are critics and writers (H.L. Mencken, Karl Kraus, Edmund Wilson, George Bernard Shaw), renowned thinkers (Nietzsche, Voltaire, Schopenhauer, Diogenes naturally, suicidal shit-disturber Socrates), comedians (W.C. Fields, Groucho Marx, George Carlin, Lewis Black and Dennis Miller and Rick Mercer and other professionalized ranters), and all manner of fictive grumpy old men (Larry David's various fictional personas, Moe Howard the stooge and Moe Szyslak the *Simpsons* bartender, Martin Crane, those two wiseasses on the balcony on *The Muppet Show*). You get the point. Beyond wit, brainpower, and the propensity for dispensing first-rate zingers, such personages share another conspicuous feature. Historically, the awesome power of curmudgeondom has been almost exclusively wielded by those who are male.

A list of female curmudgeons, historical and fictional, is undoubtedly shorter, if no less distinguished: Dorothy Parker,

Fran Lebowitz, Joan Didion, Patricia Highsmith ("mean as a snake," as a friend once memorably described her), Darlene from *Roseanne*, Sophia from *The Golden Girls*, to name some personal favorites. One might wish to simply attribute this shortage to the historical marginalization of women generally, with the natural consequence that their visibility in such roles is diminished. That is, given the civilization-long history of sexism, it would follow that there are fewer prominent female curmudgeons, just as there are fewer female Oscar-winning filmmakers and fewer female prime ministers of Canada.

But that same long, ongoing drama of sexism has another consequence. Historical expectations around femininity, female sexuality, and what it *means* to be a woman have made it a harsher prospect to be a curmudgeon of the female-identifying variety. Where men are acculturated to be assertive, women are conditioned to passivity. As writer Elizabeth Wurtzel, herself a fine modern iteration of the distaff curmudgeon, writes that as soon as a woman "lays down the option of my way or the highway, it's amazing how quickly everyone finds her difficult, crazy, a nightmare: a bitch."

Simply put, when a man is curmudgeonly, he's seen as witty, acerbic, caustic, clever, and, at worst, misanthropic. When a woman expresses those same tendencies, she's seen as bossy, pushy, overbearing, bitchy, or worse.

On a fateful March night in 2013, while overseeing operations at her flagship restaurant The Black Hoof, Toronto restaurateur and author Jen Agg tweeted, "Dear (almost) everyone in here right now . . . please, please stop being such a douche."

In her first book, *I Hear She's A Real Bitch* (a kind of *Kitchen Confidential* resto-autobiography from the managerial perspective of a woman), Agg describes it as "the tweet that would forever haunt me." The responses came fast and furious, as is so common on Twitter. Retweets and replies chided Agg, or accused her of being ungrateful. Lots of grammatically suspect stuff like:

"Sounds like somebody needs a hug."

"What not to tweet"

"tweeting for people not to be a douche is a very douchy
    thing to do"

"Biting the hand that feed you?!"*

"Good ol' Toronto Customer Service."

And, courtesy of one of the city's more well-known restaurant critics:

"File under 'Own worst Jenemy.'"

"It's craziness!" she recalls, years later.** "It was a very carefully worded tweet." And indeed, the anti-patron sentiment did

---

*   Note: This is the sort of joke that must *seem* clever, what with the biting/hand/feed wordplay and the accompanying context of a restaurant. But given that Agg and her staff are the ones responsible for dispensing the food, wouldn't it be more accurate to say that it was the rude customers who were biting the hands that fed them? Twitter, man. So thoughtless.

**   All unattributed quotes are from a conversation with Mrs. Agg, at her Toronto restaurant Grey Gardens.

stir up Canada's *Globe and Mail* newspaper, which used the incident as a launchpad for a larger trend piece, claiming that "the culture war between restaurant staff and their patrons is heating up." It also cemented an image of Agg that's been hard to shake (even if she bothered to try): a world-class bitch.

It's a word that sticks to Jen Agg like dog hair to a high-pile rug. "Toronto restaurateur Jen Agg reclaims the b-word," read one review of the book, published by a Canadian women's lifestyle magazine. Even more than her restaurant's thoughtful menu, stiff cocktails, and utterly pleasant, cool-without-being-conspicuously-cool atmosphere, Agg's attitude turned her into a foodie iconoclast.

Agg rejects her characterization as a curmudgeon, or misanthrope, or hater. Agg has wielded her status as a "bitch" or "attention-seeking whore" (her words) into a book deal, packed restaurants, and a platform for advocating for gender equality in the service industry. If she was going to be made into an enemy, then she'd rather weaponize that status for the sake of good. A fine rule for any aspiring hater.

She now finds that her reputation as a bitch or snipe or meanie is largely recirculated as a way of getting her attention. She recalls one review of her restaurant Grey Gardens, in which a critic who has never met her made broad characterizations about her persona. Stuff like, "She reminds me of a hard-bitten diner owner in a '40s detective movie—the kind who doesn't appreciate your tough questions and makes a show of spitting in your coffee." Agg has no love for these sorts of food critics, who foreground her personality over her restaurants. She variously characterizes them (without naming names) as "lumps of potatoes" who "nobody cares about and nobody respects." She's savvy enough with social media to know that such broadsides are lodged in order to generate a response, which in turn drives traffic and "eyeballs" to the review itself. And in her kindness, she sometimes takes the bait.

But it doesn't mean it gets under her skin. She is like Frederick the Great in the Seven Years War, fighting on several fronts and winning them all. As she puts it, in the extended melee between restaurateurs, patrons, and critics, she has already won. "I live a really good life," Agg boasts. "I'm renovating my beautiful home into an even more beautiful home. I pretty much only have cashmere sweaters. I dress from head to toe in rag & bone.* I have great friends. My husband's hot and has a great dick. I have a great life."

Jen Agg has managed to transmute not just her own animosity but also the animosity directed against her into a vitality. One gets a sense that, at some level, it sustains her, like Al Pacino's cokey cop in Michael Mann's *Heat*, who claims: "I gotta hold onto my angst. I preserve it because I need it. It keeps me sharp. On the edge. Where I gotta be."

Here is the image of the model curmudgeon: demanding that people rise to her standard, pushing what passes as acceptable behavior to create a new standard of acceptability. Agg's anger, productively yoked and directed, keeps her on the edge. Where she's gotta be.

---

* Fashion label rag & bone is known for US$250+ T-shirts. I only know this because I had to look it up. I swear.

— *How to Hate with Care* —

When I need to rouse myself from the boggy torpor of daily life and get those anger-pistons pumping in my heart, need to get to that place where I gotta be, there's one surefire catalyst: *Entourage*.

From the tail end of the opening credits with the sound of Jane's Addiction front man Perry Farrell, whose voice is like a phosphorus grenade exploding in my ears, repeating the phrase "Oh yeah" to the trite resolutions of its idiotic plots and all the volleys of "bro, bro, bro . . ." in between, HBO's *Entourage* is a TV show I, pardon me, fucking *haaaaaaaaaate*.

Like Nickelback or anchovies on pizza, *Entourage* is a thing you're supposed to hate, reflexively and pre-theoretically. In short: The series follows the duskily handsome Hollywood super-hunk Vincent "Vinny" Chase (Adrian Grenier), a charming Queens, New York, regular neighborhood guy who is happy to let his considerably less handsome half-brother (Dillon) and childhood best friends (Ferrara, Connolly) ride his extended coattails. *Entourage* has often drawn comparisons to *Sex and the City*, another HBO comedy that indulged glamorous "lifestyle porn" and was known for its frank discussions about sex and friendship.

The key difference, perhaps, is that *Sex and the City* served a quasi-progressive agenda. However trite or obnoxious the characters, women had rarely been depicted with such candor and so, we're told, the show is important. *Entourage* brooks no delusions of importance. The culture has long been flooded with images of smirking male decadence and entitlement. Where *Sex and the City* could be viewed as a corrective to precisely this culture of masculinist entitlement, *Entourage* can only be viewed as a corrective to *Sex and the City*, the televisual equivalent of an upper-body-burly pickup artist interrupting a woman mid-sentence to say, "Well, actually, men are allowed to have fun, too."*

Plot-wise, *Entourage* is defined by its two-steps-forward-one-step-back storytelling that sees minor hiccups resolved almost immediately, the low-key dramatic conflicts in place purely to bind its bros closer together. As I wrote when reviewing *Entourage*'s improbable big-screen spinoff movie in 2015, "The lavish chauvinist reverie of icy cold Bud Crowns, gyrating full-frontal nudity and impromptu Pharrell concerts is never ruptured as our four pals roll along their totally frictionless storylines. Not even for one second is it plausible that their trifling personal predicaments won't resolve themselves, as if by the magic of friendship and faithful stick-to-itiveness." Or as Connolly's E puts it one episode, summing up the show's writers' bible, "It'll work out. It always does."

Such lifeless dramatization and grating characterization— it is pretty much impossible to conceive, even ontologically, of a show that would use the word *bro* more than *Entourage*—has cemented *Entourage*'s place in the firmament as an object of nonpareil cultural scorn. When actor Martin Landau passed away in July 2017 and online obits mentioned his appearances on *Entourage* (in which he played flustered, terminally out-of-touch,

---

*   To *Entourage*'s minimal credit, its core foursome is more believable than that of *Sex and the City*. Because the other three are all dependent in one way or another on Vince's fame, it actually makes sense that they hang out. In watching *Sex and the City*, one is sometimes troubled by the unlikelihood that Samantha would *ever* be friends with Charlotte. Though I suppose Carrie is the vector through which the others relate to one another, much like Vince. Anyway.

old Hollywood exec Bob Ryan for a handful of episodes), many balked, as if a screen legend's legacy was being tarnished by mere association with the show.

For years, I had encountered *Entourage* in small doses: watched intermittently and skeptically with university roommates, read about in various think pieces, absorbed by osmosis in a culture in which the catchphrase "Hug it out" or even just the name "Turtle" passes as currency. Then a few years ago, egged on by a particular persuasive and harebrained online theory maintaining that the show was an elaborate and deeply cruel long con to sink its cast's career prospects outside of the show, I found myself binging the entire series through a streaming TV service. Or, to use the contemporary parlance, I hatewatched *Entourage*.

At the risk of getting back to banging the technological-determinist, medium-is-the-message song-and-dance about how the way we engage with things comes to shape the things themselves, such streaming services have (in my experience, anyway) a tendency to instill a type of televisual Stockholm syndrome in the viewer. The thinking goes, "Well, I've already wasted three hours on this trash, might as well waste another twenty-seven." Working through the series over a few weeks, my mind started opening a bit, like a real-time expanding brain meme. "Maybe this show isn't so bad," I found myself thinking. "Some of the performances are actually pretty good." Before long it was, "Hmm . . . maybe it's not just aspirational Hollywood bro-porn, but a comment on precisely that: a deep satire of Hollywood decadence, like Altman's *The Player* for a generation raised on

FHM and Monster Energy syrups instead of *Playboy* and Johnny Blue."

Such acrobatic thinking tends to dominate watching a show (or movie) you don't particularly like. Hate-watching, as a cultural practice, becomes a form of authorship. And if the spectacle of hate-watching is embodied by one modern writer, it's Drew Magary. A novelist and culture critic for the website Deadspin, he has penned so-called "Hater's Guides" to everything from Taylor Swift to the Oscars, the Williams Sonoma catalog, *Avengers* movies, college football, and even the abstract notion of "other parents" ("Parenting is like driving in that everyone else out there seems to suck at it"). Magary uses hating a thing as a way of understanding it, and of engaging with the stuff that everyone seems to be compulsively talking about. "I try to hate with care," Magary explains. "If it's just open contempt of an otherwise fine thing, it can be a turnoff."

Magary's writing, which he describes as "service journalism wrapped in insults," additionally fights a two-front war: against the prevailing, frictionless positivity of certain publications on websites on one hand, and against the more violently nasty online tone on the other. "Some places have to be uncritical for the sake of access," he says.* "But I think the dark side of the internet has gotten much more notice: trolling, deliberately bad takes, etc. With Trump in charge, that vindictive corner of the web is really the prevailing ethos of America right now." Using humor, snark, and (most importantly) an actual knowledge of the things he's raspberrying, Magary's Hater's Guides manage

---

* All unattributed quotes here are from an e-mail interview with Mr. Magary.

to save hating from open trolling. Instead of sheer, destructive negativity, they provide a productive alternative to blind, stupid positivity. Magary is not so much hostile, or even ambivalent, to the things he hates on: he's more of an anti-fan.

The anti-fan is the shadowy doppelgänger resulting from the modern ascent of fandom as the de facto mode of cultural appreciation. It's not that anti-fans necessarily reject fandom itself. Rather, they mobilize their energy against certain cultural texts while savoring others. (Think back to old Armond White, who lambastes Paul Thomas Anderson while lauding Michael Bay.) The phenomenon of anti-fandom has long been overlooked, under the presumption that—unlike active fan cultures, which are exhaustively studied in sociology, cultural studies, and other academic fields—they don't really know or care about the things that they hate. They are often perceived as merely a mass of negative energy, or sprawling entropy, that opposes certain fandoms in a broad, indistinct way. As Jonathan Gray, a professor of media and cultural studies at the University of Wisconsin–Madison has attempted to prove, nothing could be further from the truth.

In his extensive interviews with fans and anti-fans of *The Simpsons*—as massive a cultural touchstone as is conceivable, shy of other massively popular all-American preoccupations like baseball or cheeseburgers—Gray discovered that even those who didn't like the show had intelligent, thoughtful opinions about it. After all, to dislike something, one most dislike something *particular* about it. I, for example, hate *Entourage*. But I hate *Entourage* knowing pretty much everything there is to know about it.

Gray cites an interviewee named Vivi who offers "insightful commentary, and all the while marking that while she did not like *The Simpsons*, it had a definite meaning to her and played a definite role in her life." Indeed, some anti-fans even organize in structures that reflect more positively oriented fandoms. They shared jokes on online "hatesites" (which, I should stress, are not at all the same as sites dedicated to racial or ethnic or other intolerable hatreds) and can even gather to collectively consume the entertainments they swear are beneath their contempt.

Yet in his research, Gray also found that anti-fans often form oppositional opinions about certain entertainments by consuming ancillary, additional commentary: reading articles, watching TV programs *about* TV programs, and so on. In the case of *The Simpsons* in particular, such anti-fandom may crystallize as a result of the early-1990s moral panic around Bart Simpson being a back-talking bad boy. As a kid, I myself was briefly banned from watching the show after saying to a family friend, "I'm John Semley. Who the hell are you?"* From a different point on the cultural spectrum, Gray cites the kerfuffle around the publication of Salman Rushdie's fatwa-scoring novel *The Satanic Verses*. Many anti-fans who hadn't even read the book were calling for the author's death. It's easy enough to call to mind any number of other widespread waves of cultural trepidation, from the 1980s "Satanic Panic" around heavy metal way back to the reportage around copycat suicides perpetrated by Romantic Saxon youth following the publication of Goethe's *The Sorrows of Young Werther*.

As such examples suggest, anti-fandom and hate-engagement is by no means a new phenomenon. But it's becoming increasingly popular. In a 2017 article for the *BBC*, Jennifer Keishin Armstrong

---

*   Following much moping and shrill protest on the part of yours truly, the anti-*Simpsons* injunction didn't stick.

claimed that hate-watching has become even more common, encouraged by the insta-reacts of social media: "Despite the embarrassment of rich, beautiful storytelling on TV," she writes, "many of us indulge in exactly this sort of time-wasting habit: hate-watching has reached new heights. Fed by almost endless options for shows to watch, bolstered by the snark contest that social media has become, viewers now regularly revel in finding plot holes and analysing awfulness just as much as they delight in quality programming."

Pulitzer Prize–winning *New Yorker* TV critic Emily Nussbaum described the conflicting feelings at play when she watched NBC's *Smash* as far back as 2012. "I realize my vehemence is slightly suspect," Nussbaum writes. "I mean, why would I go out of my way to watch a show that makes me so mad?" Think even further back, to my earlier look at the tradition of chucking rotten tomatoes at stage performers: the act requires foresight to (a) purchase fruit; (b) let that fruit rot; and, most importantly, (c) know that you will not enjoy the performance going into it. To answer Nussbaum's question, we go out of our way to watch (or read or listen to) things that make us mad precisely because they make us mad. We gravitate to shows like *Smash* or *Entourage* willingly, with rotten tomatoes in hand.

With hate-watching, this tomato-hurling impulse often zeroes in on recurring targets. The fawning celebrity lifestyle porn of *Entourage* offers a perfect example. It shares its vast panorama of indulgence with many other definitive hate-watches: *Sex and the City*, *Gossip Girl*, *The O.C.*, *The Bachelorette* (a show that has merited several noted academic, critical, and fan studies in recent years), and other programs depicting the astonishingly easy existences of the super-wealthy and otherwise upwardly mobile. There is a leveling effect at play here. By making fun of the lifestyles of the rich and famous, whether real or fictional,* cultural capital comes to replace traditional wealth. The noxious mores of the upper-crust one percent are checked by eye rolls and snarky tweets. The savvy practice of watching something you hate—or watching something precisely *because* you hate it—functions, so the thinking goes, as a kind of cultural intervention.

Hate-watching (or hate-reading, or hate-anything) is a reflexive gesture that feels pointedly contemporary. And not just because of the inescapable attitudinal finger-trap that is irony,** which tends to further ensnare the more one valiantly works against it. It is yet another function of that broad Catholicism of taste—or rather, the rejection of taste altogether as gauche or classist—discussed earlier. In a culture that prizes the middle-brow, that takes pride in elevating the modest virtues of any premium cable drama or the most recent iteration of the children's cartoon hero Spider-Man, even poor taste becomes a performance. Websites regularly round up the nastiest zingers from reviews of Michael Bay movies (reviews that appear to have zero net effect on his films' box office); countless podcasts

---

* Though I suppose the fictionally rich and famous characters in *Entourage* and similarly styled shows are played by factually rich and sort-of-famous actors, and it's really *them* we're mocking for taking part in such programs at all.

** I often think of the *Mr. Show* sketch in which a disaffected '90s slacker, when mocked for wearing a T-shirt paying tribute to a corny horror movie called *The Return of the Curse of the Creature's Ghost*, shrugs and replies, "I'm only wearin' it cos I hate it." In *Mr. Show*'s misanthropic wiseass comic milieu, such an explanation proves perfectly satisfactory, and bears no further interrogation.

dedicate themselves to bad movies, or recapping bland TV shows, or trying to convince people to listen to Phish.

If anything, professing to *hate* a thing while ostensibly enjoying it (or at least consuming it, as one might consume, say, a thin protein gruel concocted to sustain basic metabolic functions) feels more righteous than devising some cockamamie rubric for redeeming it, or for insisting that it is, in fact, good. Yet, in both cases, the self is merely surrendered to the machinations of the culture industry. Enormous television production companies hardly care if you're watching a thing because you like or dislike it, any more than McDonald's might care if you purchase a Quarter Pounder Combo every single day just to plunk it in the trash. But however modest the revolt, liking something that "everyone" (a broadly defined, largely phantasmic concept) is supposed to hate feels usefully obstinate—a staking out of new, defiant terrain.

Hate-watching makes hating feel invigorating again. And not just in the way that one feels when watching a show like *Entourage*: the piss and vinegar pumping in the veins; the face getting flushed, as it might when one bears witness to a wholly unlikeable specimen who practically cries out for a corrective smack across the head.* It invigorates in the sense of opening up

---

* The Germans, *natürlich*, have a word for such a person:
Backpfeifengesicht, translating roughly into "a face in need of
a slap." Fans of compound German loan words reading this
note may wish to adapt the term to apply to hate-watch-worthy
television. Let's call such programs *Backpfeifenfernsehsendung*,
for "a slappable TV program." Fair warning, though: deploying
the term *Backpfeifenfernsehsendung* at a cocktail party, or wherever,
risks making one a textbook *Backpfeifengesicht*.

the range of possibility. It pushes back, even in the most facile way, against the middlebrowing of the culture: yes, we'll take part in this inescapable conversation about premium cable and a musical in which the founding father raps, but we'll only do so to tell you we *haaaaate* it. As Gray's *Simpsons*-hating Vivi explained in an interview: "Even though I don't watch this show, I don't like this show, uh, I have to know about it to a certain degree . . . otherwise I will be excluded from the conversation of my friends."

Anti-fandom, as an expression of the hater instinct, provides a vector through which the like-minded, those unified in their distastes, can relate to one another.

Unlike Jonathan Gray's illuminating anti-fan Vivi, I consider myself a rather substantial *Simpsons* fan. Or at least a fan of the show's so-called Golden Years, generally defined as seasons 2 through 6 (or 8 or 9, depending on who you're talking to). This means I have a near-total recall of the second-season *Simpsons* episode "Principal Charming" in which the hapless Springfield Elementary administrator, Principal Skinner, falls for one of Marge Simpson's terminally single twin sisters, Patty. After a night out to a bad movie and a lousy restaurant, the unlikely couple fall into each other's arms, united in their shared hatred of the same things.

Granted, it's not exactly the stuff of hopeless, hearts-in-the-eye-sockets romance, but following the revision of *High Fidelity*'s "It's what you like, not what you *are* like" maxim, it serves to predict the ways in which shared distastes and dislikes can provide a common bond. Because Principal Skinner is pretty much right.

It very often *is* nice to hate the same things. Or, at least, it seems that way.

In a 2017 episode of ABC's massively popular televised cavalcade of venture capitalism, *Shark Tank*, a young entrepreneur pitched what CNBC called "the most cynical dating app ever." It was called Hater, software that allows users to "Find Love through Hate." The app's creator, a reformed Goldman Sachs trader named Brendan Alper, claimed he got the idea while writing a comedy sketch about people bonding over their dislikes. It's an appealing idea: Instead of first dates where couples gush about *Game of Thrones* spoilers, they shit-talk the hype about *Game of Thrones*. Cupid bends his arrow into one of those naughty l'il devil pitchforks. Mean-spirited sparks fly. Nine months later, a bouncing baby boy named Jon Snow Sux Assssss is born into this cruel world.

Here's how Hater works: Users swipe either left or right, Tinder-style. But not on prospective mates. On *things*. You can hate chewing tobacco, or watery salsa, or the Internet Explorer web browser, or Donald Trump (this one seems, unsurprisingly, very popular). You can also hate more abstract concepts, like "people that hate corporations, but have iPhones," or "When someone else takes the fry I mentally claimed," or even "America." After supplying the app with enough hatreds (or un-hatreds, providing you swipe left), you're then paired with prospective matches who hate the same stuff. In keeping with the theme of fostering connections through mutual hatreds, Hater's logo is an inverted heart.

Even in a crowded market of digitized dating and hookup options, Hater struck a chord. "The name is pure genius," said real estate mogul and "Shark" Barbara Corcoran. "Because it's contrary. And even your upside-down heart, I love." Alper claimed that the idea of matching couples based on dislikes, instead of mutual interests, was backed up by science. In the sense that anyone with access to the internet can retrieve a scientific (or pseudo-scientific) study to back up pretty much any asinine claim, this is certainly true.

A 2006 article in the interdisciplinary journal *Personal Relationships* found that "sharing a negative—as compared to a positive—attitude about a third party is particularly effective in promoting closeness between people." This is in large part because "sharing negative attitudes is alluring because it establishes in-group/out-group boundaries, boosts self-esteem, and conveys highly diagnostic information about attitude holders." Here again, negation is wrought toward positive ends, with couples finding solace in their exclusion from certain large social groups. It's the same basic attitude that animates all those *They Live by Night-*, *True Romance-*, *Badlands*-style love-on-the-run movies, even beyond the couples' shared predilection toward criminality. You know, the whole "It's you and me against the world, baby!" Hating builds community. It fosters love.

Granted, the Hater app isn't meant to be exhaustive. More a novel icebreaker built on shared distaste. Which is a fine thing, because taken to its logical extent, Hater's premise strikes me as insufficient—and even to the eyes of this cynic, more than a bit cynical. If it's juvenile, and a little asinine, to base relationships purely on shared likes, then it's just as silly to use dislikes as a comparable grounding. Sure, couples might hate-watch the Oscars or *Entourage* for a while, but that's hardly enough to sustain a healthy, passably adult relationship.

The productive commingling of love and hate is better expressed in Jonathan Gray's illuminating studies of anti-fandom. There, fans and anti-fans were found coupled together, often in healthy long-term relationships. One watches *The Simpsons* for its satire, another to know enough about it to carefully hate it. Instead of unifying in a shared hostility, such a coupling is defined by an entanglement of low-key antagonism. Hating becomes acceptable, even cherished, as the superficiality of taste is flattened. I can, for example, appreciate that someone finds heavy metal music obnoxious or adolescent, even if I don't. It's not like Hate and Love are two sides of the same coin. The relationship between the two is not dichotomous but dialectic: They are entwined, challenging and refining and reforming one another.

Hating becomes a thing to be admired, as loving so often is. And if love (as Shakespeare so often put it) is blind, i.e., animated by a pure passion that somehow precedes reason, then hate must be reasonable, purposeful, deeply informed. To hate in such a way is to practice the art and craft of thought itself.

It's not about what we like or don't like, but what we *are* like—hatreds, distastes, warts and all.

Like Rocks toward the Gatehouse — *(or The Problem of Post-Critique)* —

Because I worry I'm getting a bit mushy, I want to move away from dating apps and learning to love through hate, and get back to the more material stuff of politics. Or, more specifically, the intersection of politics and culture, the point at which criticism attempts to inflect the real world.

In July 2000, the Palestinian-American scholar and critic Edward W. Said was traveling through Lebanon with his family. While there, he took part in a protest against the state of Israel, joining fellow Arab protesters in lobbing rocks across the Lebanon-Israel border, in the general direction of Israeli border security guards stationed at a nearby gatehouse. Given the distance of the gatehouse, there was little threat that any of the stones would do any damage. The protest was purely symbolic.* Said described throwing the stone as a "gesture of joy."

I would have been fourteen when this happened, more interested in collecting concert T-shirts and scouring the internet for acne treatments. I first heard about the incident years later, while studying Said in university. At that time—and, I imagine, still today—Said was taught primarily in the context of his 1978 book *Orientalism* and its titular idea: his sustained examination of how Western culture has created images of "The East" that invariably serve imperialist agendas. Said's conception of orientalism struck me as fascinating. I'd never given much thought to how such stereotypes and clichés of foreign cultures serve power. But more significantly for me, it vitally connected the real-world politics of imperialism to the stuff of art and literature, essentially inventing the field of postcolonial cultural studies.

---

* For the record: For reasons of personal safety, I would advise against throwing rocks at heavily armed soldiers, and recuse myself from any responsibility w/r/t what happens to your person should you decide to whip a rock at a border patrolman strapped with a bunch of guns and ammo. While such a gesture may be "purely symbolic," the consequences may prove all too real.

As someone whose interest in culture (books, movies, music, and, to a far lesser extent, art) had always seemed drastically at odds with an interest in politics, I found Said's theories electrifying. The image of Said, a vehement critic of the Israeli occupations, lobbing a stone toward the border seemed similarly encouraging, however symbolic. Here was a guy taking action to support his theories, taking up sticks and stones where words had proved insufficiently hurtful.

Ditto Adorno and Horkheimer's book *Dialectic of Enlightenment*, in which two Jewish scholars escaped Nazi Germany and applied a sustained critique of media propaganda to the field of American entertainment; it's a book I have often described in conversation as "life-changing."* And I suppose it's true. Though, really, what sort of "life" did I really have at nineteen, when I first encountered the likes of Adorno, Horkheimer, and Said? Not much of one, honestly. More of an inchoate state of highly squanderable potential. Perhaps it's fairer to say that such books were less life-changing and more life-*giving*. They sparked a sustained intellectual interest, invested me with a highly critical politics, and instilled me with a vague sense of purpose.

The serious, sustained, and characteristically suspicious analysis of certain works of art or culture (or *texts*, to use the more somber academese) had the potential to reveal what Fredric

---

* So indebted is my worldview to this book that I have hesitated, as much as is humanly possible, from referring to it for *this* book. I'm so in the bag for it that I operate under some anxiety that as soon as I dip into it, I'll end up just reproducing the whole of the text verbatim, like that guy in that Borges story who replicates *Don Quixote* word-for-word out of whole cloth.

Jameson called the "political unconscious." Thus, the job of the critic was not the thumbs-up/thumbs-down appraisal of whether things are "good" or "bad" but rather the "unmasking of cultural artifacts as socially symbolic acts." Following this, everything— I mean *everything*, from Hollywood movies to Victorian novels to the patter wrapping the side of a throwaway Starbucks cup— became a site of ideology. The slightly absurd, terminally slur- ring Slovenian philosopher and critic Slavoj Žižek is especially adept at this. It's as if he has a special pair of corrective lenses* that decode and demystify the hidden codes of late-capitalist, imperialist experience. With a bit of reading and consideration, I, or anyone, could contort my gaze to see the world with simi- lar clarity.**

Now—older and either wiser or more cynical, or all three— I look at that photo of Said's symbolic gesture of joy and wonder if the rock will ever hit the gatehouse. I am sometimes over- whelmed by pessimism. That despite the best efforts of critics and scholars to insist otherwise, criticism, however ruthless, cannot actually change the material reality of social and politi- cal life. This existential crisis in certain strains of critique, and the shared shrugging, "What's the *point?*" malaise, has even birthed a new tendency in academia, termed "post-critique." As

---

* To wit: A favorite structuring metaphor of Žižek's is the sunglasses of John Carpenter's sci-fi action film *They Live*. They allow the working- class hero to magically decipher the barely hidden ciphers of modern advertising as well as distinguish between a mind-controlling power bloc of extraterrestrial origin and the "real" people subjugated to their plan of world dominance through subliminal enslavement.

** At the risk of tipping my hand, this is also the modest aim of this book. And the aim of most books, I'd imagine. No?

articulated by French sociologist Bruno Latour, decades of liter-ary, cultural, and broader textual critique have pushed critical minds into irrelevancy. Latour lays out the problem in a series of rhetoric, like an apostle petitioning God for a sign: "Is it really our duty to add fresh ruins to fields of ruins? Is it really the task of the humanities to add deconstruction to destruction? More iconoclasm to iconoclasm? What has become of the critical spirit? Has it run out of steam?"

Beyond serving as a job-creation safeguard for potentially irrelevant academics, the scholarly emergence of post-critique has a trickle-down effect into the wider culture—as certain academic ideas often do, by way of plundering philosophy and cultural studies undergrads who smuggle them into newspaper movie reviews and long-form lit mag essays. After all, if the people whose whole profession it is to be critical in the most abstractly intellectual way are feeling the pinch of insignifi-cance, what hope is there for the rest of us mugs straining to apply the critical disposition to the stuff of daily life?

The prospect can feel totally pointless. It is not only because, as discussed earlier, the ruthless and vigilantly suspi-cious attitude deployed by criticism has been co-opted by cer-tain paranoid attitudes in mainstream Western life.* It is also because there may be, as the French philosopher Jacques

---

* Latour reserves particular animus for the prominent French philosopher Jean Baudrillard, who claimed, mere months after 9/11, that the Twin Towers *literally* collapsed under the nihilistic weight of financial capitalism itself. In this moment, Baudrillard stooped from respectable intellectual to "jet fuel can't melt steel beams" conspiracy monger who has origami'd his Sorbonne degree into a tinfoil hat.

Rancière has put it, "no criterion for establishing a correspondence between aesthetic virtue and political virtue." Put even more despairingly, the "revolutionary" or even plain "political" potential of art and entertainment has pretty much never, ever translated into actual, real-world revolutionary or political change. Art can be provocative, or reflective, but can it be actually, manifestly transformative? It's a hard case to make without playing the proverbial Pollyanna, coming off totally naive or, worse, like an aspiring artist pleading their case before a grants commission.

This misgiving is further compounded in the wake of recent goings-on, like the U.K.'s Brexit vote and America's election of President Donald Trump. Any belief that a thorough, hypercritical, left-progressive cultural politics might lead to a comparable conventional politics (i.e., voting, legislation, etc.) was effectively sucked into the black hole of political darkness that resulted from the reemergence of a renewed conspiratorial, populist, ethno-nationalist politics.

Put even more bluntly, and despairingly: Why should we believe in the ability of art or culture to reshape politics and society when such a reshaping has literally never happened? Why be ruthlessly critical and productively contrary when doing so often proves historically defeatist, and defeating?

The obvious, empowering answer, the one that's meant to get that piss and vinegar pumping through the veins, is that such a stance is fundamentally noble. Like Said hurling a rock at some guards he stands no chance of hitting, a critical disposition may be valuable precisely *because* it is pointless—because it suggests a self-ennoblement and uprightness against a culture that slouches onward. Quite simply: The contrarian, the curmudgeon, the hater rejects consensus, sloppy thinking, and the debasement of principles because it is the *right thing to do*. At the very least, they are the beautiful losers whose eternal failures are validated by the courage of their convictions. They are the ones who attire themselves for an international flight in well-pressed fineries while everyone else trudges through security checks in hoodies and accommodating athleisure wear. As Christopher Hitchens puts it in his epistolary treatise *Letters to a Young Contrarian*, "such a life is worth living on its own account."

However, to the truly honed critical mind—to any real hater—such an axiomatic answer likely proves insufficient. I mean, I sure hope it's insufficient. Pretty much the whole point of this book is to remind you to ask, *"Is it?"* anytime someone insists that something is self-evident. And yet, that presumption of self-evidence is a bedrock principle for pushing past the despondency and existential fretting of post-critique and mounting a final, last-ditch defense of the virtues of disagreeability.

And so, reader, you must permit me to talk about КoЯn.

Gotta Have Faith (or Nu Metal Is Actually Bad, Though)

In this sprawling cultural Bulk Barn of dashed-off op-eds, under-cooked think pieces, and wholly unconsidered opinions, there are bound to be some rotten takes: thoughtless, uncritical, frankly flabbergasting opinions that can't even be bothered to feign rigor. But there are bad takes, and there are *bad* takes. Like the one that I've been unable to shake since reading it a few years ago on a heavy metal blog: "In Defense of Nu Metal."

Nu metal (sometimes stylized, per excessive heavy metal convention, as nü-metal) is a largely maligned musical subgenre, even by the standards of heavy metal. It features extreme down-tuning; basses slung so low they're dragging on the asphalt; an unfortunate fusion of alternative music, metal, funk, and hip-hop; and even more unfortunate interventions like stock rap choruses and a form of guttural, nonsensical vocal improvisation called "psycho-scatting" (ugh). Nu metal emerged in the mid-1990s, popularized by acts like Limp Bizkit, Staind, P.O.D., Papa Roach, and Bakersfield, California, outfit KoЯn—arguably nu metal's progenitors.

Whether or not nu metal sounds like garbage is, perhaps ultimately, a matter of taste. What rankled more than the *blumppty-blippity-blum* bass lines and growled vocals was its ethic. In short, it *had* no ethic. Grunge, widely credited with saving rock and roll in the early '90s, traded on fuzzy sonic noise, sensitive lyrics, and wounded, aching front men cast in the Kurt Cobain mold, appealing to generations of mopey outcasts. Nu metal pitched itself to the outcasts who would rather rage, growl, and break stuff. As Steve Hyden wrote in his definitive 2011 analysis of nu metal, the music "convinced the losers and rejects that *they* were the bullies, and it was high time they found somebody weaker to fuck up for a change." Where grunge artists struggled with the wages of success—or at least had the decency to *pretend* to—nu metal bands raked in zillions with their self-persecuting shtick.

When the media (justifiably) called out KoЯn or Limp

Bizkit for the misogynist, homophobic[*] lyrics, the bands doubled down. They worked the whole "bands you love-to-hate" thing like skilled entrepreneurs of their own hype. If the media, or parents, or fuddy-duddy teachers didn't like them, it wasn't for any good reason. It was because the bands, like their fans, were woefully *misunderstood*. And so these bands benefited from an era dogged by clichéd appraisals like "Eminem is actually a brilliant businessman" and "Marilyn Manson is actually really smart." Yet unlike Eminem (or even Manson, at least on those first four records), nu metal was all pyrotechnics, hysteria, and empty macho posturing.

Among those would-be gatekeepers who loathe nu metal, it is sometimes given credit for expanding the appeal of hip-hop and rap. A 2008 *Guardian* reappraisal claimed that these bands "did far more to break down the artificial barriers between 'urban music' and rock than any of their more critically acceptable counterparts." This is, at best, generous. At worst, it's pure fantasy. Any number of other entertainments commingled elements of hard rock and rap: 1993's sound track to the thriller *Judgment Night* (which saw, among other crossovers, Pearl Jam and Cypress Hill on the same track), Ice-T's rap-rock project Body Count, Public Enemy and Anthrax teaming up on a version of "Bring the Noise," Aerosmith and Run-DMC singing "Walk This Way," and Blondie name-checking Fab 5 Freddy and Grandmaster Flash on the 1980 chart-topper "Rapture."

As the near-perennial reappraisals of nu metal suggest,

---

[*] That Limp Bizkit's breakout single was a growled-up cover of George Michael's "Faith" is, at the very least, *extremely* rich, if not wholly contemptible.

there's a recurring desire to want to salvage the subgenre from its own well-earned contemptibility. I should be able to sympathize with this. I mean, as a preteen, I compulsively listened to Limp Bizkit's first two albums and wore the same glow-in-the-dark *Follow The Leader*–era KoЯn T-shirt to school circa Grade 7 as often as the laundry schedule permitted. Yes, I admit it. I loved KoЯn when I was twelve. And want to know how I know they're bad? Because *I loved them when I was twelve.* I responded to them precisely for the reasons Hyden describes—a desire to feel persecuted without risking seeming sensitive, and without actually being at all persecuted—and because it proved a suitable sound track for exciting a bunch of pimply adolescents in the locker room of the local hockey rink. They were all angry and pissed off about nothing. Just like me.

This no-calorie nothingness was even more present in Limp Bizkit's . . . er . . . oeuvre. The band was led by Fred Durst, a hyper-macho cartoon "bad boy" whose backward caps and pointy facial hair barely concealed a seething male frailty. Many of their biggest hits preemptively attacked their own "haters," in a bid to rebuff criticism while simultaneously making a platinum-selling band seem like hard-done-by skid martyrs. See, for example:

> "Now all the critics want to hit it / To shitcan how we did it / Just because they don't get it / But I'll stay fitted / New era committed / Now this red cap* gets a rap from his critics" —from "Take a Look Around"

---

*   A reference to Durst's trademark red New York Yankees cap, itself a symbol of his faux underdogism. What underdog roots for the Yankees? It's like rooting for McDonald's.

"You want to mess with Limp Bizkit? / You can't mess with Limp Bizkit" —from "Rollin' (Air Raid Vehicle)"

"Let me hear you pigeons run your mouth now / Shut the fuck up!" —from "N 2 Gether Now"

"I can see it when you laugh at me / Look down on me / You walk around on me" —from "My Way"

etc., etc., etc., ad nauseam.

Yet despite such transparent effrontery, it somehow worked. Not only did Limp Bizkit become an enormously popular band despite their badness, their attitude helped shift the terrain of pop music to become critic-proof. Beyond their own musical (de) merits, the nu metal acts are contemptible because they helped usher in a new era of pop music post-critique.

There is one perfect example—a clear line from Limp Bizkit's "persecution" to what is surely the definitive pop song of this decade, and certainly of this epoch, of cultural appreciation. I'm talking about "Shake It Off," sung by Taylor Swift and cowritten by Swift and two scraggly-looking and moistly hirsute Swedish gentlemen (Max Martin and Karl Johan Schuster aka Shellback), from Swift's 2014 album *1989*.

Beyond being intoxicatingly catchy and eminently sing-along-able,* "Shake It Off" encapsulates the attitudes of the very

---

*   This is not me being sarcastic or even coolly evaluative, either. When the song came out I listened to it, pretty much exclusively, for a week. It put a literal skip in my step. I mean, what am I? Made of stone?

cultural milieu it entered into when it gained #1 chart positions in Australia, Hungary, the Czech Republic, Canada, Slovakia, the United States, and elsewhere. Lyrically, "Shake It Off" addresses media criticisms that a young pop star like Swift (and Swift specifically) are regularly subject to: that she stays out too late, is vacuous ("got nothing on my brain"), etc. In an ingenuous turn, the song robustly pushes back against critics of Swift, and of pop music in general, with its earworm of a chorus:

> 'Cause the players gonna play, play, play, play, play
> And the haters gonna hate, hate, hate, hate, hate
> Baby, I'm just gonna shake, shake, shake, shake, shake
> I shake it off, I shake it off

Swift essentially invokes the old singsongy childhood comeback, "I am rubber, you are glue," invoked as a spell to ward off insults by suggesting that any meaningful opprobrium slung by the critics will be automatically deflected back to the slinger.

"Shake It Off" is sort of like that old Guns N' Roses song "Get in the Ring." Consummate hard rock bad boy Axl Rose calls out the "punks in the press" who mock him and his band, going so far as to explicitly call out journalists who have besmirched Rose's apparently good name. Except instead of deliberately antagonizing the Mick Walls at *Kerrang!* and Andy Sechers at *Hit Parader* and Bob Guccione Jrs. at *Spin* (who Rose accuses of being aggrieved and emasculated because his father, *Penthouse* magazine founder Bob Guccione, is more sexually experienced), Swift preemptively insulates herself from such critics in the first place. Not only that, she makes even these hypothetical critics seem like total idiots for lodging their putative, and at the time pretty much wholly imaginary, criticisms.

"Shake It Off" is the perfect modern pop song not just because of its more obvious merits, but because it's pretty much bulletproof. Or, more accurately, critic-proof. Swift was the red-cap-wearing Fred Durst recast in the image of a bubbly, beautiful, radio-friendly pop star. Disliking "Shake It Off" was impossible, because Swift & Co. had already safeguarded themselves against that dislike. It's like when the movie *Superbad* came out and, in its title alone, protected itself from disses, leaving would-be haters tripping over themselves, all, "More like *Superba*—uh, never mind . . ." "Shake It Off" revealed the defensiveness and self-reflexivity of our modern era of poptimism and generalized cultural enthusiasm. One risks revealing oneself as totally foolish and out of touch if they dare to not like a thing, or if they can't just suck it up and succumb to the seductive throb of the mass cultural wavelength. It's a song that turned hating against itself.

A similar trend in critical recuperation has emerged around Canadian punch-line band Nickelback: another righteous critical punching bag whose music, persona, etc., merits no attention whatsoever. And yet outlets like *Vice* dispatch fleets of staffers to concerts at beer-branded amphitheaters, where they can register shock and sly amusement at the idea that this band "everyone hates" has fans. To this, the skeptic, the curmudgeon, the hater can do little but smack their head with the butt of an open palm and blurt, "Duh." *Of course* a platinum-selling heartland hard rock band that sings about blow jobs and has their singles played in heavy radio rotation and over the PA systems at pro sports games has fans. Nickelback's popularity is the result of the machinery of the culture industry firing on all cylinders. The function of criticism—or even the looser "cultural journalism"— should be to jam a spanner in the works, not to prostrate at the altar of the machinery and ironically shrug, "Huh! Who knew!"

What "In Defense of Nu Metal," or "In Defense of Nickelback," as a subgenre of modern think piece reveals is a compulsion to want to redeem everything within a governing program of likeability. To find the good and redemptive in absolutely anything. Some seemingly irremediable bad objects can weather this process—like when everyone started frying Brussels sprouts in bacon, rendering a once daunting, lime-green inedible perfectly palatable. Nu metal cannot benefit from the same process. We should refuse it. We should cast it out, like an Old Testament father sending his ne'er-do-well kid to live by his wits in the unforgiving desert. And more importantly, we should be perfectly OK with there being Bad Things. As Noam Chomsky, one of history's fiercest critics and arguably America's foremost public intellectual, once put it: "You have to take some things on trust or you can't survive."

Every generation has its joke acts: The Archies, Billy Joel, Foreigner, Phish, Hoobastank (the name alone!), and that's OK. Bad things aren't only inevitable. They're vital. And not just in some woolly, Manichaean, light/dark, yin-yang kind of way. The looming specter of big, bad bands helps us outline and nurture our more private passions. Next to Nickelback, pledging allegiance to other pop mediocrities, such as Taylor Swift or The Killers, almost feels like a subcultural, subversive loyalty. "Sure I like that one Imagine Dragons song. But at least I don't like Nickelback!"

The endurance of such bands, their stubborn refusal to go away, is encouraging. They're the hard, inedible lump of Yorkshire pudding at the cultural omnivore's pop buffet. More than being a meme, a joke, or critical shorthand for the objectionable, they are a bad band. And as such, they carry the weirdly buoying promise that there will always be bad bands. In their badness, bands such as Nickelback, Limp Bizkit, and KoЯn generate an opportunity for rejection, a chance to get one's hate on.

Against the creeping malaise of a post-critical culture of consensus, they offer not just the died-in-wool contrarian but also the merely sensible to stand up and, like Melville's Bartleby, defiantly proclaim, "I would prefer not to." They catalyze a crucial sentiment: dissensus.

Dissensus and the Return — — *to the Aesthetic Dimension*

Another banger of a word. Like *curmudgeon*, *dissensus* sort of sounds like its definition. I mean, it's got "diss" right in the front there!

Strictly speaking, dissensus is (as one might guess) the opposite of consensus. It means (per *Merriam-Webster*) a "difference of opinion." The *Oxford English Dictionary* traces the word back to the 1960s, a time of generalized dissent (if such a term even makes sense) ranging from the Civil Rights, gay rights, and feminist movements to anti-Vietnam protests, French student revolts, drugs, the New Hollywood, Dylan, youth culture—you get the idea.

I first came across it in a feature in *The New York Times* in which in-house film critics A.O. Scott and Manohla Dargis "reflected on the state of the movies in our state of disunion." It's the sort of writing I tend to respond to: stuff that tries to excavate the latent politics in Hollywood blockbusters and prestige biopics, regarding culture as a kind of fun-house mirror reflecting a warped vision of political reality.

Dissensus, as both a word and an idea, crops up a lot in the writing of Jacques Rancière, a French thinker. He is sometimes described as an "anti-philosopher," both for his bickering back-and-forth with other of the more-esteemed contemporary Franco-intellectuals (Alain Badiou, Jean Baudrillard, Jean-François Lyotard) and for his apparent desire to destroy the field of philosophy altogether. (To wit: Rancière's breakthrough book, *The Ignorant Schoolmaster,* mounts a provocative case against the very idea of pedagogy and the conventional wisdom that teachers actually have anything worthwhile to teach anyone.)

Rancière describes dissensus as "the essence of politics." He doesn't merely mean that politics is about healthy debate and the reconciling of difference. Rather, dissensus is the moment when discontent ruptures the existing order, creating a "gap in the sensible" through which new political ideas, models, and subjects can enter. Where consensus, by its very nature, hides what is different or deemed unacceptable, dissensus pushes outcast, marginalized, or disagreed-upon notions to the fore. The fundamental value of dissensus is articulated in Polish revolutionary Rosa Luxemburg's famous pronouncement that "freedom is always and exclusively freedom for the one who thinks differently." For a good example of dissensus in action, imagine a political protest. It serves as a physical, visible manifestation of a more generalized *sense* of malady or injustice. We literally witness an aggravation that had hitherto gone unseen.

For many thinkers of the pre-post-critique school, art and culture can provide similar manifestations of dissensus. For Herbert Marcuse, art didn't merely reflect political and social reality. It *anticipated* it. Marcuse was smart enough to know that art's ability to catalyze social change was "inexorably indirect, mediated, and frustrating." He goes on to say in his book *The Aesthetic Dimension* that there is an inherent "element of despair" in this. It may be hard to argue against such despair. But such thinking rails against the defeatist belief that art, culture, and critique never constitute sufficient challenges to the social and political order. It holds—however naively— that such practices *can* and *do* change the world.

Let's imagine a starving man begging for food. It no more makes sense to wax philosophic on his condition than it does to hand him a copy of some Rimbaud poems and say, "Here. This'll help." Marcuse knew this very well. He also knew that worthy art—and to this I might generously add the more generalized categories of culture and, perhaps even, entertainment—had the ability to transcend the social, the political, the limits of the real. Art operated through a "dialectic of affirmation and negation," which rejects the stifling conformism of what *is* and opens the boundaries of what is possible but, as yet, *is not*. This is a noble aim and far more radical and sophisticated than the wan, anemic, self-consciously virtuous, despairingly likeable liberal art that is praised for being "precisely what we need *right now*" or whatever. Writing of the hopefulness of critical thinking itself as a "disruptive force," Christopher Castiglia sets the stakes of literature, in recognizable Marcusean terms, as a "springboard

[for] turning the unreal into a source of hopeful world-making."

Thus, literature, music, all art can constitute a site of dissensus—a space where one can howl "NO!" or acquire courage to learn to prefer not to. The late Edward Said's rock may never hit the gatehouse, but the image of him throwing it may well awaken others to the social/political power of such a gesture, or the sheer emancipatory joy of rock throwing. Progress is not a process of consensus and accord, but of argument, disputation, and rejection. Even if the realm of culture and critique is a mere sandbox, in which the hater can play and grow before moving into the harsh concrete jungle of realpolitik, it is a necessary one. The aesthetic dimension is the space, the abstracted realm, in which one learns how to consider, how to admire, how to disagree and undermine, how to think for oneself.

This spirit of dissensus, rejection, agonism (as distinguished from mere antagonism), and contrarianism is energizing. It is the daft and ultimately affirmative spirit of optimism expressed through ruthless criticism, and through acts of ostensible negation. It is the refusal to accept things as they are. It is the desire to make coherent demands, to command through weaponized opprobrium that the world rise to meet you.

It's the unscratchable itch; the vigilance of piss and vinegar; the skepticism and suspicion that stands up to consensus, to conformism, to sheer idiocy. It's the acuity to critically undermine any assumption, to look at what is and bawl, in a rising tenor quavering toward full falsetto, "Tell me whyyyyyy!"

This is what it means to be a hater.

- *Letter to a Young Hater* -

My dear X,

Before we go our separate ways, there's still some work to be done. Which is why I thought I'd take a second to address you directly. Also, it's fun to write in the style of an epistolary missive! "My faithful companion. . . ," "My dear good fine sir. . . ," and so on. It's like reading *Dracula*.

Anyway, X, old bean. Have you ever read Christopher Hitchens's book *Letters to a Young Contrarian*, in which the late professionalized pot-stirrer and cigarette-smoker offered his "advice to the young and the restless" that might "help them avoid disillusionment"? That was a big book for me when I was a teenager. I very much admired him, at least before he became a hardened neocon performing pseudo-intellectual PR for the George W. Bush administration.*

Nowadays, admitting to liking Hitchens feels vaguely unfashionable, like still caring about Ricky Gervais or U2. But they all (Hitchens, Gervais, U2) boast achievements, despite

---

* You may, X, if you are keen, trace Hitchens's imperial fetishism back even further. Say, to 1992, when he penned an essay for *The Nation* decrying Columbus Day protests, chalking up the violent conquest of Indigenous lands to the forward march of history itself, and so about as worthy of protests as a "climatic, geological or tectonic shift."

subsequent slumps into irrelevance. And anyway, what kind of freethinker would I be if I wasn't willing to risk looking unfashionable? Plus, Hitchens always went to bat for Noam Chomsky, despite disagreeing with the eminent professor and activist's views, and, more importantly, did so at a time when Chomsky was being all but no-platformed by the mainstream media.

So I'd be lying if I said I wasn't still able to scrape Hitchens's books for value and insight. And I'd be lying even harder if I denied that there is, perhaps, an even greater insight to be gained from the life of one of modern history's more staunch, self-styled haters—the guy who literally played devil's advocate against the prospective canonization of Mother Teresa. And so, X, I'm shamelessly pilfering the format of Hitchens's enlightening, intermittently frustrating book as a means of addressing you now.

And so. X. X, X, X . . .

In this modest volume I've tried to lay out a few things for you. First, there was an abridged history of contrarian thought. Then an argument for how consensus—both as a form of internal accord and of society-wide collective nodding—has come to dominate the fields of culture and politics, degrading the character of that culture and those politics, in turn. I then outlined some of the problems facing the contemporary hater in an era when the naysayer as romantic hero has crossed political lines, succumbed to resentment, and slumped into the modern figure of the troll. Finally, I tried to offer some cases where hatred, or the curmudgeonly character, can be used productively: to inspire, to elevate, to emancipate.

I have attempted to illustrate how the figure of the hater suffers a bad rap. Sometimes, this rap is well-earned. But at other times, the animosity thrown back at the hater (which is more than a bit ironic on its own accord) speaks to a deep-seated conservatism and conformism of thought, a valuing of consensus over dissensus. People who say things other people don't like are rarely treated kindly. Back in the day, they'd be poisoned with hemlock or crucified or burned at the stake for heresy. These days, they're more likely to suffer torrents of abuse online, have Rotten Tomatoes users call for fatwas, or have their Twitter DMs flooded with hateful rhetoric.

There is a persistent myth that the move from print to online culture has led to a "democratization." In his book *So You've Been Publicly Shamed*, about social media shame rituals, British journalist Jon Ronson says of this move, "Egalitarianism is its greatest quality."

This, X, is a load of bunk. While these technologies can serve to give rise to the voiceless, they can just as often serve to enable (and bogusly ennoble) the fouler instincts of people who are already (over)represented in society. Not everyone who says something thoughtful, asinine, or straight-up hateful is some freethinking radical whose silence is required for a return to normalcy. Oftentimes, their opinions are the *most* normal, articulating plainly the fear-mongering, racism, xenophobia, and undifferentiated mean-spiritedness that define our civilization. And many of them, X, are just jerks.

I get anxious being overly prescriptive. This is, in part, because performing the hard work of telling people what to think sort of cuts against this book's larger "think for yourself!" mandate. It's also because I'm deeply wary of conclusion and resolution.

Per the dialectical movement of thought, and of human history itself, resolution only holds until the instant it is challenged, and then synthesized with that challenge, and then that new resolution is challenged again. Coming to anything like a meaningful conclusion is like (per the cliché) hitting a moving target or (per an even better cliché) attempting to catch a greased pig. But with all that in mind, I'd like to offer you, X, a few warnings and admonitions in your pursuit of the hater's life.

Remember that challenging convention, and idiocy, should proceed from a place of kindness and resounding fellow-feeling; that hatred should only be energized by a deeper reservoir of love. Think of that scene in *Twin Peaks* when snarling, cynical, sniping FBI agent Albert Rosenfield lets his misanthropic guard down and confesses, "I am a naysayer and hatchetman in the fight against violence . . . I reject absolutely revenge, aggression, and retaliation. The foundation of such a method . . . is love." There's wisdom there. A weird, cryptic, pseudo-gnostic, distinctly *Twin Peaks*-y wisdom. But wisdom nonetheless.

Keep in mind the dialectic relationship between hate and love. But also keep in mind, per the wisdom of Elie Wiesel, that the opposite of love is not hate, and the opposite of hate is not love: The opposite of both is indifference. Indifference softens the mind into an acceptance that things are OK as they are. Or worse, that they're not OK, but it's irrelevant because there's no way to effect change, or to meaningfully oppose. Indifference is the opposite. Indifference is the enemy.

Be wary of the black dog of resentment, which, at every turn, stalks the curmudgeon, the grump, the autodidact, the hater. Resentment turns the haterist impulse inside out, calcifies the mind, wrings dissent into useless animosity. Here it is useful to think of Hitchens, whose tragedy is his about-face from progressive revolutionary atheist to cheerleader for American empire in his late life. What once scanned as a playfully per-verse fascination with conservatism as a revolutionary force (see: the time he called Margaret Thatcher "surprisingly sexy") curdled into a full-bore endorsement of military expansionism and Crusade-like wars against Islam.

As the evolution of the modern troll illustrates, what begins as a curiosity, or even an ironic fascination, can with rotten thinking, when the veil of irony and reflexive-cynicism drops, reveal itself as utterly sincere. A spirited contrarian can slump into a raving crank and, ultimately, further sag into a mindless menace. Avoid this at all costs. It would be a shame to have to hate-watch yourself as you slumber through life.

Don't be afraid to take things on faith. Like, not necessar-ily *faith* faith. Claims of "God told me to!" rarely weather healthy skepticism any more than comparable claims like "The devil made me do it." But the present makes mincemeat of skepticism. It uses suspicion as a pretense for calling into ques-tion the character of reality itself. Look no further than the slogan of Russian propaganda media network RT: "Question everything." Question, yes. But don't be afraid to have beliefs, convictions, axioms, well-earned opinions, and attitudes that can not only console but also help deepen and enliven your thoughts.

If this all sounds too airy-fairy (or worse, disingenuous), then here's another one: Be funny. Be vulgar and rude. Use humor to afflict the comfortable, and comfort the afflicted. The myth that "the left is love" is generally propagated by enemies of progress in order to make the hopeful seem naive, silly, and weak. It's obscene. And a good way to fight back against it is with obscen-ity. Harness that gurgling meanness, that skepticism and direct it toward worthy targets. Your disagreeability can be virtuous, X. But only if you render it so.

Finally, X, it is probably obvious that I have to incorporate the wisdom of others, from philosophers to film critics to *Simpsons* characters. I have done so, primarily, because I consider myself something of an autodidact: a wide and voracious reader whose ideas and outlook are cobbled together from the hard work of others. My hope is that such acquired insight has been wielded like a lantern, to pierce the gathering fog and light the darkness. My worry is that I've used the hard work of others less like a lantern and more like a drunk uses a lamppost: as something to prop himself up against. In fairness, and humility, I recognize that it's probably a bit of both.

Still, it feels fitting that I offer the last word in this book to someone wiser, wittier, and likely a good deal meaner than me: Austrian critic, satirist, and top-shelf hater Karl Kraus. "Hate," Kraus wrote, "must make a person productive. Otherwise one might as well love."

Adios for now.
Your friend,
John

P.S. X, I'm serious. *Lulu* is worth a second look.

◄ NOTES ►

PART 1
— *Friends of the Devil* —

Thomas Aquinas quote
Summa Theologica, Pars Prima Secundae, Parts I–II.

"ally of the status quo"
Christopher Hitchens, *Hell's Angel.* TV Documentary. Directed by
Jenny Morgan. UK, 1994.

Diogenes Laërtius (no relation) writes
Diogenes Laërtius, *Lives and Opinions of Eminent Greek Philosophers*. 1925.
New York: G.P. Putnam's Sons, 23.

"It was through that . . . a philosopher."
Ibid, 51

sentenced to "home-staying."
Ibid

"I would have you stand from between me and the sun."
Plutarch, *The Life of Alexander the Great*, trans. John Dryden. 2004.
New York: The Modern Library, 14.

If constructing the future . . . with the powers that be.
Karl Marx, "Marx to Ruge: Kreuznach, September 1843," reprinted at:
https://www.marxists.org/archive/marx/works/1843/letters/43_09.htm

— *Metacriticism and the Rotten Fruit of Consensus* —

"demoralized by tomatoes."
http://query.nytimes.com/mem/archive-free/pdf?_r=1&res=9D0DE1DD153
8E033A2575BC2A9669D94629FD7CF&oref=slogin (accessed Feb. 22, 2018).

". . . a perfect shower of tomatoes."
Ibid

". . . to concessions for private privies."
Juvenal, *The Satires of Juvenal*, trans. 1958. Rolf Humphries. Bloomington:
Indiana University Press, 35.

". . . trademarked rating system were taken."
https://editorial.rottentomatoes.com/article/an-oral-history-of-rt-part-one-
the-beginning/ (accessed Feb. 22, 2018).

". . . movies that people hadn't even seen."
Qtd. in Erin Carlson, "Rotten Tomatoes Shuts Down *Dark Knight Rises*
Comments," *The Hollywood Reporter*, July 18, 2012.

"What he doesn't get . . . superheroic things."
Ed Power, "Black Panther first review: 'It is expected to stand for something
bigger than itself—the strain is visible.'" *The Irish Independent*, Feb. 6, 2018.
www.independent.ie/entertainment/movies/movie-reviews/black-panther-
first-review-it-is-expected-to-stand-for-something-bigger-than-itself-the-strain-
is-visible-36573275.html (accessed Feb. 22, 2018).

— *Upworthiness and the Dangers of Being so Damn Agreeable* —

Donald Trump told *Fox News*
Qtd in "Trump credits social media for his election," *Politico*, Oct. 20, 2017.

". . . the spectre of a bubble."
"Bursting the Facebook bubble: We asked voters on the left and right to swap
feeds," *The Guardian*, Nov. 16, 2016.

"selecting relish over mustard."
Nicholas Negroponte, *Being Digital*. 1995. New York: Alfred A. Knopf Inc., 164.

"fantasy of abundance."
Jodi Dean, *Blog Theory: Feedback and Capture in the Circuits of Drive*. 2010. Malden,
MA: Polity Press, 41.

"It's like reading a book by a fool."

"Bursting the Facebook bubble: We asked voters on the left and right to swap feeds," *The Guardian*, Nov. 16, 2016.

". . . an obstacle to their triumph."
Gustave Le Bon, *The Crowd: A Study of the Popular Mind*. 2002. Mineola: Dover Publications, Inc.

"the fail is strong in this one"
Shared by the popular (in Ontario, Canada, at least) Facebook page "Ontario Proud" in March 2018.

"15 Reasons Why Pizza Is Actually Really F*cking Good For You"
Published by the website *Elite Daily* in 2015.

". . . encounter and work with negativity."
Byung-Chul Han, *In The Swarm*, trans. Erik Butler. 2017. Cambridge, Mass: The MIT Press, 22.

ideas of conflict and harmony themselves.
Barbara Ehrenreich, *Natural Causes: An Epidemic of Wellness, The Certainty of Dying, and Killing Ourselves to Live Longer*. 2018. New York: Twelve Books, 112.

". . . what I hate I do."
Bible, Romans 7:15.

"live in the same contradiction."
Albert Camus, *The Rebel: An Essay on Man in Revolt*, trans. 1991. Anthony Bower. New York: Vintage Books, 272.

". . . and dies with a sword in hand."
Arthur Schopenhauer, *Essays and Aphorisms*, ed. and trans. R.J. Hollingdale. 1970. New York: Penguin Books, 42.

elimination of freedom itself.
Ibid, 288

PART 2
— The New Tastelessness —

"... a thousand distastes"
Paul Valéry, *The Collected Works of Paul Valéry: History and Politics*, Vol. 10, trans.
D. Folliot and J. Matthews. 1971. Princeton: Princeton University Press, 471.

"Taste ... symbolic sub-spaces."
Pierre Bourdieu, *Distinction: A Social Critique of the Judgment of Taste*, trans.
Richard Nice. 1985. Cambridge: Harvard University Press, 173.

Warhol's boxes of soap pads
The American art critic Arthur Danto has written extensively on Warhol's
Brillo Box, using the work as a launching pad for grappling with higher-order
questions about what even constitutes a work of art. See, for example,
The Philosophical Disenfranchisement of Art. 1986. New York: Columbia
University Press.

ascension of Miller High Life
A 2017 *Business Insider* article on High Life's growth in the beer sector accounted
for it thusly: "Your dad's favorite beer is making a huge comeback thanks to
hipsters—and execs are thrilled." http://www.businessinsider.com/miller-
high-life-is-becoming-more-popular-2017-6 (accessed June 5, 2018).

"... the sociology of taste."
https://nplusonemag.com/issue-16/the-intellectual-situation/too-much-
sociology (accessed June 5, 2018).

demystification sociology requires
Ibid

Jeff Bezos cops the jargon of sociology
Qtd in. https://nplusonemag.com/issue-16/the-intellectual-situation/
too-much-sociology (accessed June 5, 2018).

Deep-Fried Chocolate Broccoli:
Premium Cable, Poptimism, and the Extreme Middle Brow

"... how good they may be for me."
www.nytimes.com/2011/05/01/magazine/mag-01Riff-t.html
(accessed June 7, 2018).

". . . personal opinion and analysis."
Merriam-Webster, "think piece." https://www.merriam-webster.com/
dictionary/think%20piece (accessed May 27, 2018).

"journalistic, think-piece nature"
Buckley Barry Barrett, *Churchill: A Concise Bibliography*, 2000. London:
Greenwood Press, 66.

". . . pay for this kind of storytelling."
Ian Leslie, "Watch It While It Lasts: Our Golden Age of Television,"
Financial Times, April 13, 2017.

"Fuck the average viewer."
The Culture Show, "Series 9, Episode 7," BBC2, November 2008.

Anna Leszkiewicz
Qtd. in Caroline Crampton, "Why we like podcasts that break down
TV episode by episode," *The New Statesman*, December 15, 2016.
https://www.newstatesman.com/culture/podcasts/2016/12/why-
we-podcasts-break-down-tv-episode-episode (accessed March 14, 2018).

". . . logical organization, length"
Qtd. in *The Art of the Personal Essay: An Anthology from the Classical Era to
the Present*, ed. Phillip Lopate. 1995. New York: Anchor Books, xxiii.

Why a 'Black Panther' Movie Is Revolutionary.
Tre Johnson, "Black Superheroes Matter: Why a 'Black Panther' Movie Is
Revolutionary," *Rolling Stone*, Feb. 16, 2018. www.rollingstone.com/movies/
news/black-superheroes-matter-why-black-panther-is-revolutionary-w509105
(accessed Apr. 18, 2018).

". . . Just get it out there."
Dave Schilling, "How to Write a Think Piece," *Vice*, Dec. 22, 2013.
https://www.vice.com/en_ca/article/9bzyj3/how-to-write-a-think-
piece (accessed Apr. 18, 2018).

"Poptimism. . . seals of approval."
Saul Austerlitz, "The Pernicious Rise of Poptimism," *The New York Times
Magazine*, Apr. 4, 2014. https://www.nytimes.com/2014/04/06/magazine/
the-pernicious-rise-of-poptimism (accessed Apr. 18, 2018).

". . . compassion for the common man?"
Kent Jones, "Life Goes On," *Physical Evidence: Selected Film Criticism*. 2007.
Middletown: Wesleyan University Press, 11.

"... Bruce Springsteen and Beyoncé."
A question posed, albeit rhetorically, in Jody Rosen's 2006 *Slate* essay "The Perils of Poptimism." http://www.slate.com/articles/arts/music_box/2006/05/the_perils_of_poptimism.html (accessed June 3, 2018).

"... are thus entitled to be less so."
Marcel Proust, "Notes to *Sesame and Lilies*," *On Reading Ruskin*, trans. and ed. Jean Autret, William Burford, and Phillip J. Wolfe. 1987. New Haven: Yale University Press, 152.

text becomes narrowly "intelligible."
Susan Sontag, *Against Interpretation and Other Essays*, 2013. New York: Picador, 2013. eBook edition.

a mental scheme of categories
Ibid.

"... mediocrity pays to genius."
Ibid.

— *The Sleeper Has Awokened* —

"socially conscious criticism"
www.vox.com/culture/2017/4/20/15179232/socially-conscious-criticism (accessed Apr. 12, 2018).

"progressive" and "reactionary"
Robin Wood, "An Introduction to the American Horror Film," *Planks of Reason: Essays on the Horror Films*, revised ed. Berry Keith Grant and Christopher Sharrett. 2004. Lanham, Maryland: The Scarecrow Press, Inc., 107–141.

toxified society with its sameness
Max Horkheimer and Theodor W. Adorno, *Dialectic of Enlightenment: Philosophical Fragments*. 2002. Stanford, California: Stanford University Press.

the aesthetic form as such
Herbert Marcuse, *The Aesthetic Dimension: Towards A Critique of Marxist Aesthetics*. 1977. Boston: Beacon Press, ix.

seen as too vivid and corrupting
For more on this, check out Tom Gunning's edifying essay "Flickers: On Cinema's Power for Evil." Tom Gunning, "Flickers: On Cinema's Power for

Evil," *Bad: Infamy, Darkness, Evil and Slime on Screen*, ed. Murray Pomerance. 2004. Albany: State University of New York Press, 21–38.

". . . or clangingly missing it."
www.villagevoice.com/2018/01/23/2017-pazz-jop-surprises-slowdive-yes-taylor-meh (accessed Apr. 12, 2018).

"an erotics of art" and "culture based on excess, on overproduction"
Susan Sontag, *Against Interpretation and Other Essays*. 2013. New York: Picador. eBook edition.

damning accusation of *pretentiousness*
As Dan Fox notes in his lively essay *Pretentiousness: Why It Matters*, calling someone or something "pretentious" is often a reflexive gesture: "The pretentious flaws of others affirm your own intellectual or aesthetic expertise. Simultaneously, their fakery highlights the contours of your down-to-earth character and virtuous ordinariness." Dan Fox, *Pretentiousness: Why It Matters*. 2016. London: Fitzcarraldo Editions, 127–128.

PART 3
— To Thyself Be Enough —

". . . writing about movies to writing against viewers."
https://hazlitt.net/feature/critical-failure (accessed Mar. 18, 2018).

"the enormity of life itself."
www.nyfcc.com/2013/05/bay-watch-armond-whites-transformers-2-review-for-cityarts/ (accessed Mar. 18, 2018).

". . .as a problem *is* the problem."
https://nowtoronto.com/movies/armond-white-is-the-kanye-of-film-criticism/ (accessed Mar. 18 2018).

". . . criticism with a flaming sword."
www.filmcomment.com/blog/bombast-ad-hominem-ad-nauseam/ (accessed Mar. 18, 2018).

". . . encouraging them to experience catharsis."
www.nypress.com/what-we-dont-talk-about-when-we-talk-about-movies/ (accessed Mar. 18, 2018).

often fails in the presence of fact
"How empty is theory in presence of fact!" in Mark Twain, *A Connecticut Yankee in King Arthur's Court*. 2016. Woodstock, Ontario: Devoted Publishing, 154.

undertaken with both frankness and sincerity
Henry James, "The Art of Fiction" in *The Critical Tradition*, 3rd edition, ed. David H. Richter. 2016. Boston: Bedford/St. Martin's, 298.

—— *The Contrarian Deformation* ——

". . . like 4chan that later fused with the alt-right"
Angela Nagle, *Kill All Normies*. 2017. Washington: Zero Books, 31.

". . . and coax free porn from each other."
http://gawker.com/346385/what-the-hell-are-4chan-ed-something-awful-and-b (accessed Apr. 24, 2018).

"We actually elected a meme as president."
Qtd. in www.washingtonpost.com/news/the-intersect/wp/2016/11/09/we-actually-elected-a-meme-as-president-how-4chan-celebrated-trumps-victory/?utm_term=.c03c7b4ccd8b (accessed Apr. 28, 2018).

". . . an arena for angry minds."
Richard Hofstadter, "The Paranoid Style in American Politics, *Harper's*, November 1964.

New York Protestant Vindicator
Qtd. in Henry Fish, *Jesuitism Traced in the Movements of the Oxford Tractarians*. 1842. London: Hamilton, Adams, and Co., 12.

"the unbelievable is the only thing that can be believed."
Hofstadter, "Paranoid Style."

"the paranoid mind is far more coherent than the real world."
Ibid

". . . laws of political gravity do not apply."
David Neiwert, *Alt-America: The Rise of the Radical Right in the Age of Trump*. 2017. New York: Verso Books, 4.

". . . people that makes the phenomenon significant."
Hofstadter, "Paranoid Style."

". . . Trump's message even as they ostensibly scrutinized it."
Yascha Mounk, *The People vs. Democracy: Why Our Freedom Is in Danger & How to Save It*. 2018. Cambridge, MA: Harvard University Press, 144.

— *The New Irrationality (or I Fucking Hate Science)* —

"Quarks are quirky beasts"
Neil DeGrasse Tyson, *Astrophysics For People In A Hurry*. 2018. New York: W.W. Norton & Company, 22.

". . . still engaged in productive research."
Sergio Simondo, *An Introduction to Science and Technology Studies*, 2nd edition. 2011. Hoboken, NJ: Wiley-Blackwell. ebook edition.

". . . the truth or falsity of their content."
Hofstadter, "Paranoid Style.

PART 4
— *Reconsidering the Curmudgeon* —

In his 1755 *Dictionary of English Language*
Samuel Johnson, *Johnson's Dictionary: A Modern Selection*, eds. E.L. McAdam, Jr. and George Milne. 2005. Mineola, 142.

". . . Offense is their only defense."
Jon Winokur, *The Portable Curmudgeon*. 1987. New York: Plume, 1.

". . . Of all that breathes and moves upon the earth."
Homer, *The Iliad*, trans. Stanley Lombardo. 1997. Indianapolis: Hackett Publishing Company, Inc., 345.

". . . crazy, a nightmare: a bitch."
Elizabeth Wurtzel, *Bitch: In Praise of Difficult Women*. 1999. New York: Anchor Books, 30.

". . . and their patrons is heating up."
www.theglobeandmail.com/life/food-and-wine/the-rise-of-dining-aggression-dear-table-2-we-think-youre-kind-of-rude/article10958714/ (accessed Mar. 23, 2018).

". . . reclaims the b-word"
www.chatelaine.com/living/jen-agg-i-hear-shes-a-real-bitch/
(accessed Mar. 23, 2018).

". . . makes a show of spitting in your coffee."
https://torontolife.com/food/restaurants/the-critic-grey-gardens-
wine-bar-kensington-market-jen-agg/ (accessed Mar. 23, 2018).

— *How to Hate with Care* —

". . . friendship and faithful stick-to-itiveness."
www.theglobeandmail.com/arts/film/film-reviews/with-entourage-
hollywood-fails-in-its-transparent-attempt-to-make-itself-likeable/
article24747551/ (accessed Apr. 3, 2018).

". . . everyone else out there seems to suck at it."
https://deadspin.com/the-haters-guide-to-other-parents-507454898
(accessed Apr. 5, 2018).

". . . played a definite role in her life."
Jonathan Gray, "New Audiences, New Textualities: Anti-Fans and Non-Fans,"
International Journal of Cultural Studies, Vol. 6, Issue 1, 71. March 1, 2003.

". . . as they delight in quality programming."
www.bbc.com/culture/story/20170616-the-joy-of-hate-watching (accessed
Mar. 21, 2018).

". . . a show that makes me so mad?"
Emily Nussbaum, "Hate-watching 'Smash,'" *The New Yorker*, April 27, 2017.
https://www.newyorker.com/culture/culture-desk/hate-watching-smash
(accessed June 27, 2018).

". . . excluded from the conversation of my friends."
Gray, "New Audiences, New Textualities," 71.

"the most cynical dating app ever."
www.cnbc.com/2017/11/27/shark-tank-mark-cuban-invested-200000-in-
dating-app-hater.html (accessed Mar. 21, 2018).

". . . And even your upside-down heart, I love."
Shark Tank, Season 9, Episode 12. Episode 909, ABC, November 26, 2017.

". . . diagnostic information about attitude holders"
https://onlinelibrary.wiley.com/doi/abs/10.1111/j.1475-6811.2006.00109.x
(accessed Mar. 21, 2018).

— *Like Rocks toward the Gatehouse (or The Problem of Post-Critique)* —

"gesture of joy."
Qtd. in www.nytimes.com/2000/10/19/nyregion/columbia-debates-a-
professor-s-gesture.html (accessed Mar. 25, 2018).

". . . cultural artifacts as socially symbolic acts."
Fredric Jameson, *The Political Unconscious*. 1983. New York: Routledge, 5.

". . . Has it run out of steam?"
Bruno Latour, "Why Has Critique Run out of Steam? From Matters of Fact
to Matters of Concern" in *Critical Inquiry*. 2004. Chicago: The University of
Chicago, 225.

". . . between aesthetic virtue and political virtue."
Jacques Rancière, *The Politics of Aesthetics*, trans. Gabriel Rockhill. 2010.
London: Bloomsbury, 62.

"such a life is worth living on its own account."
Christopher Hitchens, *Letters to a Young Contrarian*. 2001. New York:
Basic Books, 35.

— *Gotta Have Faith (or Nu Metal Is Actually Bad, Though)* —

". . . somebody weaker to fuck up for a change."
https://music.avclub.com/part-9-1998-you-re-either-with-korn-and-
limp-bizkit-1798224287 (accessed Mar. 28, 2018).

". . . their more critically acceptable counterparts."
www.theguardian.com/music/musicblog/2008/feb/06/whyitsworth
celebratingnume (accessed Mar. 28, 2018).

". . . some things on trust or you can't survive."
Quoted in Chris Hedges, *The Death of the Liberal Class*. 2010. Toronto:
Vintage Canada, 37.

— *Dissensus and the Return to the Aesthetic Dimension* —

". . . movies in our state of disunion."
www.nytimes.com/2017/09/07/movies/movies-politics-conservatives-liberals.
html?ref=todayspaper (accessed Mar. 30, 2018).

"the essence of politics."
Rancière, *Dissensus: On Aesthetics and Politics*, ed. and trans. Steve Corcoran. 2010.
London: Continuum Books, 38.

"gap in the sensible"
Ibid

". . . the one who thinks differently."
Rosa Luxemburg, *The Russian Revolution*. 1940. New York: Workers Age Publishers.

"inexorably indirect, mediated, and frustrating."
Herbert Marcuse, *The Aesthetic Dimension*. 1977. Boston: Beacon Press, xii.

"element of despair"
Ibid, 1

"dialectic of affirmation and negation"
Ibid, 62.

". . . into a source of hopeful world-making."
Christopher Catiglia, "Hope for Critique?" in *Critique and Postcritique*, eds.
Elizabeth S. Anker and Rita Felski. 2017. Durham, NC: Duke University
Press, 225.

AFTERWORD

"help them avoid disillusionment"
Hitchens, *Letters*, xiii.

"egalitarianism is its greatest quality."
Jon Ronson, *So You've Been Publicly Shamed*. 2015. New York: Riverhead
Books, 271.

". . . . Otherwise one might as well love."
Karl Kraus, *Half-Truths & One-and-a-Half-Truths: Selected Aphorisms*, ed.
and trans. Harry Zohn. 1990. Chicago: University of Chicago Press, 57.

◄ ACKNOWLEDGMENTS ►

First and foremost, I'd like to thank my kind, thoughtful, judicious editor, Justin Stoller at Penguin Random House Canada, for helping develop this project from the ground up. We originally met to kick around another idea, but Justin, apparently, recognized something more valuable in my seething distemper and writhing annoyance. So thanks, Justin, for helping me shape that distemper/annoyance into something (hopefully) productive.

And hey, speaking of editors—I'd also like to thank the editors at various outlets who gave me the time and space to develop certain ideas appearing in this book and, even more importantly, for allowing me to sustain a living as a writer. So: to Sarmishta Subramanian at *The Literary Review of Canada*; Barry Hertz, Craig Offman, Mark Medley, Domini Clark, and Clifford Lee at *The Globe and Mail*; Adrian Lee at *Maclean's*; Manny Howard at *Salon*; and Drew Nelles (formerly) at *The Walrus*.

Some of the ideas in this book fermented over years, in various articles commissioned by these editors. The sections on think pieces, poptimism, and "woke criticism" appear in different forms in an essay published in *The Literary Review of Canada* ("Did virtue and the think piece ruin criticism?," April 2018) and a *Salon* essay ("The Utility of Snobbery," January 2018). The stuff about hate-watching, and hate-watching *Entourage* in particular, appeared in a different form in *Salon* as "How to re-watch

Entourage" (July 2017), and the section on pop science and scientism also appeared, in an earlier version, in *Salon* as "I F***ing Hate Science" (May 2017). The comments about Nickelback, Limp Bizkit, and the process of critical redemption of Bad Things took shape in a *Walrus* essay on Nickelback ("Too Bad," March 2015). I am extra-indebted to my assigning editors on these pieces, for helping me to develop some of the threads drawn out herein.

Thanks also to Nicole Winstanley, Tonia Addison, Kara Carnduff, Andrew Roberts, Eleanor Gasparik, Chandra Wohleber, and everyone at Penguin Random House Canada for helping to bring this book into the world. I'd also like to thank literary agent Sam Hiyate and the team at The Rights Factory for their hard work on the backend.

On the more personal front, a hale and hearty shout-out to my friends and family, and everyone who indulged me as I bent their ears with my griping and moaning as I worked through writing this book (to say nothing of my more generalized griping and moaning), especially: Lee, Jonah, Courtney, Dory, Ed, Michael, Lauchie, Doyle, Laura, and anyone else gracious enough to suffer the spikier, more utterly disagreeable edges of my personality.

I'd also like to thank the team of developers of Bethesda Game Studios for their fantastic work on the immersive fantasy-adventure game *Elder Scrolls V: Skyrim*, which offered me hours of reprieve from the stresses of writing, and even more hours of distraction from stresses same.

Thanks abound to Raina, of course, for your unwavering, frankly unbelievable love, support, patience, and perpetually replenishing kindness. And the laughs.

Finally, and maybe most importantly, my boundless thanks and appreciation to anyone who reads this book, and who might glean something of value from it. Hold your angst tight. Stay on the edge. It's where you gotta be.

THE CORPSE OF ST JAMES'S

The Dorothy Martin Mysteries from Jeanne M. Dams

THE BODY IN THE TRANSEPT
TROUBLE IN THE TOWN HALL
HOLY TERROR IN THE HEBRIDES
MALICE IN MINIATURE
THE VICTIM IN VICTORIA STATION
KILLING CASSIDY
TO PERISH IN PENZANCE
SINS OUT OF SCHOOL
WINTER OF DISCONTENT
A DARK AND STORMY NIGHT *
THE EVIL THAT MEN DO *
THE CORPSE OF ST JAMES'S *

* *available from Severn House*

THE CORPSE OF
ST JAMES'S

A Dorothy Martin Mystery

Jeanne M. Dams

This first world edition published 2012
in Great Britain and in the USA by
SEVERN HOUSE PUBLISHERS LTD of
9–15 High Street, Sutton, Surrey, England, SM1 1DF.
Trade paperback edition first published
in Great Britain and the USA 2013 by
SEVERN HOUSE PUBLISHERS LTD.

British Library Cataloguing in Publication Data

Dams, Jeanne M.
  The corpse of St James's.
  1. Martin, Dorothy (Fictitious character) – Fiction.
  2. Detective and mystery stories.
  I. Title
  813.5'4-dc23

ISBN-13: 978-0-7278-8185-4 (cased)
ISBN-13: 978-1-84751-440-0 (trade paper)

All Severn House titles are printed on acid-free paper.

Severn House Publishers support The Forest Stewardship Council [FSC],
the leading international forest certification organisation. All our titles that
are printed on Greenpeace-approved FSC-certified paper carry the FSC logo.

Typeset by Palimpsest Book Production Ltd.,
Falkirk, Stirlingshire, Scotland.
Printed and bound in Great Britain by
MPG Books Ltd., Bodmin, Cornwall.

This book is dedicated to the memory of Christopher Dean, late chairman of the Dorothy L. Sayers Society and dear friend. Without his help many of my books could not have been written. He and his delightful wife Christine provided me, over the years, with counsel on everything from British English to Buckingham Palace protocol, and with gracious hospitality whenever I visited the UK. I will miss him more than I can say.

FOREWORD

Dorothy L. Sayers described her final novel, *Busman's Honeymoon*, as a 'love story with detective interruptions'. This book might also be described in those terms, but in this case the beloved is London, city of my dreams. My love affair with London goes back more years than I care to say, dating back to when my parents took me there as a gift upon my graduation from college. I fell in love on the spot and have never changed my mind. So if there's rather a lot of travelogue interspersed with a bit of murder here and there, don't say you haven't been warned.

ONE

'And this is the celebrated Bloody Tower, where they say the Princes in the Tower were murdered by their wicked uncle, King Richard the Third.'

I must have made a face or some sort of protesting noise, because the Beefeater turned to me with an amused expression. 'Ah,' he said, 'there's a lady who doesn't believe it. Been doing some reading, have you, madam?'

'*Daughter of Time*,' I murmured. 'A very persuasive argument.'

'So I've heard. I don't suppose we'll ever know the truth of it, will we? Now on your left—'

'What are you talking about?' asked one of my guests in a whisper.

'Tell you later. We mustn't be rude to our guide.'

I was touring the Tower of London for the umpteenth time, shepherding two visiting Americans, house guests of my good friends the Andersons. Tom and Lynn had another obligation that day and had been grateful when I offered to play hostess and show them some of the obligatory sights of London.

'My dear, you are a *saint*!' Lynn had said. 'You'll be bored to tears. All those appalling tourist attractions!'

'Not I. I'm besotted with English history and English royalty, as you very well know. Besides, when you're tired of London—'

'You're tired of life. Thank you, Samuel Johnson.'

It was quite true, though. Yes, London is dirty and noisy. Yes, it's full of foreigners. You can hear virtually every language known to man as you walk its crowded streets or negotiate its old and inconvenient railway stations. But the great old grey city teems with life, and for those with eyes to see, and even a modicum of appreciation for history, there's a new delight around every corner. There's the pub where the aforementioned Johnson used to take his ale of an evening and propound, Boswell faithfully taking down every word (or inventing them, as I've often suspected). There's the house where Charles Dickens once lived, and over there Robert Browning, and there Dorothy L. Sayers. In some neighbourhoods the blue memorial plaques decorate nearly every wall. In that hospital, inside *those very walls*, Florence Nightingale tried against formidable odds to elevate nursing to an honourable profession. Over there is the tiny museum devoted to the history of Judaism in England, and there the huge Museum of London. And when you're tired of looking and walking, and your sense of awe is sated, you're only a few steps away from a café where you can get lovely tea and cakes, or a pub where you can get an even lovelier pint.

So even though, nowadays, the café might be operated by Starbucks, and the pub might have Budweiser on offer, I still adore London, and I truly love showing people around what I've come to think of as 'my' London.

It isn't, of course, possible to cover everything in a short time. Unlike the sailors in *On the Town*, who tried to see all of New York 'in just one day', when one day is all the time I'm given, I stick to the royal tour. Show me an American who isn't fascinated by the House of Windsor, especially since William and Kate's wedding, and I'll show you an American who isn't planning to visit England anyway.

I should perhaps explain myself. My name is Dorothy Martin and I'm an American, born and raised in Indiana, who lived my whole life there until the death of my first husband. We had planned to move to England when he retired, having spent vacations in various parts of the country for many years. When Frank died, I was too numb to do anything but follow already-laid plans to move to the small cathedral city of Sherebury, and that opened up a new life for me. I've lived in Sherebury ever since, and have been happily married for some years to Alan Nesbitt, a retired chief constable and an utter dear.

My American friends visit us a good deal, as do friends of friends, so for first-time visitors I've worked out a route that covers in a day all the can't-miss London high spots. On pleasant days, if my guests are young and fit, we do most of it on foot. From Victoria Station it's an easy walk up

Buckingham Palace Road to Birdcage Walk. (Birdcage Walk! I ask you. Who could fail to be enchanted by a street name like that?) That's where the Guards live, as in 'Changing of the'. If it's a day for the ceremony, we stand there by the barracks fence and watch the Guards muster while the band plays. One gets a much better view of the pageantry there than at the palace gates, where the crowds are always about twenty deep.

Then back to Buckingham Palace for the tour, if I've been able to get tickets. The tours run from late July through September, and are well worth the stiffish admission price. Even if you've seen lots of stately homes, this one is super special. It is, after all, still a family home for perhaps the most famous family in the world. I doubt that a visitor has ever glimpsed the Queen whisking out of sight at the end of a corridor, but one lives in hope!

After the palace tour, and perhaps a break for tea or a pint, we walk back up Birdcage Walk, with St James's Park on one side (if we're lucky, we see a pelican or two) and find ourselves in Parliament Square, with its statue of, among others, Abraham Lincoln. That always amazes American visitors, and touches most of them deeply. Myself, I have to blink away tears. But that's often a problem for me in this part of London. Here, just a few feet away, is Westminster Abbey, burial or memorial site for countless people whose lives have profoundly affected mine. One can't move inside without stepping on the grave of someone breathtakingly famous. Charles Dickens, Jane Austen, the Brontës, Benjamin Britten, Winston Churchill. Chaucer, for Pete's sake! There's even a statue of Martin Luther King, Jr, right there on the west front of the Abbey.

And just over there, looming ahead, golden in the sunshine, are the Houses of Parliament. Never mind that it's a Victorian structure, a replacement for the old Palace of Westminster that was destroyed by fire. It still represents the foundation of my own democracy, the idea of government by elected representatives, and I get teary again whenever I see it.

I guess I'm just sentimental. I cry at parades, too, and my throat tightens so much I can't sing some patriotic songs.

Having looked over the Abbey and gazed in awe at Big

Ben, if we haven't worn ourselves out touring the palace we then head for the culmination of the day, the Tower of London. It's much too far to walk, so we have our choice of the Tube, a riverboat if a convenient one is leaving about then, or a cab. I leave the decision to my guests, who may or may not be adventurous. My own choice would always be a tour boat, because London seen from the river is quite different from London seen from the streets, and the Thames is after all the way royal prisoners were taken to the Tower . . .

There I go again, caught up in history.

The weather on this early September day was not very pleasant. Although no actual rain was falling, something between a heavy mist and a fine drizzle hung in the air. The English call it a mizzle, a word which, with its echoes of 'miserable', I find quite appropriate. We opted for a cab, to heck with the expense. My tourists were inclined to be grumpy about the dampness, but I pointed out brightly that the weather kept the crowds down, and we'd have a much better chance of seeing the Crown Jewels without waiting in a long queue. That cheered them up a bit. I think their feet were hurting them. I know mine were beginning to complain.

However, Alice and Joe were troupers, and at their first sight of a Beefeater they forgot about the weather.

'My gosh!' said Alice in a stage whisper. 'Do they dress like that all the time? I've seen pictures, but I thought it was just fancy dress for special occasions.'

Our guide heard, and was amused. 'Actually, madam, these are our everyday uniforms, known as "undress". The dress uniform, the one you've seen on the gin bottle, with the gold bands and ruff and rosettes and all, is worn for those special occasions you mention, and is, incidentally, extremely uncomfortable.'

The weather had done its work, and visitors to the Tower were few enough that our small party had a Beefeater all to ourselves. He explained that they are properly called Yeomen Warders – not to be confused with the Yeomen of the Guard, Gilbert and Sullivan to the contrary notwithstanding. 'But everyone calls us Beefeaters; not to worry, madam.'

We saw it all. The famed wing-clipped ravens, whose

departure from the Tower would, according to legend, bring about the fall of the kingdom, were their usual raucous selves. Our guide wasn't the Raven Master, but he had quite a stock of stories about the birds. 'They have to be sacked sometimes, you know, if they get to be too rowdy. One liked to eat the television aerials, so he was booted out. And one developed a taste for beer and managed somehow to get out and take up residence at a neighbouring pub!'

We all laughed at that, but when the guide began to get into the history of the Tower, we were quickly sobered. The Traitor's Gate, through which several notable prisoners were brought to be tried and executed, looked suitably ominous on that grey day, and we were silent for a moment after the pitiful story of Anne Boleyn.

'I've heard she was very beautiful,' said Joe after the pause. 'How old was she?'

'No one knows for certain when she was born,' said the Beefeater, 'but she may have been as young as twenty-nine.'

'And never knew her daughter would become the most powerful monarch England would ever have,' said Alice sadly.

'Don't you suppose she knows now?' I asked softly, and our guide smiled at me.

My guests were suitably awed by the Crown Jewels, although I must admit I found the old display (which you can glimpse in the movie *Gaslight*), more imposing than the present one. I suppose the new one is more secure, and sadly, security must be a primary concern these days.

We were all tired and footsore by the time we finished the tour. Fortunately I know a very pleasant pub nearby, and when we were seated over our pints and sandwiches in the Minories, Alice brought up the brief exchange about the Princes in the Tower.

'Oh, dear, it's one of my hobby horses, I'm afraid. For years history books said that Richard the Third killed his two little nephews, but some historians took a different view. Then an author named Josephine Tey wrote a book called *The Daughter of Time*, which set out, in a fictional framework, the alternative explanation that Henry the Seventh was responsible for the boys' death.'

I went into a little of the history, but I was losing my audience. 'Right, then,' I said, setting down my empty glass. 'Let's get you two tired people home. There's no end to the history one can unearth in London, but now isn't the time to do it.'

'Well,' said Alice apologetically, 'maybe we have had enough bloodshed for one day. History does seem to be just one long succession of murders, doesn't it?'

I laughed at that. 'I suppose the long years and decades when all was going well and nothing much happened don't get recorded by the historians. Not interesting enough!'

I was to remember that remark, and ponder about that word *interesting*. In the sense of the old Chinese curse, perhaps?

TWO

That rainy September day presaged a wet autumn and a dreary winter with little snow, but a great deal of rain and sleet and mist and general unpleasantness. Spring was just beginning to make some welcome overtures in late February, when the letter arrived.

The outer envelope enclosed another, a large one in cream-coloured stock so thick it was nearly card stock, with, on the back flap, the letters ER embossed in gold.

'What on earth . . .?' I held it out for Alan's inspection.

'Well, my dear, there's one way to find out, isn't there?' He pulled out a folded note and then the contents of the imposing envelope, and then, eyebrows raised, handed it all to me.

'. . . invite you to attend . . . George Cross . . . twenty-third of May . . .' I read it once, and then again, and then glanced at the handwritten note on the bottom. I frowned in puzzlement. 'Alan, what *is* this all about?'

'It's about an honour, Dorothy. A whacking great honour. You remember last summer, when Jonathan jolly nearly bought it, rescuing that little girl?'

'Of course I remember!' I shuddered. Jonathan Quinn, a

Scotland Yard inspector and a good friend of Alan's, had been investigating a house suspected of harbouring terrorists, when shooting and a fire had broken out. In the middle of the worst of it, Jonathan had seen a small face at an upstairs window. At great risk to his own life, he had broken into the house and rescued the child, who was in the end unhurt, at least physically. Jonathan had been shot at and badly wounded, so badly that there was grave question about his survival.

The story had touched the hearts of millions, not only in the UK but all over the world, and when it became apparent that Jonathan was permanently unfit for further duty as a policeman, gifts and offers of employment had poured in. Jonathan had refused the gifts, with a good deal of embarrassment, or so I understood from what Alan told me. He was still trying to decide about employment, his pension from a grateful nation being quite insufficient to support himself.

'You met Jonathan when you were doing that stint at Bramshill, didn't you?' Very early in our marriage, Alan had served as temporary commandant at what was then called the Police Staff College at Bramshill, a very lovely Jacobean manor house in Hampshire.

'Yes, and you first met him there, too. He was very keen on his job, and already making a name for himself with the Met. It's a great pity.'

'At least he's alive, which was pretty iffy there for a while.' I looked again at the rather daunting invitation. 'I don't suppose there's any money connected with this "whacking great honour".'

Alan looked slightly shocked. 'My dear woman, the George Cross is beyond price! It's the highest civilian honour awarded in this country, and jolly few of them have ever been given.'

I made suitably awed noises, still wondering how the poor man was going to buy his tea and biscuits. 'Why has he invited us to the ceremony?'

'He has no family, I believe,' Alan said thoughtfully. 'No brothers or sisters, as I recall, and he never married. Too wrapped up in his job. Really, Scotland Yard was his life. He's always given me far too much credit for his rapid rise, and I've suspected he views me as a sort of father figure. Actually, I'm a bit touched.'

Alan looked away, and I smiled to myself. An Englishman is even more reluctant to display emotion than his American counterpart.

We lost no time in replying, including an invitation for Jonathan to join us afterwards for the best luncheon London could provide. 'Although he may not eat a lot,' Alan told me. 'The last I heard, his tum still wasn't quite in full working order.'

I started planning what on earth to wear to the palace, and the Ivy afterwards. At least I didn't have to worry about a hat. The problem was finding an outfit that worked with one of my many hats and didn't make me look as if I were going to Royal Ascot.

The great day dawned inauspiciously as to weather. Chilly and wet, with an angry sky promising more rain and probably thunder, it nevertheless failed to dampen my spirits. Alan and I had taken the train into London the night before, since driving in London is not only a penance, but also very expensive, what with parking and the congestion charge. We would have had to take a cab to the palace anyway. And besides, I wanted to be fresh and look my best for the occasion. 'I know it's not about me,' I told Alan. 'But it's the one time in my life that I'll get to see the Queen, up close and personal, and I intend to milk it for all it's worth.'

We had opted to spend two nights at the Goring. That venerable hostelry is way out of our class, but besides its convenient location just around the corner from the palace, it has beautiful, comfortable rooms and an attentive staff, and if that weren't enough, it was the hotel where the Middletons stayed just before Kate and William's wedding. This occasion wasn't quite that posh, but we felt it rated high enough on our life list to justify the expense.

Alan was inclined to be a bit cross as we were dressing in our lovely room. That meant he was nervous, but being English and male, he wasn't about to say so. I didn't mind showing my own nerves. I dropped my earrings twice, once perilously close to the drain in the bathroom sink. I dithered over whether my dress was appropriate, though fortunately, having brought only the one upscale outfit, I couldn't change my mind.

Neither of us was in any state to want breakfast, nor did we drink as much coffee as usual. 'Because,' I said to Alan, 'it would be perfectly awful to need the loo right in the middle of the ceremony.'

'Don't even think about it,' he said. His tone wasn't exactly a growl, but it was about as close as Alan ever comes.

We were much too early at the palace. The doorman at the Goring was very efficient at whistling up a taxi, and in fact, had it not been for the rain, we could easily have walked the short distance and still arrived early. However, the palace staff were no doubt accustomed to the nerves of guests, and showed us to the Ballroom with courteous aplomb.

We'd been in it before, accompanying our friends on tours of the State Rooms. But arriving as an invited guest felt completely different. Chairs were set in neat rows, leaving a broad aisle up the middle towards the dais at the end. An orchestra in the gallery at the back of the room played softly as the guests came in, everyone as subdued as if we were in church.

'Where's Jonathan?' I whispered, craning my neck.

'Those receiving honours go to a briefing room where they're told what's going to happen.'

'Oh.' After a pause, 'I think I'm going to cry,' I whispered.

'Stiff upper lip, old girl,' he murmured, and patted my hand.

It seemed a long time, but eventually everyone was seated and the music changed. Five men in elaborate uniforms marched in and took their places on the dais.

'Beefeaters?' I said to Alan, surprised. 'What do they have to do with it?'

'Shh! Not Beefeaters. I'll tell you later.'

We stood, and the Queen entered, and they played 'God Save the Queen', and my eyes were swimming. I fumbled in my pocket, discovered I'd forgotten a tissue, and nudged Alan, who handed me his handkerchief with a tolerant smile.

And then the herald, or page, or whatever they call him, spoke the name 'Jonathan Quinn,' and Jonathan entered, walking stiffly and carrying a cane, but erect and unassisted. He bowed and the Queen came forward to him, smiling, and fixed his medal to his chest. They spoke for a moment, then a handshake, a bow, and Jonathan went off somewhere.

I'm afraid I don't remember much of the rest. There were many more honorees, though none as exalted as Jonathan, and they tended to blend together. I believe that the Queen had a little conversation with each of them before shaking hands. I remember the handshakes, because they surprised me; I'd had some notion that one never shook hands with the Queen.

It was all over in about an hour, and we were directed to a room where we could meet Jonathan and take him off to lunch.

Our friend was looking a bit pale, and I thought he was probably in pain, but he denied it. 'No, no! Never better! It isn't every day one shakes Her Majesty's hand, is it?'

'It certainly isn't every day that someone is awarded the George Cross, old man,' said Alan. 'Or did they decide to take it away? I don't see it.'

Jonathan held out a leather box, and opened it for our inspection. 'They took it off and put it in here for safe keeping. I gather one doesn't simply flash it about on the street.'

I was secretly rather disappointed. I expected the 'highest civilian honour' to be something elaborate, perhaps even jewelled. This was a small, rather plain silver cross with some sort of medallion at the centre, hanging from a blue ribbon. Not, I thought, very impressive at all. I made politely admiring noises.

I've been told I'd never make a poker player. Jonathan gave me a twisted smile. 'Not much, is it? To look at, I mean. But then, I don't quite see why they gave it to me at all. I was only doing my duty.'

I looked at the lines of pain on his face, his shaking hand, his pallor, and my throat closed up again. Even Alan had to clear his throat before he could speak.

'Your duty, Jonathan, was to try to contain an explosive situation, to keep injuries to a minimum, and if possible to aid the military chaps to apprehend the terrorists. Saving that child was a pure act of gallantry, and I'll hear no more nonsense about not deserving this award.'

'You said they weren't Beefeaters, Alan,' I said, to change

the subject. 'They certainly have the exact same uniform. Explain.'

'I'm afraid the explanation may leave you as confused as ever. They're called – the ones we saw today – the Yeomen of the Guard. And yes, their uniform is almost exactly like that of the Yeomen Warders, the ones at the Tower. The palace ones wear a sash draped from one shoulder, the only difference I've ever noted.'

'And Gilbert and Sullivan . . . well, mostly Gilbert, I suppose . . . compounded the problem when he called the Tower ones by the wrong name. You're right. I didn't need to know.'

'But now you do. And I suggest, Jonathan, that we make our way out and head for the Ivy before Dorothy and I both perish of starvation. We were too agitated to eat our breakfasts, young man, and all on your account.'

We descended the grand staircase, very slowly because of Jonathan's bad legs, and paused at the bottom to catch our breath, or at least for Jonathan to catch his.

The foyer was milling with honorees, guests and staff. After Jonathan had recovered, we picked our way through with care, lest Jonathan be accidentally buffeted and lose his precarious balance. One of the staff members materialized by his side, and said, 'Let me help you, or you'll never get through that lot, Cousin Jonathan.'

'Oh,' said Jonathan, his voice rather flat. 'Jemima.'

'You'd forgotten I work here, hadn't you?' The young woman laced her arm through his and propelled him through the crowd, smilingly but firmly making way. Alan and I trailed in their wake until we finally reached the quieter haven of the Quadrangle.

'All right, then? Good!' The young woman hesitated a moment. 'Jonathan, come and see me one of these days. We haven't talked in a long time.' Someone frowned at her. Her boss, possibly? She sketched a wave and vanished, leaving Jonathan to the mercy of the media, who requested an interview.

Jonathan complied, reluctantly, and escaped the moment he could. He was plainly uncomfortable in the role of hero.

'I didn't know you had a cousin, Jonathan,' said Alan as we crunched across the immaculate gravel.

He scowled. 'Honorary,' he said briefly. 'Her mother was a good friend of my mother's, and we called her Aunt Letty. By extension, therefore . . .'

'Ah. I see. Pleasant young woman.'

Jonathan scowled again. 'Bit of a pill, if you want the truth. In and out of trouble when she was a girl. I rather lost touch with her when my parents died, but I know her mother was greatly relieved when she snagged the job at the palace. I don't believe they pay terribly well, but she does live in, so she's under a certain amount of supervision.'

'I'd think it'd take a brave girl to misbehave under the Queen's eye,' I commented. 'I have the distinct impression Her Majesty doesn't miss much. Look, we'd better find a taxi. You look like you've been on your feet long enough for one day.'

'Actually, I left a wheelchair somewhere. The quacks want me to use it still, but I don't, at least not unless I really have to. And I'd be damned if I'd sit to receive an honour from the Queen, so I told someone to keep it for me.' He looked around vaguely, as if expecting to see his chair behind a bush, and lo!, the someone appeared, wheeling it – with some difficulty – across the gravel.

'We waited for you at the lift, sir,' said the man, somewhat reproachfully.

'Yes, well, I managed. As you see.'

Jonathan refused to sit in it until we had left the gravel, but his face when he finally sat down told me how much that stubbornness had cost him.

I thought I could see how he had summoned up the courage to save that child.

'Right,' said Alan. 'Now to find a taxi.'

'I wonder,' said Jonathan tentatively, 'if you'd mind terribly if we walked for a bit. In a manner of speaking, that is,' he added, looking down at his chair. 'I . . . the palace is a bit . . . the rain has stopped, and I'd like some fresh air, if it's not a dreadful bother.'

'I feel exactly the same way,' I said with a sigh of relief. 'Claustrophobic. It's a perfectly lovely, spacious cave, but a cave, nonetheless. Let's walk through St James's Park, Alan.

Squirrels and ducks and pelicans are exactly what I need just now.'

The traffic around the palace is always incredible. Taxis and other vehicles whizz around the Queen Victoria Memorial in an unending stream. There are pedestrian traffic lights, controlled by push buttons, but they emit a rapid, threatening beep-beep-beep that seems to shout 'Hurry! Hurry!' My heart was in my mouth, with all those impatient engines ready to move the moment they were given the green light, but we managed to cross two streets safely and then, in seconds, were in the shelter of what is, for me, the loveliest park in London.

It was high noon, and the park should have been crowded with people: children begging their parents for ice cream and throwing crumbs to the greedy ducks, lovers strolling arm in arm, the elderly sitting on benches attracting crowds of hopeful pigeons and the odd squirrel looking for a handout. St James's is one of the royal parks, which simply means they're owned by the Crown. Anyone can enjoy them, and thousands of people do, every day. Not today, though, what with the rain. Soon, if the sun came out, the throngs would descend, but now we had the place nearly to ourselves. We wandered happily, looking at the soggy flowerbeds and smelling that spring smell of damp earth and new growth, unmatched at any other time of the year. Finding a path leading into a more densely planted area, we passed through the unlatched gate and found ourselves so shut off from the sounds of London that we might have been in the country.

Just beyond some bushes that weren't yet fully leafed out lay the lake. The waterfowl were happily going about their business. As a gorgeous swan flew in for a landing on the lake, its great wing-beats thudding like horses' hooves, I watched, enchanted, leaning on a bench.

'Tired, love?' asked Alan.

'Tired of walking. These are not exactly walking shoes. Yes, I know I thought this was a wonderful idea, but now I need to sit and rest for a bit. I'm thirsty, too. Alan, you could get me something cold to drink if the refreshment stands are open. Jonathan, you stay here and keep me company. I want to hear about how your recovery is coming.'

'Oh, I'm doing well,' he said briskly. But as Alan walked out of earshot, he sighed. 'Who am I trying to fool? It's been hell, Dorothy.'

'I thought so,' I said quietly. I tried to keep my voice neutral. Too much sympathy, and either Jonathan would start to cry, or his defences would kick in and he'd try to laugh it off.

'Not so much the pain. Oh, it's bad, but I can live with it.'

'I never knew exactly what your injuries were.'

He laughed, a sound conveying no amusement. 'Do you want the complete catalogue? It ranged from gunshot wounds to internal injuries to smoke inhalation to concussion to various broken limbs, but it's worked out at two game legs and touchy plumbing and a wonky brain. I black out from time to time.'

I swallowed hard. 'What are your doctors telling you about the prognosis?'

'They've done all they can. Now it's therapy and exercise and all that. They tell me it's all on my plate now. And to tell you the truth, I don't care.'

'No?' The neutral tone was getting harder.

'Why should I work and sweat, trying to make my legs do impossible things? Why should I eat what they tell me, hoping my insides will eventually be normal, and try to avoid stress that plays the devil with my mind? Why *should* I care? I'll never be able to work again, anyway. I'll never be fit for police work.'

'And so?'

He had been staring at the ground. Now he looked up at me, his face full of anger. 'And so there's no reason for me to keep on living, is there?'

'No? I'd have thought a man who'd won the George Cross would have more courage than that.'

He winced as if I'd slapped him. As, in effect, I had. I hated doing this, but I went on. 'You weren't afraid to risk dying, back when the little girl needed you. You dove right in and did what had to be done. So why are you so afraid to risk living?'

'Are you suggesting there's something to live for?' His voice was savage.

'Oh, don't be tiresome, Jonathan. Of course there's

something to live for!' I gestured in a wide sweep. 'The lake, flowers, trees. Pelicans, for heaven's sake! Don't tell me you'd throw away your chances of ever seeing a pelican again. Just *look* at them, with those ridiculous short legs and that huge beak! They're one of God's great jokes, like ostriches and camels. And people.'

'You want me to strain every muscle I have left, in torture, for the sake of pelicans.'

At least he didn't sound self-pitying any more.

'Exactly. Pelicans, and wood ducks, and cats and lilacs and a cuppa and a lovely pint. *Life*, Jonathan, in all its infinite variety. I know you've been through more agony than anyone should ever have to endure. I know you're depressed about losing your job – and, incidentally, I certainly hope you're getting some treatment for the depression. But the point is that the Metropolitan Police isn't the only possible job in the world for a young, intelligent man, especially one who's just been awarded the highest honour his country has to offer. You can find another job, if you do work and sweat and swear and ache and do whatever you must to regain your strength and mobility. And then you can see the world again, instead of just your own misery.'

'And pelicans.'

'Definitely pelicans.'

'Pelicans?' said Alan quizzically, returning with orange drinks for all of us.

'Dorothy seems to think they're one of the most important life forms,' said Jonathan.

'Dorothy also thinks she's going to perish of starvation if someone doesn't feed her soon,' I moaned melodramatically. 'A taxi, a taxi, my kingdom for a taxi!'

'You don't have a kingdom,' observed Alan, holding out his hand to help me up.

'Neither did Richard, shortly after those immortal words. Onward, troops.'

I got stiffly to my feet, dropping my paper cup as I did so. Orange drink splashed over my feet and on to the hem of my wildly expensive, pale blue dress.

'Damn!' I said emphatically. 'This stuff never comes out! And how can I show up at the Ivy with an orange hem? Alan, it's rolled under that bush. Get it for me, will you? I don't need to litter, on top of everything else.'

He reached under the bush, fumbled about and stopped. His face, as he stood up, wore a most peculiar expression.

'Dorothy, do you have your mobile?'

'Yes, in my purse. Why?'

'Ring for a policeman, then, please.'

'We have two of them right here, Alan. You and Jonathan.'

'We need one in active service. Unless I'm hallucinating, someone is under that bush, and I don't think she's alive.'

THREE

I t didn't take long for a constable to arrive; there's a station actually in the park. After that things got complicated.

To start, the constable wasn't very happy with us. 'This area of the park is not open to the public, sir,' he said to Alan. 'You should not have opened the gate.'

'It was not shut,' said Alan briefly.

'Ought to have been, sir. Shut and locked.'

'Well, it wasn't,' I said crossly. 'It was wide open, and the path looked inviting, and we walked in.'

'And exactly how did you discover the body, sir?' asked the constable, ignoring me completely.

'My wife dropped her drink. The cup rolled under the bush. I bent to pick it up and felt a foot.'

'Ah, yes, sir. And may I ask your name, sir?' the constable went on, his attitude a perfect blend of courtesy, authority and suspicion.

'Alan Nesbitt, Chief Constable, Belleshire, retired.' He took out his identification, and the poor young policeman swallowed, but persevered gamely.

'Yes, sir. And your companions?'

'My wife, Dorothy Martin.' I silently pulled out my driving licence. 'And our good friend, Jonathan Quinn, Chief Inspector, Scotland Yard, retired.'

Jonathan stood shakily to pull his wallet out of his pocket, and dropped the leather case containing his medal. The case fell open, and the sight of the George Cross gleaming in the watery, intermittent sun completed the constable's demoralization.

'Yes, sir. And madam. I— will you excuse me for a moment?'

He moved away and pulled out his mobile phone.

'Poor man,' I said in an undertone. 'He doesn't know what to do with us. I'm the only one who's not important, and he's scared to death of putting a foot wrong.'

'Good for him,' said Alan callously. 'A stone's throw from the palace, he needs to learn to be on his toes. VIPs are thick on the ground hereabouts.'

Jonathan said nothing, but sat back in his chair, tension radiating from his stillness. He wants desperately to be a part of this investigation, I thought.

I cleared my throat. 'Alan, what exactly did you see under that bush?'

'Not much. I was feeling about for your cup. I didn't want to get down on my knees to look, and get mud on these trousers.' He'd worn his best suit, naturally, for the auspicious occasion that now seemed to have happened so long ago. 'I felt something hard, realized it was a high-heeled shoe, felt a little farther, found the foot in the shoe, and stopped.'

Jonathan could keep quiet no longer. 'Temperature?' he asked.

'Neither warm nor cold.'

'Rigor?'

'Quite stiff. Several hours, I'd say at a guess.'

'Yes. Before dawn, then, probably. It would have been terribly risky in daylight.'

I thought it was time to remind them of my existence. 'Old or young?' I asked.

'My dear, I didn't look at her!'

'The shoe,' I said impatiently.

'A stiletto heel, three inches at least. I suppose that makes her young.'

Jonathan struck his hand on the arm of his chair. 'I can't stand this!'

Alan said nothing, just shook his head. His frustration was

almost as great as Jonathan's, but he'd learned to deal with it in his years of retirement. For Jonathan, the pain of being sidelined was new and raw. I bled for him.

The constable returned. His fresh face was a delicate shade of pink. 'Sirs, madam, I've been instructed to allow you to leave, with our thanks. If I could just have addresses . . .'

'I think we would prefer to stay,' said Alan smoothly. 'Mr Quinn and I would feel we had failed to do our duty if we left without making a complete report to your superior.'

'Well, sir,' said the constable, looking trapped, 'I was told . . . and it won't be very pleasant for the lady . . .'

'I do assure you, young man, that I am not unacquainted with the recently deceased.' I used my best Victoria Regina voice and vocabulary. 'And in any case I prefer to remain with my husband.' A little echo of the late Queen Mum thrown in for good measure.

The constable knew when he was beaten. 'As you wish, then.' He looked around, and with deep relief said, 'Ah. Here's the Chief Superintendent now.'

As the constable murmured a few words to his superior, Jonathan made no obvious movement, but I thought he braced himself. Then the approaching man called out, 'Quinn!' and he looked up.

'Sir!' said Jonathan, and that single syllable was laden with meaning. The top note, I thought, was pleasure.

'Good to see you, Quinn! I won't ask how you're getting on. I expect you're sick of the subject. I'm damn glad you're here, man. And you, sir,' he added, turning to Alan and offering him a hand. 'We've not met, but your reputation has preceded you. Carstairs.'

They shook hands. Mr Carstairs went on, 'I was, as you will have gathered, Quinn's chief. They thought I'd want to be here. I'm sure you can imagine how much he's missed. Now tell me, both of you. As you've elected to stay on the scene, what have you observed?'

Well, there I was again, being ignored while the men went over the few salient facts, over and over. I shifted restlessly on the bench, which was getting extremely hard. And extremely hot. The sun had decided to come out in full force, and combined with the high humidity, it made the temperature very uncomfortable, especially clad as I was in a long-sleeved dress and an elaborate hat. I fished Alan's handkerchief out of my pocket, wiped my brow, and sighed.

Alan cleared his throat. 'Chief Superintendent, let me introduce my wife, Dorothy Martin.'

Mr Carstairs smiled broadly and held out a hand. 'Ah, yes, the Miss Marple of Belleshire! Your reputation, too, has spread far and wide. I think your husband was gently reminding me, just now, that you might have some insights into this little matter.'

'Hardly,' I said, and if I sounded frosty, I felt I had good excuse. 'I've really seen nothing. From what Jonathan and Alan have said, I gather a young woman is under that bush. I must say, it seems a very odd place to leave a body. It was bound to be discovered soon.'

'We don't yet know that there has been foul play, Mrs Martin.'

'Right. She crawled under there in the middle of the night, for reasons of her own, and just happened to die there.'

'Dorothy,' said Alan, frowning.

Carstairs held up a hand and said, 'All right, all right! Obviously we must have a look at the lady, but I agree the circumstances are suspicious. To say the least,' he added hastily. 'For one thing, as the constable told you, this is an area of the park that is closed to the public. He said you found the gate open?'

'Ajar, at any rate,' said Alan. 'I saw no lock, and certainly no sign forbidding entry.'

'There is normally a sign, and a CCTV camera. Presumably the sign was removed and the camera vandalized by the murderer, assuming this is a murder.'

By now, the small area was swarming with policemen, most of them in plain clothes, going methodically about the business of documenting the crime scene. One of them spoke to Carstairs. 'Finished for now, sir. The body can be moved. There are some recent footprints; we've covered them and will take casts.'

'Those will probably be mine,' said Alan. He sat down and

held both feet out for examination. 'Sorry to complicate your task, but I didn't know this was a crime scene when I trampled over it. I'd give you my shoes straight away, but I've nothing else in London to wear, and we're staying until tomorrow.'

'If you wouldn't mind taking one off for a moment, sir, I can do a quick comparison.'

It was done. The policeman nodded to Carstairs and returned the shoe. Alan put it back on and stood.

'Right,' said Carstairs. 'We can get on with it, then.' He gave me a worried look. 'Are you quite sure you'll be all right, Mrs Martin?'

'If you're expecting me to faint or be sick, I can assure you I'm not likely to do either. I have seen dead people before, you know. It isn't my favourite thing, but I feel a vested interest in this one, and I'd like to know what I can. If there's something really horrible you think I'd rather not see, tell me and I'll look away.'

'Nothing like that, sir,' said the policeman who was apparently in charge of the initial collecting of evidence. 'Not that we could see, anyway.'

'Very well. Mind you, Mrs Martin, if you were anyone else, I'd turf you out of here. Right, Bob. Let's have her out from under there and see what there is to see.'

My first impression was that she was very young, too young to be dressed as she was. Her skirt was long and swirly and sophisticated, her top tight and low-cut, designed to display an impressive bust, not her slender, undeveloped form. The three-inch stilettos would have suited a woman of twenty-five. There was nothing especially terrible about her appearance, no obvious wounds, no visible blood. Her clothes were dusty and disarranged, but otherwise in good condition. She had long bleached-blonde hair, beginning to darken a bit at the roots, and wore quite a lot of make-up. Her fingernails were long and blood-red.

'Poor child,' I said. 'Trying so hard to be grown up and sophisticated, and this is how it all ended.'

'That's how it strikes you?' asked Carstairs, sounding interested. 'I'd have put rather a different interpretation on it.'

'A prostitute? Well, it's possible, but somehow I don't think so. Her clothes are "dressed up" but not tawdry. Everything is expensive. Is her handbag under there still?'

The other policemen shook their heads, and the man called Bob said, 'Nothing else of any size. We'll do a closer examination, but there's certainly no handbag.'

'Which obviously makes identification harder.' I shook my head. 'Poor child,' I said again. 'What killed her, do you have any idea yet?'

'At a guess, I'd say she was smothered. There's a bit of bruising about the mouth, and her lipstick is smeared. A number of explanations for that, but there are some indications in her eyes, as well.'

I knew about the tiny haemorrhages in the eyes that could occur in cases of either smothering or strangulation. 'No bruises on her neck?'

'Not that anyone's found yet. We'll know a lot more when she's been examined.'

I sighed. 'Looks like an evening out gone wrong. Sad, and sordid, and quite definitely *not* my cup of tea. Thank you, Mr Carstairs, for indulging me. I won't get in your hair any more.'

Someday I'll learn not to make rash promises.

FOUR

Our reservation at the Ivy had long since lapsed, and the maître d' was inclined to be haughty about our failure to cancel. His tone changed once Alan had explained the situation, but he remained firm. So sorry, sirs, madam. There were simply no tables available. Perhaps in another two hours, though even then . . .

'Alan, let's just go back to the hotel. They have a wonderful restaurant, and I don't think I'm quite up to the Ivy, anyway, after . . . all that.'

All that, as both men understood, comprised a morning of excitement, pomp and pride, followed by the striking contrast of murder. None of us was feeling terribly festive.

We were, however, hungry, so when we reached the Goring and had freshened up a bit, we presented ourselves at the dining room door, only to be told by a distraught concierge that we had missed lunch by half an hour. 'But meals are always available in the bar, if you'd like something light. Or afternoon tea begins soon in the lounge, though I fear we may be fully booked. Or we can send something up to your room.'

'It's a conspiracy,' I said, trying to laugh about it. 'All of London is determined to keep us from our food. No, I didn't mean you,' I assured the concierge. 'Not your fault, but it's not ours, either. Unavoidable. I vote for the bar, if that's all right with the rest of you?'

The barman was genial. 'I understand we've some starving Americans, have we?'

'One starving American and two starving Englishmen. And since it's been a pretty trying day so far, perhaps we'll start with a glass of sherry?'

'Certainly, madam. We've some lovely Amontillado, if that suits.'

'Admirably.'

We ordered our meals of sandwiches and salads, and sipped our sherry. I for one would happily have kicked off my shoes, but I realized the Goring was not that kind of place.

Alan lifted his glass. 'I propose a toast to Jonathan, a verray parfit gentil knyght!'

Jonathan acknowledged the toast with a little duck of the head, and muttered something deprecating.

'Jonathan, I'm so sorry the day turned out this way,' I said after clinking glasses with Alan. 'It was meant to be a celebration, and then it was spoilt.'

'Hardly your fault, was it?'

'I could have insisted we leave and turn the whole thing over to Mr Carstairs. He looks quite capable.'

'He's very good. The best there is, saving your presence, sir.' He nodded to Alan.

'Oh, for heaven's sake, Jonathan, we're long past the "sir" stage. What's got you going all formal on us?'

'Sorry, s— Alan. It's been rather an unsettling day.'

I looked at him more closely. His face was a bit pale, and

he slumped in his wheelchair. 'It has,' I agreed, 'and you're tired to death. Alan, let's feed this man and send him home. He's had enough for one day.'

I was ready for collapse, myself. Once we'd had our food and sent Jonathan on his way, in a taxi Alan insisted on paying for, we went wearily back up to our luxurious room, and at last I could take off my shoes. 'Alan, I'm worried about that boy,' I said, blissfully stretching my toes.

'Hardly a boy. He's thirty-two, I believe.'

'Oh, one foot in the grave, I see. No, from where I sit, he's a boy, and he's in a bad state.'

'The pain, you mean? Or his financial situation?'

'All of that,' I said with a frown, 'but a lot more, as well. He talked to me while you were off getting the drinks. He's extremely depressed; thinks he's washed up, useless. That's really why I was so intrusive about sticking around to see the body. I thought he'd show some enthusiasm at being included in an investigation again. The old fire horse would perk up at the sound of the bell. He didn't, though, once his first interest waned.'

'No, he was remarkably quiet the rest of the afternoon. Ah, well, he was tired.'

'As am I. Oh, Lord, it's way too early to go to bed, and too late to take a nap.'

'It is never,' said Alan, removing his tie, 'too late for a nap.'

It was, though. I slept far too long, and although Alan and I had our supper at a pub, with more beer than I usually allow myself, I had a very hard time getting to sleep. I kept thinking about that poor girl under the bush. Who was she? Why had she dressed that way, in those outlandish shoes and so much make-up? Was she a tart, as Chief Superintendent Carstairs had suggested? No mother, I thought, would have wanted to let the girl go out looking like that, although I knew mothers sometimes had little influence over girls that age. Not for the first time, I realized that my childless state had some compensations.

Perhaps she'd run away from home? If so, it had been recently. She had seemed healthy and well nourished, and her clothes had been clean when she'd put them on.

Had she been raped? It seemed likely, given the way she was found. But a royal park, even at night, seemed an odd place for an assault. Surely they were patrolled? But she had been in an unfrequented, indeed a forbidden area. And why was that gate unlocked, the camera vandalized?

The police will know, I told myself, turning over and punching the pillow for the tenth time. The police will do their job. It's none of your business.

Alan grunted, almost as if agreeing in his sleep.

I got up to go to the bathroom, an all too frequent necessity at my age. All that beer didn't help. I drank a glass of water to deal with the thirst that comes after too much alcohol, and crept back into my comfortable bed.

But how are they going to begin, since they don't know who she is? London is an enormous city, and a haven for those who want to lose themselves. Though that isn't so easy nowadays, I thought, turning over again. Computers, email, cell phones, all those other 'hand-held electronic devices' the airlines are so fond of telling you not to use – everything leaves a trail. People are easy to trace. If she ran away from home, somebody will have reported her missing. They'll find out who she was. Leave it to them, Dorothy. Leave it.

I turned over once more, and this time, I slept.

I was wrung out in the morning, but an excellent breakfast helped a good deal. It always does. Considering my too-generous figure, I've always envied those heroines who can't eat when they're upset and are always being told they're 'too thin'. Not I. I find good food a comfort in most circumstances. Still, I nodded off in the train going home and woke, with a stiff neck, only when Alan nudged me to say ours was the next station.

Our new dog, Watson, was as usual ecstatic to see us back, but our two cats, Emmy and Sam (officially Esmeralda and Samantha), were inclined to snub us, although they'd been well cared for by our wonderful next-door neighbour, Jane Langland. 'We've only been gone for two days, for Pete's sake!' I informed Sam, who uttered a blood-curdling Siamese shriek and marched stiff-legged out of the room.

'So nice to be back amongst one's loving family,' Alan commented.

'She'll get over it. As soon as you've unpacked, Alan, I need to do some laundry. Back to real life.'

'Mmm. I thought I'd go and see if David's got that book I ordered. Can I get you anything while I'm out?'

'You might take my dress to the cleaners, see if they can do anything about that wretched stain. And pick up something for dinner. We're a bit short of groceries. Get something you like, that's easy to cook.'

My husband, having been a widower living alone for some years before we met, is thoroughly domesticated. He knows how to shop and indeed how to cook, and sometimes takes over meal preparation when I'm busy or tired. Besides, the Shorebury Tesco is two doors down from the police station, and I knew he was dying to find out what was happening with the London investigation. It isn't easy to put an old racehorse out to pasture, or at any rate to keep him there.

I was putting the second load of clothes into the machine when the phone rang.

'Hello, Mrs Martin?'

'Yes?' The voice sounded familiar, but I couldn't quite place it.

'Quinn here, Jonathan Quinn.'

'Oh, Jonathan! I hope you're feeling better. I thought you seemed a bit green around the gills yesterday.'

'I'm fine.' It was the automatic response, meaning nothing. 'Is the Chief at home?'

'No, he's gone out for a bit. Shall I have him call you?'

'No!' He cleared his throat. 'No, actually it was you I wanted to talk to. Look, are you going to be there for a little while?'

'All day.'

'Well . . . um . . . could I come round to see you? Or could we meet somewhere?'

'That would be lovely, but where are you? I couldn't get another train to Victoria for an hour or so.'

'I'm in Shorebury. I . . . this is embarrassing, but I'd like to speak with you alone. Can you suggest a place? I don't know the town very well.'

Curiouser and curiouser. I thought for a moment. 'Well, there's the tea shop in the Cathedral Close. Alderney's. It has stairs; can you manage?'

'I will manage.' He sounded grimly determined.

'All right. In . . . fifteen minutes?'

'Bless you. I'll be there.'

Alderney's was one of our favourite places, but Alan was safely at the other end of the High Street. He wouldn't be popping in to Alderney's.

But whatever could Jonathan want to tell me that he didn't want Alan to hear?

FIVE

'I know who she is. Was.'

Jonathan dropped his bombshell in the middle of the teacups at Alderney's.

I stared at him open-mouthed, unable for once to say a word. Watson, at my side as usual, whined softly, sensing that I was upset.

'I know you thought I was in pain. And I suppose I was, but it was the shock more than anything else. Dorothy, I don't know what to do.'

I took a deep breath and looked around the room. It wasn't very crowded at this time of day, between lunch and teatime. We could easily be overheard. 'Well. Maybe we'd better go out into the Close. I know a couple of nice, private spots.'

We found one of them, a bench sheltered behind a huge rhododendron. It wasn't very near Alderney's, and I worried about Jonathan walking so far, but he limped along, leaning heavily on his cane, his mouth set. 'I left my chair at the station,' he said. 'Too conspicuous. And I try to walk as much as I can.'

I thought he had overdone it, but I wasn't his mother. We sat, Watson still protectively at my side. He wasn't sure he trusted this fellow. 'All right, then. You'd better begin at the beginning.'

'I told you about my honorary Aunt Letty.'

'Mother of that woman in the palace.'

'Jemima. Yes.' He paused.

'What about her?' I asked after a moment.

'Sorry. This is . . . difficult.' He swallowed, stared into the distance, and then resumed his story. 'I owe Aunt Letty a lot. My parents were . . . not abusive, just rather distant, especially my father. They packed me off to school after my eleven-plus exams, and after that I saw them only in the holidays. It was Aunt Letty who would come to visit, bring me little treats, listen to my schoolboy woes. It was Aunt Letty who encouraged me when I said I wanted to join the police. My father was dead set against it. He was a snob, you see. He was a shopkeeper, in a small way to start, but eventually with quite a large chain of upscale supermarkets.'

'Quinn's! There's one in the new shopping centre on the edge of Sherebury, and I go there whenever I need something special. I never made the connection.'

'Yes, well, that's where he got the money to send me to public school. But he wanted bigger and better things than "trade" for me. Said he'd educated me to be a gentleman, and he'd be damned if he'd see me turn into a copper. That sort of thing.'

'Ouch.'

'Yes. And he'd have prevailed if it hadn't been for Aunt Letty. She worked on my mother, and Mother worked on Father, and the decision was delayed for a year. And then they were both killed in a plane crash. On their way to Mallorca,' he added with a wry smile. 'He hated hot weather and had no use for ancient ruins, but he thought it was a fashionable place for a holiday.

'So then I inherited all that money and could do as I liked. And if that sounds callous, remember I scarcely knew either of my parents. They had never troubled to give me any attention, only money and things.'

'No substitute for love,' I agreed, thinking privately that I needn't have worried about Jonathan's finances.

'No. So I set up a trust for Aunt Letty. Her husband had died by that time, and she didn't have much money. She didn't want to take it, said she didn't need charity, but I insisted; told her it wasn't charity, but love. Then I put in for Hendon, was accepted, and that was the beginning. If it hadn't been for Aunt Letty, I'd have been forced into Oxbridge.'

'Forced? Surely in this day and age . . .'

'You never knew my father. Remember he held the purse strings. He who pays the piper, et cetera. I'd have been miserable at university, but that was where I was headed until that blessed woman instituted the delaying tactics.'

'OK. I've got the picture. You look upon Letty as a surrogate mother. What does that have to do with the body in the park?'

'Everything. She was Letty's granddaughter. Jemima's daughter.'

'Good heavens! But what . . . why . . .?'

'I don't have any answers, Dorothy. I only know I recognized her the moment I saw her. She looks exactly like Jemima at that age.'

'But why on earth didn't you say something? The police are wasting hours trying to identify her!'

'Don't you think I know that? But follow it through for just a moment. I tell them she's Jemima's daughter Melissa. They go to the palace to question Jemima. There'll be suspicion. They'll find out that Melissa was illegitimate. Even in this day and age, that puts a stain on Jemima's character. She has a responsible job, Dorothy, for the most conservative employer in the kingdom, and she can't afford to jeopardize it. For the first time in her life, really, she seems to have fallen on her feet. She was in all kinds of trouble when she was younger. Well, Melissa was one of the troubles. Now she's working for the Lord Chamberlain's Office and lives in the palace. She's got a lot to lose!'

'I thought you said you'd forgotten she worked there.'

'She said that. I hadn't forgotten. I was just hoping to avoid her. We never got on as children, and as adults we've not had a lot to do with one another. She can be . . . difficult.'

'And yet you recognized her daughter at once.'

'I told you. She looks – looked – just like Jemima at that age. Even the clothes. Jemima liked to wear that sort of arty get-up. And in any case, Letty phoned me yesterday morning,

just before I had to go to the palace. I'd invited her to the
ceremony, as my only "parent", but she called to say
she couldn't come, because Melissa had run away again.'

'Still, it could be a coincidence. Lots of young girls look
alike. Until their characters have formed—'

'But that's the other thing, you see. Those shoes she was
wearing, and the make-up and all. That's just the sort of thing
Jemima would have done, tried to make herself look important.
Like mother, like daughter.'

'Jonathan, you have to tell Chief Superintendent Carstairs.
At once.'

'How can I? I've thought about this all night. I would
unleash . . . God knows what. The palace nabobs are particular
about their employees, and there are other things in Jemima's
background that wouldn't bear scrutiny. Drugs, that sort of
thing.'

'Jonathan, forgive me, but I have to ask this. How sure are
you that Jemima's past is . . . well, past?'

At that he looked even more miserable, and he'd looked
bad enough before. 'I don't know, but Letty's been very hopeful
for the past couple of years. She believes Jemima's walking
the straight and narrow, and she's a pretty savvy woman.
Besides, they screen palace employees pretty rigorously. She
would have had to pass a drugs test and a background check.
But don't you see? Just a hint of unjustified suspicion, and
Jemima could get sacked, and revert back to her old ways.
She's a volatile personality, and a fragile one. Dorothy, I can't
do it!'

I sighed. I had a strong premonition. 'And why have you
come to me?'

'You're unofficial. Could you help me? I know you've done
this kind of thing before. The Chief was forever boasting about
you when we were at Bramshill.'

'Really!' This was an entirely new insight. I'd always
thought Alan somewhat disapproved of my sleuthing. Certainly
he became upset when I put myself in danger, as I had more
than once. The idea that he was proud of me . . . I shook my
head to clear out the confusion. 'But what you're asking is
absurd, Jonathan. For one thing, I have no way on God's green

earth to ask questions at the palace, where you seem to think this is all centred.'

'But you see, that's just what I *don't* think. Melissa ran away – she's done it before – and came to London and somehow got herself killed. But when Carstairs finds out who it was in the park, he'll have no choice but to question Jemima. That's why we need to find the killer before he gets that far.'

I ran my fingers through my hair, and Watson whined again. Whatever was happening to upset me, he wanted it to stop. 'Jonathan, listen to what you're saying! You're suggesting I go behind my husband's back, pry into matters that don't concern me in the least, muck up a police investigation into a nasty murder, and probably end up detained at Her Majesty's pleasure! You need your head examined, if it hasn't been already.'

He looked wretched, pale and in obvious pain. His eyes reminded me of one of Jane's puppies, wondering why it was being reprimanded.

'Look.' I ran my hands through my hair again. 'I do understand why you're upset. I do, truly. But you're asking the impossible. If there were no other barriers – and there are dozens – I would never, ever get into something like this without telling Alan.'

Jonathan sighed. 'You can tell him, if you have to. I wanted to talk to you first, but I was going to him next. He's retired. He doesn't have to follow procedure.'

'He may not have to, but he does. Regular Army all the way.'

'Army?' Jonathan looked confused.

'Never mind. An old American expression. It just means he's a straight arrow – sorry, he goes by the rules.'

'Then I've no hope.' He stood, painfully, leaning heavily on his cane. 'I can do nothing by myself except, perhaps, warn Jemima of the storm that's coming. Thank you for listening.'

'No!' I caught his arm as he was about to limp away. 'No, I can't let you just leave. Come home with me, have something to eat, or drink, or whatever, and let's figure out a way to talk this over with Alan. He might have an idea.'

'What?'

'*I* don't know! I just know he's come up with solutions to impossible problems before. Maybe he can do it again. And if he doesn't, you'll be no worse off than you are now.'

'Will he think he has to tell Mr Carstairs? About the body?'

'We won't tell him everything. Trust me. I won't lie to my husband, but over the years I've acquired a knack for . . . let's say, editing the truth a bit.'

Jonathan actually smiled, and limped slowly across the Close to the gate leading to my street.

SIX

Alan had returned home. 'There you are! Couldn't think where you'd got to. And Jonathan! What a pleasant surprise.'

But he looked at me with a quick, questioning frown.

'Jonathan has come to us with an extraordinary story, but I'm not going to let him tell it just now. The silly man has been walking all over Sherebury, and he's ready to drop. I'm going to tuck him up in the parlour with a nice cup of tea, and then I'm going to check out what you've found for our dinner.'

One of the things that made Alan such a good policeman was his quick perception and sensitivity to atmosphere. One of the things that made me fall in love with him was his understanding nature. He said only, 'When Dorothy gives an order, Jonathan, there's nothing to do but obey. Have a nice rest. Snooze, if you like, and we'll call you when dinner's ready.'

'Are you going to tell me what this is about?' he asked in an undertone as he put a piece of beef on the cutting board and started to cut it into strips.

'Not yet. After we eat. Stir-fry?' I asked, looking at the array of vegetables on the counter.

'Quick, easy, healthy. You want to whip up a marinade?'

We had our pre-prandial drinks in the kitchen while the

meat marinated, and then I set the table while Alan finished cooking the meal. In less than an hour all was ready, and I went in to wake Jonathan.

He woke at a touch. 'Something smells good.' He spoke with assumed enthusiasm, but his face was still drawn and worried.

'I hope you're feeling a little better. Dinner will help. And we're not going to say a word about you-know-what until after dessert.'

'Yes, ma'am.' His attempt at a cheeky grin was heart-rending.

Conversation at the dinner table was a bit strained. I didn't want to talk about the Investiture, or indeed anything that happened the day before. Other obvious topics were also taboo. I knew Jonathan didn't want to talk about his heroic rescue of the little girl, or his slow recovery, or his plans for the future, or anything that was on all our minds. Alan saved the day, finally.

'Oh, Dorothy, I meant to tell you. I ran into Bob Finch in the High Street, and he said he wanted to get started on the garden again.'

'Was he sober?'

Jonathan looked a little startled.

'As a judge. I don't know if he's taken the pledge, or his mother finally put the fear of God into him.'

'Bob has a drinking problem, as you will have gathered,' I told Jonathan, 'but he's an excellent gardener when he's conscious. I hope he's on the wagon for a while, at least, because he's right. The garden needs his tender touch.'

Almost anyone in England can hold forth on gardens, and gardeners, and flowers, for any length of time, so the subject took us safely through our fruit and custard. I made coffee and took it through to the parlour.

'Now,' I said, mentally girding my loins. 'Jonathan came to me today with a hypothetical question, or rather a scenario. We'd like your opinion about its . . . um . . . likelihood.'

'I see,' said Alan, giving me a look I knew all too well. 'Carry on.'

'Well, suppose – no, Jonathan, let me tell it my way,' I said, as he started to interrupt. 'I read a lot of crime fiction. I'm good at this sort of story. Suppose, Alan, that a crime were committed. A murder, let's say. And suppose further that there were a member of the public who had some information that might help the police. Naturally he – or she – would want to tell them as soon as possible.

'But what if that information might lead the police down an entirely wrong path, and might in fact jeopardize innocent people, people dear to the heart of the member of the public? Would he be justified in keeping the information to himself until he had a chance to look into the matter more closely?'

Alan had begun to frown. 'How certain is this hypothetical member of the public that the information would mislead the authorities?'

Jonathan opened his mouth, but I rushed in before he could speak. 'Not certain, I should think. But let's say that the assumption is reasonable.'

Alan's frown deepened. 'When I was still an active member of the force, I can't tell you how many witnesses hesitated to tell me something lest I "draw the wrong conclusion". I'm sure you've had the same experiences, Jonathan. My reply to them was always that they must let me be the judge of that.'

'And did they always tell you?' I asked.

'Usually. Not always.'

'And did you ever draw a wrong conclusion?'

'Sometimes. Not often. We are trained to sift the wheat from the chaff, as you well know. And sometimes their silence led me in the wrong direction.'

'Ah. So you say that the outcome is by no means certain, either way.'

'I also say that withholding information from the police is a serious matter, sometimes liable to prosecution. Your hypothetical person would do much better to get the whole thing off his chest.'

'I see. And suppose that this person decides, instead, to investigate on his own until he can see which quarter the wind's in?'

'And perhaps seeks the help of friends in his investigation?' The frown was now pronounced.

'Well, nothing could be more likely, could it?'

Alan sighed, long and heavily. 'Dorothy. You've been very careful to give me no useful information. I suppose you thought I'd feel obliged to act on it, and you're quite right. I would.'

I opened my mouth, and Alan held up one finger.

'A moment. I said I would feel obliged to act. I didn't say what action I might take. Even when I was actively serving, I used my own judgement about what information to pass along to my superiors, and when. Now. I assume we're talking about yesterday's discovery in the park. I would very much appreciate it, Jonathan, if you would tell me what you know about this affair.'

Alan in his chief constable mode was formidable indeed. Jonathan nodded his head. 'I see that I must, sir. Although . . . well, you'll understand when I tell you everything.'

He related the whole story, as he had told it to me. 'So you see, sir, why I said nothing yesterday. I owe everything to Aunt Letty, and this will destroy her.'

'I told you before, young man, less of the "sir". I'm not your boss any more. I'm not anybody's boss. I hope we're your friends, Dorothy and I.'

Jonathan nodded again.

'And therefore, as your friends, I hope we can help you find some way out of this mess. It's none of your doing, to begin with, but Lord, boy, you are in a dilemma, aren't you?'

'I am, Alan.' He forced a smile. 'It's far from the first time Jemima's got me into trouble.'

'All right, now, let's get this perfectly clear. Do you or do you not think your cousin . . . all right, your honorary cousin . . . had anything to do with her daughter's death?'

'No, I don't. I have nothing whatever to base that statement on except what I know of Jemima, but she's been a fiercely protective mother, that I do know from what Letty's told me. Not a wise mother, mind you. She hasn't given Melissa the kind of direction a child ought to have. But she managed to keep her warm and fed, even when that was really tough, and she protected her from her own boyfriends, to use the term loosely.'

'But where did the child live?' I asked. 'With Jemima living at the palace . . .?'

'With Letty. In West Sussex. A village called Bramber.'

'But she must be frantic with worry!' I was appalled. 'Jonathan, you must tell her at once!'

'Melissa's run away before,' he said wearily. 'It always turned out she was staying with friends, or had gone to London to shop. I'm sure Letty is calling them all, but she's . . . she's a realist, Dorothy. And she's not young.' He said that almost apologetically, looking at Alan and me. 'After a while, I think a sort of numbness set in. She knows Melissa always comes home in the end.'

'But this time,' Alan said sternly, 'she isn't coming home. Dorothy's right, Jonathan. Phone your Aunt Letty.'

'And if it gets back to the authorities?'

'Unless she's called in a missing persons report, it won't. Not for some time, at least. And you don't think she's likely to have done that.'

'No. Yes, you're right. I haven't been thinking very straight. Excuse me.'

He took his mobile phone into the next room to make the difficult call. I was silent.

'It's a pity for the boy,' said Alan at last. 'That this should happen on the very day he was honoured by his Queen.'

'Yes.'

The voice from the next room was low, but agitated. We both tried not to listen, though Watson pricked his ears. He didn't care much for this human, but he always wanted everyone to be happy.

'This is taking more courage than going after that little girl,' I said presently.

'Yes. Moral courage is always harder than physical courage. There's no adrenalin flowing, only the determination to do what's right.'

'And it's harder when you're not even sure which course is the right one. That boy has a lot of guts.'

'Well, we knew that, didn't we?' Alan drew a small, imaginary cross on his left breast, just as Jonathan came back into the room.

'I'll have to go to her,' he said. 'She took the news as well as could be expected, but she needs someone with her. Do you know when the next train leaves for Shoreham? I think that's the closest station.'

'Nonsense. We're driving you. Bramber isn't far. We've been there, Dorothy. Remember that marvellous old house?'

'Oh, yes! St Mary's. The Deans took us there. It took my breath away. Just let me get my bag, and a hat, and we're off.'

We stopped at the railway station to pick up Jonathan's wheelchair, which Alan wrestled into the boot, and then set off down the country roads that led to Bramber.

'Jonathan,' I said into a silence that was threatening to become awkward, 'what about Jemima? Will Letty phone and tell her the dreadful news?'

'We talked about that. Not right away, she decided. Jemima doesn't even know about Melissa running away this time. It's all such a pity!' He struck his armrest in frustration. 'She was wilful and wayward, but she was bright. She could have made something of her life!'

'How old was she?' I asked gently.

Jonathan thought about that, counted on his fingers. 'Fourteen,' he said finally.

'Dear God.' That was from Alan, and I knew he was thinking about his daughter when she was that age.

After another few miles, Alan cleared his throat. 'What are your plans, Jonathan?'

'I don't have any, s— Alan. Except to try to give Letty whatever comfort I can.'

'I have a bit of information that may help you,' Alan replied. 'Dorothy, I meant to tell you as soon as I got home, but . . . well. At any rate, I stopped at the police station before I did the shopping. I thought there might be some news. They haven't done a complete autopsy yet, but I can tell you, Jonathan, that Melissa – if it is Melissa, we still haven't proved that, have we? – the girl in the park, at any rate, died of asphyxia, almost certainly suffocation, from other indications. Some foreign matter in the mouth. They haven't determined what, as yet, but possibly a scarf or something of that sort, something soft. But the part that your Aunt Letty might find of some comfort, Jonathan, was that she had not been raped.'

Jonathan and I let out a simultaneous long breath. 'That's a relief!' I said. 'I had been imagining . . . well, never mind.'

'However,' said Alan, and my nerves tightened again. 'She was not a virgin. She was, in fact, about three months pregnant.'

This just got worse and worse. 'I don't suppose they could be wrong . . . no, of course not. But Alan! At age fourteen!' I turned around to glance at Jonathan in the back seat. He sat so still I thought for a moment he'd gone to sleep, until I saw his hands clenching and unclenching in his lap.

'Old enough,' Alan said roughly. 'One mistake, that's all it takes. It's happened before.'

'Are you going to tell Letty that, too?' I asked. 'Jonathan, I wouldn't. She doesn't have to know, and it would hurt her terribly.'

'No, Letty doesn't have to know,' said Alan, sounding weary. 'But Jonathan, I'm afraid this will put a great deal more pressure on Jemima, when the police work out the connection.'

'Pressure?' Jonathan sounded very far away.

'Carstairs is going to want to know who fathered the child.'

'Oh,' said Jonathan politely.

I remembered what he said about his blackouts under stress. We were coming up on a tiny village, with an attractive pub. I looked at Alan. He nodded and turned into the car park. 'Come on, Jonathan,' I said. 'Coffee.'

He came with us like an obedient child. We ordered coffee for all of us. Alan never drinks any alcohol when he's driving. And though coffee at that hour keeps me from sleeping, and I would have appreciated the soothing influence of a glass of wine, I felt I needed all my wits about me, to support Jonathan in the coming ordeal.

Jonathan came to himself after half a cup. 'Sorry. I guess I was a bit . . .'

'Gobsmacked,' I supplied. 'And no wonder.'

'And you've been more than kind. But I really do need to move on. Letty will be wondering about me.'

'And probably worrying something's happened to you, too. Her world has suddenly become very insecure. Off we go, then.'

Alan often has a Thermos in the car. He poured the rest of the coffee into it, begged two paper cups from the publican, and packed us back into the car.

It took only a few minutes to get to Bramber and find Aunt Letty's house.

'We'll come in if you want,' I offered, while Alan wrestled the wheelchair out of the boot. 'Or wait for you and take you home.'

'I think this is something I have to do alone,' Jonathan said. 'And I'll stay the night. Letty would like me to, I think. You're right about her feeling insecure just now. But she's a tough lady. I think she'll handle this better than I will, if you want the truth.'

He struggled out of the car, refusing any help. A light went on over the front door of his aunt's cottage. Jonathan turned to me. 'Dorothy, I can't thank you enough.' To my great surprise, he kissed my cheek. 'Alan, I think you know what your help means. I'll be in touch as soon as I can.' He unfolded his chair with the expertise born of long practice, and rolled up the flagged path.

Coffee or not, I slept most of the way home.

SEVEN

I woke the next morning to a blue sky and birdsong, and a moment of the sheer joy of living on such a glorious spring day, until the memory of the past two days washed over me. Then I would just as soon have turned over and pulled the covers over my head, but I knew I wouldn't sleep. Watson was alert to my wakefulness, but he has learned not to be overly animated first thing in the morning. He greets every day with vast enthusiasm, but has realized that his humans don't always share his mood.

Alan was already up, so I shrugged into a robe and went down to the kitchen. He had just finished making coffee and silently handed me a cup.

'Mm,' I said in thanks, and drank it, hoping it would brighten my outlook.

Alan handed me the *Telegraph*. I glanced at the headlines, according to which the world was just about to fall apart, again, and then turned inside to the London news.

'No progress,' said Alan. 'No identification of the body yet. They've kept your name out of it, anyway.'

I poured myself another cup of coffee. 'Thought I was irrelevant. A woman.'

'Toast?' Alan asked.

'No, thanks. Alan, what are we going to do?'

He sighed. 'I don't know.'

When Alan is dressed, his hair neatly combed, his chin freshly shaved, he looks far younger than he really is. Now, in rumpled pyjamas, his hair sticking up in spikes, his face covered in greying stubble, and with doubt and worry written all over him, he looked every day of his age. I was seized with compassion.

'I wish I didn't think we had to do something, but we do, don't we? But what a can of worms!'

At least that made Alan smile, as he often did when I came up with some colourful American expression. I love his Brit-speak, too.

'Are you duty-bound to tell anyone what Jonathan has told us?'

'Not really. It's up to my own conscience, which I must say is sorely strained. On the one hand, I have no more right than anyone else to withhold information. On the other, Jonathan has a very good point. When an investigation involves the palace, even tangentially, everyone works four times as hard, or at least tries to create that impression. Every stone would be explored.'

'And every avenue turned over. Yes. So the only question is, really, what can we do, the three of us, to get at the truth quietly?'

'I have no contacts at the palace,'said Alan.

'Well, neither do I, for heaven's sake! But Jonathan does.'

'Jemima. Is it a good idea to involve her at this stage?'

'She'll have to be involved soon. She's the girl's mother!'

'We think she is. It isn't proven.'

Alan can sometimes sound irritatingly like a policeman.

'Well, we're never going to prove it unless someone identi-fies her, are we? And we can hardly ask them to call Jemima in to look, without giving away the show. But what's to prevent Jonathan from showing her some of the pictures they took at the scene? They're not too awful, really, no blood or anything like that.'

'You forget, Dorothy, that Jonathan has no access to those photos.'

'I'll bet they'd let him see them. Or you. You were both on the scene. You were both well-respected police officers. The respect isn't gone just because you're retired and Jonathan is invalided out.'

'It would soon be lost if they caught either of us out in a stunt like this!'

His voice was getting louder. We were on the verge of a quarrel.

'But look, Alan. Suppose Jonathan asks Mr Carstairs if he can look at the photos. Carstairs will almost certainly say yes. And I'll bet it wouldn't be hard for him to make a quick copy.'

'And if he gets caught doing that?'

'He can make up something, I'm sure.'

'I won't encourage him to lie, Dorothy. Lying by saying nothing is one thing. A deliberate untruth is another.'

We seemed to be at an impasse. I could think of no way to find out anything further without a firm identification of the body, and there seemed to be obstacles in every path to that identification.

'All right,' I said slowly. 'Try this. I go to Carstairs. I say, with perfect truth, that I'm particularly interested in this case, and I'd like to see the pictures, because I didn't really get a good look at the time. Then I'll choose the best one, the clearest and least disturbing, and ask, as a special favour, if I might have a copy. I don't suppose he'll ask why, but if he does, I'll hint something. I won't lie. I think he'll let me have it, because I'm ultra respectable – I'm your wife, after all – and known to take an unusual interest in crime. If I play it right, I imagine he'll be rather amused and inclined to let the nosy old lady have what she wants.'

Alan pondered.

'I'm not official, you see,' I pursued. 'I know you and Jonathan aren't either, not now, but I never was.' And as he still said nothing, I added, 'Please don't tell me not to do this, Alan. For Jonathan's sake.'

'And if I do say no?'

'Then I'll try to find another way. I won't go against your wishes, Alan. We don't have that kind of marriage. Yes, I've fallen into situations you didn't like, but they were because of bad luck or poor judgement. I've never deliberately done anything you specifically asked me not to do.' At least I couldn't think of any instances, and I prayed he couldn't either. He's not the sort of man to give orders unless he thinks I'm putting myself in jeopardy. I admit, once or twice I've not told him what I planned to do, in case he objected, but that's justified.

'You're very good at misdirection, however. You should have been a conjuror, or perhaps a con artist. All right, my dear. You know I don't *want* to stand in your way. It's just that . . .'

'I know, love, I know. And I promise I'll be discreet.'

The guffaw that followed that remark made him choke on his coffee.

Now that I felt like eating again, I made us a modest cereal-and-fruit breakfast. Alan tries hard to keep fit, and I watch my weight when I can. Usually I watch it inch up.

'Once you get the picture,' Alan asked over a third cup of coffee, 'what are you going to do with it? Take it to Jemima?'

'Good heavens, no! I wouldn't have a clue how to go about visiting someone at the palace. No, I'll give it to Jonathan, and he can take it from there. By the way, did you think to get a phone number for Aunt Letty? I don't even know her last name.'

'I did. Shall I tell him your plans? I'd planned to phone him this morning anyway, to see how Aunt Letty was feeling.'

'And how he's feeling himself. Good heavens, Alan, that boy has been through way too much these past few days! Not to mention his physical pain.'

'I suspect he's trying to do too much, physically. Needs to prove something to himself. So am I to tell him, or not?'

'Tell him, by all means. Maybe not the details, on the principle that what he doesn't know can't hurt him, but tell him I'll try to get him a photo in the next day or two. And Alan, would you call Mr Carstairs and tell him to expect me?'

'That conversation will tax all my powers of diplomacy. When shall I say?'

'This afternoon, if it works for him. I can catch the next train.' And *diplomacy*, I thought with an inner smile, was just another word for stretching the truth. Men and semantics!

I made a quick call myself, to Lynn Anderson. 'Are you going to be home in a couple of hours? I'm making a quick trip to Town, and I want an invitation to lunch. There's lots I'm dying to tell you!'

Alan came into the room just as I was clicking off my mobile. 'And dare I ask just what you're going to tell whom?'

'Fear not. I told you I'd be discreet. I just begged lunch with Tom and Lynn, and I'm going to tell them about the Investiture. I don't think they've ever been to one, and as much as they try to be blasé about the royals, I know they'll eat it up.'

'Just as long as . . . No. I won't tell you what to say. I may protest a good deal, my dear, but in the end I trust to your good judgement.'

That earned him a kiss, and what with one thing and another, I very nearly missed my train.

Tom and Lynn live in a delectable Georgian house in Belgravia, a stone's throw from Victoria Station. They're American expats like me, have pots of money, and are very dear friends from way back. They've also been of great help in several of my forays into criminal investigation, and it was going to take all my fortitude not to tell them what I was up to in London.

We made it through lunch safely enough on the Investiture. They wanted to know all the details, and were amused at my confusing the Yeomen of the Guard with the Yeomen Warders. 'But of *course*, my dear!' said Lynn in the Philadelphia accent she's never quite managed to lose. 'Everyone does exactly the same thing. And it's all Gilbert and Sullivan's fault.'

'And the uniform. Really, I wonder if they were once part of the same unit, or something. It seems too much of a coincidence otherwise. The next time I go to the Tower—'

'Which, God willing, won't be for ages,' Lynn put in.

'—I'll ask one of the Beefeaters. I do feel safe calling them that, since everyone does.'

'You might not have to wait that long, D.,' said Tom, who had been listening indulgently. 'I know one of the Yeomen of the Guard. You could ask him.'

'Really?' I said, trying hard to conceal my deep interest. 'Does he work at the palace?'

'None of them exactly "works at the palace". They're the Queen's official bodyguards, but their duties are purely ceremonial.'

'Do they live at the palace, then?'

'I don't think so, but I have no idea, really. Why this sudden interest in a bit of royal trivia?'

'You know I love all things royal,' I said lightly. 'How do you happen to know this man, anyway?'

'Friend of a friend of a friend. You know how these things work. And you're evading my question. What are you up to this time, D.?'

'Oh, dear.' I glanced at my watch. 'Look, I honestly can't tell you right now. I'm due at . . . I have an appointment in fifteen minutes, and traffic being what it is, I'll be late if I don't leave this minute. I'll tell you all about it as soon as I can.'

'And that's the price of the name and phone number of my tame Yeoman,' said Tom, showing me down the elegant staircase.

EIGHT

I made it to Scotland Yard with exactly one minute to spare, and was shown into Mr Carstairs' office immediately.

I don't know quite what I expected. Something out of

Dickens, I suppose. I should have known better. New Scotland Yard is a sixties vintage office building, all glass and steel and anonymity, and the offices match; bland, indistinctive.

'Mrs Martin, what a pleasure! Would you like some coffee?'

'I just finished lunch, thank you.'

'Ah, well, just as well, perhaps. Our coffee is not always . . . however. How can I help you? Alan was a bit mysterious about your mission.'

'I feel a bit silly about it, to tell you the truth. I know you're terribly busy, and I shouldn't be bothering you.'

'Not at all.' It was the polite reply that meant: *Do get on with it.*

'Well, as Alan may have told you, it has to do with the incident in St James's Park.'

'Ah, yes. Do you perchance have some information for us? I'm afraid we haven't got much forrader with it.'

'Oh, dear. I'm sorry to hear that, and sorrier still that I can't help. I actually came to make a request, which you're going to think very silly and stupid, I'm afraid.'

'I doubt that, Mrs Martin. You are not a silly or stupid woman.'

Uh oh. He wasn't going to buy a ditzy act. 'You may change your mind after I tell you what I want. I know you're busy, so I'll come straight to the point. I'd like to look at the pictures your people took yesterday. I never did get a really good look at the poor child.' I stopped there, fearful lest I say too much.

Mr Carstairs frowned. 'Is there some particular reason?'

'None you'd think adequate, I suspect. You know of my interest in crime. If I were much younger, I think I might make a good investigator; officially, I mean. As it is, I simply like to know as much as I can about any crime which touches me. I suppose it really comes down to being nosy.' And that was the gospel truth, if not all the truth. Lying by omission, as Alan rather brutally called it.

Mr Carstairs looked at me very thoughtfully, and then picked up his phone. 'Oh, Latham, bring me the St James's file, would you?'

'Sounds like something diplomatic,' I said brightly. 'The Court of St James's, and all that.' I had remembered that ambassadors to England were called to the 'Court of St James's', an archaic usage from back when St James's Palace used to be the monarch's residence.

'Yes, well, we're calling this one the Corpse of St James's.' I smiled. 'Appropriate, if a bit macabre.'

'But then you enjoy the macabre, as you said.'

Why did I have the uncomfortable feeling that this man could see straight into my mind? While I was trying to think of some safe reply, the sergeant, or whoever he was, came in with the file, and Mr Carstairs opened it and placed the photographs before me.

They weren't pretty. True, there was no explicit evidence of violence, but a young girl lying crumpled in the dust was a pathetic sight, at best. They were in colour, so her pallor was more evident than I had remembered.

Her eyes were open. I hadn't noticed that at the time, or maybe they had closed them before they moved her out from under the bush. I suppressed a shudder and turned to other pictures that didn't show her eyes.

I lingered over one. It was a good clear picture, showing her face but taken from an angle that made the open eyes less obvious.

'Now I'm about to ask something truly outrageous, Mr Carstairs.' Take the initiative away from the adversary whenever possible. 'I would like a copy of this picture. Is that possible?'

He was silent for a long time. Well, I know that technique, too. I waited him out.

'I have always had a very great respect for your husband,' he said finally, 'from back in the early days, when I was just getting started, but he was in the very highest echelon already. He's an extraordinary policeman, Mrs Martin.'

'And an extraordinary man,' I said steadily.

'Were it not for that . . .' There was a long pause. Again I didn't break it, though my nerves were stretched to their tightest.

'You may have your copy. I'm sure I can trust you not to make unwise use of it.'

'Certainly.' We both stood at the same moment. 'Yes, I've

taken up far too much of your time. And thank you so very much.'

He told me to take the picture to an office on the ground floor, where he would instruct someone to make the copy for me. He was picking up the phone as I left, and I was quite sure I was under observation until I left the building, an envelope in my handbag and my heart trying its best to hammer its way out of my chest.

There are some pleasant pubs near New Scotland Yard. I made my way into the Sanctuary House (well named, I thought), ordered a half of bitter, and sat with it untouched while I phoned Aunt Letty's house.

Jonathan answered on the first ring. 'Dorothy? Alan said you might phone.'

'Yes. Jonathan, can you come to London? Or would it be better if I came to you?'

'You have—'

'Yes. I don't want to talk about it on the phone, especially a mobile.'

'Alan suggested it might be best if you came home, and Aunt Letty and I could drive there.'

'I'll be on the next train.'

I phoned Alan on the way, telling him when to meet me at the station.

'Success?' he asked.

'Yes. I'll tell you all about it when I get there.'

Alan had tea laid, so when we got home there was only the kettle to boil. Waiting for Jonathan and Letty, I sat down in the squashiest parlour chair and let my breath out in a whoosh. The afternoon was chilly, even if it was May, and Alan had kindled a small fire.

'That bad?' asked Alan without, I thought, a great deal of sympathy.

'Every bit that bad. I think that man has X-ray eyes. I swear he knew exactly why I was there and that I was hiding something important. What did you tell him when you called?'

'Only that you wanted to see him about the body in the park. He's quite capable of drawing inferences.'

'Well, all I can say is, I'm glad I wasn't a criminal facing him. I felt quite guilty enough as it was.'

'What did you tell him?'

'Essentially nothing. I didn't lie, if that's what you mean. Actually, it was you who turned the tide.'

'I! I said only that you wanted to see him. I told you.'

'No, it was nothing you said, it was you, yourself. He said he had great respect for you, and apparently my connection with you was enough to satisfy him I was trustworthy. He took his time about it, though, and for a while there I really thought I was going to have to make up some reasonable story.'

It was perhaps a good thing that the doorbell rang just then, and Alan went to admit Jonathan and his aunt while I hastened to switch on the kettle.

When I came in with the tea, Jonathan was sitting on one side of the fire and his aunt on the other. They both looked a bit pinched, and as if they were glad of the warmth.

I studied Letty covertly under cover of pouring and handing out tea. She was a small woman, probably undernourished as a child in those difficult years of austerity following the war. In fact, she looked exactly like the dauntless English ladies one meets everywhere. Her short hair, just beginning to go grey, had a tendency to curl in unexpected places. She wore a no-nonsense skirt and blouse, with no-nonsense shoes. I had seen her double on every market day in Sherebury, carrying what used to be a string bag and was now plastic or canvas, walking everywhere, buying with careful thrift, stopping now and then for a word with a friend. She was the backbone of England, strong, purposeful, dependable. Her exterior was rather severe, even rigid, but there was something about those curls that hinted at a softer core.

Jonathan started to stand, and I made a gesture. 'You're comfortable, Jonathan. Please don't get up.'

'Then let me introduce my Aunt Letty. Letty Higgins, Dorothy Martin.'

'I'm happy to meet you, Mrs Martin. And you know Jonathan and I are no relation, really. It's a courtesy title.'

'It's a title of great affection, or so I understand. I'm Dorothy, please, and may I call you Letty? I confess, after all Jonathan has told us, I'd find "Mrs Higgins" a terrible strain.'

'Please do. Jonathan has been telling me how kind you've been to him, over the years and especially now.'

'Letty, I hope you know how sorry we are, Alan and I, for your terrible loss. Nothing we can say will help, I know.'

'Thank you,' she said with great dignity.

I was sure she said no more because she was afraid of breaking down. I looked at Alan, uncertain of what to say or do next.

He cleared his throat. 'Mrs Higgins—'

'Letty.'

'Letty, then – I imagine Jonathan has told you the awkward position he's been placed in.'

'A sworn police officer with information he dare not give the police. Yes.'

'Quite. And he has therefore enlisted our aid, Dorothy's and mine, to try to uncover the truth behind this terrible crime.'

'He has told me. I must say I don't altogether approve. It seems to me he has no right to ask you to undertake actions that are questionable, if not downright illegal.'

'I understand and honour your objections,' said Alan, his stately language cutting off my protest. 'But we have talked this out, the three of us, and decided there really is no choice. Jonathan and I are no longer officially with the force, and Dorothy never had any official standing. Within limits, we feel we can act according to our consciences.'

'In other words,' I said, no longer able to keep silent, 'we're going to do what we think needs to be done, and hang official policy. So that's why I went to London today, and I managed to get a photo of . . . I'm sorry, Letty, but of the body Jonathan thinks might be your granddaughter.'

'Do you wish me to identify it?' Her voice had nary a quaver, but her hands tightened in her lap. I was glad she'd put her teacup on the table beside her.

'No!' said Jonathan. 'I'm going to take it up to Town tomorrow and show it to Jemima. I hate to do it, Letty, but she has to know about Melissa sometime. This way we'll know for sure, and can start trying to find the man who did this.'

'Man? What makes you think it was a man?'

Letty was sharp.

'Was she raped, then?' she went on stoically.

'No,' said Alan. 'Quite definitely not.'

'Then why are you presuming it was a man? I understand she was suffocated, with a scarf or something of the sort. A woman could do that as easily. Melissa was a slight child, always afraid she was too fat, not eating enough.'

'That's true enough, Letty.' Jonathan tried to save the situation. 'You're quite right, a woman could have done it, physically.'

'Then why did you say *man*? You're careful about that sort of thing, always have been from a child. Pedantic, even. You'd have said *person* if you weren't sure.'

Jonathan threw up his hands. 'I didn't mean to tell you. Honestly, I don't know for sure. I mean the Met doesn't know for sure. But . . . well . . .'

'The girl was pregnant, Letty,' said Alan quietly. 'About three months. It's a reasonable assumption that the man who was responsible for that might also have been responsible for her death.'

Letty closed her eyes. Her hands relaxed, deliberately. She opened her eyes again, picked up her teacup, and drank deeply.

'Do you think,' she asked when she had put the cup down, 'that I might have a little sherry?'

NINE

'She was always a wild child,' Letty said when I had poured sherry for all of us. 'Always, from the very first. She needed a father's influence. Jemima did the best she could, but she was only seventeen, and working to support her daughter. She was a good mother, in her way, but she was too young, and . . . well, I'll say it before Jonathan does . . . she's too much like me for us ever to have got on well.'

'She's not in the least like you,' said Jonathan. 'You're

level-headed and generous. Jemima . . . I'm sorry, Letty, but you know Jemima was always a handful.'

'I know, dear. So were you, you know. You had to have your own way, always.'

Jonathan looked astonished, but grew silent, probably considering what she had said.

Alan tactfully brought the discussion back to the present. 'I believe Melissa lived with you?'

'When Jemima looked like getting the job with the Lord Chamberlain's Office, she was of two minds about it. She's always been obsessed by art, and living in a palace full of beautiful things was like a dream come true. On the other hand, she couldn't have Melissa with her, and Jemima worried about leaving the child with me.'

'Was there ever any thought of sending her away to school?' Alan asked.

'We couldn't well afford that, and in any case . . .' She hesitated.

'Melissa wouldn't have put up with school discipline for a moment,' Jonathan finished. 'Bramber is a tiny village. It seemed better for her to stay there with Letty and go to the comprehensive.'

'But she ran away?'

'Several times,' said Letty with a sigh. 'The first time was last summer. She took some money from my purse and caught the train to London, and went to the palace. She was determined to move in with her mother. Obviously that wasn't possible, but Jemima begged a bit of time off and took Melissa on a tour of the palace, since it was one of the days the State Rooms were open to the public. I suppose Jemima hoped Melissa would begin to understand why her mother loved working and living there, even though it meant separation from Melissa. It didn't work. They had a furious row, which was overheard and noted with displeasure, and then Melissa did the unforgivable – slipped away when there were a lot of other tourists gawking at the art, and went roaming about on her own.'

'She didn't! But that isn't allowed, surely?'

'Not exactly,' said Letty drily. 'I'm not sure, in fact, how she managed to get away, but she was gone for some little time.'

'You're not saying . . . she didn't try to steal anything, did she?'

'No, apparently she was simply storming away from her mother, with no thought but to get away. That isn't easy to do, however, in that maze of palace rooms. So she was found eventually. She was dressed down pretty severely and summarily ejected, and told never to come back. Jemima very nearly lost her job over the incident, and was told that in future she would have to see her daughter somewhere else, well away from the palace.'

'And did she?'

'Oh, yes. Jemima came home on her days off whenever she could. She was frightfully worried about Melissa, and asked if I thought she should chuck her job and find one nearer Bramber, where she could have Melissa with her. But Melissa was having none of it. She wanted to live in London. She was sullen with her mother, and often with me. It was all very difficult.'

'I expect she was at that age where girls hate their mothers,' I said. 'I never had any children myself, but I remember the turmoil of my own emotions when I was an adolescent. I've often said I wondered why Faust wanted his lost youth back. I wouldn't have it as a gift.'

'You said that was the first time she ran away,' said Alan patiently. 'And the other occasions?'

'Two more, before this one. At least, two more that I know of. It's possible there were others. She spent a good deal of time away from home, with her friends, she said. But unless she was away on a school day, when the school would report it, I wouldn't necessarily know she'd been somewhere she didn't want to tell me about.' Letty sighed. 'I thought I was right in allowing her a good deal of freedom, but . . .' She raised a hand in a hopeless gesture and then let it drop.

'And the other episodes you knew about?' Alan persisted.

'She came home voluntarily the one time, just when I was thinking about calling in the police. No explanation, no apologies, just walked in the house the next afternoon, as if she was coming home from school. Said she'd spent the night with friends, and I must have misplaced the note she'd left. But she wouldn't tell me what friends. I wouldn't have approved if I'd known she was planning an overnight. I don't care for most of her friends. But I didn't believe her, anyway.'

'And when was this incident, Mrs . . . Letty?'

'Let's see.' She looked at Jonathan.

'Last August,' he said promptly. 'I remember it perfectly, because it was only two days before . . . well, all this.' He gestured to his legs and the cane by his chair.

'Yes, August. And then the next time she admitted going to London. That was in February, and a nastier, sloppier time of year to run off on holiday one couldn't have imagined. She said she needed new clothes, and certainly she came home with some, but she flatly refused to tell me where the money came from. It wasn't from me, this time. I'd kept my bag locked up ever since the first time.' Her hands had begun to clench again. 'I tried, God knows I tried. I suppose I'm just too old to understand an adolescent. When Jemima was that age we fought, certainly, but we loved each other, even through the worst bits, when she was making the wrong friends and the wrong choices. But I couldn't seem to do anything right with Melissa. She resented me, resented living in a village, resented everything.' A tear made its way down Letty's cheek. I silently handed her a tissue.

Alan looked questioningly at Jonathan, who took a deep breath, straightened his shoulders, and said, 'Letty, this is horrible for you. We don't have to continue now.'

'Yes, you do,' she said. 'You three are the only ones who know any of the truth about Melissa's death. You have to find out what you can as soon as you can. Don't you think I know anything about police work, boy? I do watch the telly, after all. What else do you want to know?'

'When did you miss her this time?'

'She didn't come home from school on Tuesday.'

The day before we found her. I couldn't keep the lump out of my throat.

'I tried to phone the school,' Letty went on, 'to see if she'd been kept late, but everyone had left by the time I rang. Then next morning I did talk to someone, and they said she'd not been there at all the day before. I should have called the police then, but to tell the truth I'd got used to her misbehaviour. I was more angry than worried.' Her voice shook, but she continued. 'If I'd said something then . . .'

'We think the crime had already been committed by then,' said Alan. 'Don't reproach yourself.' It was useless advice, and he knew it. Letty would reproach herself to the end of her days about everything concerned with Melissa. He went on briskly. 'We'll need the names of her closest friends. She might have told them the truth about her forays into London.'

'I'll tell you what I can, but it's only first names. You'll have to go to her teachers for addresses and telephone numbers. I told you I didn't like her friends. I could see her going the same way Jemima did; drinking and drugging and running wild. I didn't make the mistake I did with Jemima, though, forbidding her to see them. I knew she'd just defy me, and I didn't want to drive her away. So I encouraged her to bring them home, even though I didn't care for the way they dressed or the way they talked. She did, a few times, but I knew she thought I was too strict and she'd have more fun at their homes.'

Jonathan wrote down the name and location of the school. 'Is there anything else, anything at all, that might give us a hint about the baby's father?'

Letty shook her head slowly. 'She said very little to me about her interests. I suppose she thought I was too old to understand. Maybe I was.'

'You're not old, Letty,' said Jonathan, 'and stop thinking any of this is your fault. The little brat was impossible, you know she was. You did the best you could.'

'But,' said Letty bleakly, 'it wasn't good enough.'

I invited them to stay to supper, but I wasn't surprised when they declined. They were both emotionally drained and needed some time alone. So after they left I scrambled some eggs and whipped up a batch of what I still call biscuits, and Alan and I talked.

'She sounds like a thoroughly rebellious and unruly child,'

I said. 'I don't think I'd have been as patient with her as Letty apparently was. I'd have been strongly tempted to administer a good smack now and then.'

'That sometimes works with younger children, as you'd know from teaching,' said Alan. 'I don't think it's usually successful with a teenager. As you pointed out, it's a tough time of life for all concerned, and she does sound extraordinarily difficult, I agree.'

'I feel terribly sorry for Letty. She thinks she's failed the girl.'

'It isn't easy being a parent, even a surrogate one.'

'No. Frank and I eventually realized that childlessness had its points, and I've been forcefully reminded of it by all this. Alan, you noticed the one date, didn't you?'

'February. And this is May. Three months.'

'I wonder if Letty made the connection.'

'I was watching her pretty closely,' said Alan. 'I saw no sign that she did, then, but she's no fool. She will.'

'And then she'll berate herself even more, for not managing to keep Melissa at home. Only she couldn't have, not without chaining her up. I wonder where she got the money to travel to London, though. Train fares aren't cheap.'

Alan was studiously silent.

'Oh, no! You don't think . . .'

'Carstairs thought she was dressed like a tart.'

'But she wasn't, not really. I told Chief Superintendent Carstairs, remember? Her clothes were of good quality, and not especially flashy, certainly not tawdry. It was just the shoes, and the make-up. No, I think whoever gave her the baby also gave her money for clothes and railway tickets.'

'It's all guesswork.' Alan ran a hand down the back of his neck in a familiar gesture of frustration.

'Everything always is at this stage. Maybe we'll learn more when Jemima identifies the photo.'

'You do realize that when we have a positive ID, we'll have to insist that Jemima talk to Carstairs.'

Well, no, I hadn't quite realized that. I put down my fork.

'We've been justified, if at all, in pursuing this ourselves only because we couldn't be absolutely certain that the body

was Melissa's. When it is certain, we'll have no excuse at all.'
He was looking at me steadily.

'No. I suppose not. That is, no, of course not. But . . . but
what will happen to Jemima?'

'If she goes voluntarily to the police, very little, I would
imagine. They won't have to come to her, at the palace, and
if everyone is careful, she may not get into too much trouble.
This isn't her fault, after all.'

'Yes, but scandal . . . Alan, what if those awful tabloids get
hold of it? What a story it would make! "Family of hero
involved in palace sex scandal!"'

'Jemima isn't Jonathan's family.'

'Right. And the papers would eventually print a retraction,
in very small print on page seventeen. I'm really scared of
what will happen when the whole thing is in the hands of
Carstairs.'

'Dorothy, will you ever learn that you can't fix everyone's
problems? The world is going to produce trouble and misfortune
and suffering, sometimes for people we know, and sometimes
we can do nothing about it except sympathize.'

'I do know, but I don't have to like it. I hate feeling useless.
Alan, would you mind terribly if I deserted you for another
day? I'd like to go back to London.'

'You know I wouldn't mind, but why? Are you going to try
to talk to Jemima?'

'Not yet. No, today at lunch Tom told me he knew one of
the Yeomen of the Guard. Oh, heavens, I just can't help feeling
silly saying that. It just sounds too G and S and fairy-tale.
Anyway, I gather these Yeomen don't live at the palace, and
since they only work part-time, maybe they just live in their
own homes somewhere. I didn't have time to get the man's
name, and Tom was going to check on his address for me.' I
didn't mention that I was going to have to bribe him with the
story. 'It's the only trace I have of any kind of palace contact,'
I went on, 'and I want to follow it up. Because I really, really
think, Alan, that the palace is at the heart of this whole mess.'

'Dorothy, I do most sincerely hope you're not suggesting
the involvement of royalty?'

'Certainly not! Though I don't know why I say that. The

Lord knows that the royals have involved themselves in a good many unsavoury affairs over many centuries, not excepting recent ones. But I'm talking about the palace itself. It's such a huge place, and it has such a huge staff, and I imagine hundreds, if not thousands, of people are in and out of there every day. And we know Melissa was there at least once. I just . . . oh, Alan, you know I'm good at talking to people and finding out things. I need to talk to some people at the palace, and this is the only way I might be able to get a foot in the door.'

'Then, my dear, I wish you the very best of British luck. Now, are you ready for a wee noggin and some mindless television?'

TEN

Before I went to bed I phoned Tom and Lynn. 'It's no go, D.,' said Tom. 'My Yeoman friend has taken himself off to Spain for a little holiday, and plans to stay for the running of the bulls in July. So says his daughter, who deeply disapproves of the whole thing.'

'I should say so! Oh, well, it was a thought. Thanks, anyway.'

Alan looked at me enquiringly.

'The man's gone to Spain.'

'Ah, well. Come to bed, love.'

I moped for much of the next day. In the afternoon Alan took himself out of the depressing atmosphere with the excuse of needing some exercise. I wandered around the house, picked up a book and put it down again, went into the kitchen to see if there was some comfort food around, left again in disgust, telling myself I'd just had enough lunch to choke a horse, and besides I was up two pounds the last time I dared weigh myself. I was about to find some straws to weave through my hair, à la King Lear, when a knock sounded at the back door.

Jane! Of course, Jane! She would listen to me, offer me pithy advice, make me feel better . . . I opened the door.

Not Jane. Bob Finch, sober and with a stern eye.

'Come to do what I can with the garden, missus. You've let it get into a shockin' state, y'know.'

'I do know, Bob, but the weather—'

'Weather's been fine, past few days.'

'Well, yes, but . . . we've been away a lot.'

'Gallivantin' to London and that, I 'ear.'

Bob has strong ideas about the way Shderebury people should behave. He makes some allowances for me, as I'm an American and can be presumed not to know any better, but two trips to London in less than a week were plainly at least one too many.

I didn't ask how he knew. The Shderebury grapevine is extremely efficient.

I followed him out into the back garden. He was right, I had let it go. The weeds were crowding out the tulips; the daffodils were leaning their spent blooms and yellowing leaves all over everything, and I couldn't even see the low-growing primroses. Bob shook his head.

'You been gettin' mixed up in a murder again?' he asked accusingly.

'Well . . . in a way, I suppose. It's a good thing for you I do that sort of thing occasionally, you might remember.'

For I had proven Bob innocent of some nastiness, a few years ago.

'Yeah, well. That was 'ere. London's another story.' He knelt beside the path and began pulling up weeds by the handful.

I sighed. 'It certainly is. I don't know London well enough, don't know enough people who live there, and certainly not in Buck—' I stopped myself, but too late.

'Buck 'Ouse, is it? Don't you get mixed up with them royals, missus. Never know what they're goin' to get up to next.'

'Bob, I have never in my life met a member of the royal family, and it's unlikely that I ever will.'

'Wotcher doin' at Buck 'Ouse, then?'

When he's sober, Bob is observant, and persistent. One day I'll learn to keep my mouth shut. I suppose. 'Nothing, really. I just wanted to learn something about the way the staff operates, but nobody will give me the time of day.'

Bob lovingly freed an attractive clump of green leaves. I didn't know what they were, but something nice, I guessed from the tender way he was treating them.

'Course,' he said, 'there's the bloke I know wot works there.'

'At the palace? You know somebody who works at Buckingham Palace?'

'Looks after the corgis, don't 'ee? An' 'as the scars to show it. Nasty little buggers, they can be.'

'Really! But the Queen loves them.'

'Reckon they're smart enough to be'ave around 'er.' He got up, groaning loudly, moved a couple of feet, and got to his knees again. 'So do you want t'talk to 'im, or dontcher? Mind, he's not much for talkin', and not much for ladies, specially furriners.'

'Well, I don't care. I want to talk to him. What's his name? Should I go to the palace and ask for him, or what?'

Bob gave me the sort of look I once reserved for lazy nine-year-olds in my classroom. ''Angs out at the 'Orse an' Groom, don't 'ee? I can give you 'is mobile number, see if 'ee's in Town. 'Cause see, the Queen takes them dorgs wiv 'er when she moves abaht from one palace to the next, an' Joe, 'ee 'as to go along. So it's only if she's at Buck 'Ouse.'

'Well, she certainly was a few days ago. I saw her.'

'Thought you said—'

'I said I never met her. I sat in a room with about two hundred other people and watched her award honours. We're not exactly on first-name terms.'

'First name's all she's got, innit?' said Bob with a triumphant grin, and moved on down the border.

Alan came home while Bob was still working. I had gone into the house to see about dinner.

'I'm home, love, and ready for a drink. How about you?'

'In a minute, as soon as I get this in the oven.' I'd made one of my almost instant recipes for chicken breast. Really, it is the most versatile meat. Add a little of this and that and stick it in the oven, and voilà.

When I came into the parlour, Alan had already poured tots of bourbon for both of us, and had settled in his favourite chair.

'Enjoy your walk?' I asked. 'You were certainly gone long enough.'

'The car needed some attention, and I stopped at the police station.'

'Did you learn anything interesting?'

'We're going to need new tyres soon.'

I made a face and waited.

'Confound it, Dorothy, there's nothing to learn. Everything's at stalemate until they know who she is. I've left three messages on Jonathan's mobile, but he hasn't phoned yet. We've got to do something very soon, Jemima or no Jemima.'

'Indeed. Well, listen, Alan. Here I've been looking all over the place for a palace contact, and he's grubbing in our garden at this very minute!'

'Bob Finch?'

'Bob Finch. He's got a pal who looks after the Queen's dogs, so when she's at the palace, so is he. They travel as a retinue, as it were.'

'Literally in our own back garden. Well, well. I presume you're going to talk to the chap?'

'The trouble is, we don't know whether he's in London at the moment. Is the Queen still there, do you know?'

'Easy to find out.' He put his glass aside and picked up that morning's *Telegraph*, turning to the Court Circular at the back. 'Hmm . . . the Duke of Edinburgh . . . the Prince of Wales . . . here we are, the Queen. Well, she was certainly busy in London yesterday, doing all the normal things. Hospitals, charities, what have you. And it's over a month to Royal Ascot. I'd say the chances are good she's still there. Do you have contact information for this fellow?'

'Bob gave me his name and mobile number. "Joe Smith, 'ee is, in't 'ee, and don't take no sauce about it, neither."'

Alan laughed at my feeble attempt at Cockney. 'Do you think, my love, that it would be as well for me to go with you this time?'

'I certainly do. Bob said the best place to meet him was a pub called the Horse and Groom. I gather it's near the palace.'

'I know it. Quiet, tucked away in a hidden corner of Belgravia. Not perhaps the setting I'd have imagined for a friend of Bob's, but the beer is good. That probably explains it. Yes, I do think, if you can set something up with Mr Joe Smith, I'll accompany you.'

'Oh, no. You're going to set it up. I got the distinct impression Joe chooses his friends, and might not cotton to foreign women. I'll come along for the ride. Here's his number, and the phone.' I cravenly retreated to the kitchen to dish up supper.

'Well?' I asked when I came into the dining room with the chicken and a salad. Alan had set the table and brought a bottle of white wine from the fridge.

'Well.' He sat down and spread his napkin on his lap. 'The gentleman was apparently at the Horse and Groom, and had been for some time, I believe.'

'Oh, dear.'

'Quite. He was inclined to be truculent, but that may simply have been the drink. The burden of his song, insofar as I could understand it, was that it was a free country and if I liked to come along and have a pint in the same establishment he was occupying, it was no business of his.'

'This is the edited version, I presume?'

'Very considerably abridged and expurgated. I said we'd be along on Monday, but Dorothy, are you sure you want to do this? The fellow sounds like a lout, and I can't imagine he'll be of any use at all.'

'He's Bob's friend,' I argued, 'and Bob isn't a lout, though he can sound like one when he's in his cups. It's our only chance, isn't it? Jonathan is bound to have talked to Jemima by now, and the spit is going to hit the fan any time now. If we can't find out anything useful from good old Joe Smith, we'll just have to call it quits and tell Jonathan we tried our best. Speaking of whom, you haven't heard from him, have you?'

'Not a word, and I tried twice more. I wish I knew what he was playing at.'

'He's been under a terrible strain for months now,' I said. 'Maybe it's just suddenly caught up with him, and he's pulled the covers up over his head.'

'Fine time to climb out of the water, after he's dragged us in with him,' said Alan, in a fine flouting of metaphor agreement. 'More wine?'

Alan resolutely refused to discuss the matter for the rest of the evening, but as we tried to read and watch television and relax, the phone sat, screamingly silent.

ELEVEN

'I am getting very tired of trains,' I said next on Monday morning. We'd spent a quiet Sunday at home, taking some comfort from the usual lovely Eucharist at the Cathedral, but though we'd kept our problem off the spoken agenda, it hadn't been far from our minds. This morning we'd decided to go into town much earlier than was necessary to meet the truculent Joe Smith, in the hopes that we could track down Jonathan. We had no idea whether he had returned to his flat in London or was still with Aunt Letty; she wasn't answering her phone, either.

'That could mean anything,' I said drearily as the train moved through an uninspiring countryside. Rain streamed down the dirty windows, all but obscuring the view of sodden pastures and fields and misty oast-houses, making the latter look more than ever like witches' hats. 'If the worst has happened and the news is out, they could be hiding from the media. Or they could be hiding from the police, if they're still trying to keep the lid on the thing. Or they could have been tracked down by the murderer and silenced.'

'Have some chocolate,' said Alan, handing me his usual cure for my glooms.

This time I refused to be placated. 'Oh, I admit the last idea is foolish, but it's infuriating that the man got us into this and has now disappeared. He should have told the police the minute he recognized the girl. Or we should have gone to the police the minute he told us.'

'Yes, dear,' said Alan, and buried his nose in his newspaper.

There are times when I could smack the man.

Victoria Station was even more hectic than usual, which is

saying a good deal. The floor was wet and dirty, and I had to hang on to Alan's arm to keep from slipping. It wasn't yet lunchtime, but queues were already forming at the many fast-food stalls on the ground floor.

'I want some coffee and something sweet, and I don't want to eat it standing up,' I informed Alan. 'Let's pop into the Grosvenor.'

'It isn't the Grosvenor any more,' he reminded me.

'Yes, it is.' I pointed to the sign. 'They've changed it back. Anyway, whatever it's called, it's *here*, and I'm tired and cross, and I want a little pampering.'

The Grosvenor Hotel is one of the grand old ladies of London, a relic of the glory days of rail. In Victoria's day, railway hotels, attached to the major stations, were the last word in luxury. Many of them are gone now, but the Grosvenor, though showing her age, maintained for years a kind of faded opulence. Now she's been given a wash and a brush-up, and she's certainly convenient; there's a hotel entrance actually in Victoria Station.

We went through the lobby to the lounge and talked a somewhat reluctant waiter into coffee and chocolate croissants. We could have had identical fare in the station for a quarter the price, but we couldn't have sat in plush chairs and wiped the chocolate from our faces with linen napkins.

'Right,' I said, looking regretfully at the last pastry crumbs on my plate. At home I would probably have licked a finger and blotted them up, but I do know how to behave in public. 'So we try first to find Jonathan?'

Alan pulled out his phone. 'I'll try calling him one last time.' He punched in the numbers, and I saw his expression change. 'Jonathan? Alan here. I've been trying to reach you.'

That was the English restraint at work. I would probably have said, 'Where the hell have you been?'

'I see,' said Alan, nodding. 'Yes. Yes.' He clicked the phone off and put it in his pocket.

'That wasn't terribly informative, dear. What did he say? Where is he?'

'In hospital, St Thomas's. If you've finished, let's go.'

We took the Tube, which at that time of day can be much faster than a taxi. On the way, Alan told me a little.

'He fell. I don't know where, or anything much about the circumstances.' He looked around the crowded car, and I understood. Discretion was required.

'Did he injure himself badly?'

'He didn't say much. We'll know more when we see him.'

He was sitting up by his bed, in a four-bed ward that looked like hospitals all over the planet. He was pale, but that was his usual state.

'So, old chap,' said Alan, 'how are you?'

'Not so bad, considering.' He dismissed the subject with a wave of his hand. 'I'm sorry I haven't been in touch. I'm sure you've been wondering . . .' He looked around the ward with the same expression Alan had worn in the Underground train.

This non-communication was getting frustrating. 'Jonathan, tell us what *happened*! We've been worried sick about you.' That wasn't quite true. We'd been annoyed. But I didn't want to say that to an invalid.

'Really, it's nothing serious. I was at . . . I was visiting Jemima, and fell, that's all. Bruises and grazes, nothing worse.'

'Then why are you here?'

'Dicey medical history. But truly, I'm doing quite well.'

'You don't look it.' I was rapidly getting past being either sympathetic or tactful. 'You look perfectly dreadful. But since you're insisting you're fine, can you walk? Or wheel your chair?'

'Dorothy,' Alan began in a reproving tone.

I turned on him. 'We can't talk here, and we need to talk. Now.'

'I'm allowed to move about the floor.' He gestured to his wheelchair, folded against one wall. 'There's a small lounge at the end of the unit. I don't know if it's any more private.'

It was deserted, at least for the moment. Alan and I sat on the plastic chairs that were cleverly moulded to no human contours I could imagine.

'Now,' I said in a low voice. 'You went to see Jemima.'

'Yes, and a hell of a time I had getting her to come out of the palace to see me. I couldn't go inside, you know.'

I nodded. 'Yes, the terrorists have a lot to answer for. Sometimes I think they've won, they've changed life so completely. But you managed to prise her out, eventually. And showed her the picture.'

Jonathan closed his eyes. We waited.

'Yes,' he whispered at last. 'It was bad.'

My sympathy returned. I exchanged glances with Alan. We waited some more.

'I told her the whole story,' he said finally. 'I thought she was going to faint when I showed her . . . but when she was better, I asked her a few things. It's much harder when you know the family, isn't it?' he said to Alan. 'I've never faced that before, and I thank God I'll never have to do it again.'

'It's best to keep it as impersonal as possible, I found,' said Alan, keeping his own voice impersonal. 'So you asked the usual questions?'

'Did she know of anyone who had reason to harm Melissa? Had Melissa said anything? The critical one: when had she last seen her daughter?' His eyes closed again. We were getting to the worst part, I thought.

'It was on Tuesday. Melissa must have come straight to her when she left Letty's that morning. And she told her about the pregnancy.'

'Oh, dear.' I felt a little faint myself. The shock to a mother of hearing that her fourteen-year-old daughter was pregnant . . . no, I couldn't deal with that. I swallowed, to try to ease my dry throat, and asked, 'Did Melissa say who the father was?'

'No. Of course Jemima asked. Melissa said she wanted an abortion, and it didn't matter who the father was.'

'Wait. Was this in the palace?' asked Alan.

'No. Melissa wasn't allowed inside, you remember. For that matter, no one is who isn't official, but Melissa wasn't even allowed to go on a tour, after the time she made a scene and ran away. No, she phoned her mother from the street and asked her to come out. I gather it wasn't convenient, and Jemima was irritated. So, when Melissa refused to tell her who the father was, Jemima . . . well, she lost her temper and told Melissa she was telling lies to get attention, and she could turn right around and go home to Letty, that she, Jemima, washed her hands of her.'

'And those were the last words they exchanged. Oh, poor Jemima!' I was nearly in tears.

Alan struggled to return to the impersonal note. 'And I suppose that was what she wanted to talk to you about when she spoke to you after the Investiture.'

'Yes. She thought I might have some advice, or might be able to talk sense into the child.' He looked down. 'Child. I suppose that's not an appropriate term, is it, when she was going to have a child of her own. Or not have it, as the case might be.'

There was nothing I could say, nothing anyone could say, that would make the situation any better.

After a long pause, Alan asked, 'Is Jemima going to Carstairs with the identification?'

'She's going to talk to her superior, see what the repercussions might be. The woman is a battleaxe. I doubt she'll get much sympathy. Or that's what she planned to do when I saw her. I didn't intend to be out of touch for such a long time.'

'You never told us,' I reminded him. 'What actually happened?'

'Jemima was leaving. We'd been talking just over the way, at the edge of the Green Park. She was angry and confused and upset, and I was afraid she'd ignore the traffic. She looked ready to run across the street without waiting for the crossing signal. So I tried to run after her, and I tripped over my own cane. Sheer stupidity.'

I don't know quite why, but I didn't believe him. Something was going on, something nebulous . . . 'Jonathan, do you think Jemima would see me if I asked? Not near the palace, I mean, but somewhere else?'

He shrugged. 'You can ask.' He moved a hand towards where his pocket ought to be, and remembered he was wearing a hospital gown. 'Letty will give you her mobile number. The palace number is only for emergencies.'

'How is Letty?' Alan asked.

'Bearing up,' said Jonathan briefly. 'She's been spending a lot of time here with me.'

That explained the unanswered phone. 'Does she have neighbours or friends who will help?'

'She has neighbours. I don't know how much help they'll be. They mostly thought Melissa was a huge pain, so they won't be too sympathetic that she's gone. Relieved, probably.'

A nurse came up then, scolded Jonathan for being out of bed too long, and whisked him off.

TWELVE

'I hate hospitals,' I said when we had escaped into the fresh air.

'Yes,' said Alan. 'Where shall we go to get the taste out of our mouths? A spot of lunch? We don't have to meet Joe for at least another two hours.'

'You'll find it hard to believe, but I'm not hungry. Let's go back to Green Park and walk. Then we'll be close to the palace and the pub, when the time comes.'

'It may rain again at any time.'

'We have umbrellas.'

St James's Park has a good deal more shelter than Green Park, in case of rain. Alan knew why I didn't suggest it.

The Green Park, as it's officially called, is at its best in April, when drifts of daffodils spread across its expanses of grass, and make me go all Wordsworthian. The rest of the year it pretty much lives up to its name, and today, still early in the season and after a rain, it looked and smelled . . . well, green.

The benches were all beaded with water. Alan, anticipating the problem, had bought a newspaper in the Tube station, and spread it over the seat.

'Restful,' I said after we had sat in companionable silence for a while. Our silence, that is. Around us, children shouted, dogs barked. Traffic noises came from Piccadilly and, farther away, The Mall. But somehow the grass and trees isolated us.

'You're in need of some rest, aren't you, love?'

'Not as much as Jonathan is,' I said with a sigh. 'He looks awful, and it isn't just pain. Alan, he lied to us.'

'He didn't tell us all the truth,' said Alan. 'There's a difference.'

'Lying by omission, you called it.'

'About how he met with his accident,' he went on, ignoring me.

'At least about that. Do you think the rest was true?'

'As far as it went. It was painful for him, too painful to be a made-up story. His one fault as a policeman was always that he had trouble masking his feelings.'

'I can relate. But why would he lie about his accident?'

'Obviously,' said Alan, 'because he doesn't want us to know how it really happened. Which means someone else is involved.'

'Jemima.'

'It all comes down to Jemima, doesn't it? And if she knew her daughter was pregnant, and she and Jonathan quarrelled about it . . . He contradicted himself, did you notice? At first he said he just fell, then that he tripped over his cane.'

'I missed that. I was so horrified by the rest of the story. But Alan, you're surely not suggesting . . . her own daughter?'

'It's not as uncommon as you'd like to think. You know perfectly well that the first suspect in any murder case is a member of the family. A spouse, if there is one, but mother, father, brother, sister . . . unpleasant, but true.'

'The first recorded murder was a fratricide,' I said soberly.

'Jonathan isn't necessarily lying to protect Jemima,' Alan went on. 'He may have been injured by someone else, or in a way that he finds too embarrassing to relate.'

'He wouldn't lie over something that was just embarrassing,' I argued. 'At least not to us. He respects you, Alan. He *reveres* you. Yes, he does, don't look at me that way. He'd only lie about something really important.'

'Like what?'

And there we were stuck. Neither of us could think of something Jonathan would want to conceal, after he'd already told us so much.

The Horse and Groom was small and not very crowded, but

what clientele there were, were exclusively male. I was very glad I had decided not to go in by myself.

Joe Smith spotted us before we identified him.

'You'll be Bob Finch's friend, then?'

The voice came from a rather dark corner. I shaded my eyes and saw him – a small man with a countryman's face and an air of deep suspicion. We approached.

'And who's this, then?' He glowered at Alan, with a sideways nod of his head towards me.

'This is my wife, Dorothy Martin.'

'Thought you said your name was Nesbitt.'

Alan smiled genially. 'Alan Nesbitt, sir. I see your glass is empty. Will you have another?'

'Don't mind if I do,' said Joe Smith, his manner edging a point or two away from hostility. He waved a hand towards a chair in what I took as an invitation to sit.

When Alan came back with three brimming pints and several packets of crisps (what we Americans call potato chips), Joe relaxed even more. 'Cheers, mate,' he said, raising his glass. He downed half its contents in one swig while I took a genteel sip. By now I really was hungry, and beer on an empty stomach wasn't such a good idea. I helped myself to a handful of crisps.

'You'll be wondering why my wife and I wanted to talk to you,' said Alan.

Joe shrugged. 'So long as you're buyin', mate, don't know as I care.'

'Well, then, what can you tell me about life in the palace? Seems a rather extraordinary place to live.'

'Can't tell you about the family, y'know. Took me oath.'

'Does that include the corgis?'

'Ah, them!' He raised a trouser leg to reveal a bandage on his ankle. 'See that there? That's just the latest. That's Emma did that. Rest of 'em behave themselves, mostly, but Emma, she's got it in for me.'

I couldn't stay silent. 'Does the Queen know Emma bites you?'

'Can't talk about the Queen,' he said, and polished off the rest of his pint.

Alan gave me a '*Keep still*' look. 'How long have you lived at the palace, Joe?'

He considered. 'Twenty years come Michaelmas.'

'Then you must have seen a good many corgis come and go.'

'Corgis, and people. I don't just work with the dogs, you know. I'm a footman, and we do all sorts of things.'

'Are you allowed to talk at all about your work? The kinds of things you do all day? Most of us never get a glimpse inside the ordinary workings of the palace,' Alan added.

Joe looked pointedly at his empty glass. Alan rose, lifting his eyebrows at me. I put a hand over my almost full glass, but mouthed 'food'. He gave a tiny shrug and went to see what he could do.

'How did you get to know Bob Finch, Mr Smith?' Surely that was a safe topic, something he wouldn't mind talking about, even to a woman.

'We were at school together, weren't we? Village school, mind you. Donkey's years ago, that was.'

'Was that near Sherebury?'

'Brockhurst.' He named a village a few miles from the Cathedral city. 'Lived there all my life, till I came to London.'

I wanted to ask why he came to London at all, but Alan returned with the beer and more crisps. He handed the packets to me with an apologetic look. 'They don't do much in the way of food, it seems.' He turned back to Joe.

'You were about to tell me what, exactly, a footman does. Besides ride on the back of carriages.'

'Bit of everything, really. No two days alike. I used to drive a bus. Same thing, day after day. Couldn't stick it. There's parts of this job I could do without, like the corgis. But most of it is interesting, and I got me mates to talk to.'

Ah. If there was any point to this conversation at all, which I was beginning to doubt as I ate my substitute for real food, we were approaching it. His mates. I kept my silence while Alan probed.

'I expect you've made a good many friends in twenty years.'

'Like I said, the people come and go. A few stay on, but there's not many been there as long as me. Couple of the women.'

'I don't suppose you've ever come across a woman named Jemima? I don't recall her last name, but I think she works for the Lord Chamberlain's Office.'

Joe's face had darkened. 'You a friend of hers?'

'Friend of a friend,' said Alan. 'I don't actually know her.'

'She's a troublemaker, that one,' said Joe. 'Anyone'll say the same. She's got a kid needs a good smack on the bottom. Ran away from a tour one time, right through the palace, and her mum never stopped her. Could've run into one of the family, couldn't she?'

'Oh, dear,' I ventured to put in. 'You can't have that sort of thing, can you?'

'Too right we can't! If it happens again, the woman will be out on her ear, I can tell you that. And not many tears left behind, either.'

'She doesn't have friends?' Alan took up the conversation again.

'One or two. She doesn't mix much.' Joe applied himself to his beer. 'If you're going to report back to your friend, you can tell him I said she's a good worker. She can put on a smile for visitors, butter up the mucky-mucks when she has to. I'll give her that. And she knows a lot about the art that's all over the place. Wants to get into that side of it, as I hear. Curator, something like that. But she's nervy, short-tempered with anybody she thinks beneath her. And that's most of us. No, nobody'll be very sorry, or surprised, when she gets the sack.'

He put down his glass with a thump. 'Ta very much. Time to take the darling puppies for their walkies.'

And he was gone.

'Well, I must say that wasn't very much help,' I said as I finished my glass. 'Can't we find one single person who's willing to gossip about what goes on inside those gilded halls?'

'We've only tried one so far,' Alan reminded me. 'You're cross because you're hungry.'

'The crisps didn't do much for me,' I admitted.

'Very well, let's find some sustenance and plan our next moves.'

THIRTEEN

We found tea at one of the many small hotels that dot the area around Victoria Station and the palace. It wasn't the Ritz, but there was good strong tea and enough carbohydrates to keep me happy for a while. Alan, as usual, was right. My mood improved markedly after my third scone.

'There are really only two courses open to us at this point,' said Alan, tenting his fingers in his familiar lecturing pose. 'We've exhausted our one resource at the palace. Obviously the employees are well-trained and loyal. No one's going to talk to us, unofficial as we are. So –' he ticked off our options on his fingers – 'we can go to the police with what we know, or we can go to Jemima and demand some answers.'

'I'm in favour of the latter,' I said, wiping strawberry jam off my fingers. 'I don't know if we'll get anything out of her, because she's bound to be in a pretty fragile state, but we're not getting anywhere. If she can't, or won't, give us any information, we'll have to go to Carstairs and let the chips fall where they may.'

'And I don't mind telling you,' said Alan as he stood and fished out his wallet, 'that I'll feel mightily relieved when we've done that. This business of acting ex officio is not my cup of tea.'

'It's as bad as that time back in Indiana, isn't it?' We had visited my hometown on a memorable occasion when we wound up investigating the death of one of my dear old friends, and Alan was frustrated by his lack of police powers.

'Worse, because there I didn't have to worry particularly about stepping on anyone's toes. Here in London the toes are thick on the ground.'

'And some of them,' I added grimly, 'might even be able to boot us off to the Tower.'

'They don't imprison people there any more, as you very well know.'

'I was using the term metaphorically.'

We had headed up Buckingham Palace Road, and when the palace came into sight, my stomach began to clench, and I regretted that last scone. 'Do you have her phone number?'

'No.' Alan pulled out his mobile. A quick call to Letty produced Jemima's number. He punched it in while I waited anxiously.

'Yes, good afternoon. My name is Alan Nesbitt. We met a few days ago at the Investiture; I was with your cousin Jonathan. It's quite urgent I speak with you.' He had spoken rapidly, probably fearing she would hang up. Now there was a brief pause. 'Now, if it's at all possible. I'm just outside the Forecourt.' Pause. 'Yes. Five minutes? Oh, and my wife is with me.' He pocketed the phone.

'That sounded hopeful.'

'She wants to meet at the Canada Gate. Shall we?' He gave me his arm as we negotiated the busy crossing.

The Canada Gate is one of those pieces of useless decoration that I so love in London. It isn't really the gate to anything, since there is no fence on either side. You go around it, not through it, to get into Green Park. But it's perfectly gorgeous, gilded everywhere the designers could think to put gold, and quintessentially 'royal' in impact. It does not, however, have any handy benches nearby, and my feet and knees were beginning to complain. I hoped Jemima wouldn't keep us waiting long.

She did not. She came striding towards us within seconds after we arrived at the gate, and every movement of her body showed us she was furious.

'How dare you!' she said the moment she was near enough to be heard. Her tone was low and menacing. Plainly she would have preferred to scream at us. 'You wait days to tell me my only child is dead, and now you have something "urgent" to tell me? Well, I have something to tell you, both of you. You can both go and—'

'Jemima.' I laid a hand on her arm. She had ignored me until then, but she whirled and shook off my hand.

'No, but just listen a minute,' I said in my most soothing tones. 'If you're still angry after you hear what we have to say, you can shout, scream, whatever you want, but let's go sit down and talk about this like reasonable people.'

'I don't feel like sitting down!'

'No, but I'm a great deal older than you are, and I do need to sit, so please.' I gestured to a nearby set of steps and smiled. It took an effort, but I smiled, and it helped. With a grimace, Jemima marched off to the steps and sat, arms folded, chin out. *I dare you to change my mind.* She didn't say it aloud. She didn't need to.

I sat down next to Jemima. Alan stepped back and let me take over. 'I think, Jemima, that you may not quite understand what's happening here.' She opened her mouth, but I shook my head. 'No, you promised to listen.' She hadn't, but she closed her mouth again. 'Alan and I, along with Jonathan, have been risking a good deal on your behalf. We have, all three of us, withheld information from the police. That is very much against the law. We have done so to try to save you from their attentions and, worse, from the attentions of the media.'

She was at least listening now. I went on. 'You've had a dreadful experience. I won't try to pretend that I understand how you feel, because I never had children. I do not, from personal experience, know what you're going through, but I do know it's been horrific, and my heart bleeds for you. But my dear, think how much worse it would be if the press made a meal of it!'

'And you think you can do something to stop that.' Her voice was flat, her face full of cynicism.

'I don't know,' I said honestly. 'We can only try. If we can present the police with a solution to the crime before they even know you're involved, we have a chance. You know yourself that if they come here to question you, or even ask you to come to them, some of the gutter press are going to get hold of it. They're completely unscrupulous about how they get information, and how they use it.'

'And how do the pair of you propose to solve the crime all by your sweet selves?' Her voice dripped sarcasm. I tried hard to keep my temper. She's under a terrible strain, I kept repeating to myself.

'The three of us. Don't forget Jonathan. And don't forget that he was one of Scotland Yard's best detectives before he was disabled. And Alan was the senior police official in Belleshire until he retired. And even I have some detective instincts; I've helped solve a number of crimes, as you may not know. The point is, though, that we can do nothing without your help. That's what we're here to ask for. Your help and cooperation.'

There. I'd made my speech. Now it was up to her.

She sat for a long time, looking anywhere but at us. Expressions flitted across her face so fast I couldn't interpret them, but none of them were happy.

Finally she said, 'Why should I trust you?'

'Because we're your only hope.' Alan spoke for the first time. 'I must tell you that if you can't help us, we will have no choice but to go to Scotland Yard with what little information we have. And then—'

'"Cry 'Havoc!' and let slip the dogs of . . ." Fleet Street,' she said unexpectedly. 'Oh, I may not have gone to the right schools, but I'm not completely ignorant.' She made a gesture of hopelessness. 'All right. I don't see that you can do the least good, but all right. I'm so tired,' she added, and suddenly began to cry.

I couldn't think what to do. The Green Park is not an ideal place to have a good cry, especially not for an employee of the palace. There were no hotels or cafés nearby into which Jemima could be hustled. Alan solved the problem. He strode to the street and, with the lordly manner he can command when necessary, hailed a cab.

'Not supposed to stop here,' the cabbie called through the window.

'Emergency! A woman is ill!' A constable was approaching, but before he could send the cab on its way the three of us had bundled inside.

'Hospital, then, mate?' asked the cabbie.

'No. Drive on while I think a moment.'

I handed a fistful of tissues to Jemima, who was sobbing by now, and said, 'Tom and Lynn. Phone them, Alan, and see if they're home.' I gave the address to the driver, while trying to come up with plan B if the Andersons weren't there.

'Lynn will be waiting for us.' Alan clicked the phone off.

'You're taking me to see someone?' wailed Jemima. 'I can't—'

'You can't cry comfortably in public, and you can hardly go back to work in that condition. These are very old friends of ours, and I assure you they won't turn a hair.'

Jemima drew a long, wobbly breath, and her next sob morphed into a hiccup.

Lynn was waiting at the door, and showed Jemima to a bedroom immediately. 'You just cry as long as you like, and when you're ready to face the world again, there's the bathroom. The towels are fresh.'

She closed the door and gestured with her head, and we all retreated to the sitting room.

'Now. Before you say a word, tea or a drink?'

'After the kind of day we've had, a drink, please!' Alan nodded his agreement, and Lynn returned with a large tray, laden with glasses, a variety of bottles, a siphon, a pitcher of water and an ice bucket.

'I still keep to American ways in that respect, anyway,' she said. 'Help yourself.'

I poured myself a tot of bourbon and added one ice cube. 'Where's Tom?' I asked when I had taken a restorative sip.

'Out doing whatever mysterious things he does in the name of "business". I don't ask. I called him, though, and he's coming home. Meanwhile, tell me what's going on. If you can,' she added.

I looked at Alan. He nodded. We both knew that Lynn was utterly trustworthy. We quickly summarized the unhappy story. 'Since we learned all this, Alan and I have been trying to talk to someone, anyone, at the palace. The only remote contact we had was absolutely no help. So we finally decided we had to try to get Jemima to talk. With the result you see.'

'The Cliff Notes version. OK,' said Lynn, leaving Alan bewildered.

'American college term. I'll explain later,' I said.

'But did she tell you anything before she dissolved?'

'Not a thing. She was hostile at first, and then when we finally broke down her resistance, everything came crashing down on her.'

'And this interesting interview took place where? Surely not in the palace!'

'No. We met her in Green Park.'

'Good heavens! Out there in front of God and everybody?'

Alan smiled. 'I doubt God cared very much. He's seen worse. We were more concerned about "everybody". Some of the palace staff might have been there, one never knows. And Jemima has a reputation for creating scenes. They have not been well received by her employers.'

Lynn choked slightly on her gin and tonic. 'I will *never* cease to be amazed at the English gift for understatement. You're saying the Queen was not amused?'

'I trust the Queen knew nothing about it. I get the impression they keep her well wrapped in cotton wool. But Jemima's superiors, whoever they may be – we've not met them – threw her daughter out on one occasion and said she wasn't welcome back.'

'Her daughter. The one who was killed.' Lynn was no longer smiling.

'Yes. And we're no nearer knowing who did it than we were when this all started.'

'So the obvious question is, did Jemima do it herself?'

FOURTEEN

'**N**o, I didn't.'

Jemima had come into the room unnoticed, with Tom in the doorway right behind her. Alan was the one who coped. 'Well, that's good to know, because it was always a possibility, wasn't it? And what can we get you to drink? Do sit down.'

'I don't want to sit down, and I don't want a drink. I'm leaving.'

'No, you're not.' Alan stood and loomed over her, all six-feet-something of him. 'Not until we get some answers.'

'You have no right to keep me here! Accusing me of murdering my own child!'

'So call the police,' said Tom, who is not a small man himself.

'My *dear* girl, show some sense,' said Lynn. 'The minute the police learn about you and your daughter, you're going to be their very first suspect. And don't tell us you couldn't have done it. Of course you could. Easily. She trusted you. You could have approached her with a pillow, and she'd have thought you were playing.'

'I don't want to talk about it.'

'But you're going to have to,' I said, trying not to sound as exasperated as I was. 'To us, or to the official police. And they won't be offering you refreshments, I can tell you that. Look here, Jemima. I don't think you killed your daughter, and neither do the rest of us. We all suspect that the man who was involved with her also killed her. We need to know who that man was. Now, choose your drink, and answer some questions like a sensible woman.'

Reluctantly, she poured herself a healthy tot of gin, added some tonic, and sat back, looking at her lap.

'Yes.' Alan sounded very much like a policeman. 'Let's go back a few months, to the first time Jemima ran away from home and came to see you in London. That was about a year ago?'

'A bit less. Last July.'

'Tell us about it.'

She shrugged. 'Nothing to tell, really. She came, with some idiotic story about how dull it was in Bramber, and how she wanted to live in London. I told her it was impossible. She flew into a temper and stormed out.'

'No, no,' said Alan. 'We know all that. I want the details, please, from when she first arrived. Were you expecting her?'

'No! I don't . . . I didn't encourage her to visit me here. I went home whenever I could, but that week I was particularly busy. There was an Investiture coming up, and you know I have duties for that sort of thing. No, she simply turned up, about ten, I think. In the morning, anyway. I suppose she caught the first train out of Shoreham or South Lancing. She came straight to the palace and rang me up from just outside.

'I told her I was too busy to spend time with her, but she insisted, so I managed to get her into a tour. I thought we could talk a bit while we went round, and I'd still be available if I was needed. It didn't work. She went on and on about how she hated Bramber. We'd been over it all before. I live at the palace. I'd rather have taken a job that let me live where I pleased, but jobs aren't so easy to find, and there's a good deal of prestige attached to a palace job. And flats in London cost the earth. I told her all that. I'd told her before, but she wouldn't see reason. She stormed and shouted, and I lost my temper and shouted, too. And that's when she simply ran out of the room and vanished.'

'And this was at what time?'

'I wasn't looking at the clock. I was upset.'

'But you were also busy. Think about when you were able to get back to work.'

'Well, not then! Because Mrs Sedgewick, my boss, had heard the row. She was in the Ballroom checking some of the arrangements for the Investiture, and we were in the State Dining Room, not that far away. I'd told Melissa to keep her voice down, but she was getting louder and louder, and her language . . . well, that sort of thing just isn't supposed to happen in the palace. Mrs Sedgewick was just coming to tell me off when Melissa ran out of the room. Then we had to hunt for her. People simply cannot roam about the palace as they please, and it's a huge place. Over seven hundred rooms, you know. It's a rabbit warren.'

'How long did it take you to find her?' Alan persisted.

'That was the thing! It seemed like for ever. There are guards stationed in all the rooms open to the public, but she'd gone through a door that was supposed to be locked, and right off the tour route. And something had gone wrong with the CCTV cameras that day.'

Alan raised his eyebrows. 'Some serious breaches of security there.'

'Yes, well, it happens, doesn't it? It's not the first time, and it won't be the last. You remember that man, years ago, who made it all the way to Her Majesty's bedroom? Everyone does their best, but the only way a building that size and that complex can be truly secured is to keep all the doors and windows locked, and every single person, including all the employees and guests, checked in and out every single time, and make sure all the technology works perfectly all the time. It's impossible.'

Alan brushed that aside. 'So Melissa was missing for how long?' he persisted.

'I tell you I don't know!' Jemima was getting exasperated. 'Why does it matter? It was long enough to get me into serious trouble, I'll tell you.'

'It matters,' I said quietly, 'because of what she might have done and whom she might have met in that time.'

'But . . . you can't mean . . .'

'I don't know what I mean, except that we're talking about what might have been a critical time in Melissa's life. She was angry with you, she was fleeing pursuit in an extremely glamorous setting . . . and she was thirteen years old, a time of one's life when emotions are notoriously unstable. How was she, emotionally I mean, when you saw her next?'

Jemima bit her lip. 'She was crying. Well, she was in a pretty unsympathetic atmosphere. They'd found her, finally, in the garden, trying to get away, but all the doors were locked, and . . . well, you've seen the wall.'

Indeed I had. High, solid, and topped with spikes and barbed wire. Not intended for climbing.

'So they'd taken her to the security office, and since she was under age, they'd sent for me while they questioned her. And searched her, in case she'd stolen something. They hauled her over the coals for ages. It was dreadful! I was furious with her, but I was also pretty upset with the way they were treating her. I suppose it was after two before everything calmed down. Unless you count the rocket I got for at least another half an hour. I thought I was going to be sacked. Mrs Sedgewick would have done, I think, but *her* boss intervened, said it really wasn't my fault. I've been on probation ever since, though.'

'And Melissa left on her rampage . . . when?' Alan was back to his timetable.

'Oh. Well, I wasn't looking at my watch, but we'd started the tour at ten, and we weren't quite halfway through.'

'So you see, you do have an idea about time. Apparently Melissa was at large in the palace for at least two hours.'

'Something like that, I suppose.'

'And did she meet and talk with anyone during that time?' I asked, not expecting any satisfactory answer.

Jemima shook her head. 'I don't know. It wasn't one of the questions the security people asked. They wanted to know where she'd been, and she couldn't tell them much, not knowing the names of the palace rooms. She did mention some of the art, but the house is stiff with art. "A room with a lot of paintings and clocks" narrows it down to five or six, at best. But I wouldn't have thought her mind would be on a chat.'

'Did the staff talk about the incident later?'

'Oh, it was all over the house in an hour! They talked, all right, but not to me. I overheard bits now and then, but . . .'

She trailed off and I took up the conversation. 'Jemima, have you any close friends at the palace?'

'Not really.' She lifted her glass and took a healthy swallow. It was nearly empty. 'The Lord Chamberlain's Office is a separate department from the rest of the household, and we don't mix much.' She looked down at her hands again.

'It must get pretty lonely.'

'I'm too busy to think about that very much.' She paused. 'At least I was. Now I'll probably lose my job. I've been gone from my office for over an hour now, and you can be sure Mrs Sedgewick has noticed.'

'We'll do our best to smooth that over,' said Alan. 'But Jemima, we need you to think. You say you overheard comments about Melissa's escapade. What were people saying?'

'I tried not to listen. They're hateful, all of them!' The gin seemed to be loosening Jemima's tongue. 'They . . . they

called her a little slut, said she was headed for trouble. Some
of them know I used to . . . get into some trouble myself when
I was young, and said she was taking after me. I hate them
all!'

'Why would they say things like that?' I asked gently. 'Was
it her clothes, or her language, or . . .?'

'I don't know! I suppose she overdid the make-up a bit.
She was tall for her age, and beginning to develop a bit of
figure, and she wanted to look older. You know how it is at
that age.' She looked at me doubtfully, as if wondering whether
I'd ever been a teenager.

'How well I remember! A woman spends her whole life
wanting to be twenty-five.' I suddenly remembered that Melissa
would never be twenty-five. Lynn gave me a reproving look,
which I deserved. It had been a stupid remark. But I ploughed
on. 'What I was getting at was this: do you think any of the
staff had seen Melissa flirting with some young man while on
her palace odyssey?'

'She was thirteen!' Jemima set her glass down with a thump.
'The staff are all much older. The youngest footman must be
twenty, at least. Besides she was too angry to think of anything
else. She gets into . . . she used to get into these huge rages,
tantrums, almost. When she was like that she was blind and
deaf to everything.'

I sighed. 'I understand what you're saying. But Jemima,
someone seduced your daughter. Someone got her pregnant.
I'm sorry to say it so baldly, but it has to be said. I thought
it might be someone from the palace, but if you don't like
that idea, who was it, then? Have you no idea at all?'

'Some lout from school, probably. What on earth does it
matter?'

I bit my lip. I hated to do this to her. 'Jemima, listen. I
know this is impossibly hard for you. But we want, we need,
to find out who killed Melissa. She was killed in London. Your
mother says the last time she ran away was three months ago,
and that she admitted going to London. The timing is right.
So you're right, it could be some boy from her school. But
why would he come to London? Nothing about that makes
sense.'

'But nothing about anything makes sense! And nothing matters any more, nothing! My daughter is dead, and it's my fault!'

That tore it. Jemima's sobs escalated into full-blown hysterics. By the time we had calmed her down, there was no way I could make myself ask her any more questions. I wasn't sure she had any useful answers, anyway.

Lynn wanted to put her to bed, but Jemima was having none of it. 'Are you sure you're well enough?' Lynn persisted. 'Forgive me for saying so, but you look dreadful.'

'I have to get back to the palace. I don't know what excuse I'm going to use. I can't lose my job on top of everything else.'

'You'll have to say you're ill,' said Alan. 'It's not so far from the truth. And Jemima, the time has come. I need a list of the people working in the palace that day who might possibly have fallen within Melissa's erratic orbit. And then I need your permission to take this information to Chief Superintendent Carstairs.'

I held my breath. But she shook her head.

'I can't let you do that. It's not just about me and my job, honestly. I'll probably lose that anyway. It's . . . oh, well, damn it, I suppose I do have some loyalty to the dear old much maligned royals. It can't be pleasant living in a goldfish bowl, and really the Queen can be quite decent. So no, if there's any way to keep scandal away from Buck House, I'd rather do it that way.'

'It will be much harder,' Alan warned. 'None of us has any authority to question anyone, and we can't go about kidnapping all our witnesses.' He smiled at Jemima, who managed a tiny smile in return. 'However, the sentiment does you credit. How soon can you get me that list?'

'If you get me back to the palace within ten minutes, and I can sneak into my office without the dragon noticing, I may be able to claim I had a headache and had to lie down for a while. Then I can find out some names of the youngest footmen and phone you tonight.'

'Not just the youngest,' I said as we made our goodbyes to Tom and Lynn and hurried down the stairs. 'Pay attention to the best-looking ones, and the friendliest.'

'They're none of them friendly to me,' she muttered.

'Taxi!' Alan called.

FIFTEEN

We were both exhausted by the time we got home. The house was chilly, and Sam and Emmy were querulous. We had been away from home entirely too much of late, and they told us, at some length, that they felt unloved and neglected. I wanted only to go to bed, but I felt obliged to sit on the couch with a cat on either side and pet them until they purred their forgiveness. Alan, meanwhile, built a fire against the chill that had come with the morning's rain, and then disappeared into the kitchen, followed by an alert Watson.

When the cats had purred themselves to sleep, and I was near that state myself, Alan came back from the kitchen with roast beef sandwiches on good, crusty bread. 'I'm not hungry,' I said, massaging Sam's favourite spot behind her left ear.

'I know. Neither am I. But we have to stay up to wait for Jemima's call, and food will help. Try it, at least.'

Once I bit into a sandwich, I discovered I was ravenous. I ate it all, except for the fragments of beef that Sam and Emmy claimed as their due. Cats can, at times, be magnificently oblivious to human mental distress, though they are usually attentive to physical illness. Their indifference can be refreshing. Dogs, on the other hand, are never indifferent to their humans, or to food. Watson got his share, too.

The food did help. A cup of coffee would have helped still more, too much, in fact. I wanted to sleep tonight. I wanted to sleep right now. I was nodding off, a cat in my lap and a dog on my feet, when Alan's mobile rang. I jumped, and the animals scattered.

'Ah, Jemima. First of all, were you able to placate the dragon?' Pause. 'Good. Now, what do you have for me?' A lengthy pause, while Alan wrote on a notepad. 'Excellent. Now, have you any suggestions for how to approach these gentlemen? Do they frequent the Horse and Groom?' Pause, punctuated by various assenting noises. 'Good. Yes. Yes. Goodnight.'

I was wide awake by that time. 'Well?'

'Four names. Young and/or good-looking footmen. They are apparently not as hostile to Jemima as the others, or at least as she thinks the others are.'

'I suspect a good deal of it is her own attitude. If she'd loosen up a bit, she'd find it easier to make friends.'

'Yes. Well, at any rate, these four prefer another pub, the Bag O' Nails.' He paused. 'Jemima gave me their phone numbers.'

I was very tired. I sat silent for a long time. Watson came back and sat at my feet, feeling I was in need of a comforting dog. Finally I said, 'Tom and Lynn have a spare room. Shall we ask if we can use it for a few days?'

'I'll phone them. Go to bed, love.'

I went.

I slept later than usual the next morning. It felt like the first time in weeks I had been able to indulge myself. Alan brought me a cup of coffee when he thought I was about due to wake. 'Feeling better, my dear?'

'Mmm.' I sipped the magical brew.

'I would have let you sleep longer, but I was afraid you'd wake with a headache.'

'Mmm.' I needed a bit longer to surface. Alan kindly left me alone with my coffee.

I had showered, dressed, and begun nibbling on a piece of toast before my dear husband asked me to face the day.

'If you can bear another train ride, love, I've talked to Tom and Lynn. They'll be delighted to have us stay with them for however long we need to. Jane will look after the cats.'

'And Watson?' The dog looked up at the mention of his name, his tail wagging hopefully.

'Watson comes with us. I'll actually feel better about you meeting potential murderers if he's with you.'

I know dogs don't understand much English. But I'll swear he had a smug expression on his face.

Watson is the first dog I've ever owned, so I don't know if

dogs are allowed on American trains. I rather doubt it. But dogs are very important people in England, so they're welcome nearly everywhere. The Queen's corgis aren't the only dogs to be treated like royalty.

We packed for a week. I hoped we wouldn't be away that long, but the way this investigation was going, it might take us at least a week to learn anything important. That meant taking a week's worth of dog food and treats, and Watson's favourite toys, as well as his food and water bowls, and the bags and scoop to deal with his less pleasant artefacts.

'We need a diaper bag,' I said, surveying the growing stack of impedimenta. 'It's like travelling with a toddler.'

'No bottles or rattles,' said Alan. 'Otherwise, I agree.'

We caught the train with about ten seconds to spare. Watson baulked at the last minute, not at all sure he wanted to climb those nasty-looking steps into a place he knew nothing about, but we managed somehow. 'Never been on a train before, have you, old boy?' said Alan, sounding like a doting papa. It seemed a reasonable assumption. We found Watson, or rather he found us, as a mature dog, after his previous owner died, so we didn't know a lot about his background. I was a little uneasy about how he might behave on the journey, but once he observed that we were calm and comfortable, he decided that a train was acceptable, and went to sleep at Alan's feet.

'Do we have a plan of action once we get there?' I asked Alan. The carriage was deserted except for the three of us.

'Not really. We'll phone the first man on the list, find out when he's available to talk to us, and go from there.'

'Oh, I *wish* it weren't all so nebulous!' I pounded the arm of my seat in frustration, and Watson woke for a moment. 'It's all right, dog, But . . . oh, Alan, every day that passes means the Met will have a harder time working the case, and every day makes me feel guiltier about not telling Carstairs everything.'

'I know. I keep on trying to think what else we could have done, and finding no other course. But if we learn nothing in the next day or two, we'll have no choice but to go to Carstairs.'

'And take our lumps.'

Alan shook his head wearily. 'Whatever "lumps" he doles

out will be minor, compared to the beating I'll give myself, if this case is never solved.'

There was no possible reply to that.

Tom and Lynn's house is within easy walking distance of Victoria Station, but not with two large suitcases, Watson's carryall, and Watson himself. Alan bundled me and the luggage into a taxi. 'I'll take the old boy and meet you there. We could both use the exercise.'

'You'll probably get there first,' I said. The traffic was even worse than usual. It was high tourist season in London, and besides the cars and buses and taxis, bewildered travellers were afoot everywhere, speaking every conceivable language and getting in each other's way.

'I don't know,' I murmured. 'Maybe Sam Johnson was wrong after all.'

'Beg pardon, madam?' said the driver.

Tom and Lynn received us with the minimum of fuss, showed us our room, made much of Watson, and then left us to our own devices. 'Because,' said Lynn, 'this is business. We'll have a wingding when you've put the puzzle together. Meanwhile, here are two house keys and a key to the garden. Come and go exactly as you like. We're here when and if you want company, but otherwise ignore us.'

'I'm glad they have such faith in us,' I said, sitting down on the bed. 'I'm not as optimistic.'

'Need some chocolate?'

'No.' I stood up again and started to unpack. 'Alan, I don't mean to be grumpy, but what I need is not sympathy, but an idea. A direction.'

'Then leave that silly unpacking and come for a walk with me.'

Alan so seldom issues an order that I was startled into dropping the jacket I was hanging up, and following him out the door.

Belgravia is one of the loveliest areas of London. If you ever saw the old television series *Upstairs, Downstairs*, you know exactly what it looks like. Streets are lined with elegant Georgian houses, set off by gleaming black iron fences and small potted trees by every front door. Many windows sport boxes full of cascading flowers, and here and there a small garden occupies a square. These are fenced and gated, for use only by the residents.

Watson was very interested in the smell of the garden opposite the Andersons' house. 'We have the key,' said Alan. 'Shall we?'

'Did you bring a bag, just in case? I can't imagine what they'd do to a dog that fouled a path in this neck of the woods.'

'Not the dog, the owners. Shot at sunrise, I imagine. I have a bag.'

We wandered through the garden. There wasn't a lot to it, really, just a few patches of grass, bushes, gravelled paths. We let Watson off the leash and he wandered happily, sniffing, checking out all the other dogs that had visited there since time immemorial.

Somewhere in the distance there was a hint of martial music. 'Is there a parade or something?' I asked.

'Dorothy, we're very near the palace and Wellington Barracks. It won't be the Changing of the Guard, that's in the morning, but they're probably practising for something.'

The sound came and went, now borne to us on the wind, now buried under traffic noise. The beat of the drum was the one constant, the pattern changing from time to time but the rhythm as steady as my heartbeat.

Rhythms. Patterns.

'Alan, we're missing something. Something critical. I don't know what it is, but there's a thread to this somewhere, if we could only find it. I've been thinking about it a lot. Well, all the time, really. I have begun to think it's naïve to suppose that Melissa just happened to come to visit her mother, just happened to run away and roam the palace for hours, just happened to meet someone, just happened to get seduced by him. Somewhere there's a pattern, I know it. If only I can figure out what it is!'

Watson brought a mitten for us to inspect. It had apparently been lying under some bush since last winter, or perhaps the winter before that. The child who had lost it had probably outgrown it long ago. I tossed it for him to retrieve and he trotted off in pursuit.

'You have a point, Dorothy. Why was Melissa so determined to live in London? That may be at the heart of the matter.'

'Maybe. We're groping in the dark. It could be nothing more than just a young girl's boredom with a village, living with a grandmother and wanting some freedom.'

Alan was inclined to object. 'But she'd actually have had much less freedom in London. Especially with her mother working at the palace. A girl her age needs much closer supervision in a city these days. Plainly Letty let the child get to school and back on her own. That simply wouldn't be safe here.'

'She might not have realized that.'

'But Dorothy! The child wanted to live at the palace. That would never have happened, but you'd think she could see that her freedom would be severely curtailed, living in that fortress.'

'Mmm.' Watson brought the mitten back. I tossed it again. 'Alan, where is Jonathan from? Where did he grow up, I mean?'

'I don't actually know. He was living in London and working for Scotland Yard when we first met him. I suppose I assumed he was from Bramber.'

'That's where Letty lives now. But it would have been an awfully small house for her and her husband and Jemima. It's only a cottage, really. And then, Jonathan said his father was a shopkeeper who started small but then built a big business. If there are two shops in Bramber that's one more than we've ever seen. Hardly a place to start an empire.'

Alan thought about that. 'I think you're right. Do you think it's important to know where he and Jemima grew up?'

'I don't know what's important! I just . . . there's an itch somewhere, Alan. I need to know more about the . . . the back story. Hercule Poirot always said that the most important character in any murder was the victim, and that once one understood the victim, one would find the murderer. Or something like that. I don't feel we know anything, really, about Melissa, and I think we need to get to know her really well before we can work out why she died.'

'Well, it's a direction, at least, and that's what you wanted. What we wanted, really. Let's see if Jonathan is out of hospital and ready to tell us the story of his life.'

SIXTEEN

J onathan's 'flat' was very small, a glorified bed-sitter, and almost painfully tidy. The front room held a daybed, made up with military precision, a table with one straight chair and a bookcase with a miniature television, a laptop and a CD player on top. One corner had a tiny sink, a microwave, an under-counter refrigerator and one cupboard for food, utensils and tableware. There was a door leading, I assumed, to a bathroom. There was no back room.

Jonathan sat in his wheelchair, and motioned me to the bed. 'It's far more comfortable than the chair, I assure you. Sorry, Alan.'

'You're very . . . cosy here,' I said.

Jonathan grimaced. 'I've only noticed how small it is the past few months. Yes, I could easily afford a better place, what with my inheritance. But until I . . . had to retire, I was almost never here except to sleep.'

There was that hesitation again, as if he weren't sure how to refer to his horrifying experience. Or didn't want to.

'Yes. Well. Jonathan, we need to talk.'

'Yes. Would you like some tea?'

'Not right now, thank you,' said Alan. 'We'd like to ask you a number of questions, Jonathan. I don't have to tell you that you need answer none of them.'

'I've nothing to hide. If some answers can help you find Melissa's murderer, fire away.'

'All right, then.' I bit my lip. 'You're not going to like this one, though. What really happened two days ago, when you fell?'

He sighed and looked down at his hands. 'I might have known I couldn't fool either of you. You're too good at reading people, both of you. You've been trained to do it, of course, Alan.'

'And with me it comes from natural nosiness, plus years of teaching school and "I didn't do it, Mrs Martin, honest!" The kids used misdirection, too. Which is what you're trying to do now. What happened, Jonathan?'

'I think Jemima pushed me.'

'You *think*?' Alan sounded extremely sceptical.

'I'm not sure. I might have slipped. I don't do stairs awfully well.'

'Where was this? Not in the park, was it?'

'Actually it was. We had gone to sit on those steps to the side of the Canada Gate?'

'Yes, I know them.'

'There was nobody much about, so we could talk there. Jemima didn't want to talk in a pub or anywhere like that, which was a good thing, really. I knew she might react badly when I showed her the picture. But she didn't want to get too far from the palace, either. She was like a cat on hot bricks, worried about her job, worried about Melissa. So the Canada Gate was a logical place . . .'

'But . . .' I prodded. Jonathan was finding it very difficult to come to the point. I knew it was painful for him, but we had to stop treating him with kid gloves.

He swallowed. 'But when I told her about finding . . . about what we found in the park, and showed her the picture, she screamed. Not a loud scream, and there was plenty of traffic noise to cover it. And she seemed so faint, I thought we ought to sit down. And the only place to sit was the steps.'

'So that wasn't when she pushed you?'

'I honestly don't know that she pushed me. But at any rate, no, that isn't when I fell.'

He paused. Alan and I remained silent. Finally he went on.

'I'm not being deliberately obstructive, you know. This is very difficult.'

'Take your time.' Alan's voice was gentle. I wondered if that was an interview technique, or if he was genuinely sympathetic to Jonathan's distress. Whichever it was, it worked.

'Yes. It was at the very end of our talk. Well, it would be, wouldn't it?' He made a face. 'Obviously she wouldn't go on talking to me after that. I told you what she said about the last time she saw Melissa.'

I nodded and shuddered. Jonathan went on.

'Well, when she told me what she said to Melissa, I was furious. I said . . . a lot of things I shouldn't, hurtful things. It was unforgivable. Jemima was upset anyway, and she simply went spare. I don't know if she meant to slap me, or if she was going for my face, but I shied away . . . and that's when I fell down the steps.'

I didn't have the nerve to ask, but Alan did. 'Exactly what did you say, Jonathan?'

He looked absolutely miserable. 'I told her it was her fault. I said if she hadn't been hell-bent on living in London, living at the palace, none of this would ever have happened.'

I must have looked my shock. Jonathan flared up.

'I *said* it was unforgivable! Don't you think I regretted the words the moment they were out of my mouth, and every moment since? I'm thankful I was hurt. It should have been worse.'

Alan got up to get Jonathan a glass of water, and to give him time to regain his composure.

I persevered, much as I hated to keep hitting the sore spot. 'Beating yourself up isn't helpful, Jonathan. The point is, was it true, what you said? I had the impression Jemima took this job because it was what she could get. Was there more to it than that?'

The rage had left him as quickly as it had come. He sat back, pale and spent. 'Yes, it was true. Not about it being her fault, I mean. Not really. But she was determined to come to London, and the palace was her idea of the perfect place to work.'

'But why?'

'Because of the art.' He frowned in puzzlement.

Ah. Something clicked in my head. I couldn't have said why, but I felt we were getting somewhere, at last. 'We don't know about the art, Jonathan. At least, we know a little about the art at the palace, and someone said Jemima was interested in art, but we need to understand the connection. I think you'd better tell us, starting at the beginning. Where did your family, and hers, grow up?'

'Brighton. But what does that have to do with . . .?'

'I don't know. But Alan and I think we need to know more about Jemima and Melissa, and your childhood is a place to start.'

'Jonathan,' said Alan gently, 'I know your personal involvement in all this has clouded your judgement, not surprisingly. But try to remove yourself from the equation and go back to thinking like the excellent policeman you are. Remember the things they taught you at Hendon, the things I taught you at Bramshill. Tell us everything you can about Jemima.'

It was exactly the right approach. Jonathan lost that strained look. A little colour came back to his face. 'Where shall I begin? "I am born" à la David Copperfield?'

'If you like. If you think it relevant.'

'Possibly not. But I suppose I could go back to my first memories of Jemima . . . it must have been when she was about three. I would have been five.'

The two had been playing, or rather Jonathan had been teasing Jemima. 'I remember thinking she was a great nuisance. I suppose I was jealous of the attention Aunt Letty gave her. Natural enough. Letty was her mother, not mine. But I never had much attention from my own parents. Anyway, Jemima had a toy, or something . . . no, it was a book. One of those soft books one gave a child, made of some sort of cloth, with bright pictures or colours . . . I don't really remember. But I took it away, and she screamed the place down.'

'It sounds as though your interaction with Jemima hasn't changed a lot over the years,' I said.

'I suppose not,' said Jonathan. 'I hadn't actually thought about it that way.'

'All right, we have your first memory,' said Alan. 'Go on.'

'There's nothing more for a while. I do remember, or I think I remember, being at Letty's house one day when her husband came home. Fred was always rather useless, I'm afraid. I can see that now, looking back. Then, I just thought he was stupid. He came home drunk that one time and fell into the front room. I'd never seen anyone drunk before, and I wasn't sure what was the matter. I remember being frightened.'

'Was he abusive when he drank?'

'Not that I ever saw. I don't remember seeing bruises on Letty or Jemima, either. I think he was just lazy and lacking in ambition. I know Letty worked very hard to keep the family afloat.'

'What did she do?'

'Housekeeper at the Old Ship. Do you know it?'

'Very well. Dorothy and I have stayed there several times. Lovely old building, but hard to keep in good condition, I'd have thought.'

'It was. Still is, I suppose. Letty did very little of the actual cleaning, but she had to supervise those who did. It was hard work, and though she was paid a bit more than the cleaners, there were no tips. She struggled.'

'Were there no family members able to help?' I asked.

'Not that I ever knew. Jemima had an uncle, her father's brother, who was comparatively well-to-do, but he disapproved of the way Fred's family lived, disapproved of Letty's job and Fred's drinking, thought Jemima a wild young thing – which she was, to be fair – and wouldn't help them at all. In fact, in a way he made things far worse.'

Jonathan sipped from his glass of water and went on. 'You see, Uncle Roger had a son, Bert, a little older than Jemima. We went to school together before my parents sent me away to school, and became close friends, but we couldn't see each other a great deal out of school. Bert's father kept him on a tight rein. I used to feel sorry for him. He wasn't allowed to go anywhere with his mates, or do anything unless he was under supervision.'

'So, he went wild, too,' I put in.

'Of course he did. I thought you never had children.'

'I had hundreds of children during my years as a teacher,' I retorted. 'I saw what a rigid approach could do to them. Some knuckled under, turned into little pale shadows afraid to move lest they incur the wrath of their parents, or parent; it was usually a stern father who did the damage. I don't know if any of those poor girls – they were almost all girls – ever regained their self-confidence and became whole people.

'Those who went the other direction, who rebelled, strained against their bonds, went in all sorts of directions. The most intelligent of the boys – the rebels were almost all boys – sometimes turned out all right in the end. One or two even achieved brilliant careers. Those were the ones who were not so much running away from their upbringing, as running towards some goal that simply could not be denied, something they simply *had* to do. They had a passion in life, a purpose, and nothing their parents could say or do made the slightest difference.'

'That was the case with Bert,' said Jonathan. 'I could understand it myself, because all I ever wanted, from the time I first thought about what lay ahead in my life, was to be a policeman. But I wasn't as strong as Bert, or perhaps I cared more about conformity. It took Letty to change the course of my life. Bert didn't have a Letty, so he went off the rails. And he took Jemima with him.'

'Oh! I hadn't realized . . . he was allowed to spend time with her? I thought you said the two families didn't get along.'

'They didn't. At least, I think Letty got along quite well with Roger's wife . . . I can't recall her name. She was never in the picture much. She was one of those pale shadows you talked about, so thoroughly cowed by her husband that she wouldn't say boo to a goose.

'But Roger despised his brother, and wanted Bert to have nothing to do with any of the family. As cousins, though, the two children were bound to meet on occasion. Jemima was only a year or two younger than Bert, and very pretty. I didn't like her at all back then, but even I could see her beauty. And when they found their shared passion, it would have taken barbed wire to keep them apart.'

'Passion? At the age of . . . what, ten?' My voice was rising to a squeak in spite of myself.

Jonathan almost laughed. 'Not that sort of passion. Not then, anyway. Their passion was for art.'

SEVENTEEN

'Art!' I smacked my forehead. 'The palace! Joe Smith told us, remember, Alan? He said she knew a lot about the art, "wanted to get into that side of it". That's why that palace filled with priceless art was her Mecca, the ideal place to work, even though she had to leave her daughter behind to do it.'

Alan shook his head sadly. He didn't say 'misplaced priorities'. He didn't have to.

'But Jonathan, that might make sense in a woman of thirty or so. But children at age ten? Seems strange to me.'

'It's a long story,' said Jonathan, sighing, 'and I'd really like some tea. Let me make it, and then we'll go on with the saga.'

I wanted to make the tea for him, but I realized he had to do it for himself, had to prove to himself that he could do normal things. So I watched him move painfully around his minute kitchen, put mugs on a tray, go through the whole ritual.

When we were settled, with steaming mugs in our hands, Jonathan took up the tale. 'It began in The Lanes. You know them?'

Alan and I nodded. 'The Lanes' designates an area of Brighton that used to be renowned for its antique shops. Now most of the shops are gone, moved to other areas or turned into junk shops, but years ago there were beautiful things for sale, at very high prices indeed.

'Then you know the quality of the merchandise that used to be on offer. And you'll remember that Jemima lived in a household with no money to spend on anything except absolute necessities. Bert was somewhat better off. His father made a decent living, but his rigid view of life meant that there were no lavish expenditures on his son. He had to be taught that life was real, life was earnest, and good things had to be earned.'

'A genuine Calvinist,' I commented.

'Yes, but without the faith to back it up. There were no needlework mottoes of "The Lord Will Provide" in that house, I'll wager, though I was never inside it. No depending on the Lord. Bert had it drilled into him that the only way to succeed in life was to work, hard and constantly, with no time out for nonsense like music or art or sport or literature, or anything that might be enjoyable.'

'No wonder they went off the rails, he and Jemima! What a terrible way to bring up children!'

'I suppose he thought he was doing it for the best. But you're right. Both he and Jemima rebelled badly, and once they saw what money could buy in The Lanes, they simply had to have some. So they began to steal, first from their parents' purses and wallets and the housekeeping money, and then from any source they could find.

'I had gone off to school by the time they got into real trouble. Jemima began dealing drugs to get money. Just marijuana at first, but I think cocaine after a while.'

I was too appalled to speak. Alan said sharply, 'How old was she?'

'Twelve, I suppose. She was caught, almost at once. She was too young to be clever about covering her tracks, but given her age, nothing much happened to her. She had to do some community service of some kind. Letty was devastated. She understood, in a way, but she could not condone. What she did do was arrange various jobs for Jemima – babysitting, dog-minding – jobs that would keep her off the streets and give her a little spending money.'

'Hardly enough to buy antiques in The Lanes, I wouldn't have thought.'

'No, but enough to buy inexpensive prints, reproduction china, that sort of thing. You'd have thought that would satisfy a child, but it only fed her obsession, her passion for the real thing. Whenever I came home for school holidays, she'd come to see me and try to wheedle some money out of me. My father, oddly enough, gave me a generous allowance. I suppose he wanted to make sure the other boys at school knew I was the son of a wealthy man. Anyway, I usually gave in. Jemima was a cute kid, and she was Letty's daughter, and she was a beautiful little liar.'

I was growing more and more disturbed. 'Jonathan, nothing you've said has given me any confidence in Jemima's integrity. Quite the reverse, in fact. And I'm wondering, with a background like that, how on earth she landed a job at the palace. Don't they do security checks?'

'Of course they do!' Alan ran a hand down the back of his head. 'And with a record like that, I can't imagine why they'd have anything to do with her!'

'Ah, but she changed!' Jonathan was almost beginning to enjoy himself. 'You see, she and Bert eventually managed to put enough money together to buy something they'd always wanted, a nice pair of Staffordshire dogs. They split the purchase, each taking one of the pair. And that evening they sneaked out together to celebrate. They were wild with delight over their success, and they had a little wine, and one thing led to another . . . and Melissa happened.'

'Oh, dear,' I said weakly. 'That must have made matters much, much worse.'

'You'd think so. But in fact it was the turning point. Jemima's not stupid, you know. She realized that she had a child to support, and she settled down to do it. She's always tackled life as if she was fighting tigers, and this was no exception. She had no marketable skills, so she set out to acquire some, took a secretarial course and landed a job with Quinn's.'

'With your father!' I said, amazed.

'He was dead by that time, and the man who took over didn't care who an employee was, so long as she was competent. Jemima was all of that. She had an unexpected talent for organization, and it wasn't too long before she was managing the business end of the catering department.

'I got all this second-hand, you understand. I had finished at Hendon and made it into the Met, the very lowest rungs, but climbing one step at a time. I kept in touch with Letty, naturally. She'd inherited that house at Bramber – from an ancient aunt, I think – and with a tiny annuity and what I had set up for her in trust, she managed, but she couldn't have

Jemima and Melissa living with her. The house was too small, and she wanted Jemima to make it on her own.'

'Which she was doing, apparently,' I put in.

'Which she was doing. Melissa was old enough for school, which helped a bit. Jemima had to have a childminder only part of the day. Even so, she was away from her flat more than Letty thought she should be, because she was still mad for art. Took classes in art history, that sort of thing, and applied for jobs in galleries.'

'Where was Melissa's father all this time? Bert, was that his name?'

'We all assumed it was Bert, though Jemima would never say. I was appalled by that. Her own cousin. I was sure the baby would turn out to be an idiot or something, but she turned out all right.' Jonathan stopped, remembering how, in the end, Melissa had 'turned out'. He drank his tea, cold by now, and resumed.

'Anyway, Bert had pretty much dropped out of the picture. He had helped out when he could, at the beginning, but he was just a kid, and he wouldn't have dared approach his father. He got a job in one of the local galleries, and did well enough there to go to London. I assume he's still there. I've not heard from him in ages.'

'Would he have helped Jemima get the job at the palace?' asked Alan.

'Possibly. I really don't know.'

I exchanged glances with Alan. He nodded. 'I think we need to talk to him,' said Alan, 'about that and several other things. He lives in London?'

Jonathan shrugged. 'I suppose. As I said, I've lost touch. It's possible Jemima might know.'

'And his surname is Higgins, I assume, as he's the son of Letty's brother-in-law?'

'It was. He may have changed it, I suppose. It's not a classy-sounding name, is it? And the circles he moves in . . .'

'Phone Jemima.' It was not a suggestion.

Jonathan fished his mobile out of his pocket and punched in a number. 'No answer,' he said eventually. 'She always answers. I can't imagine . . .'

Alan ran a hand down the back of his neck once more, then stood and looked Jonathan straight in the eye. 'All right, my friend. It's obvious that Bert Higgins must be found. It's also obvious that the two or three of us, working on our own, can't do it. This is a job for the Met. It's time we told Carstairs the whole story.'

'But . . . Jemima . . . the palace . . . the scandal . . .' I protested.

'I hate it as much as you do, Dorothy.' Alan looked grim. 'But it's that or risk a murderer going free. We must tell him. Now.'

'Couldn't we try Jemima again?' I pleaded. 'She might know where Bert is. It's worth a try.'

Alan pulled out his phone, pushed buttons. 'Voicemail,' he said. 'Let's go.'

We were a sad and sorry trio an hour later, leaving Carstairs' office. He had greeted us cordially, but once Alan launched into our story, the emotional climate became arctic. The Chief Superintendent ignored me completely, turned the occasional chilly glare on Jonathan, and said absolutely nothing throughout Alan's narrative.

'I see,' he said when Alan had finished. His jaw worked, as if he had a great deal more to say. Alan's exalted one-time rank, however, kept him silent. 'Yes, sir. I'm sure you will excuse me, as I now have a great deal to do.'

A curt bow to me and to Alan, another icy glare at Jonathan, and he strode out of the office, leaving us to find our way out.

'There's a pub just around the next corner,' I said, finally. 'Can you walk that far, Jonathan?'

'I know the place. I can get that far.' He limped along. He'd left his wheelchair at his flat, not wanting to appear in it before his erstwhile boss. Now I thought he was regretting it.

None of us said another word until we were seated at a small table in the Sanctuary House, with pints in front of us. I took a large, refreshing gulp of mine and said, brilliantly, 'Well.'

'We deserved every word he didn't say,' said Alan, with a grimace. 'We've been bloody fools.'

Alan almost never swears. I agreed with his sentiments, and his mood.

'What do we do now, troops?' I asked when I'd finished my beer and reluctantly decided against another.

'The very first thing is to phone Jemima,' said Jonathan. 'I should have done it the moment we left the Yard, but I wasn't thinking very straight.' He pulled out his mobile and punched in some numbers.

I rolled my eyes at Alan. 'We should have thought of that,' I whispered. 'They may be with her right now.'

'It's still going to voicemail,' said Jonathan, sounding doomed.

'We have to trust them to be discreet,' said Alan. 'They won't start a palace scandal if they can help it.'

'The question is, will they be able to help it?' I wasn't optimistic. Scandal is the life blood of a tabloid, and dearly as I love England, I think the bottom-feeders in their press corps are much, much worse than their cousins in America. 'We're really left with only one thing to do. Jonathan, phone Letty and ask her to meet us at the station in Shoreham. We need to be with her when the police get in touch with her, and we need to pick her brains.'

I put in a quick call to the Andersons, telling them to expect us back when they saw us. Alan hailed a taxi; Jonathan wasn't up to the walk to Victoria Station.

We said little on the journey. What was there to say? We had tried our best to help Jemima by keeping her name out of the murder investigation. It had been a foolish undertaking from the start, worse then foolish, verging on the criminal. And we had failed. We were simply not equipped to deal with matters involving the palace.

If it did involve the palace. I still wasn't totally convinced about that. Certainly, Melissa could have run into someone while she was abroad on her illicit tour of the palace, met someone who later took advantage of her naïveté and dragged her into an affair. And certainly we'd have to check on that list of footmen that Jemima had provided. But it didn't sit right with me, somehow. There was something wrong with the scenario, and I wanted to get to the truth.

Or I wanted someone to get to the truth. It looked, now, as if it was likely to be the mighty forces of the Met, and as long as they handled it discreetly, that was perfectly fine with me.

Of course it was.

EIGHTEEN

We looked for Letty at the station, but couldn't see her. Jonathan finally spotted her car in the car park.

'Oh, no!' he cried.

'What's the matter . . . oh.' For I had seen what he saw. There were two people in the front seat, and the passenger was Jemima.

'You idiot!' Jonathan lowered his head to Jemima's open window and spoke in a low, furious voice. 'Don't you know running away is the stupidest thing you could have done?'

Her expression went blank. 'I haven't the least idea what you're talking about. I didn't run from anything. I came to Letty for a little rest. I told the dragon my daughter had died and I needed some time off, and she gave me a few days' compassionate leave.'

'Then you haven't seen the police?'

'No! What are you talking about? What have you done?'

Jemima was growing more and more agitated, and Alan intervened. 'Perhaps it would be best to discuss this in a less public place. I think we'll all fit in the car, Letty, if we squeeze a bit, and when we get to your house we can talk. Until then, Jemima, please be assured that nothing dire has taken place.'

Alan is not given to lying, and that, in my mind, classed as a whopper, but I followed his lead and tried to force Jemima into idle conversation on the short ride to Bramber.

'Jemima, Jonathan tells us you're an expert on art. Do you have a favourite period? Myself, I've always loved the Impressionists.'

'They're all right, but I prefer the Renaissance. Jonathan, what were you talking about?'

'The Renaissance?' I ploughed on. 'Now that covers a pretty broad field, and I'm afraid I'm relatively ignorant about it. Are we talking painting, sculpture, architecture . . . what?'

'Painting and the decorative arts, really, I suppose. Jonathan, tell me!'

I put on my schoolteacher voice. 'Really, Jemima, it will be much better if we wait until we can discuss this calmly. Meanwhile, I actually do know a little about the decorative arts. Have you ever heard of the Thorne Miniature Rooms at the Art Institute of Chicago?'

'I don't want . . . oh, all *right*.' She gave a dramatic sigh. 'Yes, I know what you're talking about. I've seen pictures, heavily retouched, I'm sure.'

'Oh, no, I know the pictures you mean, and they're absolutely accurate. You wouldn't believe how perfect the scale is, and how carefully each tiny detail was planned. She was a very wealthy woman, Mrs Thorne, although not in the same league with your boss.'

'My boss? The dragon?'

'I think she means Her Majesty,' said Alan, with the hint of a smile in his voice.

'Oh. Well, nobody's in her league, are they? She doesn't have to deal with miniature furniture and tapestries; she has the real thing.'

'And you love them, don't you?'

It was the wrong thing to say. Her love of all those beautiful things had led her to the palace, away from the care of Melissa, and in one way or another, that decision had led to tragedy.

As Jemima began to sob, Letty pulled her car into the minuscule parking space next to her house. 'You'll all have to get out on my side; sorry. Come along, love, you're skinny enough to slide under the steering wheel.'

Jemima clung to her (much smaller) mother like a child with a skinned knee.

I heard Alan say, in an undertone, 'Jonathan, let me do the talking.'

Letty, in her no-nonsense way, settled Jemima down enough that she sat quiet in an armchair while Alan laid out the whole story, ending with the need to find Bert. 'And in a city the size of London, it's plainly impossible to find one man without using the resources of the police. Unless you know where he is.'

Jemima shrugged. 'I don't even know *who* he is nowadays. He changed his name when he went to work with his first London gallery, I do know that. I used to get Christmas cards from him, but it's been a long time, and I don't remember his posh name.'

'Did he not help you get the job at the palace?' I was honestly surprised.

'Bert Higgins hasn't helped me with anything for a very long time.' She sounded not so much bitter as utterly weary. 'We were kids in love with beauty, never with each other. When we got a pair of Staffordshire dogs, at auction, we were over the moon, couldn't believe we'd actually done it. That was why we . . . well. We never actually meant all that much to each other. I didn't blame him for going off, well, not much, anyway.'

'I did,' said Letty. 'You faced up to your responsibility with a child. He never did. Left you high and dry.'

'He had his horrible father to deal with. I don't blame him. Not now, at least. He didn't have you, Mum.'

She leaned over to give Letty a kiss, the first sign I had seen in her of any softness. Then she sat up straight and said to Alan, 'Right. Now. What can I expect?'

As if in answer, the telephone rang. Her face filled with apprehension, Letty answered.

'Yes? Yes.' She made a face and nodded at us. 'Yes, she's right here. Would you like to talk to her? I see. In a few minutes, then.'

She sat back in her chair and sighed. 'They're on their way, love.'

'How did they sound?'

'Non-committal. Very official.'

Alan spoke. 'Now listen to me, all of you. I'm going to answer the door when they arrive, and introduce myself. I'll make it quite clear that I am here only as a friend of the family, which is true enough, but my former rank will keep them on their toes. Jonathan, don't volunteer your former rank, but don't lie if they ask. In fact, no lies from anyone, please, but say no more than necessary. Understood?'

When Alan speaks in full chief constable mode, people obey. We all nodded and sat silent, our hearts thudding, waiting for the police to arrive. I don't know about anyone else, but I was praying.

The knock when it came was neither loud nor threatening, but we all jumped. Alan opened the door. 'Good afternoon, Inspector, Sergeant. My name is Nesbitt. I'm the retired chief constable of Belleshire, and a good friend of the Quinn and Higgins families. Won't you come in?'

If Alan had hoped the police officers would be disconcerted by that little speech, he was disappointed. They had obviously been warned in advance that CC Nesbitt was meddling in this affair. Gravely polite, they introduced themselves, showed their identification, and came into the small room.

'I'll get chairs,' murmured Letty. The five of us had taken up all the available seating.

'Please don't bother, ma'am,' said the woman, apparently the senior officer of the pair. 'We can stand.'

'I'm sure you can, but you'll be more comfortable sitting,' Letty retorted, and went to retrieve the kitchen chairs. Jemima started to stand, to help her, but Alan shook his head ever so slightly, and she subsided.

The woman cleared her throat and spoke to us all. 'I'm Inspector Bradley and this is Sergeant Dalal. We are with the Sussex police, and are assisting the Metropolitan Police in their investigation into the murder of Melissa Higgins. May I assume that you are Jemima Higgins?'

It wasn't much of a guess. Jemima was the only young woman present. She nodded. 'I am.'

'And you are her mother, Letty Higgins?'

The inspector had spoken to me. I shook my head, and Letty, returning with two chairs, said, 'That's me.'

'Ah. Then you will be Mrs Martin, I take it, and you are Jonathan Quinn.'

We all nodded dumbly. I thought we looked as if we belonged in the back window of a car.

'Well, then. Thank you, Mrs Higgins.' The inspector sat on

one of the chairs and nodded to her assistant, who moved the chair quietly into the most inconspicuous spot he could find and pulled out a notebook and pencil.

'First of all, Ms Higgins, my condolences on the loss of your daughter.'

'Thank you.' Jemima's words were barely audible; she pulled a tissue out of her pocket and tried to stem the flow of tears.

I hoped Inspector Bradley would be merciful. Jemima was exceedingly fragile. I thought about saying something, but Alan cocked an eyebrow at me. I bit my lip and remained silent.

'Can you tell us why you failed to report your daughter's death to the police?'

Whoa! That was hitting her between the eyes. Letty put her hand on Jemima's arm.

Jemima swallowed hard before she answered. 'I work and live at Buckingham Palace. I was afraid that any police investigation would bring the media down on me and create a scandal.'

'Were you concerned that you might lose your job?'

'Partly that, but mostly I just wanted to protect the palace and the royal family. Not that they have anything to do with any of this, but you know how the media can twist things.'

'Exactly what are your duties at the palace?'

'I'm with the Lord Chamberlain's Office. We deal with the ceremonies connected with the royal family, at Buckingham Palace and elsewhere, but I work only at the palace. There are a good many ceremonies!'

'Indeed.' The inspector smiled. 'But can you be a little more specific about what you do?'

The impersonal questions were calming Jemima, I was glad to see. She had stopped shredding the tissue in her hands. Letty quietly took it away and handed her a clean one.

'It's a lot like organizing a huge wedding, several times a month. Someone must see to the invitations, to the housing of guests if it's that sort of do, to the menu if there's food, to the details of the ceremony itself. I don't do any of the planning, actually. That's done in much higher echelons, and in a sense there's not a lot to do there, because most of the ceremonies haven't changed in years. Centuries, maybe. Take the Investiture last week, for example.' She glanced at Alan, wondering if she was saying too much, but he smiled and nodded.

'My specific duty that day, after I'd checked the Ballroom to make sure everything was ready, was to help greet those being honoured and direct them to the briefing room. There were about a hundred of them, so three of us were assigned to that little chore. Then after the ceremony was over I had to help shepherd everyone out. But the real work was done ahead of time: preparing the invitation lists, making sure all the medals were ready, in the proper order, checking on the music – oh, a thousand details. I don't do all that, but all of us on the staff have to know, in general, what's going on and what needs to be done. We're expected to be able to step in wherever needed.'

'Sounds like hard work.'

'It is, but I wouldn't trade it for anything. Working at the palace, I mean. I'd actually like to get into the Royal Collection Department, but those jobs aren't going begging, and I . . .'

She made a futile little gesture and stopped speaking. Inspector Bradley leaned forward. 'I thought you said you weren't terribly concerned about losing your job if a scandal arose.'

Jemima didn't reply immediately. When she did, her voice had sunk once more to a whisper. 'I said that wasn't my chief concern, and it's true. I do love my job, but . . . going to work there . . . leaving Melissa behind . . .' She couldn't continue.

'We can come back later if you prefer,' the inspector said quietly to Letty, but Jemima shook her head vigorously.

'I think she'd rather get it over,' said Letty. 'If you'll just give her a minute?'

'Certainly. Mrs Martin, do you think you could take her to another room where she could wash her face and so on? Meanwhile, Mrs Higgins, perhaps you could tell us a few things about Melissa.'

I would have liked to hear that, but the inspector plainly wanted Jemima to be chaperoned, and I was the obvious candidate.

She refused my hand to help her up, and led the way to Letty's small bathroom. 'I'll be all right,' she said indistinctly. 'It was just . . .'

'I know. You think this is all your fault. It isn't, you know.'

'Yes, it is! If I hadn't been so stubborn, hell-bent on that job and no other, if I'd stayed home with Melissa—'

'Everything in the garden would have been rosy? You never had the slightest trouble with Melissa before you went to London? I find that hard to believe.'

She dismissed my remarks with a shaky wave of her hand. 'I don't care if you believe it or not. Oh, we quarrelled. Mothers and daughters do. But there was never anything really serious until I went off and left her with Letty.'

'Uh-huh. Melissa was a lot like you, wasn't she?'

'I . . . what do you mean, like me?'

'I mean she was rebellious, strong-willed, intelligent . . . and passionate about beauty. Just like you.'

She looked at me for a moment, stunned, and then sank to the floor and started to cry in earnest. This time I let her cry. She needed the release.

When her sobs had abated, I handed her a facecloth wrung out in cold water, and a fistful of tissues.

'I look frightful,' she said when she had mopped up and looked in the mirror. That was a good sign.

'Yes,' I said frankly. 'Your eyes are red and the lids are puffy and your nose looks like you've had a bad cold for a week. Better have some more cold water.'

'I can't tell if you're trying to irritate me or make me laugh,' she said shakily, and ran the water.

'Either. Both. Anger is a more useful emotion than sorrow, you know. Up to a point, it sharpens your wits and gets the adrenalin going. You're going to have to go back in there and face them, and you'll need all the armour you can find.'

'Yes.' She dried her face and took a deep, shaky breath. 'I haven't made a very good showing so far, have I?'

'A trifle spotty, perhaps.' I looked her over. 'You'll do. Off we go.'

Letty was talking when we got back. 'As I've said, I was not . . . not admitted to Melissa's private life. She kept it very private indeed. I made mistakes raising Jemima, interfered too much, tried to control too much. I thought the wiser course with Melissa was to give her a loose rein, let her make her own mistakes, work out the rebellion her own way.' She stopped for a moment, gripping the arms of her chair. 'I was wrong.'

'Mum, it's not your fault!'

'Not my fault that she ran away several times, ran away and got herself in trouble, got herself killed in London . . .'

I was about to make the same speech I'd given Jemima, but Inspector Bradley got in first.

'You mustn't blame yourself too much, Mrs Higgins. I have children of my own. Dealing with them is always a balancing act, and in the end, once they've reached a certain age, they make their own decisions. So you can't give me the names of her friends?'

'Only the few I've mentioned.'

'We'll try the school, then. Now, here's the critical question, and I wanted to save it, Ms Higgins, until you were back with us. Can either of you think of anyone who might have wished Melissa harm?'

The usual answer to that is a quick denial. Not this time. Letty and Jemima both thought hard.

'Not in the sense you mean, Inspector,' said Letty finally. 'Melissa could get up people's noses. She was rude to several of my neighbours, who understandably didn't have much time for her. She didn't care for school work, except for art, so she probably wasn't popular with her teachers. But as to harming her . . . no.'

Jemima nodded slowly. 'Exactly. Most of the palace staff who met her disliked her. They made it quite clear to me that they thought her unruly and badly brought up. Actually, they don't care for me, either. Same charges, I suppose.'

'And your other friends in London?'

'I have no friends, Inspector. In London or elsewhere.'

Before I could process that bleak statement, Jonathan, who had been entirely silent until now, said, 'You have one, Jemima.'

NINETEEN

Jemima looked at him in sheer astonishment. I'm afraid I did, too. I'd been certain that Jonathan didn't particularly like Jemima, and stuck with her only through loyalty to Letty. Now the scales fell from my eyes.

How could I have been so blind? He was in love with her! I wondered how far back it went. To when they were children, bickering, annoying each other? To the teen years, when Jemima had made her big mistake with Jonathan's best friend? He'd scarcely seen her as an adult, or so he said. And yet his sentiment was unmistakable, once I'd stopped being stupid.

I looked at him with my new understanding, and realized that he had no idea what he'd just revealed. He didn't know, himself, about his feelings for Jemima. Bratty little sister who needed protecting, that was what he thought he was feeling.

Inspector Bradley saw it, though, saw it quite clearly. She focused her attention on Jonathan.

'How well do you know Ms Higgins, Mr Quinn? Or should I say Chief Inspector Quinn, sir?'

Jonathan took a tight grip of the arms of his chair. 'As you know, I am no longer with the Met, Inspector. Mr Quinn will do. As to Ms Higgins, I knew her very well at one time, as I imagine you also know. Her mother was a very close friend to my mother, and I always viewed Mrs Higgins as my aunt, though there is no actual family tie. Thus I thought of Jemima as my cousin.'

He took a breath. 'I have, however, seen very little of Jemima – Ms Higgins – since we were teenagers. I went away to school, then to Hendon, while she stayed in Brighton.'

'Were you aware that she was working at Buckingham Palace?'

'Yes.'

Inspector Bradley cocked her head. 'And how did you know that, sir?'

'I have kept in touch with Mrs Higgins through the years.'

'And how would you describe your relationship with Mrs Higgins?' The inspector was a perfectly courteous pit bull.

'I have very great affection for my Aunt Letty.' The smile Jonathan produced was strained, but it was genuine.

'I understand. Your own parents are dead, I believe?'

'Yes.'

'So would it be fair to say that Mrs Higgins has been something of a substitute mother?'

'Very fair.' He swallowed hard. This wasn't easy for him.

'And you, Mrs Higgins, view Mr Quinn as a son?'

'The son I never had, Inspector. I'm very proud of him.'

And, her tone and body language implied, I'll fight you or anybody else who tries to harm him. In her own very different style, she was a pit bull, too.

'I'm sure you have every right to be. Very few men, or women, have ever won the George Cross.' She stood. 'I think that's all for now. Thank you for your cooperation. Please let the police know of your whereabouts for the next few days, either our office or the Met. I'm sure we'll have more questions as the investigation proceeds. We can see ourselves out.'

Our collective sighs of relief when they left rivalled the huffs and puffs of the Big Bad Wolf.

'It isn't over,' Alan warned. 'Not by a long chalk. Inspector Bradley was just establishing the background, getting a feel for the people involved. You will have noticed, Jonathan, that she asked none of the vital questions.'

'Where were we all on such-and-such a date, what were our relationships with Melissa . . . all that. Yes. The three of us are bound to be the most logical suspects. We're all the family she had.'

There it was again, that unconscious identification with the Higgins family, with Jemima. Surely he could see that, of the three of them, he was the very most likely suspect in the eyes of the police.

I jumped in with both feet. 'So, Jemima, where *were* you the night before the Investiture?'

She had recovered enough of her spirit to glare at me. 'Are you accusing me of murdering my own child?'

'No. But you have to be prepared with your answer. Fumbling around sounds suspicious.'

'Actually,' said Alan, 'it sounds normal. Most people can't remember what they had for breakfast, much less what they were doing several days ago. But go ahead, Jemima.'

'I don't even have to think about it. It was the night before the Investiture, and I was behind with my work, because of the scene with Melissa that morning. I didn't even go out for a meal, though I usually do in the evening. The food at the canteen isn't bad, but the stress level in my job is pretty high. I need to get away when I can.'

I shuddered and nodded vigorously. 'I needed to get out of the palace as fast as I could that day, after the Investiture, and I wasn't there much over an hour. The place gets to me. All that luxury, all that security . . .'

'Dorothy.' Alan reminded me that this wasn't about me.

'Well, anyway, so the last time you left the palace was . . .?'

'Sometime the day before, I suppose; the Monday. As I say, I usually pop down to one pub or another after my work day's finished, but there was nothing remarkable about that day, so I can't swear to it.'

'But you can swear to the day in question. You didn't leave the palace at all, even for a moment? I'm sorry to belabour this, but you can be certain that Inspector Bradley will press you hard on the point.'

'Only in the morning, for a few minutes, when Melissa rang me up and wanted me to meet her outside. I told you about that. I was never farther away than the Canada Gate, and I'm sure the guards noticed the row she and I had. We weren't exactly keeping our voices down.'

Her voice was getting shaky. I absolutely hated making her remember that day. Not that she could ever forget. To her dying day she would remember that her last words to her daughter had been spoken in anger. But it was time to change the focus.

'Well, that seems clear enough. Letty, what about you?'

'I spent most of the day fretting about Melissa, not getting much done. I'd pick up something and forget what I wanted to do with it. I wish now that I'd phoned Jemima. She would have told me that Melissa was in London, and I'd have stopped worrying. Mistakenly, as it turned out. But I didn't phone, so I didn't know, and I wasted the day.'

'Did you go out at all?'

'No. I wanted to be here when Melissa came back, to give her a piece of my mind.'

This was a minefield of unhappy thoughts for her, too. That was the way with murder. There were far more victims than the one who lay dead. I shook my head. 'Were the neighbours at home?'

'I have no idea. My neighbours keep themselves to themselves. They don't like Melissa. Didn't.'

'So they wouldn't be able to say for certain that you were here all day.'

'Probably not. Though my car was here, come to think of it. The Bells, the ones who live on that side –' she pointed – 'complain about my car all the time. They claim I park over the yellow line. As you saw when we arrived, there's very little room, and there is absolutely nowhere else I can put my car. I do my best, but occasionally the Bells leave their rubbish bin jutting out, and my choice is to bang into it or park over the line.'

It was clearly an old grievance, but reciting it took her mind off Melissa for a few seconds. It was useful.

'Then we come to you, Jonathan. Where were you and what were you doing that day?'

'And there we strike out, as you Americans might say. I was at home in my flat all day, fighting my nerves about the Investiture, along with my other demons. No one phoned, no one came to call. I have no alibi whatsoever.'

TWENTY

Well, that was what I had expected, but it was a blow, nonetheless. I tried to look on the bright side. 'Well, I think that's certainly in your favour. You're a policeman. Yes, I know you're retired, or sidelined by your injuries anyway, but you're still a trained policeman. If you intended to commit a murder, you'd make sure you had a rock-solid alibi. So the very fact that you don't have one . . .'

Alan sighed. 'You've been reading too many crime novels again, my dear. The perfect alibi is a virtual impossibility. Murderers, even when they're as smart as Jonathan – which, thank heaven, they usually are not – have a very hard time coming up with them. They usually depend on someone else, someone who will lie his head off for his friend, or lover. And that kind nearly always break down, since liars are, by their very nature, unreliable. Dangle a strong enough incentive in front of the chap, and he – or it's often she – will break down. Besides, it's very difficult to tell a consistent lie. So a story like Jonathan's is often the best recourse. He can't prove he was in his flat all day, but equally, we can't prove . . . that is, the police can't prove he wasn't, unless we can find someone who saw him elsewhere.'

I didn't care for the tone of this at all, and neither did Jemima and Letty.

'You're talking as if—'

'You can't believe that—'

'But Alan! You don't mean—'

We all spoke at once. Alan held up a large hand. 'No. I don't believe Jonathan to be guilty. I'm reasoning the way the Met will. They don't want to believe him guilty either. He's one of their own, and don't quibble about technicalities. But the fact is that he withheld important information from them, for days, and he is intimately acquainted with the victim's mother and grandmother, if not with the victim herself. What are they to think?'

We sat in gloomy silence.

At last Jonathan spoke. 'I've made a royal mess of things, haven't I?'

I giggled, inappropriately. 'Sorry. It's the strain, I suppose. I just thought . . . a royal mess . . . and it's all centred around Buckingham Palace . . . sorry.'

They all quite rightly ignored me. Jonathan gave a deep sigh. 'In the end, I'm hoping forensic evidence will put me right out of it. Have you heard anything further about the complete autopsy?'

'No. And I won't.'

I drew my head back. 'You mean you're not going to follow it up?'

'I mean I won't be allowed any access to information. Our actions in delaying the investigation have made me persona very much non grata with the Met. Not another particle of information will come my way, I assure you.'

Letty drove us back to the station, and we went back to London, our tails between our legs.

'Well, you're *not* going to just give up!' Lynn's voice was indignant. Watson looked from her to me, decided she was no threat, and put his head back down on his paws. 'For a start,' she went on, 'he can hardly walk! How could he—'

'He has a good deal of upper body strength, Lynn,' said Alan. 'Anyone who uses a wheelchair regularly develops powerful muscles in the arms and chest. Sorry, Jonathan, but it's true, isn't it?'

'Quite true,' said Jonathan morosely. He picked up a convenient dictionary and held it steady in front of him, without a single tremor. 'I could probably smother anyone I liked.'

We were gathered in Lynn's elegant living room that evening, drinks and nibbles in front of us. Jonathan had been ordered into the most comfortable chair and given cushions to support his legs. Alan and I sat on the couch in varied poses of despondency. Tom looked on, frowning, and Lynn gave a helpless shrug.

'I don't see what else we're to do, Lynn.' Alan took a healthy swig of his bourbon. 'We've all been shown large "No Trespassing" signs. And with no access to official records, and a firm order to stay out of the investigation . . .'

'Well,' I said thoughtfully, 'no one's actually told us that, in so many words.' The bourbon was beginning to ease my distress.

'Surely you can read between the lines!'

'I can, but . . . do you remember the movie *A Man for All Seasons*? About Thomas More?'

'I saw the play. But what does that have to do with—'

'Just wait. I loved that movie, and there's one part that I especially remember. Someone's told More about the decree or act or something that the King has drawn up, that he, More, is going to have to sign. Its intent is clear, and it would require More to violate his steadfast Catholic faith, but More, hoping to avoid infuriating Henry, says, "I know what it means. But what does it *say*?" Or something like that. He is hoping the letter of the law will give him an out. So do you see? *You* may feel bound by what you know the official police intend. But until they actually *say* it, I for one feel free to prod and pry wherever I like.'

Reactions were entirely predictable. Alan sighed heavily, Jonathan bit his lip and looked embarrassed, Lynn and Tom lifted their glasses in salute.

Alan ran a hand down the back of his neck. 'Setting aside the dubious legality of your proposal, exactly how do suppose that you can gain any information? I assume you don't plan to run amok in the palace à la Melissa.'

'Sarcasm, as my old friend used to say, is the tool of the devil. I'll do it the way I've always done it. I'll talk to people. Jemima and Letty can tell me who might know anything. And I'll start with Bert whatever-his-name-is-now.'

Jonathan's brows knitted in a scowl. 'And you'll find him how?'

'With Letty's help, and Jemima's. And yours.'

'I told you I don't know—'

'He was once your best friend. You knew his habits, his likes and dislikes. You're going to have to think about where he might have ended up. The same with Letty. As for Jemima . . . well, I'm not sure I believed her when she said she had no idea where he is. She may be trying to protect him.'

Jonathan's scowl deepened. 'I believed her. Why would she want to have anything to do with that ba— with him?'

'He was the father of her child,' I said as gently as I could. 'You may not like the idea, but there it is. She could have sought him out for financial help, or just to talk about the problems she was having with Melissa. Or there's the art connection. Bert shared her passion for beauty back then and presumably he still does. She wants to get into curatorial work. What's more likely than that she went to him for help and advice?'

Jonathan said nothing. Lynn looked at him and then at me. *Yes*, I signalled with raised eyebrows. *Isn't it interesting?*

'Well,' said Alan, getting to his feet, 'it's been a long day. Jonathan, let's get you back to your flat.'

'Nonsense,' said Lynn. 'We've plenty of room here, and an extra toothbrush. If you can manage with my husband's somewhat ample pyjamas, Jonathan, you're staying here. We'll all be brighter in the morning.'

By morning, though, my enthusiasm had waned considerably. For one thing, it was raining; a persistent, very English sort of rain that seemed destined to keep on till Doomsday. I sat up in bed, looked out the window, groaned, and plopped back down on my pillow. 'Does it really rain all the time in London, or it is just my imagination?'

'Your imagination, my dear. Or a persistent delusion.'

'Then it's a special curse, just for me. I wanted to do things and go places today.'

'I'll go and get you some coffee.'

Alan thinks my every mood can be improved by drinking something. The maddening thing is, he's usually right. The coffee and the pastries that he brought with it cheered me considerably.

'Now that you've recovered, love, what are your plans for the day?'

'Phone Letty and Jemima. Then I may have to go down and see them again. I swear, if I never see another train again, it'll be too soon.'

'I thought you liked English trains.'

'That was before I started living in them.'

It turned out, thank heaven, that I didn't have to climb on a train yet again that morning. When I phoned Letty, she told me Jemima had returned to work.

'Oh, dear. I'm not so sure that was a good idea. She's still so fragile.'

'I quite agree. However, as you will have gathered, I have very little influence over Jemima.'

'She must be a great trial to you.'

There was a pause. 'Now and then, Dorothy, your instinct fails you. You know a good deal about children, but very little about mothers. She is my pride and joy, even when I'd like to turn her over my knee.'

Oh, dear, what could I say to that? 'You're right, and I'm sorry. I was stupid. Um . . . do you think I could phone her? I mean, would she talk to me?'

'That depends on her mood at the moment. She's volatile, as you have seen.'

'Yes. Well, I can only try. Meanwhile, let me explain why I really called.'

I summarized our conversation last night at the Andersons', leaving out the bits about Jonathan's ability to have committed the crime. 'I'm the only one not bound by official don'ts, and I'm determined to pursue this. I think the cops have pretty much made up their minds Jonathan's their man, and because that's an embarrassment and even a cause of grief to them, they'll bend over backwards to give him no slack. In the end, he'll prove he didn't do it, or I hope he can. Proving a negative can be awfully hard. But meantime he'll be put through the wringer, and if the press get hold of it everything will be twenty times worse. So I need to find Bert Higgins, or whatever he's calling himself these days. And I want you and Jemima to help me.'

'Why do you think we can help you?'

'Because I'm pretty sure you and/or Jemima have a good idea where he is, or where to start looking.'

'There are dozens, perhaps hundreds, of art galleries in London.'

'I know.' I let the silence lengthen.

'Why do you want to find him so badly?'

'He's a link to the art world, and I'm convinced this whole mess has its roots in Jemima's love of art. I'll ask you a question in return. Why do you and Jemima want so badly to keep me from finding him?'

This time it was she who kept silent. Finally she said, 'I'd better come and see you. No, don't argue. I want to come to London, to . . . for reasons of my own. I'll ring you when I get to the station and you can give me directions.' She hung up before I could say anything else.

I went down to the kitchen, where Lynn was stirring a soup pot, watched attentively by Watson. 'That smells wonderful. I hope you're making a lot, because you may have another guest for lunch.' I explained. 'We're making perfect nuisances of ourselves and abusing your hospitality. I do apologize.'

'Right. Apology noted and discarded. When did you ever know me to run out of food? I'm putting lots of meat in it, because that Jonathan needs building up. I've seen fatter, healthier scarecrows.'

'It isn't just lack of good food.'

'Of course it isn't. First he nearly dies in that awful set-to with the terrorists, and then his little almost-cousin gets herself killed, and now he's probably suspected of her murder. And if that's not enough, he's suffering from unrequited love.' She had lowered her voice for that one, and I responded just as quietly.

'I'm not sure he even knows he's in love. And I'm not sure it's unrequited. I may not know much about being a mother, but I do remember being young and in love.'

Jonathan walked into the kitchen and put an end to that particular speculation. 'I just came in to thank you, Mrs Anderson, and say goodbye. I must be getting back home.'

'You must be doing no such thing. I'm making soup especially for you. And it's Lynn. And this kitchen isn't big enough for three people, not to mention one dog, so the whole caboodle of you can just take yourself off to the living room. I think Tom's built a fire, so it's nice and cosy, and you can talk all you want without me eavesdropping. Which I'm *dying* to do, but this soup needs my attention just now. Shoo!'

Watson stayed where he was. Jonathan and I shooed.

'Letty is coming to see us,' I said when Jonathan was safely seated.

'Letty? But why? We just saw her last night. And that reminds me. I'd better report in if I'm going to be here for a little while.' He made a face, pulled out his phone, and punched in what was obviously a familiar number. 'Yes, this is Chief— Jonathan Quinn. Yes. I'm visiting a friend in London.' I pushed over a note with the address, and he repeated it. 'Yes, any time. I understand. Yes.'

He put the phone away. 'They may want to come and see me again. Really, I ought to go home.'

'You're better off here for now, Jonathan. Lynn loves company, and loves coddling people, so you're truly no trouble. Your flat is small and not very comfortable, and right now you need some comfort. Now. Letty is coming because I want her to tell us where Bert is. Unless you already know.'

'I told you I don't know! And I don't understand why you're so hell-bent on finding him.'

'Yes, you do. Understand, I mean. Or you would, if you'd think about it for a minute with your police-trained mind instead of your mixed-up emotions. You're so busy thinking about how much you hate him, you're not seeing where he might fit into this investigation.'

'Why should I hate him? I haven't seen him in years, for God's sake! And no, I don't know where he is. I keep telling everybody that, but nobody believes me.'

I sighed. 'That's another good reason for you to stay here for the time being. You need time to get your head on straight. And you're somewhat less likely to be arrested if you're here among friends, including a retired chief constable.'

'My chief isn't very happy with Mr— with Alan, just now.'

'No. But Alan's rank still impresses. At least we can hope it does.'

'They're going to arrest me, though, aren't they?'

Alan came into the room just then, and sat down heavily. 'I'm afraid it's very possible, Jonathan. You don't need to be told why.'

'No. But it's going to be a huge embarrassment to them. The George Cross one week, in quod for murder the next. The media will love it.'

'That's the one consideration that may keep you at liberty for a while.'

'That, and the fact that he didn't do it,' I insisted. 'We wanted to solve this crime before the press got hold of it. Now that the police are on it with all their minions, time is slipping away rapidly. So if you'll excuse me, I'm going to try to talk to Jemima before Letty gets here.'

'Letty?' said Alan in the same tone Jonathan had used earlier. I left the two of them to sort it out and went to another room to use the phone.

I was back in a minute or two. 'Success! Jemima has agreed to meet us here for lunch. I'd better go apologize once more to Lynn.'

Lynn's dining room seats twelve easily. Tom came home for lunch, but the seven of us had room to spare, even with Watson hiding under the table, hoping a few scraps might fall.

We tried for a while to make polite conversation. Lynn did her best to sparkle, and Lynn's best is very good indeed. It all fell flat. Five of us had spent entirely too much time together lately, in circumstances that were too stressful. We finally gave up the pretence and put down our soup spoons. I decided it was time to take the floor.

'Lynn, this is a wonderful meal, perfect for a chilly, rainy day. I'm sorry we're all too worked up to enjoy it, but I hope getting together, yet again, can be productive. Letty, when we spoke this morning, you were going to tell me why you prefer to keep Bert's whereabouts a secret.'

Jemima looked startled. 'But you told me—'

'I said I didn't know. Nor did I. When you asked.' Letty sipped her water. 'That was when you first went to work at the palace. You were having a hard time making ends meet, and so was I.' She looked hard at Jonathan, who had opened his mouth. He shut it again. 'I was happy to do what I could for Melissa, and for you, Jemima, but the finances of it were . . . not easy. I thought it was high time Bert stepped up to his obligations as Melissa's father. You and I both thought he'd landed on his feet, working in a posh gallery somewhere. So I set about tracking him down.'

She looked again at Jonathan.

He raised his arms and shoulders in an exasperated shrug. 'All right, all right! Letty came to me. I was in the Met. I had resources. It wasn't too hard to find him.'

'Jonathan! You never told me!' Jemima was . . . what? Angry? Upset, certainly.

'No.' The monosyllable spoke volumes. He went on with an obvious effort. 'I told Letty.'

'Jonathan, you told us you didn't know where he was. And we believed you!' I had no doubt about my own reaction; I was furious with him.

'I didn't lie to you. I don't know where he is, now.'

'You mean he moved, or changed jobs – what?'

'I mean literally what I said. I don't know. I told Letty where he was two years ago. That was the end of it, as far as I was concerned. He may have fallen off the face of the earth so far as I know. Or care.'

'I . . . see.' I saw a lot more than Jonathan thought I did, but this wasn't the time to pursue tangents. 'It's an awfully fine distinction, young man! I'm not very fond of being told the strict truth when there's a good deal left unsaid. However.' I turned to Letty. 'Have you kept up with Bert, then?'

'No, not in the way you mean. I wrote to him, after Jonathan found him for me. I explained the situation and asked for help. I'm a proud woman, Dorothy, but not where the welfare of my family is at stake. I told him he seemed to be doing quite well, financially, working at a good gallery and living in a flat in Chelsea, and that the mother of his child was struggling. I must say he responded very promptly. He didn't want to see Jemima or Melissa, he said, but he would be happy to help with Melissa's support. Since she was living with me, he arranged for a monthly bank draft to be paid into my account. It made all the difference.'

'Mother! Why didn't you tell me? I didn't want his money. I've never wanted anything from him!'

'You weren't the one trying to bring up a child on very little, my dear.' Letty's tone was just slightly acid. 'I was happy for you in your job, but the living arrangements did make things a bit difficult.'

I tried to steer the conversation back to Bert's whereabouts. 'Do you still have Bert's address?'

'I have the address of his flat two years ago, and the name and address of the gallery where he worked then. Like Jonathan, I have no idea whether they are still good. The monthly allowance is simply paid into my bank, so there is never any correspondence.' She put a hand to her mouth. 'Oh, and I've forgotten to notify the bank that they should stop the payments.'

'Yes. Well.' Alan cleared his throat. 'The point now, Dorothy, is: why do you want to get in touch with him? We've established that he has had no recent contact with anyone in the family except for Letty, and that only indirectly. What possible use could he be to the investigation?'

TWENTY-ONE

'I don't know.' It seemed to me that today had been very full of *I don't know*. 'I have no sensible reason to offer. I just feel, very strongly, that this whole sorry mess has to do, somehow, with the art world. Bert is very much a part of that world. I want to talk to him.'

Alan managed not to roll his eyes, though I could see what he was thinking. The others looked uncomfortable. Lynn, bless her heart, raised her water glass in a salute. 'Hear, hear. Trust your instincts, Dorothy. They've been right too often in the past to be ignored. But we have to plan this. Letty, what was the name of that gallery?'

Letty eventually dredged it out of her memory. 'It's in Bond Street, I think.'

'Yes, it would be,' said Lynn, the art lover. 'I think I know it, actually. So now, Dorothy, you and I are going to organize a shopping trip. Tomorrow, I think, don't you?'

'Wait a minute,' said Jemima. 'I have the right to know what you plan to do. Melissa was my daughter, and my cousin is suspected in her murder.'

'Yes, you need to know,' I said. 'I'm guessing that Lynn wants us to go to the gallery, looking like ordinary shoppers. I couldn't pull it off, but Lynn knows galleries.' I looked around at the dining room walls, hung with paintings that were either original Impressionists or very, very good copies. 'She'll be able to convince them that she's a genuine customer.

Meanwhile, I hope to strike up a conversation with Bert. If he still works there. If he's in. If, if, if.'

'And what exactly do you intend to say in that conversation?'

This was the tricky part. 'I'll play it by ear, but my idea now is to find out if he knows anything about the Royal Collection. Not just what's in it, I mean – I doubt even the Queen knows what all she has—'

'It doesn't belong to the Queen, my dear,' said Alan. 'It belongs to the Crown. Quite a different matter.'

'I do know that. Manner of speaking.' Personally I thought the distinction rather fine, but I had the sense not to say so. 'But what I want from Bert is anything he can tell me about the curators, or guardians, or whatever they're called. The people who look after the Collection; who know about it.'

'You're trying to find out who might have met Melissa.' Jemima's voice sounded dead.

'That, among other things.'

Letty gave me a pointed look before she got up and went on her way, but I was not prepared to say any more.

At least not then and there, to Jemima and the rest. That night, though, as Alan and I were settling down in bed, and trying to discourage Watson from joining us, Alan said, 'What are you really after tomorrow, Dorothy?'

'What I told Jemima. I want to know who might have crossed Melissa's path at the palace.'

'What else?'

'You're a policeman. You don't have to be told.'

'No. Tell me anyway.'

'I think Bert may have had more to do with his daughter than anyone knows. I think those repeated visits to London might have been to see him, at least in part.'

'You're not suggesting . . .'

'Incest. No. I devoutly hope not, and anyway I have a hunch . . . well. No, but I have the feeling Bert might well put us on a path to finding Melissa's lover. And her murderer.'

'Put *you* on the path. Remember, I'm out of this. I've blotted my copybook.'

'Yes, and I know you'll carefully refrain from giving me any suggestions, or bailing me out when I get into trouble.'

'You'd better not get into trouble.'

He turned out the light, and Watson, assuming that since we couldn't see him we would not know he was jumping on the bed, proceeded to settle right in the middle.

I'd planned to get up early, but what with Watson and my uneasy thoughts, I didn't really get to sleep until the wee hours, and then I slept like a rock. Alan woke me with a cup of Lynn's wonderful coffee.

'It's nearly ten, love. If you're off on a shopping binge with Lynn, you'd better get cracking.'

'Mm.'

Alan grinned, mussed up my hair, and left me to surface in peace.

Once I'd regained full consciousness, I showered in haste and then considered what to wear. I hadn't packed with the intent of visiting an upscale gallery with an upscale lady, but I had tossed in my one and only Little Black Dress. Not so little any more, owing to my love of carbohydrates, but undeniably black and understated. With pearls it would have to do.

I headed for the stairs and ran smack into Jonathan. 'Dorothy, may I speak to you for a moment?'

I nodded and looked around. There was no one in sight, but conversation from the floor below told me Alan and Tom and Lynn were nearby. 'If it's private, we'd better duck back into your room. Alan might come up and pop into ours.'

'I don't suppose it's especially private. I just wanted to say I've been a fool, and I know it. I . . . it's jealousy, you see. I never thought of Jemima as anyone I cared about, so when I found out about her pregnancy, all those years ago, I didn't understand why I . . . well, I was watching you yesterday, your face, and you seem to have worked something out that I didn't even know until just now. I . . . I thought I was only trying to protect Aunt Letty, when all the time . . . and I've always thought of her as more like a sister, and now it's all gone pear-shaped. I don't know what to do.'

He sounded more like a lovesick teenager than a man in

his thirties. 'I can't tell you, Jonathan. You have to work it out for yourself.'

'I know. But what I really wanted to tell you was to go ahead and do what you need to do to find Bert and . . . say anything you want to him. We need to find Melissa's murderer, and if the police keep on thinking I did it, they're not going to look much further.'

'I don't know how true that is. I find it hard to believe that the Met will accept the easy answer, but I *can* imagine that they may spend a bit more effort just now trying to find proof of your guilt than looking for another suspect. And since they won't be able to find that proof, you not being guilty, it will, perforce, take up a lot of their time.'

'Yes.'

He looked so downcast I had to give him what encouragement I could. 'Don't worry too much, Jonathan. You know better than most that the police are efficient and conscientious. They don't put many innocent people in prison.'

'Not many. But there have been some. You know there have been some.'

'Yes, well, then we'll just have to trust in God, won't we?' And leaving him with what was obviously a startling idea, I went downstairs to my breakfast.

'Seeing as it's nearly lunchtime,' said Lynn with an assumed air of martyrdom, 'I'm making omelettes. Is there anything you don't like by way of filling?'

'I've never been too partial to pickled herring in an omelette, but other than that . . .'

'If I had any, I'd put it in just to spite you. Sit down now. They only take a second.'

Less than an hour later, replete, we sallied forth into a beautiful day, warm and sunny, with the smell of summer in the air.

'Are those roses I smell?'

'You ask that in England? There are roses everywhere they can possibly be made to grow, even in London. I think the nearest ones are actually in the garden two squares away, but in weather like this, you can smell them even over the diesel fumes. Hi! Taxi!'

Bond Street wasn't that far away. I was getting nervous. 'What are we going to do if he doesn't work there any more?'

'Ask where he's gone. I can play the grande dame and say I prefer to deal with Bert, personally. I don't have to give a reason. Rich bitches don't need reasons. But if he's there, then I'll get all snooty with the gallery owner and act like I'm going to spend a bundle, and you can chat up Bert while I debate about whether I like the one with the invisible white cubes or the one with the invisible black lines.'

'Oh. It's that kind of gallery.'

'Probably. Most of them are these days. Don't worry. I'll twist them around my little finger. And here we are.'

Lynn paid the driver what seemed to me an exorbitant amount of money for a short ride, and we went inside the imposing premises of the Andrews Gallery.

They seemed imposing to me, anyway. Intimidating, even. There is something about the atmosphere of a place where lots and lots of money changes hands that gives me a cold chill. Lynn was used to it and batted nary an eyelash.

A white-haired man was seated at a desk at the back of the room. Even my unpractised eye could see that it was an antique, a fine example of what Jemima would call the decorative arts. Louis the Fourteenth, perhaps, or that sort of style, anyway. The carpet it was sitting on was the sort I would have hung on a wall, had I been fortunate enough to own such an exquisite piece of weaving. I was very glad the weather was good. The thought of walking on the probably priceless rug with wet feet made me cringe.

The paintings on the walls didn't match the surroundings. I nearly giggled as I looked at one canvas that was apparently blank, though on a closer inspection it had some sort of pattern in the brushwork. Lynn's invisible white cubes.

The white-haired man rose and smiled with just the right degree of condescension. We might be customers, but he was certainly not going to be mistaken for anything so crude as a salesman. 'Good morning, ladies. Lovely morning.'

'Yes,' said Lynn crisply. 'I wonder if Bert is here this morning.' She allowed her accent to become somewhat more American than usual, and her attitude to become far less amenable.

'Bert? Oh, Robert.' White-hair frowned. 'He is no longer with us, but I assure you, madam—'

'I prefer to deal with Bert. Where has he gone?'

'Er . . . I believe he has opened his own gallery, madam. I could not say whether he is able to offer quite the standard of quality—'

'Where is it?' Really, Lynn cultivated a very nice standard of quality herself. In rudeness, that is.

'Madam?'

'Bert's gallery. *Where is it?*' She had raised her voice, as to the deaf or stupid, and was speaking with a cut-glass emphasis on each word.

'Er . . . I believe I may have the address somewhere.'

'Good.' Lynn sat down on one of the spindly little gilt chairs that were clearly there for decoration and crossed her legs, plainly prepared to stay there till she got what she wanted, if it took all day.

White-hair conceded, if with a bad grace. He went back to his desk and pulled out a rather dirty business card. 'Ah. Here we are, madam. I hope you won't be disappointed.'

'Do you?' said Lynn, and swept out, trailing invisible robes, and me, in her wake.

'Goodness!' I said as we waited for a taxi. 'That was an impressive performance, I must say. I was ready to curtsey.'

'I was always a hit in the minor roles at Bryn Mawr.'

The address we'd been given was in Chelsea, not quite as upper crust as Bond Street, but very close. 'Hmm,' I said when the taxi drew up to the kerb, 'I wonder. Didn't Letty say Bert had a flat in Chelsea? I wonder if he lives over the shop.'

We paused before the door. 'Robert Hathaway, Fine Art' was written in flowing gold script on the glass.

'Bert Higgins, Robert Hathaway. How the lowly have risen,' was Lynn's comment. 'Shall we?'

The shop was smaller than the Bond Street place, and furnished less opulently. On the other hand, I greatly preferred the art. These paintings were recognizably pictures of something or someone. Small, friendly-looking *objets d'art* sat here and there on shelves and one lovely little piecrust table. And on one corner of the mantel sat – aha! – a very nice Staffordshire dog.

No human being was in sight, but the ping of the opening door brought a voice from behind a curtain at the back of the store. 'Hullo! Be with you in a tick!'

'I might just be minded to buy something in here,' said Lynn *sotto voce*. 'I like his style.'

'*Much* nicer than old stuffed shirt back there,' I agreed.

'And what can I do for you today, or would you just like to look?' The young man was dressed in designer jeans and a white shirt that managed to be both elegant and casual at the same time. He was very good-looking, tanned and fit, and had an engaging smile.

I took a deep breath. 'Actually, I just wanted to talk to you. That is . . . you *are* Bert Higgins, aren't you?'

TWENTY-TWO

His smile faded. 'That's the name I was born with, yeah. Why?'

'I don't know quite how to tell you this, but I've become a friend of your cousin Jemima.'

Now his expression was definitely wary. 'Ye-es?'

'And . . . did you know about her recent tragedy?'

'Look, if you're trying to tell me something, just tell me, OK?'

'Your daughter is dead, Mr Higgins. She was murdered. And I'm trying to help the police find the man who did it.'

He said nothing for at least a minute, which can be a very long time. Then he went to the door, locked it, and pulled a shade over the window.

'I don't know about you, but I could use a cup of tea. Or something stronger. Let's go through to the back.'

Behind the curtain was a small, cluttered office, and behind that, a tiny, very clean kitchenette. 'Sorry, only two chairs,' he said, with a glance at Lynn.

'It's all right. I'm really just along for the ride. I'll go back out in front and take a look at your stock.' She disappeared, and I sat down.

'Tea?' asked Bert.

'Thank you, but I'm fine. You have some, though.'

'If it's all the same to you . . .' he said, and pulled a bottle of Laphroaig and a glass out of a cupboard. Pouring himself a healthy splash, he sat down opposite me at the minute kitchen table and took a good swig. 'Now. Tell me. For a start, who are you, and how did you get mixed up with my . . . with Jemima?' He took another swallow.

'My name is Dorothy Martin, and it's a long story. You might want to ease up on that a bit.' I nodded to his nearly empty glass.

He gave me a long, not particularly friendly look, and pushed the glass away.

'It all started the day of the Investiture, a week ago Wednesday. Or well, no, back a lot further than that, really. My husband and I have been friends with Jonathan Quinn for a long time.'

He looked up sharply at Jonathan's name.

'So,' I went on, 'when Jonathan was to be awarded the George Cross, we were invited to the ceremony at Buckingham Palace, and just as we were leaving, we ran into Jemima.' I narrated the rest of the day, the discovery of the body in St James's Park, and then Jonathan's disclosure the next day that he knew who the victim was. 'Now you know . . . or I suppose you do . . . that Jonathan was a fairly high-ranking officer with the Metropolitan Police before that terrible terrorist thing that left him too handicapped to serve. But what you don't know is that my husband used to be a policeman, too. Chief Constable of Belleshire, until his retirement a few years ago.'

'But . . . you're American.'

'I am. My husband is English. It's a second marriage for both of us.'

'Wait a minute. What did you say your name was?'

'Martin. Dorothy Martin.'

'I read something in the paper . . . but the name wasn't Martin. Nestle . . . Desmond . . .'

'His name is Alan Nesbitt. I kept my name when we married. I'd used it for over forty years, after all.'

'Right. But I still don't see . . . look, I'm sorry, but what does your personal history have to do with anything?'

'I think we might do better if you just let me tell my story,' I said, suppressing a sigh. 'The point of my personal history, and Jonathan's, is that when Jonathan decided not to tell the police, the official police, that the body was Melissa's, he was violating not only the law – withholding evidence is a crime, you know – but his personal code of conduct.'

'He did that? Not like him. He was always such a good little boy, was our Jon.'

'His reasoning was that Jemima's position at the palace made her vulnerable to the lower echelons of the press, and he wished to avoid scandal, if he could. And he persuaded Alan, my husband, to go along. Which is out of character for Alan, too. That was when I began to suspect that Jonathan's feelings for Jemima were somewhat different from what he supposed them to be.'

'You're not saying . . . Lord! Then that's why . . . Jon dropped me like a hot brick the minute he knew about Jemima's pregnancy. I could never understand why, but if . . . another thing, too. I wondered how Aunt Letty managed to find me, with the name change and all. But if she had a copper doing the hunting . . .'

'Yes, Jonathan was the one who found you. Incidentally, the financial support you've been providing has been a great help to Letty. She wanted you to know that you could stop sending it, now that . . . well, that you could stop. But there is something else you could do that would aid us in the present situation.'

I paused. Now I truly wanted that cup of tea he had offered earlier. I was parched from so much talking. But he was really listening now, really interested in what I had to say, and I didn't want to break the mood.

Lynn did it for me. She poked her head in from the showroom. 'Sorry to interrupt, just when you were all nice and cosy, but I'm going to run a few errands. Bert, there are two paintings I like very much, so I'll be back to talk to you about them. Does the front door lock itself . . .? Good. Have a lovely talk.'

The door pinged, and she was gone.

'Bert, may I change my mind about that tea?'

'Sure. Earl Grey or Darjeeling?

'Darjeeling, please.' I watched as he moved about his kitchenette with an economy of movement which was pleasant to see. 'Do you live here?'

'Upstairs. I have quite a nice apartment on the upper two floors, with a proper kitchen. I like to cook. But it was a bother running up every time I wanted tea or coffee or a snack, so I had this put in. Barely room to swing a cat, but it suffices. Milk? Sugar?'

I accepted both, and we settled down again. I tried to remember where I'd left off.

'You said I could help you somehow, but I don't quite see how. In fact, I don't see how you fit into this at all.'

'I told you that Jonathan and Alan decided not to give the police the vital information about Melissa's identity, in the hopes that we could clear up the matter quickly ourselves.'

'Are you a policeman . . . er . . . a police person too, then?'

I smiled. 'No. I'm a retired schoolteacher. But I've discovered an unexpected talent for snooping, and on occasion I've been of use to the police. In this case, I'm acting entirely unofficially. You see, it became necessary to tell the police everything, and they were extremely angry with us for not telling them sooner. They didn't charge any of us – Alan because he had outranked them all at one time, Jonathan because he was a hero. You heard about that?'

'One could hardly avoid it. It was splashed all over the news.'

'Had you heard about the George Cross, until I told you just now?'

'No. I'm not surprised, though. Jon was always brave, and always soft about kids. He saved a couple of them from drowning once, at Brighton, only it didn't get put about. He didn't want anyone to make a fuss about it. He deserves that medal, several times over.'

'You were really good friends, weren't you?'

'The best mate I had, ever.' Bert made a dismissive gesture. 'But you were telling me how you got mixed up in this business.'

'Well, with Jonathan and Alan both out on their ears, so to speak, I was the only one still free to poke around and see what I could find out.'

'Well, I'm sure you're a splendid Miss Marple, or whatever, but perhaps it would be just as well to leave it to the police?'

'It looks as though the police think Jonathan did it.'

'Jon! But that's . . . that's . . .'

'Ridiculous. But look at it from their point of view. He was closely involved with the family. He was in the vicinity. He was actually there when Alan found Melissa's body, and then he concealed her identity from the police. No other viable suspect has surfaced. They don't *want* it to be Jonathan, but that very fact is going to make them careful to keep him at the top of their list. And there's something else you don't know.' I debated for a moment, and then decided, in for a penny, in for a pound. 'Melissa was three months pregnant.'

'*What?* She's a child! It's impossible!'

'She was fourteen. It's entirely possible. And true, I'm sorry to say.'

He stood, turned away from me. I waited while he fought for control, thinking all the while what a pity it was that men were ashamed to cry.

When he thought he could trust himself to speak, he said, 'Are you telling me you think Jon's the father of Melissa's baby?'

'I don't think so. The police may. DNA testing would prove the matter, one way or another, but that's terribly expensive and takes a long time. No, my idea is quite different. I do think it's likely that the same man is almost certainly responsible for the pregnancy and the murder. But I'm quite sure it isn't Jonathan. And that's why I've come to you.'

He turned abruptly to face me. The signs of his tears were still there, but he was furiously angry. 'If you think for one moment that I would have molested my own daughter—'

'Oh, don't be silly. How could I possibly think that? For one thing, you're gay, aren't you?'

He simply looked at me.

'That little fling with Jemima happened before you were comfortable with your sexuality, didn't it? You might even have been trying to prove to yourself that you were heterosexual, because you knew how that father of yours would react to your being gay. My guess is that learning about the pregnancy shocked you into a reassessment. Something did, anyway, and you realized that wasn't the path for you.'

'Got it in one,' he said, and sat down again. 'Sorry.'

I wasn't sure whether he was apologizing for his tears, or his anger, or both. I shrugged a 'doesn't matter'.

'So,' he said, trying to establish an easy tone, 'going back to the last remark but five, you said you wanted my help. About what?'

'About the art world. Specifically, the Royal Collection and its minders.'

'The curators, you mean?'

'I don't know enough about it to know what I mean. Anyone who has anything to do with the collection and works at the palace.'

'At Buck House? Or the others? Windsor, Balmoral, and the rest,' he added somewhat impatiently when I looked puzzled. 'The Collection spreads out over quite a vast area, you know, all the royal residences.'

'How stupid of me. I should have known. Just . . . Buck House.' I was a little uncomfortable with the term, which smacked to me of *lèse-majesté*. Bert's hint of a grin told me he was well aware of my reaction.

'Term of affection, dear lady, I assure you. I do know a number of the staff who look after the Collection, as it happens. What do you want to know . . . and why, if I may ask?'

I leaned forward. 'This may seem as far-fetched to you as it does to Alan and Jonathan, but I'm convinced that art is somehow at the bottom of all this. It was your passion for art, yours and Jemima's, that led you into this business and Jemima into her job at the palace. I don't know if you know that she's hoping desperately to change jobs and work with the Royal Collection in some capacity. It was, if you don't mind my saying so, that same passion for art that led to . . . well, the fact of Melissa. Art keeps swirling around in my head. There's some connection, I'm sure of it.'

'It's not too much of a stretch, I suppose. You're right. Jemima was as mad about art as I was . . . as I am. And I suppose she could have passed her obsession on to her daughter. But what could that have to do with Melissa's death?'

'Just this.' I told him about Melissa's escapade at the palace. 'She was roaming that treasure house, unsupervised, for perhaps two hours.'

'You don't think she stole something?'

'No. She couldn't have. Apart from anything else, there's the security system.'

Bert frowned. 'The palace isn't a museum, you know. It's a home. A very posh home, with furnishings that would grace any museum in the world, but nevertheless a residence. The Queen would cast a cold eye, believe me, on any attempt at museum-style security; pressure pads, electronic eyes, that sort of thing.'

'I'm told the treasures don't actually belong to her, but to the Crown. I confess the distinction eludes me.'

'They belong to the United Kingdom, under the guardianship of the current monarch. Under certain circumstances she could give something away, to a visiting head of state, for example, but she cannot sell or otherwise dispose of anything. They are hers to enjoy during her lifetime. If she wishes, for example, to move a vase from one room to another, or from one residence to another, for that matter, she is free to do so. She cannot, however, decide that several of the clocks are hideous – which, frankly, some of them are – and should be given to Oxfam, though she can banish them to the attics. And if she wants to walk round with a guest and pick up a piece of Sèvres to point out a detail, she certainly doesn't want alarms to ring. So Melissa could, in theory, have made off with some small object, a snuff box, that sort of thing.'

'Right. But they searched her when they found her, so that really isn't a possibility. No, my idea is quite different. I think she met someone, someone who showed her around, was amused by her admiration and wonder, and thought she might be fun to know.'

'And you want to know if I can think of any likely candidates.' He reached for the glass holding the remains of his whisky. 'Are you sure you won't have some?'

'I'm a bourbon girl. But as I've had no lunch, I'd say no in any case. The tea was ample.'

He brooded, sipping. 'No one comes to mind at the moment, but this has all come as a bit of a shock. I still can't believe . . . I mean, I believe you, but the idea of my daughter . . . I know I abandoned her. I know I've had nothing to do with her life. At first I thought I had no choice. I was just a kid, with no job, nothing . . . and my father would have turned me out if he'd known. He hated his brother and that whole side of the family. And I hated him. He was a smooth, self-righteous prig. I liked Aunt Letty, though. Anyway . . . there wasn't much I could do for Jemima and Melissa at first, and then . . . I don't think she wanted anything to do with me, anyway, and she . . . a baby . . .'

'A baby would have been a terrible embarrassment to you in your new way of life.'

'That makes me sound like a selfish prat.'

'Yes.'

He sighed. 'Oh, all right, so I *was* a selfish prat. It didn't seem like it at the time, but looking at it now . . . OK, I could have done a lot more. I should have done a lot more. I was getting along all right. I'm not exactly rich, but I suppose I'm not far from it. And here's Jemima working some nothing job just to make ends meet, and Melissa . . .' He finished his whisky at a gulp, stood, and looked me straight in the eye. 'I'll make out a list of anyone I can think of at the palace who might have caught Melissa's fancy, and I'll get it to you as soon as I can. But I'll tell you this. If you, or the police, or whoever, catch up with the bastard who messed my daughter about and then killed her, you'd better have him safe behind bars before I know who it is. I may not have been much of a father, but I'll kill the bleeder if I find him.'

TWENTY-THREE

Lynn came back and bought her paintings and then took me back to the house. We sat around having a late snack lunch and a post-mortem. Jonathan had gone home to brood, and I assumed Letty was either with him or back in Bramber. I was glad they weren't there; it made the discussion easier.

'Did he mean it, the threat?' asked Alan.

'Oh, he meant it. At the time, anyway. Now once he's over his first shock, he may cool down. I don't know, though. He struck me as genuinely contrite about his shabby treatment of Jemima and Melissa in the past, and deeply distressed about the child's death. I may have set the cat among the pigeons.'

'Would it do any good if I were to speak to him? Along the lines of letting the police do their job, two wrongs don't make a right, and so on?'

'I doubt it. He'd be very polite and agree with all you said, and go ahead and do what he thought he had to. He seems quite a nice young man. I liked him. But there's a core of steel, it seems to me. I doubt he's easily swayed.'

'Well, then, we just have to make sure the police get to our villain before Bert does.'

'Yes, well, as Mrs Beeton is reputed to have said, first you have to catch your hare.'

The next few days were tedious in the extreme. Oh, they should have been interesting. Alan and I, sometimes in company with Watson, interviewed the palace footmen on the list Jemima had supplied, and then other men from Bert's list. My taste for beer was sated to the point that I took to ordering tonic instead. Some of the men admitted to seeing Melissa as she stormed through the palace. One of the footmen even said he had talked to her briefly, telling her she'd better get back to her mum in a hurry or be in real trouble. None admitted to any further relationship with her. Well, they wouldn't have, but it seemed to both Alan and me that they were telling the truth.

So there set in a period of waiting, something I'm never very good at. Alan and I went home to Sherebury, where we were greeted with varying degrees of indifference by the cats. Watson was happy to be home, but then Watson is nearly always happy. As long as Alan and I are around, his paradise is complete.

I was fidgety. I wanted to be doing something, but there seemed to be nothing to do. I had run out of ideas. So I puttered around the house, driving Alan and myself to distraction. Occasionally, I varied the programme by going into the garden to drive Bob crazy. He was busy setting out annuals and trying to deal with the yellowing foliage of the daffodils.

'Why don't you just cut it off? It's really ugly now that it's not nice and green.'

'You don't want to cut it off. Has to stay till it's brown. Feeds the bulbs. You could braid it if you want. Some people do.'

His tone of voice told me exactly what he thought of people who wasted their time braiding daffodils, and incidentally of people who wasted their gardeners' time with silly questions.

I went back to annoying Alan.

Meanwhile, the police machine had been grinding on, putting out public appeals, trying to find evidence that Jonathan had been in or near St James's Park at the relevant times on Tuesday, the eighth of May. They had found a number of witnesses who claimed they had seen a man of Jonathan's description 'acting very strange' that evening. None of those strange men had been limping, however, or carrying a cane, so Jonathan had not yet had to appear in a line-up, or 'identification parade' as they rather grandly call the procedure in England. Carstairs et al knew that something like ninety-nine percent of the responses they got from the general public were so much eyewash, but they had to go through the drill, if for no other reason than that the media, predictably, were giving them hell. 'NO LEADS YET IN ST JAMES'S MURDER!' screamed the headlines in the tabloids. The respectable papers,

The Times and *Telegraph* and *Guardian*, were more discreet but equally censorious, along the lines of 'It has now been nearly two weeks since the discovery of the body of a young woman in St James's Park, and the police appear no nearer . . .' Under the circumstances, I thought Carstairs was to be commended for not clapping Jonathan straight into jail and having done with it.

I said as much to Alan, who grunted and retreated deeper into the crossword puzzle. He was hating this, I knew; hating having to be sidelined, exasperated with Jonathan for putting him in this position, and annoyed with me for my relative freedom to poke my nose in.

The trouble was, I could think of no useful venue for said poking. If only some new information would surface! Surely the police, with all their resources, ought to come up with something. Then I reminded myself that even if they did, I would be told nothing about it. We were well and truly stuck.

We tended, during those days, to talk a lot about the weather.

It was a Sunday afternoon when a new idea finally emerged. Alan and I had been to church at the Cathedral, had lunched at the Rose and Crown, our favourite pub, and were back home pretending to enjoy the lovely weather and our garden, now that Bob had worked his miracles and it was in full bloom. The phone rang.

'I'll get it,' we said in unison, trying to spring to our feet. At our age, springing is not our best act. Alan, leaner and fitter, beat me by a length, but then held the phone out to me. 'For you.'

'Who?'

'Don't know. He didn't say.'

I took the phone. 'Robert Hathaway here. Or Bert Higgins, if you prefer.'

'Yes, Bert. I'm very glad to hear from you. I've been hoping you might think of someone else to question. We don't seem to be getting anywhere.'

'No. And you may be disappointed in this idea, as well. I've not come up with any more names, only the faintest hint of an idea.'

'That's a great deal more than we have here. Tell me.'

'I found this out quite by accident. And it may have nothing to do with Melissa, but I thought perhaps I should pass it along.'

I was gripping the phone so hard my hand threatened to lock up. '*Bert.*' I tried hard to keep my impatience out of my voice.

'All right, yes, I'm getting to it. You see, I happen to know one of the chaps who deal with the palace tours. That is, he isn't a guide, you understand, but he helps deal with the punters, especially the group tours, which can get a trifle unruly, especially when children are involved.'

Children. Might there eventually be a point to this rambling discourse?

'He gets especially nervous when school groups visit, as I'm sure you can imagine. All those fragile treasures . . . well, you can see what even one careless or exuberant child might do.'

I didn't trust myself to speak. I was near meltdown point.

'So there's a chap he brings in to help the regular guides with the children.'

'A teacher?'

'No. Well, that is, I suppose he teaches some art classes, but he's actually a sort of consultant. An artist himself, you know.'

'Bert, I don't know, and I wish you'd tell me what this person has to do with anything!'

'I'm trying to. He – his name is Anthony Jarvis – makes part of his living by supervising school groups on palace tours. He knows a lot about the Royal Collection. I think he'd like to be a curator, but there hasn't been an opening. He's an artist, as I said, a painter, but quite frankly he's better at talking about art than doing it, if you know what I mean.'

He stopped. I gripped the phone even harder. 'What *do* you mean, Bert?'

'Oh, haven't I said? It's a bit tricky, you see, because the chap, not the one who works at the palace, but the other one, Jarvis, is someone I used to know rather well, and even though . . . well, I still wouldn't want to embarrass him, or make his life difficult, or anything of that sort.'

'Robert Higgins Hathaway, if you don't tell me immediately what you're stalling about, I'm going to make *your* life difficult!'

'He was there that day, the day that Melissa did her little walkabout in the palace. There was a school group doing the tour, and Jarvis was with them. The chap at the palace happened to mention it to me, and I just thought—'

'And you say you know this guide – assistant – whatever he is?' I interrupted.

'Used to. He lived in Brighton when I did. That's how I got to know him.'

'I . . . see.' I didn't, actually, or not very clearly. 'Then he's roughly your age?'

'Roughly. Looks quite a lot younger, though.'

There was a pause.

'Bert,' I said, my voice weary, 'you're going to either have to tell me the story or forget about it. Half-hints are no use at all.'

A gusty sigh came down the line. 'You're right. I had hoped . . . but you're right.' Another sigh. 'This is difficult for me.'

I waited. I found I was clenching my teeth. I unclenched them.

'You see, I fancied him. He has a baby-face, and he's so . . . or at least he was, a few years ago. We used to see each other now and again, just casually, and I had high hopes that one day . . . but I haven't seen him since . . .' Pause. I thought I heard Bert swallow.

'I had moved to London by then, but I still went to Brighton now and then. The antiques trade had pretty well dried up there by that time, but I still had some connections, and I could sometimes pick up a good deal. So this one evening I popped into a pub, one of my old haunts, and there he was.'

'A gay pub?' I thought I saw where this was going.

'Well, it was when I lived there. So when I saw him, as beautiful as ever, sitting alone at the bar, I was sure this was my chance. I sat down beside him and began to . . . try to renew the acquaintance.'

'And then he broke your heart, and now you're trying to get revenge. Really, Bert!'

'No, it wasn't that way at all. The fact is, I'd made a mistake. He wasn't interested. The pub had changed ownership, and character, since the last time I'd been in and . . . he was very nice about telling me he didn't play on my team. I . . . I found the whole experience humiliating.'

'I can see how you might. But, Bert, what possible connection might this have to Melissa's murder?'

'I don't know. It's just that I used to know him, and he's from the same part of the world as our family, and . . . well . . . he was there on the day Melissa was roaming about the palace, and he is, or at least was, extremely nice-looking, and . . . oh, I said it was only the tiniest of possibilities. Forget it.'

'You're right. It's a slim lead. But as it's the only one we have, or the only one I have, I'll see if it goes anywhere. What was his name, again?'

'Anthony Jarvis.'

'Why does no one ever have a peculiar name? I could probably find an Aloysius Jacobowicz, but Anthony Jarvis! Do you have an address or phone number?'

'I'm afraid not. But I can find out the name of the school he was shepherding. I don't think he's in Brighton any more. I haven't kept track of him, for obvious reasons.'

'Yes. Well, I'll follow up, and let you know.' I clicked off the phone.

'Anything?' Alan asked, eyebrows raised.

'Probably not. Just Bert's attempt to salve his conscience about Melissa, along with a little spite about a guy who rejected him.' I gave him the details. 'There's not much we can do about it until Bert gets back with the name of the school, or we can figure out some other way to trace this person.'

'Not much *you* can do,' Alan corrected. 'I can turn the name over to Carstairs. He can track the fellow down in the blink of an eye.'

'Oh. Oh, yes, I suppose you have to do that.'

'You know perfectly well I have to do that.'

I bit my lip. 'What will he do with it?'

'Put it into the hopper along with everything else. Solving a case is like making sausages, Dorothy. You collect all the information you can, sort it out, grind it up, and hope it comes out in some recognizable form.'

'But it's such a tenuous connection. Will he even think it worth pursuing? Especially since he thinks Jonathan did it.'

'You're not thinking, Dorothy. What he does with the information is his business. It need have no effect on what you do with it. True, if there's anything to be learned from this Jarvis fellow, Carstairs and Co may get there first. But you may ask questions that don't occur to the official investigators. You almost always do.'

And if there was a hint of resignation mixed with the affection in his voice, I decided to ignore it.

Alan made his rather depressing call to Carstairs, and I settled down, with ill grace, for more waiting. Fortunately, this time the wait was a matter of hours rather than days. Bert called back before bedtime with the name, address and phone number of the school whose pupils Anthony Jarvis had shown around the palace. 'And they weren't exactly children. Sixth-formers from St Cuthbert's College.'

I remembered that 'college', in the English sense, means what an American would call 'high school', and that 'sixth-formers' were between sixteen and nineteen, in their last year or two of school before going on to university, if they did well in their examinations and could afford it.

I thanked Bert and passed the information on to Alan. 'Now what?'

He considered. 'In view of the fact that the Met almost certainly have this information already, I think what you want to do is move as quickly as possible. You have a much better chance of getting information from Mr Jarvis if you can find him before the police do. The headmaster would probably have his address and phone number, but a schoolmaster keeps early hours, as a rule, so I wouldn't try to phone him tonight.'

'I suppose he lives at the school. At least, it is a boarding school, isn't it?'

'I don't know, my dear. St Cuthbert's College is new to me, and at any rate schools have changed so much since my day, I have no idea what they're up to.'

The changes had, I perceived, not been for the better, at

least not in Alan's eyes. I decided the subject was not a happy one, and moved on. 'Well, I want to talk to him. Or better yet, see him. He might be able to tell me some things about this Jarvis person, and people talk more freely in person. Do you think, if we got an early start in the morning . . .?'

He sighed. 'You realize, Dorothy, that while I'll be glad to drive you anywhere you want to go, at any time you choose, I can't take any part in your activities. I've been quite definitely warned off.'

I echoed his sigh. 'I think it's utterly foolish. You're retired. Why on earth can't you contribute your experience and know-ledge when you want to . . .? No, I know.' I held up my hand. 'We've been over this often enough. Territorial wars. I think it's idiotic, but I do grasp the idea. But I'll certainly talk it all over with you afterwards. They can't stop that. If I can remember.' I frowned. My memory was growing unreliable at times. I could remember what Alan had worn to our wedding, and what he had given me for every birthday we'd spent together, but not where I'd put the book I was reading five minutes ago, nor last Sunday's sermon that had so impressed me at the time.

'I've come up with a solution for that little problem.' Looking remarkably like Emmy when she's just lapped up a saucer of cream, he pulled a pen out of his pocket and handed it to me.

'Take notes? Wouldn't that be a little obvious? Or even rude? Anyway, I've never been any good at shorthand.'

He went to another pocket and pulled out a flimsy wire contraption. He attached it somehow to the pen and then said, 'Put it up to your ear.'

Reluctantly, I did just that . . . and to my astonishment heard myself saying, 'But I'll certainly talk it all over with you afterwards. They can't stop that. If I can remember.'

When he stopped laughing at my reaction, Alan said, 'Spy stuff, love. I was going to get you an ordinary pocket recorder, but they don't seem to make the cassette sort any more. I found this online and it seemed just the thing. It even writes, so you can take it out and use it, and nobody will be the wiser.'

'Dorothy Martin, GSA. I love it!'

'GSA? Girl Scouts of America? I never knew—'

'Geriatric Spy Association. I just founded it, as president and sole member. Now, teach me how to use the gadget, and first thing tomorrow we're off to school.'

TWENTY-FOUR

'Where we will no doubt find out,' I said as we left Sherebury the next day, 'that Anthony Jarvis is a respectable member of society trying to drum some aesthetic sensibilities into adolescents. Poor guy!'

My spirits were high, probably because the weather was glorious. Some poet said of June, 'Then, if ever, come perfect days', and this day deserved the adjective. The English countryside, which can be beautiful even in the pouring rain, was outdoing itself. Roses cascaded over every cottage, lupines flaunted themselves in every garden, birds trilled in every copse.

'I keep expecting a couple of bluebirds to fly up with a ribbon garland to drape over the car.'

'You've been watching too many Disney films,' said Alan, but he said it cheerfully.

St Cuthbert's was situated on a hill near Hove, but inland. We couldn't see the Channel from the road, but as Alan drove towards the college I looked back, and there it was, glittering in the sunshine. 'Nice view the kids have,' I commented.

'Nice in June. I imagine it gets a trifle bleak in January, and somewhat cold.'

'Yes, well, English schoolboys are supposed to suffer, aren't they? Builds character and all that. But I thought you said this school was new?' I pointed to the magnificent building towering above us. 'I'm no architectural expert, but that's surely seventeenth century, at the latest.'

'Probably built as a manor house, fallen to the fate of so many of them, thanks to death duties. At least it's being used and maintained. As for character building, I believe this college admits girls as well. Parents will protest mightily if their daughters suffer discomfort.'

I shivered. 'And with the winds from the sea, winters are probably bitter here.'

'Ah, well, perhaps the sleeping quarters are of modern construction.'

I was silent. Alan knew what I thought of modern British construction. Some of it was brilliant, even I would admit, but post-war buildings in general were all too apt to be poorly designed and cheaply made. I've had my issues with Prince Charles from time to time, but on the subject of architecture I think he's dead right.

Alan pulled the car up on the gravel sweep at the front door. 'Do you think you're allowed to park here?' I asked doubtfully.

'I'm not parking. I'm letting you off. I'll go and find a car park. Phone me when you want to leave.'

Oh. I had completely forgotten that I was on my own this time. For a fleeting moment I wished I had Watson with me, but I banished the thought. A school was an unlikely place for a dog, even in England. And if I had to talk to an art teacher . . . I shuddered at the havoc an active dog could wreak in a room full of easels and canvases and paint.

'You have your pen at the ready, I trust?' Alan knew why I was hesitating. He can usually diagnose my moods.

'Yes, and my feet are getting colder by the moment, as you very well know. However. Onward and upward.'

Alan leaned over for a kiss, and I struggled out of the car's embrace, straightened my skirt, and climbed the four curved steps to the front door.

The door stood hospitably open, and the brilliant June sun showed me a panelled hall with a black-and-white tiled floor and a graceful staircase rising to a diamond-paned landing window. On either side of the hall doors stood open. A discreet brass plate over the nearest one read 'Enquiries'.

Well, I had some of those, all right! I tapped on the door frame and walked in.

The receptionist, or secretary, or whatever she was, a trim woman of about fifty, looked up with a brightly welcoming smile. 'Good morning. Lovely morning, isn't it? Were you wanting to visit one of the students?'

'It is a lovely morning, certainly. Actually, I was wanting to see your headmaster, if he's free.'

Her smile dimmed a fraction. 'Was there some sort of problem?'

Why, I wondered irrelevantly, do the English couch this sort of question in the past tense? It's catching, too. 'No, I only wanted . . . I only want to ask him how to find someone who has a . . . well, a rather tangential tie to the school. The college, I mean.'

'Perhaps I could help you, if you'd tell me who . . .'

'It's a Mr Jarvis, Anthony Jarvis.'

'Oh.' Now the smile was gone completely. 'Well. Um. Was it his address you were wanting?'

'That and some other information. I'd really like to speak to the headmaster. I'm perfectly willing to wait.' To reinforce the point, I sat down and planted my handbag firmly on my lap. The chair was one of those squashy leather affairs that are almost impossible to get out of, but I'd deal with that when the time came. I made myself quite comfortable and conveyed, I hope, the idea that I was prepared to sit there until Doomsday.

The receptionist gave up. 'Oh, I see. Well, Mr Davidson is teaching his seminar just now, but he'll be finished soon. If you really want to wait . . .'

A young man poked his head in the door and started to say something, then checked himself. 'Oh, sorry, I didn't know you had a visitor.'

'Oh, Colin, good. This is Mrs . . .'

'Martin,' I supplied. 'Dorothy Martin.'

'Mrs Martin, and she wants to see Mr Davidson. Could you show her to the seminar room, please? Their session should be nearly over.'

Colin nodded politely. 'Sure. I think he stayed behind to talk to Allison, but he shouldn't be long. Follow me.'

The room to which he led me had plainly been one of the drawing rooms of the manor house. It was still beautiful, with diamond-paned windows, panelling in some light wood, elaborately carved plaster mouldings, and a lovely fireplace framed in pale green marble. No doubt the floors had once been covered with priceless rugs where there was now a sensible carpet, but the room retained its charm, even with modern chairs arranged around a central table.

A man stood near the table talking, with expansive gestures, to a short, dark-haired, remarkably pretty girl, who was nodding her emphatic agreement. She carried a small book whose title read, in two lines of large letters:

ΠΛΑΤΩ
ΠΟΛΙΤΕΙΑ

Well, my Greek is limited to the alphabet, which one could hardly help learning in the American college town where I spent much of my life. It didn't take too much brain-wracking to figure out that the first word was 'Plato', and I didn't really need to try to decipher the other one. This child was reading one of Plato's works in the original. My respect for St Cuthbert's shot up.

'. . . and I do take your point, but I still think he was a dangerous man. A fascist, really, with his espousal of censorship, and his insistence on keeping the citizens firmly within their respective classes.'

Teacher and student were approaching the door. 'I beg you to keep an open mind until you have finished the dialogues. Socrates may yet redeem himself, my dear.'

He gave her a friendly pat on the shoulder as she left the room, and then turned to me. 'Were you looking for me, or one of the students?'

'For you, sir, if you are the headmaster. My name is Dorothy Martin. I was a teacher before I retired, and I'd like to talk to you for a few minutes, if you have the time.'

'Roger Davidson.' He extended a hand, and I was relieved to note that his grip, while firm, was not bone-crushing. 'Do I detect a transatlantic accent?'

'I've lived in England for some years, but yes, I lived most of my life in America, and I suppose I'll never lose the accent entirely.'

'Shall we go to my office? I usually have a cup of coffee

at this time of day; may I offer you some? Or tea, if you prefer?'

I chose tea as the safer option. One never knows about English coffee, which ranges from superb to execrable, but given the national predilections, English tea is almost always well made.

While we awaited our tea, we made polite conversation. I commented on how impressed I was with his school. 'I gather the students learn Greek,' I said with some awe. 'I didn't know anyone still taught Greek outside the universities. '

'It has certainly disappeared from many curricula,' said Mr Davidson, 'but I regard the *Republic* as one of the essential texts, and there are no really accurate translations, in my opinion. My seminar isn't required, but many of the more able students seem to enjoy it.'

'The young lady I saw certainly had some strong opinions about the book! I confess I've read only bits of it, years ago and in English, and have retained almost nothing.'

'And yet – ah, here is our tea. Milk? Sugar?'

When my tea was poured into a delicate cup and prepared to my liking, we settled back into comfortable leather chairs, I got out my notebook and pen and pressed the small button on the pen that would, I hoped, start it recording. We sipped our tea and chatted about Plato for a few minutes more, and then Mr Davidson tilted his head to one side and looked interrogative.

'Yes, you want to know why I'm here. I do apologize for taking up your time, but I'm hoping you can help me. I'm very interested in educational methods in this country, especially as regards extra-curricular activities. I'm trying to find a man named Anthony Jarvis, who I'm told escorted at least one group from St Cuthbert's when they toured Buckingham Palace some months ago. Would you have his address, by chance?'

I noted his expression carefully. There was, just for an instant, a sort of silent sigh and a look of wariness. Then he was all courtesy. 'I believe my secretary, Mrs Stevens, would have that information, although you do realize that Mr Jarvis is not in any way connected with the college. I know very little about him, though I believe he was an art teacher at one time.' Mr Davidson put down his teacup, straightened his tie and looked at his watch.

Aha, I thought to myself. You know a little more about him than you want to tell me. And you're uneasy about something. How interesting. I picked up my empty teacup, peered into it, and put it down with an expression, of, I hoped, regret.

The man was a gentleman. He wanted to get rid of me, but he couldn't ignore so obvious a cue. He lifted the teapot with an enquiring look.

'Oh, yes, please! Thank you so much. You know, I'm wondering, Mr Davidson. When I was teaching, we did educational visits outside the school – we called them field trips – but they were always escorted by the teachers themselves, with parents to help when the groups were big ones, and of course help from the experts at the museums or wherever. Is it the usual thing here in England to hire someone as a tour guide?'

'Not perhaps usual, though we here at St Cuthbert's do try to make such excursions as valuable to our students, educationally, as we can. When a recognized expert in the field volunteers to accompany our visits, we are of course quite keen on the idea.'

'Oh, then Mr Jarvis volunteered?'

'If I recall correctly, that was the case. Our art master, Mr Peretti, might remember more about the exact arrangements.' Mr Davidson looked again at his watch, more obviously this time. 'I'm sure Mrs Stevens will be able to help you with the contact information you need.'

I can be persistent, and even rude when necessary, but I thought I'd better not ignore this second, pointed signal. Mr Davidson wasn't going to tell me any more right now, and I did want to talk to the art teacher.

I stood. Mr Davidson stood. We uttered oh-so-polite insincerities. He showed me how to find the art studio on the top floor – 'Right up at the top of the house, in the old day nursery. It has the best light, you see' – and enquired solicitously as to whether I would prefer to use the lift. I said the stairs were fine and complimented him on their beauty. I left his office.

I thought about two things as I negotiated the several flights up to the studio. One was that Mr Davidson had never asked me the obvious question, which was why I wanted to know so much about Anthony Jarvis.

The other was the ever-so-slight sigh of relief he'd uttered just a split second too soon, before the office door had quite closed behind me.

Once I got to the top floor, the strong smell of paint told me I was indeed in the right place. At the head of the stairs an open door led into a large room, skylights furnishing the north light so essential for artists. Easels were scattered across the room, facing a still-life arrangement on a table; a challenging one with grapes and apples and a Venetian glass half-full of red wine, sitting on a draped piece of elaborate brocade. The students were hard at work, their faces intent. No one paid me the slightest attention.

I moved into the room, as quietly as I could, and studied the nearest painting. It was more than half-finished, and was surprisingly good. The girl had managed to convey the transparency of the glass and wine and the translucency of the grapes, and was working with fierce concentration on the mottled skin of the apple. Not quite a literal treatment of the subject, her work combined Impressionist leanings with a strongly individual style.

The man in the middle of the room, who had been strolling about, commenting here, praising there, looked up and saw me.

'May I help you?' He made his way to me, carefully avoiding the easels and stools. The students barely looked up.

'Mr Peretti?'

'Yes. And you are . . .?'

'My name is Martin, Dorothy Martin. Is there a place where we could talk for a moment?'

He shrugged. 'This lot's set for the next hour. We could pop into my office next door, I suppose.'

His office, in what must once have been a bedroom – the 'night nursery', perhaps – looked exactly the way I had imagined an artist's environment. He removed a stack of miscellaneous objects from a chair and motioned for me to sit. He perched on the edge of the desk, to the imminent danger of a pile of books and papers.

'I suppose you want to talk about dear Kevin's unrecognized artistic ability. Or Maggie's. Or Rashid's. No, not Rashid's. You're not likely to have a grandson named Rashid. Though one never knows, these days.'

'I'm not here about any of your students, Mr Peretti. I know no one who attends this school. Though I must say, from what I just saw, that I think at least one of them is exceptionally talented. That girl near the door . . .'

'Elizabeth. Yes, she's good. She may make an artist one day, if her parents don't succeed in marrying her off to a stockbroker, their most desperate hope. So if you're not trying to convince me about a budding Leonardo, what did you want to see me about?'

'Well, I'm sure this is going to sound very odd to you, but I'm doing some research about school activities in England. I am, as you can probably tell, American by birth, though I've lived in Sherebury for some time now. I was a teacher in the States, and I'm writing a book contrasting American educational methods with English ones.'

I took out my pen and notebook again, keeping the open page out of the man's sight. It contained random jottings that made no particular sense. I wrote down his name.

I had hoped for a truly boring approach, and it appeared I had succeeded. His eyes were already beginning to turn towards his studio. 'Yes, and how may I help you? I suspect methods of teaching art are much the same all over the world. One instructs in methods and then puts the little blighters to work. Most of them are dire.'

'Well, I'm actually more interested in your methods of teaching art appreciation. At least, that's what we called it back in Indiana. Art history, perhaps?'

'Again, probably very similar to the way it's done in the States.' He shifted, and a pile of papers cascaded to the floor. 'Pictures, slides, that sort of thing.'

'Ah, but on this side of the pond you have so many opportunities to see the real thing. All the wonderful museums in London alone! And then there's Buckingham Palace. Your headmaster tells me you sometimes take the older children on tours there. How wonderful for them!'

'Some of them enjoy it. Others just don't care about that sort of art. They'd choose Robert Indiana over Rembrandt any time, so for them it's a frightful bore.'

'I understand you sometimes take along an expert on the collection, to supplement the information on the self-guided tour.'

'We did once. Bloke volunteered. He knew his stuff, but . . . he wasn't entirely satisfactory. I doubt we'll do it again. Now if that's all, Mrs Um, I need to make sure the brats are still working.'

He stood, ignored the books that joined the papers on the floor, and strode out of the room.

I'd touched a nerve.

Once I'd regained the ground floor, I stopped to get Mr Jarvis's address and telephone number from Mrs Stevens, and then headed for the front door. Just as I got to the front steps I heard voices.

'What the hell did she want?'

It was a man's voice, and I thought it belonged to the art teacher. I casually leaned against the wall to tie my shoe.

'Whatever's the matter, Mr Peretti?' That was Mrs Stevens.

'She was asking too many questions about Jarvis. I want you to find out who she is and what she thinks she's doing.'

'Really! I am not an enquiries firm.'

'No? That's what it says outside your door. Enquiries. You'd better get on with it, Sadie, my dear, or—'

Somewhere nearby a door slammed. I skedaddled.

TWENTY-FIVE

When Alan had driven us well away from the school, I recounted my conversations.

'Did you record them?'

'I hope so. I pressed the right button, I think. I won't know for sure till we get home and I can listen to the thing. But Alan, don't you think the most interesting part was what they didn't say?'

'Everyone seemed to avoid talking about Mr Jarvis.'

'Even the secretary. Oh, I don't think I recorded her. But she acted funny when I mentioned him. Acted . . . as if she expected some trouble.'

'Hmmm. And it sounds as though they all shied away from any talk about London and Buckingham Palace. None of it's evidence. But I agree, it is suggestive.'

'And what it suggests to me is that there's something at least slightly fishy about Mr Jarvis.'

'Or that Carstairs' people have already been there.'

'I thought of that, but I just didn't sense that kind of reaction. There was no "But I already told the police all that" sort of attitude, just a stone wall. I wish I could find somebody who would tell me something about the man.'

'Surely the first step is to speak to the man himself, wouldn't you say?'

'You're right. I . . . for some reason I'm a little uneasy about the direct approach. I suppose, suspecting what we do . . . but you're right. I need to meet him and form my own opinions.'

I pulled out my mobile and punched in the number I'd carefully noted down. After five rings it went to voicemail.

'Not home. Or not answering.'

'Does he live in Brighton, or possibly Hove?'

'Neither. It was a London address.' I looked it up. 'Mulberry Walk, SW3. Do you know it?'

'Not to say know it. I think it's in Chelsea.'

'Hmm.'

'Lots of people live in Chelsea, Dorothy.'

'I know, I know. Still . . .'

We drove in silence for a couple of miles, pondering.

'Home for lunch before catching the train?' said Alan after a while. 'I do *not* propose to drive into London.'

'No. I mean, yes, lunch at home first.'

I found my A-to-Zed after we'd eaten a quick sandwich, and looked up Mulberry Walk. 'You're right, it's in Chelsea, a couple of streets north of the King's Road. Doesn't look like there's a tube station anywhere close.'

Alan sighed. 'Bus or cab, then. This little adventure is getting awfully expensive, my love.'

'Jonathan has lots of money. We'll bill him for expenses, once we get him off.'

'If we get him off.'

Alan drove to the railway station in Sherebury, but when I turned to kiss him goodbye, he was already getting out of the car. 'You're coming with me?' I asked in surprise. 'I thought you were keeping discreetly out of any active investigation.'

'Not if it means letting you walk into a lion's den by yourself.'

'We don't know that it's a lion's den.'

'We don't know it isn't. Get a move on, old dear, or we'll miss the train.'

The carriage was crowded, so we didn't talk about anything important on the way in. There wasn't really much to say. We were grasping at straws, and we both knew it.

It took us a long time to get a taxi at Victoria. For some reason, they all seem to vanish from time to time, though when one doesn't want one there's a long queue of them. The afternoon grew warmer by the second, and by the time we finally got to our destination, I was hot and tired and cross.

Alan rang the bell, and after a longish interval, rang it again. I pulled out my phone and called Anthony's number. Voicemail again.

I uttered a couple of regrettable words.

'Annoying, isn't it, my dear? When the universe fails to arrange itself according to your wishes?'

'Oh, go ahead. Make fun. But it tells us one thing, at least. Why would the man be hiding from us unless he had a good reason?'

'He could, you know, be out doing his job. Or buying groceries. Or communing with nature, or writing a sonnet, or taking in a matinée, or . . .'

I sighed, deflated. 'Did I ever tell you you have an annoying habit of being right?'

He grinned and took my arm. 'Now, would you like to cool off over a nice pint?'

'Would I ever! But first . . .'

'But first you'd like to call on Bert Higgins and see what more he can tell us about the elusive Mr Jarvis.'

But Bert's shop, only a street or two away, had a sign on the door: 'Closed today, back tomorrow.'

'Well, that certainly isn't very informative! Some dates would be useful. Alan, I begin to get the feeling this isn't our day.'

'Or we may be going about this the wrong way. Let's have that pint, love, and talk about other possibilities.'

The pint, tracked down at an especially pretty pub neither of us had known before, was refreshing. The place wasn't crowded, amazingly enough, and that meant a pleasant drink, but the noise level was too low for private conversation. The train home, by way of contrast, was so crowded and noisy that any conversation was next to impossible.

So we didn't get a chance to talk until we were settled at home, tired and disgruntled, with various comforting animals disposed about us.

'That,' I said, 'was a totally wasted day. No one we really wanted to talk to was available, and the only people who were didn't tell us – didn't tell *me* anything useful.'

'Mmm,' said Alan.

That's the sort of noise the man makes when he doesn't agree with me, but thinks it wiser not to say so. It can sound non-committal, or disapproving, or, with an upward lift, interrogative. No matter how he says it, it's just as maddening as direct contradiction.

'All right, so tell me what you think was productive about all the running around we did today.'

Watson, at my feet, lifted his head and whined at my tone of voice. I sounded unhappy, to his distress.

'You're right, of course, love. We didn't accomplish a great deal. But we did confirm our sense that there's something not quite right about Anthony Jarvis.'

'But we still don't *know* for sure.'

'There is, of course, one resource we haven't yet tapped.'

'Well, Bert, but he wasn't home.'

'I was thinking of something much closer to home.' He gestured with his head towards his study.

'The Internet!' we cried in unison.

I admit I was slow to move into the electronic age. My own age might have something to do with that. But now that I've understood the possibilities, I can't imagine how I ever functioned without the remarkable resources that a computer puts literally at my fingertips.

I smacked my head. 'Of course. The obvious. The headmaster at St Cuthbert's said Jarvis used to be a teacher at one time. There's bound to be something about him on the Net.'

We went to work, each on our own computer. (Yes, we have two. We haven't yet succumbed to smart phones and the like, but we do love our computers.)

I spent an hour in my small kitchen-office hopping from one website to another, growing more and more frustrated. At last I went into Alan's den, where he sat frowning at the screen.

'Alan, I'm having no luck at all. I find sites for schools all over the area, and academic directories, and all sorts of places where Jarvis ought to be, but he isn't. I can't even find any phone or address listings for him except the one in Chelsea. He has a website, but it's pretty useless. No bio or background, just self-promotion.'

'I'm finding the same pattern. You know what it means, don't you?'

'Something's being covered up.'

'And perhaps there's been a name change. There could be all kinds of reasons for that, you know.'

'Witness protection programme, something like that? Yes, I know, but all the same, it's odd. And frustrating! This is when we need the resources of the police, and they're not available to us! Do you think the Met will follow this up?'

'I wish I could say yes, but their eyes are on Jonathan. They're not going to go out of their way to find another suspect when he's so handy.'

'Is that the way the police work?' I sounded a trifle bitter.

'Sorry to disillusion you, but yes, in these days of understaffing and underfunding, I'm afraid it often is the way they work. There's always pressure from above to clear a case and get on with the next. And when the case is as explosive as this one could be, the pressure is unrelenting.'

'So.' I dropped into a chair. Watson, anxious about me again, came over and licked my hand. I patted his head absently. 'What now? I've run out of ideas.'

Alan looked at me over the tops of his glasses. 'You're tired, and you're depressed. I'd suggest you rest for a bit while I make us some dinner, and then we'll brainstorm.'

Even though he sometimes exasperates me, I often have occasion to bless the day I married this man. He knows me so well.

The rest turned into a nap, of course, but I woke when the smell of dinner became too enticing to ignore.

The dear man had concocted some sort of ragout, with beef and onions and mushrooms and baby carrots in a rich gravy. He'd made mashed potatoes to go with it, and a salad, and by the time I'd made my way through every bite, I was feeling very much better.

'It's a good thing I didn't know you could cook like this before I married you, or you'd think the whole deal was just to get a chef.'

'No, indeed, my dear. I knew you married me for my accent.'

'That, too. Oh, no, thanks, I'll just have coffee.'

Alan put the fruit tarts back in the fridge. 'They're store-bought, anyway. Pastry isn't my strong point, and I had the feeling you might not want much dessert. Now, love, while you were snoring away, I've been thinking.'

I sipped my coffee and looked encouraging.

'The source of all the troubles, in more ways than one, is Melissa's father, Bert Higgins. Or Robert Whatever-it-is.'

'Hathaway. Well, he was certainly the source of Melissa!'

'And of the information about Jarvis. Now I've begun to wonder about that. If his name has been changed, and Higgins hasn't seen him since the encounter . . . or non-encounter . . . in Brighton, how did Higgins know his present name?'

'Oh. Maybe we're wrong about the name change.'

'Quite possibly. But in any case, don't you think another little visit to London is in order?'

I sighed. 'What I think is that I'd like a little brandy with my coffee.'

The fact, I admitted to myself and finally to Alan, was that, old Sam notwithstanding, I was tired of London. Oh, not for good. There would come a time when I would want to enjoy the bustle and the glitter again, but June in the country is gorgeous. Bob was getting my garden in shape, and the Cathedral was looking at its best, and . . . well, much as I hated to say it, I wanted to stay home and tend to my knitting.

'You never were very good at knitting,' Alan observed to that last comment. 'What's really wrong, Dorothy?'

'I am genuinely tired, Alan. And discouraged. Every time we find something that looks like a promising path to explore, it leads to nothing, or at least to a place where we can go no further. I've never felt like this before. There was always something just ahead to chase, like . . . like a fox's brush. Now . . . oh, I'm ready to give up the whole thing.'

Alan took my hand, and we sat there for a long time. I finished my coffee and my brandy in silence. There seemed to be nothing to say.

The phone rang. Neither of us really wanted to answer it, but Alan finally released my hand and got to his feet.

'Nesbitt here.' A brief pause. 'I see. Thank you, sir.'

He turned to me, his face set in lines of worry. 'That was Carstairs. Jonathan's in hospital. He's tried to commit suicide.'

TWENTY-SIX

We spoke little on the way to London. Alan concentrated on his driving, and there was either too much to say, or too little.

'They didn't give me any details, Dorothy,' Alan said in response to my tentative query. 'They went to his flat to ask him a few questions, and found him unresponsive, apparently drugged.'

'Will he . . .?' The question stuck in my throat.

'They don't know yet.'

The road unrolled. Lights flew past. The long June twilight darkened into night.

'I hope someone's called Letty!' I said suddenly, sharply.

'I don't know. Probably.'

And that was all, until we hit the nightmare of London traffic.

Alan, who knows the great city well, found a car park close to London Bridge Station. 'We can get a taxi from here,' he said briefly.

'Not the Underground?'

'It'll be closing soon. A taxi's slower, but surer.'

I was all but biting my nails by the time we got to St Thomas's and found the Accident and Emergency department.

Mr Carstairs rose as we came in. 'He's going to be all right,' he said instantly.

I dropped into the nearest chair. Somehow my legs didn't want to hold me up.

'Can you tell us what happened?' Alan was keeping his voice from shaking, but I could hear the effort. He spoke in the hushed tones one uses in places where death is a frequent visitor.

'Not in any detail. He apparently swallowed a good many oxycodone capsules. We phoned him to say we wanted to talk to him for a bit, and when we got no answer, we went to the flat. That is, my people went. They found the door unlocked and Quinn almost unconscious on the bed, with the empty bottle beside him.'

'A note?'

Carstairs pulled a plastic bag out of his pocket and handed it to Alan, who read the note inside and grimaced. 'Bloody little fool!' he said under his breath.

'Let me see,' I whispered. He handed it to me.

In crisp, precise handwriting it read simply, 'Sorry for everything.' It was not signed.

'It's his handwriting,' Alan said, and gave the pathetic little document back to Carstairs.

There was a gloomy silence.

'Can we see him?' I asked finally.

'They'll let us know when he's conscious and can talk to us. I'll have to question him, of course.'

Of course. Suicide is a crime, even when it isn't successful.

A hospital waiting room may well be the most depressing place on this earth. Its stark functionality provides no cheer for the soul; no rest for the body. One is tired and uncomfortable, simultaneously bored and terrified. At our ages, Alan and I brought to the place a lot of unhappy memories, as well. We'd done this before, and the outcome had sometimes been tragic. I knew he was thinking of his first wife, as I was of my first husband. Both had died suddenly, unexpectedly, and far too young. They'd died in hospitals thousands of miles apart, but in one sense, in exactly the place where we now sat, restless and frightened.

'Coffee, love?' Alan asked after a while, gesturing at the machines in the corridor.

I shuddered. 'I'm not that desperate. A candy bar, maybe. Or a Coke.'

He brought both. The candy was stale and the Coke warm. I ate and drank anyway. It was something to do.

Hours passed.

I was too tense and uncomfortable to sit, too tired to pace. I was aching in every muscle, and nearly weeping from weariness, when the nurse came in and beckoned to Carstairs.

We all stood, Alan and I with some difficulty.

'He's conscious and rational,' she said briefly. 'One of you may see him for five minutes.'

Carstairs followed her. Alan and I sat back in our easeless chairs.

He was back in less than the allotted time, and sat down beside us.

'He confirmed that he took the capsules. There was never much doubt, but I had to make sure.'

'Did he say why?' I asked. 'Or no, I don't suppose you wanted to ask at this stage.'

'No, I wouldn't have asked. Not yet. But he told me a bit. The world has rather dumped on him of late, but the trigger tonight – last night – had to do with Jemima.' The superintendent suddenly looked a good deal more human. 'He's got a bad case, hasn't he?'

'But what did Jemima do, or say, or . . .?'

'He wasn't specific; he's very tired and feels bloody. She came to see him. I gather they had a row. We'll know more tomorrow.' He sighed. 'Meanwhile, he isn't allowed any visitors, and he's under observation.'

'But . . . he's going to be all right. You said so.' My panic started to rise again.

'In case he thinks about trying again, love,' said Alan gently.

'Oh.' I was too tired even to try to stop the tears that welled up.

Carstairs offered us a lift to a small hotel nearby. It was nearly morning, but we were too tired to drive home safely, and in any case we wanted to talk to Jonathan when he was feeling better. I slept like the dead and woke at mid-morning with a raging headache and a mouth that felt like our cats' litterbox.

'No toothbrush!' I moaned. 'And no ibuprofen!'

'You used to carry both those essentials in your handbag,' Alan said mildly. He had just stepped out of the shower. Clad in a towel, he found my bag, rummaged in it, and tossed me the items requested. 'And there's shampoo in the bathroom. You'll have to do without a facecloth, I'm afraid. This is a genuine English hotel.'

The English, as I learned many years ago to my dismay, consider a washcloth as personal as a toothbrush, and travel with their own. Many hotels nowadays supply them, but I've learned to do without when necessary.

I felt slightly better with clean teeth and a clean body, but I hated getting back into clothes that felt like I'd worn them non-stop for a week. Alan had made coffee. I don't care much for instant, but it supplied caffeine, and with the ibuprofen, took the edge off my headache.

'No biscuits, worse luck,' Alan commented. 'And it's far too late for breakfast. Would you like to go straight to the hospital, or find a snack somewhere?'

'Don't I remember a Starbucks in the hospital lobby?' That

lobby had startled me considerably, the first time I saw it. It looked more like a shopping mall.

There was indeed a Starbucks, and I lingered over an indulgent mocha and a huge muffin. Truth to tell, I was not eager to talk to Jonathan.

'I don't know how to act,' I admitted to Alan. 'What does one say to someone who's tried to . . .?' I couldn't say the words.

'What you would say to anyone else who was ill and in distress,' said my husband sensibly. 'Ask how he's feeling, and let him take it from there.'

'I suppose. It's just . . . it feels like he's a different person, somehow.'

'Buck up, old girl. You'll manage. I suspect he'll be more embarrassed than you are.'

We were told, when we announced ourselves, that Jonathan had been moved to a room, now that he was in no imminent danger. A single room, not a ward. A uniformed policeman sat discreetly in the corner, but stood when we entered. 'Mr Nesbitt. Mrs Martin. I was told to expect you. I'm to remain in the room, you know, but I'll try to be invisible.'

Jonathan made some sort of noise, a protest, I thought. I turned to him, intending to say something bright and cheery, and found myself unable to speak at all.

He looked so small, lying there flat and pale. And so very young and helpless. I put out a hand, and he grasped it. 'Let you down. Sorry.'

I swallowed hard and decided to ignore that. 'Are you really feeling all right?'

'I feel like hell. Have you ever had your stomach pumped? I don't recommend it. But I daresay I deserve it. And before you ask, no, I'm not fool enough to try it again. They're wasting manpower.'

He nodded his head in the direction of the mandated observer, who cleared his throat. 'Orders, sir.'

'I know. I doubt that Chief Constable Alan Nesbitt, retired, and his lady wife, have smuggled drugs in, but . . .' Jonathan made a weary gesture. 'Ah, hell. I've caused everyone enough trouble.'

'Are you up to talking about it?' I asked cautiously.

He lifted a hand and let it drop to the blanket. 'There was another row with Jemima. I'd thought . . . but I was wrong. She made it quite clear . . . and it just put the lid on. I had all those pills. I hadn't taken any for a long time, trying to tough it out. So there they were, and I . . .'

'You thought it was the easy way out of your troubles.' I tried to say it gently.

'In fact, old man, it's dug you in a bit deeper, you know.' Alan was speaking gently, too, and sadly. 'You can't escape the obvious conclusion.'

'Suicide as a confession of guilt,' said Jonathan in a flat voice. 'And that damn-fool note didn't help, did it.' It wasn't a question.

'What's going to happen now?' I asked. 'You can't just go back to your flat alone. Will you go to Letty's? Oh, Lord, where is she, anyway? I forgot all about her last night, but surely—'

'It appears no one thought to tell her until this morning,' said Jonathan, 'and by that time there was no reason for her to traipse all this way. No, I'm not going to stay with her. It's too much of a burden. She's had enough to deal with.'

He sounded stronger, which was a good sign. Stronger, and thinking of someone besides himself.

'They won't let you go home alone, you know,' said Alan. 'You're under a suicide watch.'

'I've told you, I—'

'I know what you've told us. The fact remains.' Alan consulted me with a raised eyebrow. I nodded.

'All right, old man. When are they going to let you out of here?'

'This afternoon, I think. I didn't take enough to cause serious damage, they tell me.'

'It would have been serious enough if they hadn't found you!' I couldn't help saying.

'Yes, well. Anyway, they need the bed, so I'm out soon. With my keeper, I suppose. Bloody waste of police time.'

'I have an alternative proposal,' said Alan. 'We'd like you to come home with us.'

It took a little persuading, but Jonathan was sensible enough to realize he had little choice. The police would not let him go home alone, and he was firm in his decision not to go to Letty. We checked with Carstairs to make sure our hospitality would meet official requirements, and finally told Jonathan to phone us when he was ready to leave.

TWENTY-SEVEN

'What do you want to do about lunch?' I asked Alan when we were out in the sunshine again. 'We probably have a few hours to kill.'

'If you wouldn't mind making do with a sandwich, I'd like to call on one Robert Higgins Hathaway. I think that young man has some explaining to do.'

The more expensive a shop is, it seems, the later it opens, and Robert Hathaway's shop was very expensive indeed. The sign wasn't on the door any more, but the shades on the door and the show window were pulled down, and no lights were visible. 'Round here,' said Alan, steering me into the narrow passageway between the shop and the one next door. It was rather more salubrious than such areas in London tend to be. Evidently Chelsea keeps not only its streets but its footpaths cleaner than do lesser neighbourhoods.

The door Alan had expected to find was there, blank and unwelcoming. It had a buzzer and an intercom, though, and Alan applied his thumb and kept it there. We could hear the raucous noise from where we stood.

Eventually a voice sounded from the speaker. 'Go away.'

'Not until we've talked to you, Mr Hathaway.'

'Who the hell are you?'

I spoke up. 'It's Mrs Martin, Bert. I'm here with my husband,' I added, in case Bert was feeling violent at being awakened.

Pause. The voice, when it came again, was a little less agitated. 'My dear lady, do you have any idea what *time* it is?'

'It is after noon, sir,' said Alan. 'We must talk to you.'

'Bloody . . . all right, all right. Give me fifteen minutes.'

It was more like half an hour before the door finally opened. A young man who bore no resemblance to Bert stumbled out, glared at us, and paused to light a cigarette and blow smoke in our faces before walking towards the street, muttering.

'Shall we?' Alan gestured to the open door. I coughed, nodded, and followed him up the narrow stairs.

Bert had managed to shower and pull on a pair of elegant jeans. He was barefoot and wore no shirt. He was standing in the kitchen area, at a fearsome-looking machine which was making noises suggestive of an imminent blast-off. 'Sorry I was rude,' he said, 'but I'm barely human until I've had my coffee.'

'Late night?' I asked brightly, looking around the flat. Glasses and bottles were much in evidence, as were over-flowing ashtrays. The air was heavy with the odours of sweat and smoke, and not, I thought, just tobacco smoke.

The disorder was a great pity, because the flat should have been beautiful. It was decorated in a clean, modern style that managed still to be warm. A couple of fine paintings hung on the white walls; a few well-chosen objets d'art brightened shelves and tables.

'I'm surprised you allow your guests to smoke in here,' I said. 'It can't be doing the paintings any good.' And then I told myself to shut up. We weren't there to talk about his habits, for heaven's sake!

'I don't usually have parties up here, for that very reason. Last night just sort of happened. Some people came by, and then some more, and some of them brought in food, and they just . . . stayed.'

His hands shook as he picked up the cup of coffee, and his eyes were bloodshot. He looked, in short, a wreck. He needed some aspirin and several more hours of sleep, not an interrogation.

I hardened my heart. Jonathan was in the hospital, and might have been dead. He was running a real risk of arrest for murder, and I was certain he was innocent. If Bert could help us find the real killer, he would just have to deal with his hangover later.

'We're sorry to disturb you,' I said crisply, 'but we need some information, and we need it now. Jonathan Quinn tried to kill himself yesterday.'

Bert spilled his coffee. 'Ow!' He grabbed a towel and dabbed at his chest. 'But why?'

Alan shrugged, with a warning look at me. 'At least in part because he is suspected of murder. The point is, several of us think he's the wrong man. We'd like to know a little more about Anthony Jarvis. For a start, what is his real name?'

With great care, Bert put his coffee down. 'So far as I know, his name is Anthony Jarvis.'

'I don't think so, Bert,' I said. 'Oh, that may be his real name now, but it isn't the one he was born with. What was his name when you first knew him in Brighton?'

'Why would you think it was something different?'

Aha! We'd been fishing, but whenever a person answers a question with a question, that person is stalling. I let Alan take over.

'There are ways to find out, Higgins, but asking you was quickest. The name, please.'

'Why should I tell you? You're not the police. And I don't want to get the poor chap into trouble.'

Alan just waited, looking steadily at Bert.

Bert picked up his coffee cup and sipped, gingerly. His hand was a trifle steadier. 'Oh, all right!' he said finally. 'I should never have mentioned him in the first place. He couldn't possibly have anything to do with this, but you're going to think . . .'

'You supply us with the facts and let us decide what to think.'

'I suppose you'll find out anyway, if you persist with this ridiculous notion. His name was Andrew Welles.'

'And he used to be a teacher?'

'I never said so!'

'No.' Alan let the silence lengthen again.

'Yes,' Bert said finally, 'at a small school. It isn't there any more. It's been merged into some god-awful comprehensive.'

'He taught art?'

'If you can call it art in a school like that. He worked with the nine-to-elevens, trying to impart some sense of line and mass. It was a lost cause, naturally.'

'You seem to know rather more about him than you implied to my wife earlier.'

'I didn't "imply" anything at all!' Bert winced at his own loud voice. He picked up his coffee cup and took a swallow. 'Look, I don't know what you're talking about. I knew Andrew for about a year. All right, I pursued him, if you want to know. So I chatted him up whenever I could contrive to meet him. I knew he hated his job. I wasn't surprised when he chucked it.'

'I thought you didn't know he had left Brighton.' Certainly I'd had that impression when Bert called.

'Well, I did. Look, that's all I know about the man, except that he's really knowledgeable about art and a decent sort of chap. And I need to dress and work out some way of feeling human by the time the shop opens, so if you don't mind . . .'

'Just one more question,' said Alan. 'How did you know the gentleman's new name? And why did he change it?'

'That's two questions. How would I know why he changed it?'

Another question answered with a question, I noted.

'As for how I knew, it's perfectly simple.' Bert took on the tone of one addressing a somewhat slow five-year-old. 'The man is an artist. He is interested in art. I sell art. He came into the shop one day to look. I didn't happen to be out front. My assistant tried to help him, but he wanted something by a specific artist, and we had nothing at the time. My assistant took down his name, Anthony Jarvis, and his phone number. I happened to glance out while they were talking, and recognized Andrew.'

'And you didn't go out to talk to him?' I put the maximum of scepticism into my voice.

'After the way he humiliated me the last time we'd seen each other? Not bloody likely!'

'But you're sure it was Andrew Welles. And he gave his name as Anthony Jarvis.' Alan likes to be certain.

'God, how many more times! Yes, I'm sure. And I think I'm going to be sick. Go!'

We went.

'What now?' I asked Alan as we descended into the Tube station.

'Suppose I send you home by train. I imagine you'll have some arranging to do, and between Jonathan and his gear, the car's going to be a bit full.'

So we made for Victoria Station. Once I got home, and after I'd tidied up the guest room and changed to fresh clothes, I sat down at my computer.

If information about Anthony Jarvis was notably lacking, there was a plethora about Andrew Welles, and it was both confusing and unsettling. He had apparently begun his teaching career working with younger children, and he'd done a lot of job-hopping. A year here, two there, always with the same age group, the intermediate ages of nine to eleven. He was a part-time art teacher at first, but then, in one school, had taken a full-time position with a class of eleven-year-olds, teaching general subjects.

All the schools were in the same part of the country, never far from Brighton, and there seemed no reason why Welles had moved around so much.

Then I found it: a newspaper account of Andrew Welles's trial for child molestation.

I scrolled down. There was no verdict shown; apparently the trial ran to a second day. I clicked a few times and found the follow-up article.

Acquitted. I wished I could see a transcript of that trial.

I also wanted, urgently, to tell Carstairs. Surely he'd find it of interest that a suspected child molester was in Buckingham Palace at a time when he might have met Melissa!

Well, I'd better consult Alan before I tried to talk to Carstairs. Meanwhile, there was the question of a meal. I finally decided to make a hearty salad and slice some meat and cheese for sandwiches. Then everyone could eat what they wanted, if they wanted. I made a quick trip to the High Street for orange juice, since wine isn't a good idea for someone suffering from depression, and bustled about vacuuming cat and dog hair away, arranging flowers.

Everything was ready much too soon, and then all I had to do was sit around and worry. I sat for a while, Watson anxiously attentive, then went to the window to peer down the street, then went to the kitchen to make sure I'd left nothing undone, then sat again. The cats, annoyed by my restlessness, disappeared, presumably upstairs to sleep on the freshly made bed and deposit fur on the pillows. Watson eventually wearied, too, and stretched out in his bed in the corner.

I fretted, imagining all sorts of disaster. Jonathan was worse. The police had decided to keep him in London. There'd been an accident on the A21.

I put the kettle on, brewed myself some tea, and forgot to drink it.

Twilight was approaching by the time they finally arrived, and twilight comes late to England in June. I forced myself to assume an attitude of calm. The last thing Jonathan needed right now was a dithery female.

Alan helped him out of the car, and he made his way to the front door, leaning heavily on his cane.

'Welcome, Jonathan.' To my horror, my voice shook and a tear threatened to slide down my cheek. This would never do!

'I'm sorry to be a bother,' he muttered. 'Frightful nuisance, I know.'

Well, that dealt with my tears. 'Jonathan Quinn, I never want to hear you say anything like that again! You are *not* a nuisance, you are an honoured guest, and you'd better get used to it! Now come in and sit down and tell me if you'd prefer tea or orange juice.'

'There's no need to bother . . .' he began.

I gave him The Look.

'That is . . . tea would be very nice, thank you.'

I exchanged glances with Alan. He shrugged almost invisibly. Nothing interesting to report.

I made fresh tea for Jonathan, poured wine for Alan and me, and set out my sketchy supper on the table. 'Come and have something to eat, gentlemen, before Watson and the cats scarf it all.'

They sat in near silence, passed food, asked for the mayonnaise and mustard.

I'd had enough. I cleared my throat. 'We're all being very discreet, and ignoring the elephant in the room. It's time we talked. Jonathan, are you able to tell us about last night?'

He put down the fork with which he had been pushing food around his plate. 'Not much to tell. Jemima came to see me. We quarrelled.'

I waited.

'We . . . I thought we were getting on better. But when I tried to talk to her about her future, she . . .'

'Of course she did,' I said with exasperation. 'Too soon, Jonathan.'

'I don't know much about women. I've never had time. And now . . . if the police hadn't come . . .'

'But they did, and a good thing, too.'

'Why? So I could be accused of murder?' The bitterness was corrosive.

'Jonathan, it's a good thing you're not in possession of all your physical capabilities. Because if you were, I'd have no problem shaking you till your teeth rattled. As it is, my conscience won't let me.'

Alan raised his eyes heavenward. 'My dear, I do think we ought to let this poor man get some sleep.'

'And how well do you think *I'd* sleep, thinking he was lying there trying to figure out how to kill himself as soon as we let him out of sight?'

Jonathan winced. 'I've told you . . . and in any case, I would never abuse your hospitality in that way.'

'But only because you're polite, not because you've given up the idea. No, you'd wait until you weren't under our roof any more, and then . . . wheel yourself in front of a lorry, or under a Tube train, or something. And it's got to stop, do you hear? I've tried to tell you life is worth living. Letty's tried to tell you. I suppose even Jemima's had her shot at you. Yes, that's right, think about Jemima for just a minute. How do you think she'd feel if she lost you on top of everything else? Don't look at me that way. She may have torn a strip off you last night, but under all the prickles, she feels the same way you do. I'm not blind, you know, even if I am an old bat. Now you eat some supper, and then we're putting you to bed, and *then*, in the morning, we're going to see what we can do about your depression.'

Jonathan, looking rather as if he'd been hit on the head with a baseball bat, obeyed.

After we'd seen him safely to his room, Alan and I retired, exhausted, to ours. 'You were pretty hard on the poor chap, Dorothy.'

'I know. And I hated to hit him when he's down. But he needs to be shaken up. He's been wallowing for so long in the slough of despond that he's forgotten how to climb out of it. I don't think he even knows there's a way out. First thing in the morning, I'm heading straight to the Cathedral to ask the Dean who's the best counsellor or psychiatrist or whatever in town. Jonathan needs professional help, and I intend to see that he gets it.'

I think Alan muttered something about 'steamroller' as we got into bed, but I ignored him.

'Dr Miller, John Miller, is my recommendation. He's a psychiatrist who specializes in treating depression, and he uses a full range of treatment, including alternative medicine . . . whatever he thinks is best for the patient. He's always very busy, but if you'd like, I could phone him and say this is an emergency case.'

'Oh, please do! I know there's no immediate cure, but if we can even get Jonathan started with someone, I'll feel a lot better about the whole thing.'

The Dean made a note. 'I've added him to the prayer list, as well. It sounds as if Jonathan needs all the help he can get. What a dreadful situation! Is he a religious man, do you know? I'd be happy to call on him, but I never like to intrude.'

'I suspect not, from some things he's said, and not said, but I'll try to sound him out and let you know. And thank you, Dean! I knew I could count on you to know the right person.'

'Any time, Dorothy. Will we see you at the concert Friday night?'

Alan and I are regulars at the Cathedral Music Series each

year, and the programme on Friday comprised music by Ralph Vaughan Williams, one of our favourites. 'We have tickets, but it all depends . . .'

'We'll hope things work out so you can be there. I've heard them rehearsing, and it's sure to be a splendid evening.' He sent me off with a cheerful wave, and I stepped out into the brilliant June morning feeling a good deal better.

Jonathan was awake and in the kitchen when I got home. He had showered and dressed, though in the same clothes he'd worn the night before. 'Sorry,' he said, gesturing at himself. 'I don't have any others with me. I couldn't think what to pack yesterday.'

'I'd offer you some of Alan's things, but I'm afraid they'd be far too big. Later the two of you will have to go back to your flat and collect enough to do you for a while.'

Jonathan made a helpless sort of 'whatever' gesture, and I didn't pursue it. 'Now, have you been able to find any breakfast?'

He shook his head wearily. 'Thank you, but I'm not really hungry.'

'That, as you know, is beside the point. Do you prefer your eggs boiled or fried?'

Again that helpless gesture. It seemed he wasn't up to making any decisions at all. I made toast and coffee, scrambled eggs, assembled marmalade and the other accoutrements, and sat and watched him while he ate about a quarter of what I'd prepared.

'That's better than nothing. You can't operate on any empty tank, you know, and this morning we're . . . drat.'

The phone was ringing insistently, and Alan was either still asleep or in the shower. I picked it up and answered with the phone number. 'Yes? Yes! Good! And the address?'

I clicked off and turned to Jonathan. 'As I was just about to say, this morning we're going to be busy. I'm taking you to a shrink.'

'You . . . I assure you, I don't need . . .'

'Yes, you do. Jonathan, I don't mean to boss you around, but at this stage, somebody needs to and I seem to be the one available. You're in a state of deep depression and you

need help, and with the best will in the world, I'm not quali-
fied to give it. Neither is Alan. Neither is Letty, dearly as
she loves you. You need a professional, and in –' I glanced
at the kitchen clock – 'fifty-seven minutes you're going to
see one. Meanwhile, we're going to buy you a new shirt
and pants, which will also make you feel better. So finish
that orange juice to top up your blood sugar, and off we
go.'

I left a note for Alan and hustled Jonathan out the door.
I can drive Sherebury streets easily enough, though given
the difficulty of parking on the High Street we would have
done almost as well to walk. We have a small Marks and
Spencer in Sherebury, and at this hour of the morning they
weren't yet crowded, so I was able in short order to find
both outer- and underwear for Jonathan. It was like taking
a child shopping, except he didn't whine. He obediently
tried on the first things I found and pronounced them acceptable, though he objected when I paid for them. 'You can
pay me back. I'm guessing you have almost no money with
you, right?'

He admitted helplessly that he didn't know. I clucked a bit.
Good grief, the sooner I got this poor man to the psychiatrist,
the better. He was coming apart at the seams.

He dressed in his new clothes, right down to his socks, and
we headed for the discreet office of Dr John Miller, MBBS,
MSc, MRCPsych.

The long string of letters intimidated me completely, but
Dr Miller's receptionist was very pleasant. 'The doctor can
see you right away, Mr Quinn. And Mrs Martin, if you'd like
to wait, we have reading material that is actually current. Or
you could come back in about two hours. An initial interview
does take a little while.'

Well, that was a very nice way of being told I was extra-
neous to this process. 'I'll come back, thank you.' I patted
Jonathan on the shoulder, and he followed the receptionist
through a door that shut firmly behind him.

I left, feeling a bit empty. I'd felt decisive action was called
for. Now I'd taken that action, and Jonathan was out of my
hands for the next two hours. Now what?

My stomach rumbled, and I realized I was literally empty. I'd been so concerned with feeding Jonathan that I'd had only coffee myself. I decided my car was fine where it was and walked to the Cathedral Close, where a pot of tea and an almond croissant at Alderney's satisfied the inner woman.

The next obvious stop was the Cathedral itself. It would be a bustling place. Tourists would be strolling about gawking at its incredible beauty, and stopping in at the gift shop to buy souvenirs. Someone would almost certainly be practising music, either the organist, or one of the groups that were performing in the concert Friday night. The clergy and staff would be going about their business purposefully.

But for me, it was always an oasis of quiet and peace. A building that has been a place of worship for many centuries holds peace like a goblet brimful of warm, golden wine, and trivial externals ripple the surface only slightly.

I made my way to the small, lovely chapel devoted to private prayer and slipped to my knees.

It wasn't until I became aware of discomfort that I wondered how long I'd been there. I can kneel for a while on my nice titanium implants, if the kneeler is well-padded, but pretty soon they begin to complain. Well, not the titanium, presumably, since it has no nerves, but the rest of the reconstruction. I pushed myself to my feet, somewhat stiff in body but much restored in mind and spirit. Overhead, the Cathedral clock chimed the three-quarters. I'd need to hurry to make it back in time to fetch Jonathan.

He was waiting for me in the outer office, looking pretty much the way he had two hours before. I wanted to ask him how it went, wanted to hear all about it, wanted, really, to be told he felt much better. But I restrained myself until I'd brought the car around for him, and then said only, 'What's he like?'

'Pleasant,' said Jonathan, and relapsed into silence.

I made sure my long sigh was inaudible.

TWENTY-EIGHT

I managed to find a private moment to tell Alan what I'd learned about Jarvis/Welles. He agreed that Carstairs must be told, and promised to do so when he took Jonathan back to his flat for clothes. As soon as they'd left, I got on the phone to Dr Miller.

'I know you can't tell me anything confidential, Doctor, but I need to know how carefully I need to tread with Jonathan. I presume the Dean gave you the background?'

'He did, and I must say you've all got yourself into a right muddle! Small wonder Jonathan isn't feeling quite the thing.'

'After the suicide attempt, how seriously do you think we need to take that risk? He's staying with us for the next week or two, and it's a big worry.'

'I always take suicide talk seriously. But in this case I think he'll be all right if closely supervised. Try to keep his mind off his troubles, feed him, keep him occupied, and watch him. Make sure he has no drugs in his possession, and don't let him go out alone. I don't believe he has the energy right now to make any elaborate plans to kill himself, but if an easy opportunity arises, he just might take it.'

'Yes, we can do all that, but it's the matter of keeping his mind off his troubles that's going to be the tricky part. You see, we're trying, Alan and I, to work out what really happened to the girl he's suspected of killing, and that means we need to ask him some questions about it.'

'Yes, I've heard about your detective . . . er . . . bent. But I'm afraid it won't do. I don't want you to bring up the subject of the murder, or of his depression. Leave that to me. I'm seeing him every day this week, though I'm having to juggle my schedule a bit. At the end of the week, we'll see where we are.'

I asked about medications, was told none had been prescribed for the moment, and clicked off, wondering as I put the phone down just what we were to talk about if his troubles were forbidden topics.

Alan and Jonathan were once again late getting home, but Alan called me to say they were stuck on the motorway and to expect them when I saw them, so I made a sandwich for supper and settled down with a spiral notebook, a pen and the usual attendant animals.

I've made lists all my life. Shopping lists, Christmas card lists, to-do lists. Just making the list gives one a spurious feeling of accomplishment. My list this time was a to-do list: How to Catch a Murderer.

Not that I put that down, but it was in the back of my mind as I wrote:

Anthony Jarvis/Andrew Welles. How to find out more about him?
Find out more about his trial. Newspaper? Internet?
Talk to head teachers at his former schools.
Go back to St Cuthbert's and find out how/why they found him for the palace tour.
Find out where he was the night Melissa was killed.

That last was really a matter for the police. If they could be persuaded to look into it. Surely, though, now that they knew about Jarvis/Welles, it could plant some doubt about Jonathan's guilt.

I made another note:

Talk to Carstairs myself about Jarvis/Welles.

I looked at that one with foreboding. The Chief wasn't going to welcome any suggestions from me. If I had to talk to him, I'd better be armed with enough solid information that he'd listen. What sources did I have, whom did I know who would talk to me frankly about a child predator?

Possible child predator, I reminded myself. Innocent until proven guilty and all that.

There were no school officials available to me at this hour

of the evening. I could try the Internet again . . . or! I had a
sudden brilliant idea. Jane!

Jane Langland had been a teacher for many years until her
retirement, and she still kept up with school matters. As far
as I knew, she'd never taught in the Brighton area, but it
wasn't all that far away. Surely she knew someone who knew
someone.

I went to my kitchen door and peered out. Her back door
was ajar to let in the balmy evening air, but there was no sign
of any visitors. Keeping my animals back with one foot, I
scurried out and knocked on her door.

'It's open,' she called in her distinctive growl. The bulldogs
set up a welcoming chorus and came to greet me as I walked
through her kitchen to her front room.

'Young man getting settled in?' was her greeting. 'Thought
he was still in London.'

She would have seen Jonathan's arrival, of course. 'He's
terribly depressed, so we're keeping an eye on him. We're all
afraid he'll . . . try to do something foolish.'

'Hmph!' Jane has little use for euphemism. 'Kill himself,
you mean. Not that stupid, is my guess.'

Since Jane had never met him, she was drawing conclusions
from who-knew-what source, but I didn't stop to question her
information. 'He tried once, Jane,' I did say. I gave her the
story, briefly. 'I've fixed him up with a psychiatrist, who doesn't
think there's imminent danger, but he needs to be watched.
And I'm not to talk to him about his troubles, but what else
is there to talk about? His mind is so full of pain and worry
he can't even eat.'

'And what are you doing about it?'

Bless Jane. She has enormous faith in my ability to 'do
something' about almost anything. 'That's why I'm here,
actually. I've got my eye on a possible suspect, and I want
you to help me find out anything I can about him. He calls
himself Anthony Jarvis, but his real name is Andrew Welles,
and he—'

'Oh. Him.'

'You know who he is?'

She looked at me over the top of her glasses. 'Not a teacher in these three counties doesn't know about him. Wrong 'un. Changed his name, has he?'

'Yes, and he's not teaching any more. Tell all, Jane.'

She got up, went to a side table, and assembled a tray with bottles, glasses and a soda siphon. 'Need a stiffener for this one. Help yourself.'

The tale she had to tell wasn't a pretty one. Before it was over I was very glad of my 'stiffener'.

Andrew Welles had a long history of suspected, but never proven, crimes against children, mostly between the ages of ten and thirteen. Mostly girls, but a few boys as well. 'Never rape, or never accused. Fondling. That sort of thing.' Jane made a face and took a healthy swig of her Glenfiddich. 'Take the taste out of my mouth.'

It was the usual story of conflicting testimony, confused and terrified children, angry parents, defensive school officials. 'Damn hard to prove these things. No one wants to put the kids through it. End of the day, he'd just be asked to resign. Only ever went to court once; acquitted. Travesty.'

'So he changed his name and set himself up as some sort of art consultant, as nearly as I can make out. He wouldn't have to have a CV for that.'

'Bastard's a damn good artist, good teacher. Bloody shame.'

I wasn't sure whether she meant it was a shame that a good teacher had ruined his career, or that he had never been made to pay for his crimes, or that so many children had been victimized . . . or all of the above.

'So I don't suppose he has a police record.'

'Would do if he'd been convicted. Wasn't, so probably not.'

'Still . . . I think the people at St Cuthbert's suspect something.' I told her about the palace tour, and the reluctance of anyone at the college to talk about it.

Jane's snort was eloquent.

'In any case, the police need to know about all this. Is there someone you know, someone maybe who taught at one of the schools where Andrew got into trouble, who would be willing to talk to Chief Superintendent Carstairs, who's in charge of the case?'

'Dozens. Want me to call 'em?'

'Please. That could be the greatest help. When Alan gets home I'll ask him the best way to proceed. And I'll try to figure out something useful I can do to move things forward. But Jane, meanwhile, what on earth am I to talk about with Jonathan?'

'Can't help you there. Talking's not my strong point. Good listener, though. Send him over here if you want. Dogs'll be good for him.'

They would be if he liked dogs. I always lose count of how many Jane has, but when they're at their liveliest, they appear to number in the dozens. And for Jonathan, a man with limited physical resources . . .

I decided not to worry about it. Jane would cope. She specializes in coping.

I went back home to my list.

I'd actually cleared up some of it, just by talking to Jane. I sat and chewed my pen for a while, and then decided to give it a rest. My brain wasn't functioning any more. I wished Alan would come home, so I could talk everything over with him, once Jonathan was safely out of earshot. I picked up a book I was in the middle of reading, and put it down again after a minute or two. I couldn't concentrate on the plot. I wandered out to the kitchen, and was immediately surrounded by fur persons, assuming that when a human is in the kitchen, it's time to eat. I got snacks for them and for me, went to the TV, decided that, as usual, there was nothing I cared to watch, and resumed what I do best: fretting.

I suppose it wasn't actually very long until I heard Alan's car, though it seemed like hours. A routine had already been established: he dropped Jonathan at the door and then put the car in our minute garage while I helped our guest in. Alan followed in a moment with a couple of suitcases. Both men were looking very tired, but I thought Jonathan looked perhaps slightly less overwrought than when he'd left after lunch.

'Right,' I said when they had dropped into chairs in the parlour. 'Something to eat, or drink, or just bed?'

'Bed for me,' said Jonathan. 'For someone who's let Alan do all the work, I'm whacked.'

'We stopped on the road,' Alan said. 'Ghastly sandwiches, and mine is still sitting like a lump of lead. I'm ready for bed, too, love.'

'Good. Me, too. I'll lock up; you two go on up.' I gave Alan a look I hoped he could interpret. Not the bedtime look we sometimes exchange, mind you, but *I need to talk to you, so don't fall asleep.*

Either it worked, or Alan simply read my mind, because he was just getting into his pyjamas when I got to the bedroom and shut the door on the animals.

I jerked my head in the direction of Jonathan's room.

'If he isn't asleep already, he soon will be,' said Alan very quietly. 'And he has a white noise machine that we brought along. Very soothing, he says.'

'Well, then.' I plopped onto the bed, fully dressed. 'Let me tell you what I learned from Jane tonight.'

I summarized the story in very low tones. 'And Jane's going to phone some people she thinks will be willing to talk to Carstairs. Do you think he'll pay attention?'

Alan considered. 'Yes, I think he will. I wasn't able to talk to him today, but I left a message, and he'll consider it. He might not have listened to you, with little more than suspicion, but if several people, independently, tell the same story, yes, he'll listen. He won't actually talk to them himself, but he'll send someone. He's a fair man, Dorothy, but in a very difficult situation.'

'Hmph!' I said, in my best imitation of Jane.

'*And,*' Alan went on, ignoring me, 'once he's digested what these people have to say, I suspect there are a few other enquiries he'll want to put in train.'

'Like where the gentleman with the various names was on the night Melissa died.'

'That, of course. But how about, was anyone resembling Melissa seen near his flat between now and last July? And particularly, where was he and what was he doing on the day in February when we know Melissa ran off to London?'

TWENTY-NINE

N ext morning we discussed it a bit further. 'And then they could follow up with DNA . . . oh, good morning, Jonathan. Sleep well, I hope?'

It wasn't my imagination. He was looking better. Rested, and far less strained. He was even walking a little better. And that reminded me. 'I forgot to ask before. What are you going to do about your physiotherapy while you're here? I wouldn't think you'd want to drop it.'

'No. I hadn't thought about it, either, but this morning I was pretty stiff until I got myself moving a bit. I suppose I'd better phone my doctor and see if he can set up something with someone in the neighbourhood.'

That was the most he'd said the whole time he'd been here, and furthermore he was taking some initiative. I felt like cheering, but instead I asked if he preferred muesli or corn flakes.

His appointment with Dr Miller was right after breakfast, so Alan drove him over, and I went back to my list. Was there anything I could do at this point, anything the police couldn't do quicker and better?

Well, not on the list, there wasn't. But I thought perhaps a conversation with Jemima might be useful. That meant going to London again. I sighed. Johnson, I thought rebelliously, never had to deal with rail travel or modern traffic.

I thought about calling to set up a time and place to meet Jemima, but there was little point until I knew Alan's schedule for the day. Given that one of us had to be with Jonathan all the time, my freedom of movement was curtailed.

When I'm frustrated, I clean house. The kitchen was sparkling and the parlour was getting there by the time the two men walked in the door.

Alan knows my habits. He looked around and raised his eyebrows. 'And what are your plans for the day, love?'

'Well, that sort of depends on yours.' I gave Jonathan a sideways look. 'I have some shopping I really need to do in London, but if that's inconvenient for you today . . .'

'Not a bit. Jonathan and I thought we'd go for a drive and do a spot of sightseeing, as it's such a lovely day. We might be gone the whole day, actually. Can you believe this lad's never seen Stonehenge?'

It was my turn to raise an eyebrow. Stonehenge is nearly a hundred miles away, by English standards a very long distance indeed. 'Then we'll hope the traffic is kind, and I'll expect you when I see you.' I also hoped they'd find something to talk about for that whole time, but men seem to be able to sustain long periods of silence without feeling uncomfortable. In any case, it was Alan's problem, not mine. 'If you'll wait a moment or two, you can drop me at the station.'

I'd phone Jemima from the train. It would be nearly lunchtime when I got to Victoria Station. Maybe we could have a nice lunch and a talk.

Her phone rang and rang and finally went to voicemail. Drat. She was probably doing something important and had it turned off. I left a message and tried to concentrate on the newspaper someone had left on the seat.

Three attempts later, I'd accepted the fact that she wasn't going to answer. Well, now what? I could hardly go to the palace and ask to speak to one of the staff.

Could I?

Nothing else occurred to me as I made my way through the heavy foot traffic in the station, buffeted on all sides by tourists who were rolling heavy luggage, trying to figure out where they were going, and conferring about it in at least four languages I could recognize and many more I couldn't. I was swept by the tide out on to Buckingham Palace Road headed towards the palace. I gave a mental shrug and answered an anxious query from the timid little Japanese lady waiting beside me at the traffic light. 'Straight ahead about three blocks, on the left. You can't miss it, really. Or just follow me. I'm going that way.'

When we neared the palace, I pointed out the Royal Standard flying over the roof, indicating that the Queen was in residence.

My Japanese lady was thrilled and went into a rapid explanation to the rest of her party, then asked where they could get
tickets to tour the palace. I was sorry to tell her that it was
never open when the Queen was there, only in late summer
and early autumn when she took off for Balmoral. They were
disappointed, but I pointed them in the direction of Wellington
Barracks, where they might, if they were lucky, make it in
time to see the Guards muster.

They fluttered off, full of thanks, and I approached the visitor's entrance in a glow of self-esteem.

Five minutes later the glow had vanished entirely. No,
madam, there was no way to get a message to a member of
the household. It was impossible to check to see if a given
employee was working that day. Perhaps I could telephone
her mobile? Oh, well, in that case . . . so very sorry, madam
. . . perhaps later . . .

I was back in Buckingham Palace Road, listening to the
approach of the band, trying to fight my way out of the crowd,
with no place to go.

I plodded drearily back to Victoria Station, bought a sandwich at a kiosk and a cup of coffee at a different one, and
consumed them leaning against a pillar (Victoria Station
doesn't feature seating for the travelling public) and pondering
the futility of life in general.

This would never do. I pushed myself away from the pillar,
dropped my cup and sandwich wrapper on the floor (Victoria
doesn't have trash cans, either, presumably because they would
be such handy places to stash bombs), and found a chocolate
croissant at yet another kiosk. Low blood sugar, after all, is
an impediment to productive thought, and besides I hadn't had
my chocolate fix for the day.

All the indulgence improved my mood slightly, but it didn't
seem to speed up my brain. I couldn't think of anything to
do. Without hope, I tried Jemima again. No answer.

Well, Tom and Lynn were nearby and might have some
ideas to jump-start my feeble mind. I looked up their number
on my phone (really, these gadgets can come in handy), and
called it.

No answer; voicemail.

Was everyone I knew away from their phones? Didn't they know I was trying urgently to reach them? What's the point of having mobile phones if you don't leave them turned on?

After a few moments of such useless fulminating I made a decision. I needed to sit down in comfort. There was the good old Grosvenor just through a door. I could sit in the lobby and compose my mind, and if I could think of absolutely nothing useful to do, I could admit defeat, go back into the station, and catch the next train home.

The lobby is really rather splendid. Lots of wasted space, with a lovely staircase, made wide enough to accommodate the huge hoop skirts popular among the gentry when the place was built, and a magnificent crystal chandelier. The place was busy, but not really noisy; the carpets and draperies took care of that. I found a lovely soft chair in a corner where I could sit and think in peace.

And finally, finally, I had an idea. I suppose it was the opulence of my surroundings that triggered it. There was one person I was pretty sure of finding in. He had a business to run, and even though I'd lunched early, it was certainly, indisputably, afternoon.

I headed for the Underground and Sloane Square Station, hoping I could remember exactly where Bert's shop was.

Actually, I might have had a little trouble finding it, if it had not been for the police car outside.

What on earth?

I crossed the street and tried to peer in the window, but a very polite constable stopped me. 'I'm sorry, madam, the shop is closed. Move along, please.'

'But Bert . . . I mean Mr Hathaway, is a friend of mine.' That was stretching the truth quite a bit, but in a good cause, I thought, if it got me some information. 'What's happened? Is he hurt?'

'I have no information, madam, Now, if you would please—'

'Constable.' It was my Victoria Regina voice again. I seemed to be using that quite a lot lately. 'My husband, Alan Nesbitt, was Chief Constable of Belleshire before you were born, young man. I am aware of police procedure, and of the fact that I am hampering nothing by asking you some questions. I repeat,

I have an interest in the welfare of Mr Hathaway. Now, what has happened here?'

He looked around unhappily, but there was no superior officer in sight of whom he could seek advice. 'I understand there's been a burglary. Place is a bit of a mess. Really, ma'am, I can't let you go inside.'

'I realize that. I might destroy evidence. But there's no reason on earth why I can't just look.'

And I moved once more to the window and tried to peer in.

'Don't touch the window, ma'am!'

'No. But it's awfully dark in there, isn't it? May I borrow your torch?'

The London bobby, rather sadly, no longer carries one of those huge flashlights that used to double as an effective weapon in case of need. Now they're issued much smaller, more efficient ones. The poor man sighed and handed me his. I shone it through the window on an appalling scene.

The beautiful rug in the middle of the floor was virtually covered in shards of china and glass. The delicate piecrust table I remembered had been overturned and broken to splinters. I moved the light around and saw that the mantel was bare. No Staffordshire dog. I assumed its shards were among the others on the rug.

'Madam!' The constable's voice was low, but urgent. I straightened and handed his flashlight back a millisecond before a man came out of the passageway beside the shop. The man, though in plain clothes, was unmistakably a policeman.

I approached him before he could do more than glare at me. 'My name is Dorothy Martin; my husband is retired Chief Constable Alan Nesbitt of Belleshire. You may have heard of him. I presume you are the officer in charge of this crime scene?'

'Yes, I—'

'I am a friend of Robert Hathaway, the man who owns this shop and lives above it. I have been unable to learn from this young man anything about what has happened here, but I am very concerned about Mr Hathaway. What can you tell me about him?'

'More to the point, what can *you* tell *me*?' asked the man, pulling out his warrant card. I didn't recognize the name, but I saw with some dismay that he was a superintendent. That meant something serious was going on.

'I? I just got here, and I've been trying to pull *some* information out of *someone* about my friend Mr Hathaway! Is he hurt? What's going on?'

'You're sure you don't already know?'

'Sir! Are you deaf, or simply unable to believe anything you're told? I do not know anything about what has happened here, and it begins to appear that I never will! If you will let me pass, I will go upstairs to Mr Hathaway's flat and see for myself.'

He moved slightly to bar my way. 'I doubt you'd learn much up there. We didn't. The flat has been virtually destroyed, as has the shop, and Mr Hathaway is not here.'

THIRTY

'So I took my courage in both hands and went to see Mr Carstairs,' I told Alan much later. Jonathan, exhausted by his day out, had gone to bed as soon as they'd got home, and Alan and I were sitting in the garden with drinks in our hands and contented pets all around us. 'I wasn't sure how long it might take the news to filter up – do things filter up? – anyway, to reach him, and I thought he ought to make the connection right away – that Melissa's father had apparently been attacked, or at least his home and shop had been, and that he was missing.'

Alan chuckled quietly. 'I'm sure he was suitably grateful.'

'He was just as stuffy as I'd expected, at first. Implied that I'd been poking around where I had no business—'

'Which you had been.'

'Which I had been.' I conceded. 'But when I told him that Jemima wasn't answering her phone, either, he began to pay attention. He can get answers out of the palace, and when he found out that she wasn't there, hadn't been all day, hadn't been given time off, and was in fact AWOL, he was even more interested. He even admitted I'd been of some use. It hurt him to say it, though.'

'But he did let you go back and look at the crime scene.'

'Under very strict supervision, let me tell you! The SOCOs had done all their work already, but even so I had to wear gloves and bootees, and could walk only around the perimeter, where I couldn't step on much. Alan, it was . . . frightening.' I took a short pull at my glass. 'The destruction was so violent. The paintings were cut to shreds, and that nice little Staffordshire dog had been smashed to pieces no bigger than *that*.' I indicated about half my little fingernail. 'I could only tell what it was because a bit of the chain was still recognizable. And some of the mess on the rug had been ground underfoot to powder. I think the rug itself may be a total loss. It looked as though it had been cut right through in places by the glass fragments. Even the walls had chunks of plaster knocked out where things had been thrown against them. I can't imagine that a bomb could have done more damage.'

'But no blood stains,' said Alan thoughtfully.

'I sure didn't see any, and I looked, believe me. Even upstairs, though the flat was absolutely trashed, I couldn't see any sign that Bert or anyone else had been injured. So what the heck could have happened?'

'You don't have any theories?'

'I do, but I'd rather hear yours. You're the expert.'

'I'm the professional,' he corrected. 'You've done some pretty expert work yourself, from time to time. However. From your description, it sounds like sheer anger and hatred at work. Not just random vandalism, destruction for kicks, but passionate fury. My guess, and remember it is just that, an uninformed guess, would be that someone who hates Bert Higgins with a white-hot hatred came there intending to kill him. Higgins was out, or escaped when he saw his enemy, and when the person couldn't destroy the man, he – or she – destroyed his world.'

'He, or she.' I swallowed a little more bourbon. 'And I saw

nothing that a woman couldn't have done. A woman on a rampage. Alan, do you think Jemima has that kind of rage inside her?'

Alan sighed. 'Almost anyone is capable of blind, senseless fury, given the right, or I suppose the wrong, stimulus. I haven't seen that sort of temperament in Jemima, but consider what she's been through recently.'

'And at just the wrong time, too, when she thought her life was beginning to get better. Alan, I don't *want* it to be her! But if she thought Robert killed Melissa . . . oh, I wish they could find her.'

For Jemima was still missing, and so was Robert.

'There's one bit of silver lining, love,' said Alan, putting his glass down. 'Jonathan couldn't possibly be involved, and that casts even more doubt on his guilt in the murder. He just might be off the hook entirely. I'll make some phone calls in the morning. And on that note, let's go to bed. I could sleep for a week.'

I got up early the next day, little as I wanted to, to look after Jonathan. He seemed to have slept well, and he ate the large breakfast I put in front of him, which was a good sign. Then I was able to keep him talking, until his counselling session, about his trip to Stonehenge.

'It really is the most amazing place, isn't it? One has seen pictures, but the reality still astonishes.'

'Exactly like the Grand Canyon,' I agreed. 'You think you know what to expect, and then you stand on the edge and say, "But I didn't know it was like *that*!"'

'I've not been to the Grand Canyon. Nor to any part of America, come to that. I'd like to go sometime, spend a week or two and see the sights.'

'My dear young man! How big do you think the country is? You couldn't "see the sights" in Indiana in a week or two, and it's one of the smaller states. A lifetime or two wouldn't suffice! I lived there for over sixty years and only skimmed the surface.' We went on bickering happily until Alan came down. I wanted badly to ask if he'd had any luck with his phone calls, but I couldn't, not in front of Jonathan.

'Beautiful day, you two,' he said, pouring himself some coffee. 'Dorothy, I thought you might care to come with me when I take Jonathan to see Dr Miller. There are some skirts in the M and S window that I think would look rather fetching on you.'

Had Jonathan known us better, he would have spotted the utter inanity of that remark. If Alan had noticed women's clothing in a shop window, it was certainly for the first time in our marriage. He notices my hats, because they tend to be noticeable, but as long as I'm clean and dressed neatly, he thinks I'm beautiful. Which is quite endearing, actually. I managed to turn my flabbergasted giggle into a cough, agreed that a little shopping would be lovely, and got out of the room before Jonathan could notice my reaction.

'So what did you find out?' I asked, the moment we had dropped Jonathan at the doctor's office.

'Let me find a place to park first, love.' The High Street was, as usual, packed with cars, so Alan had to find a car park.

'We might almost as well have gone back home,' I said as I extricated myself from the car.

'Sorry we're so close to the other chap. It's the only space I could see. And if Jonathan had seen us going in the direction of home, he might have wondered about my shopping story.'

'Just out of curiosity, are there skirts in the Marks and Sparks window?'

'I hope so. If not, they'll have changed them since yesterday. Right?'

I was free to giggle as much as I wanted as we walked back towards the High Street shops.

On this beautiful day, Sherebury presented as near to an ideal English scene as any tourist brochure could desire. Hanging baskets of flowers graced the fronts of pubs and cafés and the occasional lamp post. Shop windows sparkled in the sun. The half-timbering of the Town Hall shopping arcade contrasted beautifully with its slate roof, and over all the great grey spire of the Cathedral towered benignly.

True, many of the store fronts were jarringly modern, but there were so many people on the streets it was possible to ignore the acres of plate glass. I was doing that when Alan took my arm and pulled me to a halt. 'Marks and Spencer,' he said, and added, triumphantly, 'Skirts.'

'Mmm. They'd look good on almost anyone age eighteen and size zero. But let's stand here and look at them while you tell me. I'm dying by inches.'

'The first thing,' he began, ticking off points on his fingers, 'is that Jonathan is no longer under serious suspicion. Yesterday's incident at Bert's shop, and the continued absence of Bert and Jemima, have put a different complexion on the case.'

'Oh, Alan! I'm so glad!'

He held up a warning hand. 'I haven't told him yet, because he might want to go home, and his little respite here seems to be doing him good. I think he ought to continue seeing this bloke. Depending on how you feel about his staying on.'

'You know I'd love to have him stay, but it should be his choice, Alan. Now that he has a choice.'

'Yes. But I intend to urge him a bit, because he's not totally exonerated yet, and so long as he's here with us, he can't get into more trouble.'

'All right, I'll apply a little gentle pressure, too. But Alan, it's getting harder and harder to talk to him without referring to the case.'

'That's another thing I wanted to tell you. Yesterday he brought it up himself.'

'How on earth did you get all the way to Stonehenge?' I interrupted.

'The traffic wasn't bad until near Salisbury. So we stopped at a pub for a bite to eat, negotiated the crush in Salisbury, and headed north. We had a good deal of time to talk, and after a bit had pretty well exhausted the changing landscape and the weather. As he seemed to be in reasonably good spirits, I decided to let him choose the next topic, and he wanted to talk about you.'

'Me!'

'He thinks you're marvellous, you know. He went on and on about it. I was getting quite jealous.'

'And rightly so. But what did he say about the case?'

'Wanted to know if you'd made any progress in solving it. So I told him what you'd learned about Mr Welles/Jarvis.'

'And how did he react?'

'As one might expect. Interest mixed with mild excitement mixed with sorrow. We were discussing the death of his cousin, after all. Well, his adopted cousin, I suppose one might say.'

'And the daughter of the woman he's in love with. But Alan, did you say Jemima is still missing?'

'She was, first thing this morning. No answer on her mobile, and it isn't taking messages any more. "Mailbox full." Apparently, the people at the palace are quite annoyed, because there's some sort of diplomatic reception or state visit or something of the kind this evening, and they're short-handed without her.'

'They've tried Letty?'

'They've tried everything. Carstairs was rather more forthcoming than I expected. He told me they've put a watch on the ports, ship and air and the Eurostar.'

'Goodness! That's the treatment they give the really high-profile stuff, serial killers and bank robbers and terrorists.'

'Carstairs is taking this very seriously indeed. The profile is rising with every moment that a palace staffer is missing, and he's under a lot of pressure.'

'Yes, well, every time royalty is even tangentially involved, there's pressure. Not nearly as bad as that incident when they found the body at Sandringham, but bad enough.'

'And not just from the royal end. There's the chance, you see, that Jemima is responsible for all the trouble, after all, or that Bert is, or that they're both innocent but in danger from the real killer, who might be Welles/Jarvis or someone else they haven't even spotted yet. Incidentally, Jarvis also seems to be among the missing.'

'Stop!' I raised my hands to my head, hatless in the fine weather. One or two passers-by glanced at me, and I lowered my voice. 'Alan, this just keeps on getting worse. The more we find out, the less we know, and now everyone we could talk to has vanished.'

'Not quite everyone.' He nodded his head in the direction of Dr Miller's office.

'Jonathan? Do you think we should? Dr Miller said . . .'

'Yes, but things have changed, meanwhile. I'm going to speak to the doctor for a moment when we go to fetch Jonathan.

I'd like his opinion about Jonathan staying here, and about discussing the case, since he's now nearly above suspicion.' He turned his attention to the shop window. 'I do actually think those skirts are attractive.'

'Which only proves you still have all the proper male impulses. I'm not getting into mutton dressed as lamb, thank you. Let's go have a coffee.'

Jonathan was looking quite cheerful when we picked him up, better, really, than at any time since the Investiture. Alan stayed behind to chat with Dr Miller, and Jonathan cocked his head as we walked out of the office together, Jonathan spurning my arm and using his cane as little as possible. 'Checking up on the baby's progress?' he asked with a grin.

'Something like that. Judging strictly by appearances, I'd say you're feeling something like a thousand per cent better.'

'He's very good, this chap. He's got me to see a lot of things in a different light. Though,' he added, his tone changing, 'being a murder suspect darkens the outlook a bit.'

I bit my lip. I was aching to tell him, but thought it better to wait until Alan got back. 'Well, not as far as we're concerned, you're not. So you can just put that bright face back on and decide where you'd like to go for lunch.'

'I say,' said Alan, coming to join us, 'we stop at the market and pick up some cheese and salads and so on, and have a picnic at home. There are things we need to talk about, in some privacy.'

And not another word would he say until we were seated around the kitchen table, a small feast in front of us. Alan had poured a glass of beer for each of us, and now he raised it in a toast. 'Jonathan, this is to you. First, because you've made such progress with Dr Miller, and second because you've dropped to the bottom of the list of suspects.'

'I've . . . what did you say?' He was suddenly pale, and I was afraid Alan had broken the news too suddenly. Even good news can be unsettling.

'Steady, there! It's true. I talked to Carstairs this morning. There have been some startling developments, and though you're not quite out of the tunnel, the light at the end is growing brighter all the time.'

So we told him what had been going on in the past couple of days. He was listening so intently he forgot to eat.

'So,' I concluded, 'you're the only one who can help us at all. Everyone else has flown the coop! Now eat something, and then we'll do some serious planning.'

He looked at his almost untouched plate. 'Oh. Sorry. Everything's delicious. It's just . . . all this is a little overwhelming.'

'Of course it is. And you have no idea if any of the food is even edible; you haven't tasted it. Finish your beer . . . that is, does Dr Miller say you can have it?'

'He does,' said Alan firmly. 'I checked.'

There was Alan-the-chief-constable coming out again, dotting and crossing all the appropriate letters. I exchanged a grin with Jonathan.

'Now, then, if you two have finished flirting with each other, shall we get down to it?' Alan reached for three pads of paper by the telephone and handed one to each of us, along with pens.

'First of all, what do we know?'

Well, I would have started with what we didn't know, but I wasn't a trained policeman. And certainly the list of known facts was a good deal shorter. 'Shall we do it by name? What we know about each of the principals?'

'As good as any method,' said Alan, nodding. 'Let's start with Jemima. First, her character as we know it.'

'Prickly,' said Jonathan, with a small frown. 'Impulsive. Passionate.' He flushed a little. 'About art, I mean.'

'But passion for one thing can translate into passion for another,' I pointed out.

'No speculating at this point,' said Alan. 'No analysis. That comes later.'

'Just the facts, ma'am,' I said drily, creating a puzzled look on both their faces. 'Never mind. Old American TV show. Onward. Jemima's headstrong, and she has a temper, but she's hard-working.'

Alan waited a moment for more comments, then drew a line on his pad. 'Very well. Now. Background.'

Jonathan could do most of that. Born and raised in Brighton, daughter of his honorary 'aunt', Letty Higgins. Father pretty much a nonentity. Jemima wild as a child and teen, bearing illegitimate child at age seventeen. Already obsessed by art. Worked hard to support Melissa. Eventually landed job at the palace, sending Melissa to Letty.

I watched Jonathan covertly through this recitation. Though it was obviously hard for him, he bore up very well for someone who'd been a basket case a few days before. I made a note or two of my own, trying to make connections, but there wasn't much to work with.

'Now are we going to get to actions? A timetable?' I was getting restive.

'Not yet. The rest of the characters first.'

So we went through them all. First Letty, who wasn't suspected of anything but was clearly important to Jemima, Melissa and Jonathan, and to a lesser degree to Bert. That led us to Bert.

We split on Bert's character, at least at first. 'Charming,' I pronounced instantly.

'Ye-es,' said Jonathan. 'But . . . unreliable, I suppose is the word.'

I thought about that for a moment. 'Well – vacillating, perhaps.'

'A liar,' said Alan flatly. 'And dissolute.'

'But he runs a successful business,' I protested. 'And he helped support Melissa when Letty asked him. He can't be all that unreliable or "dissolute". What a Victorian sort of word, Alan!'

'It stands. Don't forget, he was responsible for Melissa in the first place.'

'Well, there is that,' I admitted. 'But he's still charming. At least most of the time.'

'I thought you mistrusted charm.'

'Some kinds of charm, I do, but in Bert's case . . . oh, you know me too well! Is there any more beer, speaking of dissolute?'

We noted Bert's background, so similar to Jemima's until the unfortunate circumstance of Melissa's birth led the two young parents down such different paths.

Then, at last, we came to Anthony Jarvis/Andrew Welles.

'Which name do you want to use?' asked Alan.

'Jarvis. I don't like that name as much as Welles, and I definitely do not like Mr Jarvis.'

Jonathan knew nothing except what we had told him of the art teacher with the nasty reputation, so Alan and I made quick work of his character and background. 'And for my money,' I finished, 'he's the one. He's likely to be the father of Melissa's baby, which gives him a whale of a motive for killing her. Her accusation would have put him in prison as a sex offender. He could have had the means; everyone has scarves and that sort of thing. Even a plastic bag could have done for her. And Carstairs and Co can certainly find out whether he had the opportunity.'

Alan and Jonathan exchanged a glance. 'Yes, but you see, Dorothy . . .' Jonathan began, and Alan guffawed.

'He's trying to be delicate, love, and tell you that what you've spun is thinner and much weaker than a cobweb. I don't like the chap, either, but you have nothing whatever that even comes within shouting distance of evidence. He's *likely* to be the baby's father; he *could have had* a scarf or whatever; the police will find out *if* he had the opportunity.'

'All right, all right! I know I'm not the professional here. I still think he's the one. But maybe it's time to go into actions and movements? Then maybe we can spin something a little sturdier. I'm going to make some coffee.'

THIRTY-ONE

Coffee and more coffee. Discussion and more discussion. When at last I threw down my pencil, we had a timeline of sorts, with huge holes in it; times when we knew nothing about where various characters were or what they were doing.

I sat back, exhausted. 'All right, you two professionals, tell me. Was that worth the time and effort?'

They looked at each other. They were developing an irritating habit of silent communication, shop talk without words. Alan sighed, finally. 'It cleared the decks, I think. It's perfectly obvious that these three people are caught up together in a web, whether of their own making or the work of another, we don't know.'

'We do know, though,' I said, 'that all three of them are missing. Isn't it reasonable to suppose – all right, to hypothesize – that they're together?'

'That's one possibility, certainly. And given the whole situation, it's rather an ominous one.'

I stood, with some difficulty. I'd been sitting for a long time. 'Alan, this inactivity is killing me. Isn't there something we could do? If Jemima is in danger . . .'

'Carstairs is doing everything he can, Dorothy. I know exactly how you feel. I feel the same way. But we'd just be getting in the way of the police, and we haven't anything like their resources.'

'With respect, sir.' Jonathan coughed.

'I thought we'd got over the "sir" routine,' Alan growled.

'Very well, then, Alan. I think Dorothy has a point, and with res – that is, I believe there is something we can contribute.' He gestured at the table. It looked rather as if a minor tornado had struck a paper mill, and I must have looked as baffled as Alan.

'We know these people,' Jonathan explained. 'At least, we don't really know Jarvis, but even about him, we know things that the police may not. We have inside information. I think if we were to institute a search for one or another of them, we might be more successful than the Met. If I may say so, s— Alan.'

Alan was silent, considering. Considering many things, I suspected. Jonathan's fitness, mental and physical. The danger inherent in the situation. The probability that we would further anger Carstairs, or that we would interfere with his investigation.

Finally, he said, 'You're right, both of you. The thing is, Jonathan, are you up to this?'

Jonathan looked him straight in the eye and said, 'Yes. If I run out of stamina, I can rest and start again. And I'm as fit mentally as I've ever been. This is something I can do. Something I need to do.'

'For Jemima,' I said.

'Yes. And for myself.'

His finest hour, I thought to myself. There really is something in the English character that displays its best under pressure. Jonathan hadn't looked a lot like a hero in the past few weeks, but he looked like one now.

'Well, then,' I said, swallowing the lump in my throat, 'you know Bert and Jemima the best. Where would you look for them?'

'If they've gone somewhere of their own free will, it will be a beautiful place. I'd bet on London; they're both Londoners now. And Bert has lots of money. My guess is, they've figured out who killed Melissa, and they're hiding from him. And where better place to hide, if you can afford it, than one of London's posh hotels?'

Alan and I both felt we should have thought of that. We had once had occasion to use the Ritz as a hideaway for some people who needed protection and could afford the luxury.

But there are a lot of posh hotels in London. Intimate ones like the Goring, which is absolutely wonderful, but perhaps not so good for hiding out, simply because of its size. One tends to be noticed at the Goring.

We went down the list. The Dorchester. The Connaught. Le Méridien. The Langham. None seemed quite right.

'The Ritz, then?' I suggested. 'It's big enough to guarantee anonymity, and it's certainly grand enough.'

Alan ran a hand down the back of his neck. 'Very grand, but a bit . . . flashy, perhaps? I'm not sure that two people who love art would . . . Ah. I have it, I think. Jonathan, what do you think of Claridge's?'

His face lit up. 'Yes! The very symbol of luxury and grandeur, but very, very English. Not, mind you, that I've ever stayed there, but a friend who did treated me to lunch once. He showed me his room. I've never seen the Queen's bedroom, needless to say, but I can't imagine it could possibly be any more . . .' He waved his hands about, searching for a word. 'No, I can't even describe it, except it really is the last word in luxury and good taste. Oh, yes, if Bert wanted a bolt-hole, Claridge's would be perfect. In fact, now that I think of it, he said once, when we were boys, that he'd like to live there one day.'

'Well,' I said, 'he's there, or he isn't. We can only try it. What are we waiting for?' I picked up my purse.

Alan cocked an eyebrow. 'Don't you want to change?'

'Why? Is there dirt someplace I can't see?' I twisted around to try to check the back of my slacks.

'My dear Dorothy, you look perfectly all right, and no, there's no dirt anywhere. But we're talking Claridge's. If you want to blend in . . .'

'Oh.' I was wearing a very nice pair of summer slacks, new last year, and a pretty, striped tee shirt, but I could see his point. 'Not exactly elegant, huh? I'll go find something for hobnobbing with the nobs.'

I had to rummage a bit, but I finally spotted a church dress I hadn't worn in a while, that went very nicely with my Queen Mum hat, a purple sort of cloche with violets all over it. It was really a winter hat, but never mind. It looked as respectable and upper-class as all get-out, and would, I hoped, impress the staff at Claridge's.

It impressed Jonathan, at any rate. His eyes glazed a bit, but he made no comment. Alan, who had put on his best suit, grinned at me behind Jonathan's back, and I made a face.

We were the only ones in the train carriage on the way to London, so we could talk freely. 'Have you thought out a plan, Dorothy?' Alan asked mildly. 'We can scarcely saunter in and ask for Bert Higgins.'

'I think he'd register as Hathaway,' I said primly. 'Since it seems one needs to be lah-di-da to be let in the door. Anyway, that's probably the name on his credit cards.'

'Robert Hathaway, then. They won't tell you anything about him, you know.'

'I do know. I thought we'd go to a house phone, if there is one, and ask them to ring his room. If there isn't, we'll have to go to the front desk, but I'd rather do it the other way.'

Jonathan nodded, looking very much like a policeman. I've seen that look of concentrated thought on Alan's face enough time to see the wheels turning. 'And then, once we know for certain he's there, we can work out what to do.'

We headed for Victoria.

Jonathan had refused to take his wheelchair, and I wondered

how much of his physical disability was related to his mental state. Certainly he seemed to be moving more easily, now that he was in better spirits.

We took a cab from the station. Guests at Claridge's presumably did not arrive by Underground or bus. One wondered if they had ever heard of public transport. 'Pity the Rolls is laid up,' I commented to no one in particular as we sat in a typical London traffic jam.

'Even if it existed,' said Alan drily, 'it couldn't move any faster in this mess.'

We crept up Bond Street, with me pushing the cab every foot of the way, nearly dancing with impatience as we were stopped again and yet again by the heavy traffic.

'You'd get there quicker on foot,' the driver called back to us.

'Our friend can't walk that far,' Alan shouted back. 'Otherwise we'd have taken the Tube.'

'No good for business, all this traffic,' the driver grumbled, beginning to move and then braking sharply for a messenger on a bicycle who cut in ahead of him.

I thought it was probably a good thing that I couldn't quite make out the stream of broad Cockney that followed.

It didn't take us more than fifteen minutes after that to make the five-minute drive to Claridge's, and the driver managed to reach the kerb, behind a Bentley, a Mercedes and a luscious burgundy-coloured Rolls. Suddenly my Sunday dress and hat didn't seem quite so elegant.

'*Courage, ma chérie*,' murmured Alan, and the French – good French, too – so surprised me that I forgot to be nervous. It's amazing how much I don't know about my husband, after several years of marriage.

We walked in and found a house phone with no trouble. 'You or me?' I asked Alan.

'I suppose I'd best do it. If we do manage to reach him, he might recognize your accent. But I'm not sure what to say to him.'

'Don't worry about that,' said Jonathan quietly. 'Don't say anything. Just give me the phone when he answers.'

I swallowed hard. Alan picked up the phone. 'Yes. Be so good as to ring Robert Hathaway for me, please.'

THIRTY-TWO

We waited. I could hardly breathe. Alan nodded. The phone was ringing.

First hurdle passed.

Then he handed the phone to Jonathan, who spoke into it. 'Yes, sir. Room service here. I have your order, but no one answers at the room number you gave us. May I verify your room number, please?'

A pause. 'I see, sir. Yes, I'm terribly sorry to have disturbed you. I will double-check with Reception. Thank you, sir.'

Jonathan hung up and grinned at us. 'He's in suite 329, and he didn't order anything from room service. He's slightly annoyed.'

'Well done, Jonathan!'

'Indeed,' said Alan, but he didn't sound entirely happy. 'But now what? We've found him. We still don't know if Jemima is with him. And he may become suspicious. He's hiding out, after all, and is undoubtedly nervous. If he realizes he just gave his room number to an unidentified voice on the telephone, he may be checking right now to see if someone did ring up from the kitchen.'

'You think he'll try to leave?'

'I think there's too much we don't know about the situation. I'd like to find Jemima.' He ran a hand down the back of his head in his typical gesture of frustration. 'We need to talk about this, think about it, but there may not be time. If Bert has taken fright . . .'

'All right, look. Let's go up to the third floor. There's almost bound to be some sort of lounge, some chairs, anyway, in the elevator – sorry, Jonathan, the lift lobby. We can position ourselves where we can see room 329, and meanwhile we can talk.'

It wasn't an especially brilliant plan. Depending on how much traffic there was, we might not have much privacy, and at lunchtime there was apt to be a good deal of coming and going. But nobody had a better idea, so we found the elevators and went up to the third floor.

There we hit our first major snag. Room 329, or rather suite 329–331, was at the end of a corridor, as far away from the elevators as it was possible to get, and around two corners from them. It was impossible to keep an eye on the door, or doors, without lurking in the corridor looking extremely conspicuous.

Worse, the suite was directly across the hall from a fire exit. We looked at each other in silent dismay, and retreated to the elevator lobby.

'We'll have to divide up,' said Alan.

'Yes.' Jonathan nodded. 'If you two can stay here at the lifts, I'll keep watch at the fire door.'

'But Jonathan.' I hesitated. 'I hate to mention it, but suppose Bert does try to get away, down the fire stairs. You might not be able to follow him, or . . .' I didn't want to say, *You can't run after him. Stairs are difficult for you. You might lose him.*

His smug grin broadened. 'You're being very tactful, Dorothy. But you see, I have a secret weapon.' He reached into his pocket and pulled out . . .

'Your whistle?' Alan's voice was full of both amazement and amusement. 'You've kept your whistle, all these years?'

'My pride and joy,' he said. 'It was the first piece of equipment issued to me when I joined the force. It got me out of trouble more than once when I was still doing foot patrols, and I wouldn't give it up for any price anyone could offer.'

He disappeared, limping slightly, but moving pretty well.

'I can't believe this is the same man who was ready to end it all just a few days ago,' I said in that low voice that is so much less carrying than a whisper.

'He was pining for want of something to do,' said Alan in the same tone. 'That old fire horse you've cited before has heard the bell again, and he's ready to run. Now, do we have any plans worthy of the name?'

'Not really,' I admitted. 'The trouble is that there are too many scenarios. Jemima may or may not be with him. One or both of them may be our culprit. Or they may be hiding from Jarvis, if he's the villain of the piece, or if they think he is. Or even, if he's alone in there, Bert may simply be taking a little holiday, living in luxury. And the circumstances determine what we need to do.'

'Mmm.' Another of those non-committal sounds. They don't always convey disapproval, and sometimes I can interpret them.

'You think?' I asked.

'Don't you?'

'Yes, actually I do. It's time.'

He pulled his phone out of his pocket and pushed a single button. 'Chief Superintendent Carstairs, please. Yes, I'll wait, but this is Alan Nesbitt calling. The matter concerns the St James's Park murder and is extremely urgent.'

My nerves tightened again.

'Then call his mobile, or his home, or whatever you need to do. Now, please!'

I had never heard that tone of voice from Alan. Even I was intimidated; I could only imagine the effect on the person at Scotland Yard.

'Carstairs. Nesbitt here. We have located Bert Higgins. He's at Claridge's, room 329. Jonathan is watching the door, but there is a fire escape . . . Yes, right away, if you please. Thank you, sir.' He put the phone away. 'He's coming, with men. It's a bit tricky, you know, this being Claridge's. One can't simply storm—'

Jonathan's whistle sounded, shrill and urgent.

I looked at Alan in panic. 'He's getting away!' I started to go to Jonathan's rescue, but Alan grabbed my arm and held me back. 'No! This time I'll keep you safe even if I die for it!' Then, with great presence of mind, he did what I would never have dared: took the little hammer, broke the glass and pulled the fire alarm.

'You think there's a fire?' I asked, terrified. A fire in a hotel, an old hotel . . .

'No. But that'll fetch help faster than anything. If we're lucky, there'll be someone at the bottom of the fire stairs before Bob gets there.'

'But we don't want them to . . . do we?'

'It should work. I haven't time . . . ah.'

The approaching sirens sounded clearly over the internal fire alarms and the babble of voices. Doors along the corridor opened, heads popped out. Alan said, 'I think the time has come for us to make a discreet exit. Yes, madam,' he said, raising his voice, 'I believe it's a false alarm. No need to worry. Disgraceful, the way these systems fail even in the best hotels. No, I'm afraid the lifts aren't working, but I'm sure they will be soon. I'm going down to demand an explanation and an apology.'

He hurried me along. I was going to have a bruise on that arm. 'Where are we going really?'

'To help Jonathan. I pulled the alarm because, in any well-run hotel, there is a designated gathering place in case of fire, and the staff have the duty of making sure the guests go there instead of wandering off on their own. So we may be lucky enough to have Bert, possibly with Jemima, nicely penned up where we can have a talk with them. And if Jonathan is with them, so much the better. Can you run?'

'I'll try!'

The best I could manage was a sort of trot (running on artificial knees isn't easy), but we made it down the long corridors and round the corners at reasonable speed, and paused at the fire door.

'We may not be able to get out until we get to the bottom,' said Alan. 'Will you be able to cope?'

He was referring to my claustrophobia. I gritted my teeth. 'Lead on, Macduff.'

He went ahead of me, to cushion my fall in case I slipped, I supposed. I went as fast as I could, but three flights is a good many, and I was panting by the time we reached the exit door.

It stood wide open, and a considerable fracas was going on outside.

'. . . an outrage! I am paying a king's ransom for accommodation here, and I do not expect to be treated—'

'. . . sure we can work this—'

'Don't be an ass, Bert, I'm only—'

'I told you we should have—'

Alan stepped through the door and uttered the words I have longed for years to hear from an English policeman:

'Now, then, what's going on here?'

THIRTY-THREE

S ome hours later, I still wasn't sure. We were gathered in an interview room at Scotland Yard, that being the only space big enough to hold us all: Alan, me, Jonathan, Bert and Jemima, along with Chief Superintendent Carstairs and a couple of other police officers, whose names I never did catch.

It had taken us a while to get to this point. Alan and Carstairs had first had to apologize to the Claridge's management, who were, to a man, irate to the point of fury. This sort of thing simply Did Not Happen at their establishment. There was No Excuse for such behaviour. They obviously wanted to Refer This Matter to the Police (the phrase was trembling on the manager's lips), but were thwarted by the fact that the police, active and retired, were not only present in force, but were largely responsible for the situation in the first place. The discussion went on for some time, and it took all the diplomacy Alan and Carstairs could summon to soothe the ruffled feathers.

And now we were trying to sort out just what was 'going on', and were having a rough time of it.

'If a man can't take a bit of rest, a few days off at a nice hotel . . .' said Bert wearily, for perhaps the seventh time.

'Certainly, sir,' said Carstairs genially, as he had said again and again. 'But we're wondering about the devastation at your shop and flat, and what part that played in your decision to "rest".' His tone put clear quotation marks around the last word.

'How many times! I do not, repeat, do not know what you're talking about. I know nothing about any "devastation", and would very much appreciate being allowed to go and see for myself.'

I kept still, with some difficulty, but I wondered if anyone uttering similar words to the police had ever, in the history of time, been telling the truth. What would I say, if the police were questioning me and I literally didn't have a clue? I thought I would be less worried about defending myself and more concerned about getting to the bottom of the mess. I would also, probably, cry. I hate it, but I do tend to cry when I'm extremely angry, and the tears make me angrier still.

Absorbed in my own thoughts, I missed part of the conversation, which had become repetitive and extremely tiresome. I was brought back to the present by a sudden silence, a distinct change in the atmosphere of the room. Everyone was looking at Jemima.

'I've said so from the first.' Her tone was defiant.

'But, my dear—'

'I'm not your dear, Bert Higgins, and I'm going to tell the truth.' She turned to Alan. 'I don't know why Bert is being so stupid about this. It's perfectly simple. He came to see me at the palace. I didn't want to see him. Why would I? But he insisted, so I came out, and he told me he knew who the father of Melissa's baby was.' She lost control of her voice for a moment, pressed her lips together, and looked down until she could speak again. 'He said we should go to the police and tell them, and I agreed to go with him. He wanted to stop at his shop first. He wanted to give me back the other dog.'

She looked up to see if we knew what she was talking about, and Alan and I nodded. Alan murmured something to Carstairs, who seemed satisfied and gestured to Jemima to go on.

'But when we got to the shop, it was a wreck. Everything smashed, even the . . . the dog.' Another pause.

I gave Alan a worried look. He exchanged glances with Carstairs.

'I'm all right,' said Jemima, who plainly wasn't. 'I want to get this over and go home. So then Bert told me he'd seen a man coming to the shop just before he left, and thought he'd wrecked the place. The man was the one Bert said was the father. He said it was too dangerous now to go to the police, that this man was a killer and now he was after Bert. I didn't understand, but he said we had to go into hiding so this man couldn't find us. I just kept saying we had to go to the police, and now here we are, and not before time, either.'

'And who, Mr Higgins, is this man you believe to have fathered Melissa's child and ruined your shop?'

'And killed my daughter, don't forget that! The name he's using now is Anthony Jarvis, but his real name is Andrew Welles. He's a paedophile, though he's never been convicted, and he's dangerous as hell, and Jemima and I will be bloody lucky if he doesn't kill us before it's all over, thanks to all of you!' His glare took in all of us.

Carstairs nodded gravely. 'That will be all right, sir. You will be guarded, and Miss Higgins, at her job, could scarcely be safer, now could she? It would have been better if you had come to us at once, you know.' His glance, too, addressed all of us. Alan, Jonathan and I all looked embarrassed.

But Carstairs wasn't finished. 'In fact, sir, I'd like to have a word with you for a moment. Miss Higgins, you may be excused. We have a car waiting to drive you back to the palace, where we have phoned to explain your absence. I think you will find you will not be reprimanded. Thank you for your cooperation.'

Looking somewhat bewildered, Jemima left, without a backward glance at Bert. Carstairs went on, 'Some of what I have to say might have been distressing to Miss Higgins, you see. Now. You may be relieved to know that we have been keeping an eye on Mr Welles, and he is now in our custody. It's curious, though.' He leaned forward confidingly. 'Mr Welles has admitted to improper relations with Miss Melissa, though he insists they were consensual. Given her age, that of course makes no difference to the offence. He admits to damaging your home and property, and I think you might have been right to flee from him. He's very angry with you, indeed, Mr Higgins.'

'Yes, well, I'm not exactly happy with him, am I?'

'But the curious thing to which I referred is this. He has been very candid with us about many of his activities. He says he met Melissa the day she ran away, at Buckingham Palace, and they became friendly at once. She came to see him in London repeatedly after that, and he admits he may well have been the father of her child. But he categorically denies killing Melissa. In fact, he claims that you are her murderer. And since I am disposed to believe him, I therefore place you under arrest, and caution you that you do not have to say anything, but it may harm your defense if you do not mention when questioned something which you later rely on in court. Anything you do say may be given in evidence.'

But Bert wasn't listening. He rose from his chair. 'That bastard! He hates me! You saw what he did to my home, my life's work! And he would have done it to me, if I'd been around. I'd like to get my hands on him, the bleeding—'

'Sit down, Mr Higgins.' Carstairs spoke crisply and very, very softly.

Bert sat down.

'I had given some thought to allowing the two of you a bit of conversation together. As tempers seem to be running a trifle high, however, I decided against such a meeting. I say again that you need not answer me, but I wonder if you have any idea why Mr Welles is so cross with you.'

'Because he killed my daughter, and he knows I know it! If he could have killed me before I told anyone, he'd have got off scot-free.'

'Mmm. But you had already told Mrs Martin, had you not?'

'No! I told her I knew he'd been at the palace when Melissa was there, that first time. But I had no idea he'd killed her, until . . .'

'Yes, Mr Higgins? Until when?'

'When he came to the shop, with blood in his eye, out to get me! I got away just in time! The man's a maniac, I tell you!'

'I see.' Carstairs pulled a sheaf of papers out of a drawer. 'This is the statement Mr Welles made to us a little while ago. Don't worry, I shan't read all of it to you, but you may find this bit of interest.' He adjusted his glasses and cleared his throat. 'He has just told us that he came to visit you, quote, "because I found out he'd shopped me to the old lady and I wanted to have it out with him". Then he goes on to say, "The place was shut up when I got there. He'd done a runner. Left so fast he forgot to switch off the kettle. It was just coming to the boil. If he'd been there I'd have blacked his eyes for him, maybe left a few other bruises. But he wasn't, and I went mad, just tore into the place. I don't suppose I left much untouched. A pity, too, in a way. He had nice things."' He put the papers down. 'Now if you had left before Mr Welles arrived, I don't quite understand how you learned he was the murderer of Miss Melissa.'

'I . . . I didn't have to "learn" it. I knew the moment I saw him coming. Why else would he be coming after me?'

'Ah. I see there is a further area of confusion.' He picked up the papers again and searched for a moment. 'Yes. Here it is. "I walked from my flat, because I didn't want a cabby to remember me and report to the . . . to you. I was careful to walk at a normal pace, so as not to draw attention. I was sure no one noticed me, but obviously Bert saw me coming. I suppose he was upstairs and looked out the window for some reason. He had to have gone out the back way, because I had the front door in sight almost as soon as I left the tube station." I don't quite understand how you inferred from his calm, unhurried walk that he had . . . "blood in his eye", I believe you said?'

'I . . . he . . . you have only his word for the way he walked! I tell you, I could see that he was furious, and I didn't want to have a row with him.'

'No, sir, that's not quite all we have. We have the word of several other shopkeepers in the neighbourhood, who saw and heard nothing at all unusual until they began to hear the sounds of breaking glass and so on.'

'What someone didn't see or hear is hardly evidence!'

'Not in a court of law, perhaps,' Carstairs agreed smoothly. 'But it is an interesting indication, don't you think? And as it happens we have something more.' He reached into another desk drawer and pulled out a clear plastic bag. It contained a man's silk scarf, a rather beautiful one in a deep green and blue paisley.

'Where did you get that?' Bert reached for it.

'It is yours, then?'

Bert sat back. 'I . . . I thought it was. Now I see that I'm mistaken. And I don't want to say anything more without my solicitor.'

'No comment to make about this, then?' Carstairs pulled another rabbit out of the hat.

I gasped. It was a very small, very chic handbag of the sort carried by the young. Carstairs opened it and turned it upside down. Out fell a house key, a lipstick and the latest thing in mobile phones.

'Found in your flat, sir, between the cushions of the settee, where you presumably overlooked it. The mobile is definitely Miss Melissa's.'

Bert sat silent, looking at his feet.

'Very well.' Carstairs stood up. 'I charge you, Robert Higgins, with the murder of Melissa Higgins.' He nodded to the burly policeman who had been standing silently in the corner. 'Take him away.'

THIRTY-FOUR

'He was so sure he could get away with it,' I mused. Jonathan and Jemima were sitting in the garden with Letty, Alan and me. It was two weeks later, the middle of a warm, lovely July. We'd had a leisurely tea and were trying to sort out all the details.

'He was always like that,' said both the young people, almost in chorus. Jonathan grinned at Jemima and gestured, giving her the floor.

'He was charming. He really was, you know.'

'I know,' I said ruefully. 'He charmed me. I liked him, quite a lot, at first. And he was so convincing about Jarvis/Welles, ever so reluctant to implicate him and all that. I should have remembered about Richard the Third, and history written by the villain.'

We were talking about Bert in the past tense. I had no idea what was going to become of him. There is no capital punishment in England, so he would survive, but he could spend a long, long time in prison. At any rate, so far as all of us were concerned, he was in the past.

'He claims it was an accident,' said Alan, who had spent a long time at Scotland Yard after the rest of us had gone home exhausted. 'He says he was just trying to keep her quiet, and put the scarf to her mouth because she was shouting.'

'What do you suppose really happened?' I asked, and then looked at Jemima in alarm. 'Oh, my dear, would you rather we didn't talk about it?'

'It's all right. Better now than later. I'm still sort of numb, and I want to know what happened. Maybe then I can begin to make sense of it.'

Alan tented his fingers in his lecturing mode. 'According to Welles – as that's his real name, I'm going to call him that – according to him, it was Melissa who started it all.'

'Well, no,' I said sternly. 'He started it when he started her baby.'

'Indeed. But the way things played out at the end began with Melissa deciding she must have an abortion. She went to see Welles . . .'

It had not been a successful mission, according to Welles, Alan went on. He had told Melissa that he had no money to spare, that she could always go to a National Health doctor, and that he couldn't be sure, anyway, that the child was his. She argued that she was too young for the NHS, that she had friends who'd had botched abortions and nearly died, and she wanted better care. He, Welles, had been of the opinion that Melissa simply wanted pampering, or else that she wasn't pregnant at all and just wanted money. She said, in that case she'd go to her father, who was rich . . . and she told him who her father was. Welles got the impression she'd known for a long time.

'But she came to me first,' said Jemima in a toneless voice. 'She came to her mother, and I turned her away. I thought the same as . . . that pervert . . . that she was lying just to get money.'

'And so then she went to Bert,' I said quickly. Letty had taken Jemima's hand and was holding it tight.

'And he went ballistic,' said Alan. 'That isn't quite the way he put it, but it was easy enough to read between the lines. Here was Welles, who had attracted Bert's notice and had spurned him, and had then messed about with Bert's daughter! He insisted that Melissa tell him where Jarvis was, but she refused. He says that must have been when she left her bag behind.'

'With her mobile,' I commented drily. 'Without which no teenager stirs a foot, these days. He must have hurried her out of there, or she'd never have left without it.'

'Right,' Alan continued. 'I'm only repeating what Bert said. He claims he then took her to the palace to talk the situation over with Jemima, but Jemima wasn't answering her phone.

'By then it was getting dark, according to Bert. The argument intensified. Bert half-dragged her by the hand into the park. He saw the gated area, saw that someone had vandalized the CCTV camera and the padlock, and took her in there. They argued.'

'If only I'd answered my phone,' said Jemima.

'There is never,' I said firmly, 'any point in "if only". Things are as they are, and we can only go on from where we are now.'

Alan resumed his narrative, or rather Bert's narrative. 'Melissa was, naturally, very upset by now. It had been a long and frustrating day, and in her condition she was tiring easily. Melissa started crying and shouting. Bert says he put a hand over her mouth to keep her quiet, and she lost consciousness. In a panic, he wound his scarf around her face in case she came around and screamed, dragged her under a bush, and waited for her to regain consciousness. In time he realized . . .'

'That she wasn't going to come around.' Jemima again, still in that dead voice.

'That's his story, at any rate. I think it's open to question, and the prosecution will make mincemeat of it.'

Yes. He was a good liar, was Bert. Later, out of Jemima's hearing, I'd ask Alan what he thought had really happened.

'He thought he was safe,' said Alan. 'No one had seen him, almost no one knew of his connection with Melissa. He didn't know she had told Welles. But when a too-inquisitive lady started coming round and asking awkward questions, he decided it would be useful to implicate Welles, whom he hated. That, in the end, was his undoing.'

There was a silence.

'When I talked to him about the murder,' I said, 'that first time when Lynn and I went to the shop, he acted so surprised and shaken, and swore vengeance on the man responsible. He was very convincing. I believed him utterly.'

'I suspect the surprise and anger were real,' said Alan, 'but only because you knew about the crimes and about his connection with Melissa, not because of the murder itself. His vengeance might very well have caught up with you, my dear.'

'I loved him once,' said Jemima, very quietly.

'So did I,' said Jonathan. 'He was my best friend, until . . .'

When the silence threatened to become maudlin, I stood up and stretched. 'And now the two of you are friends again, a great good coming out of a great tragedy. Not much thanks to me, I might add. I didn't really do a thing to clear this one up.'

'You persisted, my dear,' said Alan gently. 'You kept the police toes to the fire.'

'And you believed in us,' added Jonathan, giving Jemima a look that made me want to cry.

'Well, then. We have a very nice bottle of cognac inside, and I, for one, intend to drink a toast to restored friendship.'

Hand in hand, Jemima and Jonathan followed us inside.